FAMILY BIBLE STUDIES SERIES

BOOK FIVE
The New Testament Commentary

Eric C. Dohrmann

WESTBOW
PRESS®
A DIVISION OF THOMAS NELSON
& ZONDERVAN

Copyright © 2019 Eric C. Dohrmann.
www.timeseyes.org

All rights reserved. No part of this book may be used or reproduced by any means, graphic, electronic, or mechanical, including photocopying, recording, taping or by any information storage retrieval system without the written permission of the author except in the case of brief quotations embodied in critical articles and reviews.

Scripture quotations taken from the New American Standard Bible® (NASB), Copyright © 1960, 1962, 1963, 1968, 1971, 1972, 1973, 1975, 1977, 1995 by The Lockman Foundation Used by permission. www.Lockman.org

Scripture quotations marked (NIV) are taken from the Holy Bible, New International Version®, NIV®. Copyright © 1973, 1978, 1984, 2011 by Biblica, Inc.™ Used by permission of Zondervan. All rights reserved worldwide. www.zondervan.com The "NIV" and "New International Version" are trademarks registered in the United States Patent and Trademark Office by Biblica, Inc.™

This book is a work of non-fiction. Unless otherwise noted, the author and the publisher make no explicit guarantees as to the accuracy of the information contained in this book and in some cases, names of people and places have been altered to protect their privacy.

WestBow Press books may be ordered through booksellers or by contacting:

WestBow Press
A Division of Thomas Nelson & Zondervan
1663 Liberty Drive
Bloomington, IN 47403
www.westbowpress.com
1 (866) 928-1240

Because of the dynamic nature of the Internet, any web addresses or links contained in this book may have changed since publication and may no longer be valid. The views expressed in this work are solely those of the author and do not necessarily reflect the views of the publisher, and the publisher hereby disclaims any responsibility for them.

Any people depicted in stock imagery provided by Getty Images are models, and such images are being used for illustrative purposes only. Certain stock imagery © Getty Images.

ISBN: 978-1-9736-5945-7 (sc)
ISBN: 978-1-9736-5944-0 (e)

Print information available on the last page.

WestBow Press rev. date: 04/09/2019

Contents

The Gospel of Matthew 1
The Gospel of Mark 71
The Gospel of Luke 85
The Gospel of John 113
The Book of Acts 145
Romans 183
1 Corinthians 207
2 Corinthians 227
Galatians 243
Ephesians 251
Philippians 265
Colossians 273
1 Thessalonians 281
2 Thessalonians 289
1 Timothy 295
2 Timothy 307
Titus 315
Philemon 323
Hebrews 325

James	359
1 Peter	371
2 Peter	385
1 John	393
2 John	403
3 John	405
Jude	407
Revelation	411

Introduction

I want to thank Westbow Press for providing a fine, courteous and professional assistance in the development process of producing this and all the books I have written for the <u>Family Bible Studies Series</u>. Their service and final product of this series has been exceptional. I also want to thank my wife Barbara for her keen eye in the editing of this and the previous books in this series and typing them up for production.

People often wonder how authors go about writing their books. So, I thought I would give the background of how this book on <u>The New Testament Commentary For The Family Bible Studies Series</u> came to existence.

This book is actually an extension of the discovery made and produced in Book Four of <u>The Family Bible Studies Series-The Theology of the Bible</u>, the theme that connects all the books of the Bible together, from Genesis 1 to Revelation 21 and 22. That theme is <u>The Family of God</u>. With this theme in mind, <u>The New Testament Commentary for The Family Bible Studies Series</u> will give a concise explanation of each Biblical passage in the New Testament showing how the writings fit into this overall theme of the Bible. Each passage will have a summary and explanation of that Biblical writing. At the end of those summaries will be a section that will say "notes". This will include some specific details of that passage to help better the understanding of that particular Biblical passage. In my education of the Bible at Trinity Divinity School, my teachers would continually emphasize the importance of interpreting Bible passages within its own context. Another way to say this is--let the Bible interpret itself. So, I have been careful to do this and only after doing this to refer to other related Bible passages.

This book was quite an extensive project. Over the course of 30 years (as of this writing and ongoing), I have studied completely through the New Testament from the original Greek language two individual times in my own personal studies. During these years of study I have used various helpful aids to better understand the New Testament Greek language, such as grammars, lexical aids, word study books, dictionaries on the Bible and commentaries. Some of these that were regularly used are listed in the Bibliography at the end of the book. After doing these two complete studies of the Greek New Testament, I then highlighted each book again and then started with the Gospel of Matthew and wrote the commentaries of each New Testament book.

I did not spend a lot of writing on the background of each book, the author's background or the controversies involved regarding the dates and how the books came about. Bible dictionaries will cover most if not all of these topics and I encourage everyone to have some of those for your Bible library. I will usually jump right into the Biblical text and give the summary and notes on the Bible passage being presented.

It is my pleasure to present the years of study in this book and hopefully by keeping things simple and to the point, you will gain rich understanding from this in your own Bible reading and studies; and with this, to gain very practical application from the book, which is the intent of the <u>Family Bible Studies Series</u>, both for individuals and families together. The <u>true</u> riches in life are found with God and being in His Family. We find these riches in the Bible and in asking Him for them in our daily walk with Him. So thanks to our heavenly Father, our Lord and Savior Jesus Christ, and our Helper and Comforter, the Holy Spirit, for making this available to us in the <u>Family of God</u>; and the reality for them to take place in our everyday life with God.

"How blessed is the man who finds wisdom, and the man who gains understanding. For its profit is better than the profit of silver, and its gain than fine gold. She is more precious than jewels; and nothing you desire compares with her." (Prov. 3:13-15, New American Standard Bible; see also James 1:5).

All my personal studies were done using the King James, New International and New American Standard Bible translations; and all the quotes in this book are from the New American Standard Bible translation, unless otherwise stated. Highlight vss. for easy reference.

The Gospel of Matthew

Matt.1:1-17 and Luke 3:23-38—There are two genealogies of Jesus in the New Testament.

The two genealogies presented to us in the New Testament of the Bible about the lineage and the background of Jesus have two different emphasis about them. In the Matthew account we have the royal or kingly line of Jesus' ancestry. It begins in verse one, stating Jesus coming in the lineage of David to fulfill the prophecy in 2 Sam.7:12-16. Matthew completes the genealogies by stating that Jesus is the Messiah (vs.16). See also the four women mentioned in Matthew's account (vss.3, 5, 16) and one who was inferred to in the passage (Bathsheba, vs.6).

In Luke's genealogy, the passage brings out Jesus' family ancestry on earth. Coming from heaven from the Family of God as God's son (vs.38), Jesus was given to Mary by the birthing of the Holy Spirit (Mt.1:18; not the natural human birthing; Mt.1:18-25) and was born in this world to the family of Mary and Joseph. Many comments have been made to there being gaps in the ancestries provided. Yet these are given to present a continuity shown by the writers and do not present a problem from start to finish. Jesus came from the Family of God in heaven and was born into His God-chosen family on earth.

Different and yet with similarities is the Christian birthing we are born into the family that God places us in, and when one becomes a Christian, turning from one's sins and receiving Jesus the Savior and Lord into one's life, that person is born into the Family of God. Tremendous work of God on how He brings this all together indeed! See the passages of the spiritual birth that God brings about to birth a person into His Family in John 1:12, 13; 3:1-16; also, the Prayer of salvation to come into the Family of God, if you have not done so already, or know a friend who hasn't yet, in the back of the book.

Matt.1:18-25—This is Matthew's account of the birth of Jesus. His emphasis is on the virgin birth (vss.18-20, 25) in fulfillment of the prophecy in Is.7:14 in vss.22, 23; and the birthing was by the Holy Spirit (vss.18-20); and that He was from the lineage of David (vs.20); and also, He is the Savior of the world "who will save His people from their sins" (NASB, vs.21; see also 1 Jn.2:2). His given name of Jesus means Savior in Mt.1:21 and 25. Note in verse 25, the literal translation of the first part of the verse is—he (Joseph) was not knowing her until Mary gave birth to Jesus (knowing her has a stronger meaning in the original language and is stating that he had no sexual relations with her until Jesus was born. The verb here is in the imperfect verb tense in Greek (ongoing action in the past) and so, the New American Standard Bible translates this as, "kept her a virgin until she gave birth to a Son" (vs.25).

Matt.2:1-23—Chapter two presents us with further developments of how Jesus fulfilled another prophecy coming to earth and how He was miraculously protected from evil, even from King Herod of that time who tried to have Him killed. The prophecy of Micah in Mic.5:2 is a tremendous prophecy of Jesus being born in Bethlehem (small little town in Israel, over 700 years before the birth) in vs.6; how the angels helped protect Him through dreams to Joseph and the Magi (vss.12,13,19,22); and how the prophesy from Jeremiah 31:15 was fulfilled, when King Herod the Great had killed all male children of 2 years old and under in Bethlehem and surrounding countryside in Israel, to try and prevent the "King of the Jews" from living (vss.18, 2). History tells us that King Herod died not long after he gave this order to take place. Jesus was safely brought back to Israel with Mary and Joseph and they resided in Nazareth (vss.19-23).

Note: The Magi were wise men and priests from the East and were experts in astrology. They came to Palestine and declared they had read in the stars the birth of the Messianic King (BAGD, under Magi).

Matt.3:1-17—As Jesus begins His ministry of salvation to the world and inviting people into the Family of God, John the Baptist appears and prepares the hearts of the people to receive Jesus' preaching by baptizing them in the Jordan River for the forgiveness of their sins (vss.5,6). His message contains words of judgment also, if the message of God's salvation through His Son and Savior is not received (vss.7-12; see also Acts 4:12, the message the Apostles continued to proclaim). John's coming was in fulfillment of the prophecy in Is.40:3. His message to the people was to repent of their sins, because the kingdom of God was at hand (vs.2; see Jesus' message likewise in 4:17). The Jews were waiting for their kingdom to be restored to them (Acts 1:6), only now it would be offered to the whole world, to those who would receive Jesus and His salvation ministry (see Eph.2:11-22). This was a powerful message to both Jews and Gentiles, as Gentiles were used to being treated as outcasts relating to the Jews and their religion. Now, the King of the Jews (2:2) was inviting all who would receive Him to come into the Family of God and serve Him in His everlasting kingdom (vss.8, 11, 12; see Jn.1:9-13; Lk.1:26-37).

"For nothing will be impossible with God" (Lk.1:37).

John baptized Jesus, showing the start of His ministry "to fulfill all righteousness," as the other members of the Trinity, the Eternal Family of God—the Father, Son, and Holy Spirit—joined in on the celebration, ending with the Father's proclamation that "This is my beloved Son, in whom I am well-pleased" (vss.13-17; see also the prophesy in Is.42:1-4 of God's coming Servant).

Matt.4:1-25—The Holy Spirit proceeded to lead Jesus into the desert for 40 days and nights to be tempted (or tested—the Greek word here is used for both those words) by the devil—a long time to go without food (see how Moses handled his situation, going without food for the similar amount of days with God (Ex.24:18; 31:18; 34:28; Dt.9:9, 10). Sometimes, for us, God uses such an experience to prepare us for the work He has for us to do. For Jesus, He already made the earth and everything it was made of (Ps.24:1; Jn.1:3). His "food" was greater than the things that go into the stomach, as He quoted Dt. 8:3 in vs.4, and lived out in His life on earth (Jn.4:34). His ministry for the world was not to test God (vs.7; compare vs. 1), but to please God (3:17; Jn. 8:28-30); and the Kingdom was already His (3:2; 4:17; Lk.1:32, 33; Jn.18:36, 37; see also Lk.12:32-34). He countered such temptation (or testing) with the word of God and kept His focus on it in serving God (vs.10). Notice in His pleasing God the angels came and ministered to Him when it was completed (see also Matt.26:33).

His ministry around the Sea of Galilee was a fulfillment of the prophecy from Is.9:1-3 in verses 15 and 16 of this chapter in Matthew. It was in this area that Jesus began to call His apostles, as many of them were from that area (vss.18-23). Jesus' ministry of proclaiming the Gospel also came with "healing every kind of disease and every kind of sickness among the people" (vss.23, 24; 8:16; 9:35; 14:14). In the Gospel of Mark, crowds responded in amazement to His healing and gave glory to God saying, "We have never seen anything like this!" (Mk.2:12); while in the Gospel of John, officers returned to the chief priests of the Jews and said about His words, "Never did a man speak the way this man speaks" (John 7:26). The result was that large crowds of people followed Jesus, from Judea and all the surrounding areas and countryside (vs.25).

Matt.5:1-16—The Sermon on the Mount is certainly one of the most glorious declarations of God's wisdom, truth, guidance and authority, given to mankind on earth in such a concise speech, that has ever been proclaimed. Those who are spiritually poor (vs.3) can become spiritually rich through God's kingdom blessings (3:11; 11:5; Lk.12:31, 32); those who think they are "spiritually (i.e., religiously) rich" and do not receive the message and salvation of Jesus, would find themselves poor and even blind to the things of God (13:10-17; John 9:35-41; Rev.3:17-20). The ones mourning (effect of grief, vs.4) can find their comfort in Jesus and His salvation message (the word comfort is the same word for the Holy Spirit (Comforter) in the Gospel of John – 14:16, 26; see also John 16:20-22; while this may still not cover all grief experiences, God will help the one mourning and seeking Him find a way to His comfort—2 Cor.1:3-7). The meek can look forward to inheriting the earth (vs.5; Ps.37:11; meekness is being caught up with God, seeing His hand on adversity and blessing, and thus, not easily disturbed in their temper in the circumstances they face; so God would gladly turn over the earth He has made to such people, with all His promises of His coming kingdom). Those thirsting for righteousness will be satisfied (vs.6; when one seeks His righteousness and kingdom first, these plus all the things mentioned previous to this, will be added to them—6:24-33). Those merciful will reap the same (vs.7, simple sowing and reaping here—Gal.6:7; 2 Cor.1:3-7; Rom.11:30-32). The pure (Greek clean) in heart will see God (vs.8, by following His Word—3:6, 8; Ps.12:6, 7; 19:7-14; 119:9-16. As Jesus did, God's children are to share His peace with others, too (vs.9; truly the message of salvation in bringing peace with God (Rom.5:1) and peace with man—Eph.2:11-22); peace-sowers, are truly a dimension of His wisdom—vss.44, 45; James 3:13-18). Persecution for righteousness is better than persecution for evil and wrong-doing (vss.10-12; 1 Pet.4:12-19). It sows a satisfying good reward (vss.6, 12; 6:32, 33; Gal.6:7). Growing in these attributes (Beatitudes) is the way to be "the salt of the earth" (vs.13); "the light of (to) the world" (vss.14-16; John 8:12); and to "glorify our Father in heaven "with our good works" (vs.16).

Matt.5:17-48—Jesus came to earth not to put an end to the Old Testament Law, but to fulfill it and what the prophets had predicted about Him (vs.17; 11:13; Lk.24:44; Heb.1:1,2). While the strict adherence to the Old Testament Law is no longer required to be followed in the strict adherence it was to the Old Testament Jewish people for their pursuit of salvation, the Law does provide from God principles and guidelines for life for us to follow (ex. The Ten Commandments). Since Jesus fulfilled it (see Rom.10:4), now trusting in Him by faith gives us the strength to live out the appropriate guidelines for our daily life (Rom.3:19-31). For example, one may not feel compelled to let his beard continue to grow unattended (Lev.19:27), but certainly the proper care of animals would still be enforce for today (Dt.22:1-4, 6, 7; Ex.23:4, 5; Jonah 4:11; Ps.36:6; Ps.104; Rev.5:13) and continuing to love our fellowman (vss.44-48; Lev.19:13-18). Forgiveness; peace with our fellow man; the freedom and moral conviction to not commit adultery; fulfill vows we make (see Eccl.5:1-7) and all the simple things we can do to help our fellowman, are the standards for today to "love your neighbor as yourself" (vss.44, 45; vss.21-48; Eph.4:25-32).

Matt.6:1-18—Three good spiritual practices to do that Jesus brings up are personal giving, prayer and fasting. The continual guideline given here with these three practices that is repeated is to do these before God and not as a showing to man. It is not saying that man may not see us doing this; it is saying that doing it for man's attention is not the purpose of these but only to be done for and in the view of our heavenly Father. Jesus' guideline for prayer contains this same principle, all directed to our Father in heaven and the purposes of His kingdom: our daily needs of food and provision (see 6:32, 33), forgiveness (toward God and our fellowman) and being kept from evil and/or falling into it (vss.9-15). Keep in mind that the appropriate judgment and timing is important with these, as well (Eccl.8:5,6; see Book 3 of The Family Bible Studies Series—Growing In God's Wisdom, for further insights along this line of seeking God for and applying His wisdom).

Note: Verse 10, God's will is to be done on earth as in heaven. Important to think in our prayers how God's will is done in heaven and how that is appropriated here on earth.

Matt.6:19-34—Jesus declares to us to think carefully where one is going to put up their treasures in life. What is a treasure? Certainly something of value and good for future use are two contained ingredients of a treasure. He says to be careful what you see and what you take to heart (vss.19-23). The word that goes with "eye" in vs.22 in the Greek is "haplous," which means "single" (in the KJ, for its root meaning). Our eyes are two, but focus on only one thing at a time. If one focuses on "good" things, this will have good effect over one's whole being; if not, "darkness" can set in (vss.22, 23). W.E. Vines says quite appropriately—"Singleness of purpose keeps us from the snare of having a double treasure and consequently a divided heart" (for the word "single;" also see

Ps.86:11-13). What helps us also to determine this is when Jesus says you cannot serve two masters—God and material things (vs.24). Obviously, serving the Creator instead of the created thing is the right (and noble) thing to do (see the warning in Rom.1 on this for this contrast in worship; also Matt.4:8-10 in the tempters test to deceive people). That is His purpose of the earth's creation—to admire what our Creator has done (Gen.1; Ps.19:1-6; John 1:3, 10; 5:23; Rev.3:14) and provide for those living on the earth (vss.25-34). This involves the prayer Jesus gave previously in vss.9-15—seeking God's will and kingdom first and seeing our earthly needs provided (vss.24-33). Note: Three times in these verses Jesus brings up concern about being anxious (vss.25, 27, 31—eager wanting that can lead to worry). Remember His promises in these verses; and His timing is always perfect (see Mt.5:48—having moral and faithful development here).

Matt.7:1-29—Jesus finishes up the Sermon on the Mount here in chapter seven with thoughts on making proper judgment toward God and man. Jesus warns about judging our fellowman. We seldom know all the facts about situations in order to do so, as well. But we do have to make proper decisions regarding what is right and wrong using God's word as our guide to do so (Heb.5:13,14; John 7:24; Prov.21:2,3). Our analysis first must start with ourselves (vss.1-5).

The next six verses have to do with what we give to others and what we look to have given to us. In verse 6, Jesus instructs us to be careful that our giving reaches its intended goal, which involves both the giver and receiver knowing the same intent and faithful to follow it through.

What we ask for has significance in the Greek verb tenses here. In verse 7, all the initial prayers (ask, seek, knock) are in the present, ongoing tense in the Greek (i.e. keep asking, seeking and knocking). The first answer (asking) comes in a future passive tense (i.e. given from God); next, the seeking answer comes in a present tense response (i.e. keep seeking until you find it); and knocking, again, comes with a future passive answer (i.e. keep knocking (and waiting) till God opens the door; there is comfort here knowing this; keeps us on track in prayer, as well as letting God show us what <u>He</u> has for us next). Verse 8 is similar to verse 7—all the beginning prayer requests are present participles (ongoing action) and the first two answers (asking and seeking) are present tense verbs (thus, keep on doing these until the present answer arrives); and the last on knocking, once again, is a future passive answer (and so, keep knocking and waiting and watching) till God opens up the door. The present verbs involve more action on the one asking, while the passive verbs imply a little less action, but more active trust. All contain an ongoing anticipative answer from God. After all, if He will give us the best for us (Himself as well as what is best for us—see Lk.11:13 on this same passage), how do we not have great anticipation in watching how the Father will answer our prayers with His best for us (vs.11)? Knowing this, I like to say—let God surprise us. As the title of the TV show in the past said well—Father knows best.

The next eleven verses have to do with taking the right path in life (see these verses for a nice warm up to this passage (Ps.16:11; 27:4-6, 11; 119:35,101,105,128; Prov.2:6-9; 4:10-19; 16:9; Is.43:15-21). In the previous paragraph on the topic of seeking

God for the open door, God instructs us in the Bible to walk in the "righteous paths" (Ps.23: 2,3; Prov.2:6-15, 20-22; 4:10-15, 18, which Solomon was teaching to his children). The narrow gate is often not easy to take (think of narrow passage ways and roads). Broad is no problem (on the initial glance). Taking the "righteous path" often goes against the broad path; and the broad path can lead to destruction (vs.13), stumbling and darkness (Prov.4:12,19; Solomon said to his family to guard this instruction for "she is your life"- Prov.4:13; see Book 3, Growing In God's Wisdom, on wisdom's word "instruction"). But the narrow way—God's righteous path—leads to life (vs.14).

Knowing God's word keeps us from false prophets (vss.15-23), who will be detected by their words (false, not according to God's word) and by the fruit of their lives (character and actions—public and private lives). You wouldn't expect good fruit from a bad tree (vss.17, 18), so it is important to know them by their fruits (vs.20-23).

Jesus concludes His sermon and says to us to build the foundation of our lives on His "righteous paths" (hearing His words as then and now written for us in the Bible, and putting them into practice—vs.24). He says a wise man does this (the Greek word for wise is prudent—practical understanding and wise application; see also Book 3, Growing in God's Wisdom, on the description of prudence), so at times of adversity (unlike those who do not know Him (vs.23) and do not put His words into practice and can fall in times of "storms"—see also 13:19-22), their foundation will stand against the "storms of life," because they built it upon the Rock, His words and "righteous paths" for their life (vss.24-27; see also Dt.32:3, 4; Luke 6:47, 48).

Matt.8-9—In the next two chapters, Matthew now concentrates and records for us a number of the miraculous healings that Jesus performed. Along with bringing the message of salvation and the gift of eternal life by His life, death and resurrection from the dead, and invitation to come into the Family of God (John 1:12, 13; 3:16), Jesus also performed many miraculous healings in His ministry on earth. Matthew summarizes these on a number of occasions in his Gospel. Notice the descriptions of the kinds of healings that Jesus performed and the superlatives that Matthew uses in these notable passages—Matt.4:23, 24; 9:35; 14:14; 15:30, 31; 19:2; 21:12-14. These were all very powerful restorations done by Jesus in His love for mankind who are made in the image of God (Gen.1:27; 5:1; Col.3:10). Many of these healings were very complex physical and spiritual abnormalities. Matthew devotes these next two chapters to some of these healings that Jesus performed.

Matt.8:1-4—This is a brief account of Jesus healing a leper. When asking Jesus to heal him, Jesus replies back to the leper saying, "I am willing" (vs.3). Mark says Jesus had compassion on him and touched him and healed him (Mk.1:41; Matt.8:4).

Matt.8:5-13—In the healing of the centurion's servant, once again we see Jesus' willingness to heal (vs.7—note, Jesus says "I will come <u>and</u> heal him" (my underlining here for emphasis, vs.7). Note the complexity stated by the centurion in vs.6. As a man of position and responsibility in the world, the centurion was very humble in his speech (vs.8) and recognized Jesus as a man under authority like him (great faith here—wonder if there were any others who recognized the same—Jesus being sent by the Father (vs.9; 10:40)! Jesus then speaks to the crowd ("you" is plural in vss.10, 11) and wants the crowd to have such faith, with the promises of being with Abraham and Isaac and Jacob to come. Only His kingdom offers this—not the kingdom(s) of this world (vss.11, 12). As the centurion's faith was expressed, so Jesus healed him at that time (vs.13).

Matt.8:14-17—Here in the healing of Peter's mother-in-law, we see as in many other Scripture passages God's love for the family (Mk.5:19; John 11:1-45; Lk.2:49; John 4:53; Acts 11:13, 14; 16:14, 15, 29-34; Gen. 12:3; Ps.22:27, 28). Verse 15 says Jesus touched her and the fever left Peter's mother-in-law. The word "touched" in the Greek (same word with the leper in vs.3) is in the middle voice, meaning it has special interest for the subject and here, that is Jesus (in His ministry). In many of Jesus' healings the Gospel writers use this middle voice describing Jesus' healings, noting again His love and willingness to do this in accompanying the Gospel of salvation message (see the previous healing passages noted in Matthew). The result of this brought many more who were sick and demon-possessed for Jesus to heal that evening. Once again Matthew uses the superlative that all who were ill were healed (vs.16), in the process of fulfilling Is.53:4 about Jesus.

Matt.8:18-22—Instead of staying around with the buildup of a crowd, Jesus and the disciples depart to the other side of the Sea of Galilee (vs.18). Jesus is approached by a scribe and another of His disciples on wanting to follow Him. Jesus said to the scribe that he may not have a place to sleep (which was often the case for Jesus) in following Him. And, as important as the burial of one's father would be, Jesus said something else comes in priority- "Follow Me" (vss.19-22). See also the next verse 23.

Matt.8:23-27—The result of following Jesus, as the disciples found out, would bring many great challenges, plus many marvelous sights (like the one coming up) they would not forget (see John 14:26). As the disciples were out on the sea in a boat with Jesus, a great storm arose, so that the waves were covering the boat. Jesus was sleeping while this was developing (vss.23, 24; the word "storm" here is the Greek word "seismos," where we get the word seismology, the study of earthquakes. It is mentioned 12 times in the New Testament and in all the other passages is translated "earthquake(s)." NASB has a "shaking" in the margin off the side of this passage. One wonders what may have been the "cause" of this storm and if this was related or not). The disciples thought they might go down with the boat and so pleaded with Jesus to save them (vs.25). He asked them why they were frightful and He then rebuked the winds (plural) and the sea. After a great storm, there was now (literally in the Greek), "a great calm" (vs.26; from the same root word here for "calm" comes the word "smile" in Greek; and so, as poets write the saying, "the smiling ocean"—Vine, for calm). As this was certainly a great faith builder for the disciples (and relief), they marveled at what Jesus did and wondered what kind of man He really is (vs.27).

Matt.8:28-34—The healing of the demoniacs bring out one very straight forward message—the value of human life, first and foremost, over any other created thing (remember—Jesus came to save the lost). While other Gospel passages have only one demoniac, it is not hard to see that more than one could be living there and Jesus deals with the main spokesman (not hard to understand with the hierarchy of demons, as well). The response to Jesus was from the demons (vs.29), made known in verse 31, as they were fearful that their final judgment may be upon them from Him (vs.29; see Mk.1:24; Rev.12:12). Jesus allowed them to go into the herd of swine, which then drowned in the sea (Ps.50:10, 11; 104:24, 25). The herdsman reported all this to their towns people, who then came and asked Jesus and His disciples to leave (note Jesus' instruction given to the demoniac in Mark's Gospel story in 5:19, 20).

Matt.9:1-9—This passage in Matthew is the healing of a paralytic, followed by the calling of Matthew to follow Jesus. The passage begins by Jesus returning to his own city (Capernaum—4:13). The paralytic (see 4:24) is accompanied by a team of faithful helpers (vs.2). Jesus says to him that his sins are forgiven, with the helpful expression of the faith of all of them. Why does Jesus say this? To let the people and paralytic know that the Son of Man has authority on earth to forgive sins (after all, as some their teachers of the law responded, "Who can forgive sins but God alone?—in Mark's passage of the paralytic, Mk.2:7; (well said by Jesus!); and so, Jesus' authority is being exercised here; (later this is passed on to the Apostles, also—John 20:23). Simply speaking, he knew what was in the heart of man (Jn.2:24, 25) and who had a heart to be forgiven (Lk.7:47-50), very possibly seeking Him to be forgiven of sins along with his healing (a great way to seek God for it, indeed). This healing follows as well with the calling of Matthew. For Jesus knows His own and His own know

Him (John 10:14, 27; Mk.3:13-19). This faith and assurance is seen in Matthew's response (vs.9; see again 8:22, 23).

Matt.9:10-13—In Luke's account following the paralytic and the calling of Matthew, a large reception was given for Jesus at Matthew's house (Lk.5:29). With this sequence in mind, most commentators see the account in Matthew as the same, being at Matthew's house, though Matthew is not mentioned by name in the Matthew Gospel writing. As a tax collector himself, other tax collectors came to the gathering, as well as sinners (vs.11) and other people, also (Lk.5:29). Some Pharisees were there, too (vs.11). However the mix at the gathering turned out, when they heard Jesus' message they knew He was not calling to the righteous (yet, self-righteous, relying on <u>their</u> personal sacrifices, vs.13), but sinners, whom He came to save (see 1 Tim.1:15). As a result, from the very beginning of Jesus' ministry, they needed to repent of their sins, as Jesus and John the Baptist declared (3:3-6; 4:17), because the kingdom of heaven was at hand—and the King was in their midst (2:2; 27:11).

Matt.9:14-17—Jesus then speaks to the disciples of John on a question they asked Him about fasting. Regarding the common pattern of fasting by them and the Pharisees, Jesus says that as long as He (the Bridegroom) is with His disciples (the Bride) there is no need to fast. After He leaves earth and returns to heaven, then they will fast (vs.15). He goes on to say that it is time for "new wine and new wineskins" (vs.17), the time for the change from the old pattern, as He brought this out in vss.16, 17. Wine was a common drink of that day so they would be able to relate well to what Jesus said. But what was the "new wine" about? Wine took time to cure to reach its best taste and flavor. So He wasn't talking about what He is bringing some time later—He was talking about what He was bringing <u>now</u> to the world, and only to get bigger and better as time goes on (13:31-33). The "new trend" (wine) will now be based on salvation by faith in His name – the free gift of salvation and the free gift of the Holy Spirit (Phil.3:9; Jn.3:5-8, 16; 14:16-18; Eph.5:18; 1Pet.1:6-9). The emphasis is not on "patterns" and works righteousness, but now by faith and the "new life" in His name (2 Cor.3: 5, 6; Eph.5:17-20; Jn.4:23, 24; Phil 3: 3). Notice at end of His teaching how He wants <u>this</u> to be preserved (vs.17).

Matt.9:18-26—Matthew returns to two mighty healings by Jesus. Both exemplified strong faith (in heartful words and actions) and their great need of Jesus to heal their requests. The synagogue ruler is identified as Jarius in the accounts of Mark (5:22) and Luke (8:41). He wanted Jesus to raise his daughter from the dead who had just died. The passage said Jesus got up and followed him (vs.19). Along the way He was met by a lady who had an unstoppable flow of blood. She just wanted to touch His garment (in the crowd) to be healed (vs.21). Both accomplished their goal of the action by their faith (the woman at once and Jesus taking the daughter's hand, raised her to life—vss.22, 25). Notice at Jarius' house Jesus tells the noisy flute players and crowd to leave before healing her, calling the bluff of their intended actions and not in sincerity of the true grieving moment at hand (vss.23, 24). Jesus does not get caught up in the moment and actions going on but accomplishes God's will in the circumstance he faced. The news spread quickly of this throughout all the land (vs.26).

Matt.9:27-34—Matthew focuses on two healings that Jesus performed here in chapter nine—the healing of two blind men and also of one who did not speak. The two blind men referred to Jesus as the Son of David (vs.27; 1:1). Note their faith and humbleness in this statement and in great need in coming to Jesus (vs.27, 28). Their faith brought about their sight. Jesus was stern with them not to go about declaring this to others (did not want the public buildup with it) but this was hard to prevent (vs.31). With the complications that can come with some physical ailments as brought up previously, the man who could not speak needed a demon cast out of him to bring about his healing. When this was done and he spoke, two different responses came out from the crowd—a great marvelous work had been done unlike anything they were used to seeing; and a negative response from the Pharisees that Jesus had a demon (approaching very closely to the unpardonable sin—12:24, 31).

Matt.9:25-38—This Scripture passage concludes the listing of some of the healings that Jesus did in chapters 8 and 9. Matthew gives another beautiful summary of Jesus' ministry in how the healing of the sick went right along with Jesus' salvation message of the kingdom of God and to bring people into the Family of God (vs.35). Important to see the superlatives mentioned in this verse once again—going to <u>all</u> the cities and villages and healing <u>every</u> kind of disease and <u>every</u> kind of sickness (vs.35). Jesus had compassion for the crowds, seeing they were distressed (word can also mean harassed) and like scattered sheep (vs.36). He then presents a contrast speaking to His disciples—on the one had (orig. Greek), the harvest is plentiful; on the other hand (orig.

Greek), the workers are few (vs.37). Therefore, He says to them to pray to God to send out workers into the harvest (vs.38). This prepares them (and for us to pray, also) for their commissioning to enter His ministry, which He was about to send them out to do right at the start of the next chapter.

Matt.10:1-42—Jesus gives a full chapter here to discipleship and sending the apostles out with instructions in His ministry. He gave them authority (word in Greek means—the right to act, vs.1) as He has over demons and all diseases and sicknesses (vs.1, same words as in 9:35). In the names of the apostles, all are the same except for Thaddaeus (vs.3), which commentators and dictionaries (example, Unger) note to be same as Judas, the son of James in Luke 6:16. People could go by different names then, similar as can happen today. Jesus instructed them to only go to the "lost sheep of the house of Israel" (vs.6). That was not tremendously far to go (throughout Israel, though they most often walked) compared to today, for Israel is about the size of New Jersey here in the United States. So, they wouldn't need a lot of accommodations, like people travel today (vs.10). It was also said to them not to go out for the purpose of money. They could freely receive, though (vs.8: see also Luke 10:7). They were to stay in peaceful settings in their ministry, those who acknowledged their ministry (vss.11-15; example, Acts 9:43). They were to conduct the same ministry they watched Jesus do (vs.8). Note—shaking the dust off their feet was the Jewish saying of shaking off anything impure (vs.14). They were to be shrewd (Greek, practically wise) as serpents (and certainly smarter over <u>this</u> one in Gen.3:1-5; 2 Cor.10:5; 2:11) and innocent (to evil) as doves (see 3:16, 17; John 16:8). With the Lord's strength they were to endure hatred toward them and persecution (Jn.15:9, 18), completing their task of going through their country of Israel; and when brought before kings, leaders and governors, they were to trust the Holy Spirit for the things to say (vss.16-23, 27). They were to go forth continuing to confess Jesus and the gospel message (vss.32, 33), remembering a student is not above their teacher (vs.24; recalling Gen.3:4, 5; Phil. 2:5-11; note—the statement made by Jesus about Beelzebul refers back to the Pharisees statement of Him in 9:34; they were not to fear them—vs.25, 26; see 12:36, 37). Building the Family of God through the Gospel in Jesus' ministry on earth can separate members of families on earth if they do not all believe. So the heart of God is to save families (see comments on 8:14-17). Our love for God who made us and saves us and cares for us must be greater than any earthly relationships. This will be shown in our words and deeds; and those who bless Jesus' disciples in their ministry will not lose their reward from Him (vss.31, 34-42).

Matt.11:1-19—Matthew now returns to speaking about John the Baptist, whom we have not heard about since chapter 4:12, possibly because as John the Baptist said—"He must increase, but I must decrease" (John 3:30). John is in prison at the time Matthew writes this passage (see 14:1-12 for the background of John's imprisonment). The turn of events for John and the Roman government still predominating over Israel appears to have caused John to question some if Jesus was the coming Messiah or (as John was a forerunner) if the "true" Messiah was yet coming (vs.3). John had already declared about as strong as one could (and with God's revelation) who Jesus was (see John 1:29, 33, 34).

Jesus' response to John's disciples is to reiterate His works (vss.2, 5, 6). In God's eyes, this is the true demonstration of His King (2:2), but with Israel in bondage to the Romans, not necessarily what the people expected. Yet, regardless, Jesus gives John one of the highest acclamations given to man (vs.11). John appears to have performed his ministry flawlessly and sacrificially, paying the ultimate price of his life dedicated to God's service as other prophet's had done as well (14:10, 11). John was the start of a new era (vs.13; Heb.1:12; Luke 16:16). So now, those ("whosoever"—John 3:16; 1:12) who believe in his message and come to receive Jesus as Savior and Lord become even greater than him (vs.11; see Heb.1:1, 2). Instead of responding in faith to Jesus' message and not by personal works (vs.1), some were trying to force their way into God's kingdom (vs.12; "everyone" in Luke 16:16). John came in the "spirit and power of Elijah" (Lk.1:17; Jn.1:21). As Jesus was alluding to about "hearing" what He was saying (vs.15), if they had listened and received John's ministry and message, they would not have trouble receiving His (3:5, 6; Mk.4:10-12; Jn.1:7-9, 15). The best part is demonstrated in actions to back up the words of the proclamation—this is where wisdom is "proved right"—NIV (vss.19, 5, 6). Note: Jesus' analogy of playing music alludes to the beauty of His message and His and John's sacrificial lifestyle, plus Jesus' miraculous deeds He performed (vs.5), yet not many were accepting them, and even trying to claim that evil was involved (9:34; 11:18; 11:16-19). But the bottom line is God's miraculous works back up His wisdom expressed (vs.19).

Matt.11:20-24—Along with those who did not accept His message and works (see vs.7), Jesus goes on to denounce (a public rebuke—vs.20) the cities around where He was staying (cities of the north part of the Sea of Galilee), who were not repenting after hearing His message and seeing and hearing of His great miracles there. He compared (warned) them about the day of judgment—even Hades and Sodom! Even those judgments would be more tolerable than theirs (compare 13:17).

Matt.11:25-30—Jesus closes this particular discourse to this crowd with a beautiful outspoken prayer to the Father and heartfelt invitation to the people (and us; more proclamation of God's wisdom expressed in our earthly world—vs.19; the word "praise" in verse 25 (KJ—"thank") means literally—to say the same thing out openly; thus, confess, thank). Jesus gave acknowledgement to the Father for hiding these things from the wise and intelligent ones (in their own eyes) of that day and revealing them (Greek word "apokalupsis"—an unveiling, uncovering, the things of God—vss.25, 27; same word for the Book of Revelation) to babes (unsophisticated in mind and trustful in disposition—Vine, for babe; see Mk.4:9-12). This was well-pleasing in the Father's sight (vs.26; for the word "well-pleasing "see also Luke 2:14 on the birth of Jesus, and Matt.12:18). Jesus invites those who are weary and burdened (not literal weight here but "feeling the weight of something"—work, worries, individual or cares of the world, etc; see 6: 24-34) to come to Him for rest (a true aspect of God's peace—see 5:9). A yoke was a brace put over two animals to help steer them together for farming work. When one "yokes" with Jesus, one learns from Him (vs.29), growing in two particular aspects of His good character—meekness (here in the Greek—see 5:5 and James 3:13 for its description) and humility (not putting oneself above or below others—above is pride, below is false humility; see helpful guidelines on relationships in Book 2 of The Family Bible Studies Series called The Levels of Relationships; vs.29). When one thinks about this, there is not much if any strife in these two characteristics; and so, being "yoked" with Jesus (our example and source of these character traits) and putting faith in Him, one finds "rest" for your soul (vs.29). For (note a reason here), His yoke is easy (Greek word here means—fit for use, able to be used, pleasant—Vine, for easy); and His burden (same word in vs.28) is light (light in weight, easy to bear, thus, relief, compared to vs.28—Vine, for light—as to weight). A great salvation message can be found in this (see vs.27); plus, a great discipleship principle; and, also, a basic truth for everyday life.

Matt.12:1-21—Matthew now records 2 incidents regarding the Jewish Sabbath—eating grains from the fields and Jesus healing a man on the Sabbath. Regarding the first event, Jesus' disciples were hungry and began to pick grains from a field to eat, which was lawful for them to do (Dt.23:24, 25). However, the Pharisees complained because they were doing this on a Sabbath day (vs.2). Jesus gives them an example from the Bible (see 4:4, 7, 10) where David ate the bread of the temple, where only priests were allowed to eat it (1 Sam.21:6; they simply replaced it with hot (fresh) bread after David ate it; vs.4). Jesus also gave the example that the priests break the Sabbath by working on it, yet are innocent (vs.5). Jesus quotes Hos.6:6, that God desires compassion and not sacrifice as His priority (vs.7), and something (Someone) greater than the temple (and we can add, the Sabbath) is there with them, they needed to recognized—the Lord of the Sabbath (vs.8). Jesus then proceeds to heal a man with a withered hand in their synagogue on a Sabbath day, drawing a similar, only now more extreme, response from the Pharisees (vs.14). Jesus gives another great example of people pulling their sheep out of a pit if needed on a Sabbath. How much better and so important for another person to bring a needed healing to them; (see Mt.8:28-34, on God's value on each human being; also, remember Jesus' heart for healing in bringing the Gospel to mankind –Mt.4:23, 24; 12:15). Now with this extreme response by the Pharisees to destroy Him, Jesus leaves that area and proceeded to heal all those who needed so, of those who were following Him (vs.15). Also, with this statement made by Pharisees, we see the first proclamation of the Gospel to go forth to the Gentiles. Matthew now quotes the time for Is.42:1-4 to be fulfilled. Note the emphasis on justice and His quiet nature and heart to reach outcasts and the needy in this Isaiah passage being inaugurated by Jesus; (see the Trinity in verse 18; also, Book 1 of <u>The Family Bible Studies Series</u> called <u>The Family of God-Foundation</u> for a description on the character and functions of the Trinity, plus eight Bible Studies on the character of God).

Matt.12:22-45—Matthew now concentrates on this passage in his gospel writing of Jesus of Jesus' rebuke to the Pharisees. It has now reached this level of necessity to do so, due to the Pharisees response to His message and works stated in vss.14 and 24. Jesus first performs quite a complicated healing (to us, anyway) of a demon-possessed man, unable to speak or talk (vs.22). The crowds were so amazed that they wondered if Jesus was the son of David prophesied (vs.23). But notice what two blind men already said about Jesus before He healed them in 9:27; (note also the demons declaration in 8:29). Jesus speaks to the Pharisees and breaks down their statements in simple, logical thought—Satan is divided against himself if he healed this blind and mute man (implied, the sickness due to Satan's work and then healing him). Likewise, by whose name do their sons then cast out demons (vs.27, bringing the same logical result just mentioned; also, their sons couldn't do so by the Spirit of God). So, if Jesus' work comes by the Spirit of God, God's kingdom has come upon them (implied—accept or reject it, with the consequences to follow of their decision, good or bad). Instead, Jesus just bound the strong man and took back what was rightfully His (plus good health to the one He healed—vs.29). People scatter who do not follow Him, as Jesus said in vs.30 (see previously 11:7). So Jesus pronounces the unpardonable sin to the Pharisees saying what they did in vs.24 (vss.31, 32; 9:34). One might mistaken Jesus and later come to accept and receive Him for who He is; but one cannot declare God's good work of the Holy Spirit and say it is based in an evil spirit and get away with it (vs.32). This is where God draws the line in declarations about Him and His great work and words for the benefit of fallen mankind. Man must produce good fruit to please God and fill his treasure chest (mind and life) with good things, so that he may bring out good things to share with others. One's own words are to back this up, and also, sharing good things with others—as Jesus did (vss.33-37; note the previous warning along this line in 7:15-27; see also Eph.4:29, 30). The Pharisees end this incident by demanding a "sign" from Jesus (vs.38; what about the tremendous one just performed on the blind and mute man in vs.22?). Jesus said only the "sign" of Jonah will be given to them (i.e., His coming death and resurrection—vss.39, 40); and using the preaching of Jonah and the wisdom of Solomon as great examples to them of God's work, Someone even greater than these is standing in their midst (vss.41, 42, 6-8)! Even if demons are cast out of them, (fallen angels, not content with waterless (desert) places, meant originally to minister to mankind for God and now have turn against them), and not replaced by the Spirit of God, their last condition would be far worse than what it was then (vss.43-45; see Lk.11:13).

Matt.12:46-50—Jesus finishes this discourse by declaring what it means to be in His family. Jesus loved His earthly family, but they too needed to receive Him for who He is—God's Son (3:17; 14:33; 26:63, 64; Lk.3:23-38). The "sign of Jonah" (vss.39, 40) of His death on the cross for the sins of the world and His resurrection from the dead is His gift of salvation to mankind. When one then turns from their sins and receives Him into their life, they come into the Family of God (Jn.1:12, 13; 3:16, 17; see the helpful Prayer of salvation at the end of the book if you have not received Jesus yet as your Lord and Savior or know a friend who hasn't yet done so). This is the will of God to become a brother or sister and follower of Jesus (vs.50; see also previously in 7:24-27).

Matt.13:1-52—With the Pharisees plotting to take the life of Jesus (12:14), followed by the declaration of Jesus' ministry bringing hope now to the Gentiles (12:18-21), Jesus begins His teaching to the crowds in parables in Matthew chapter 13. Jesus would share more parables later again as He comes closer to His trial, death and resurrection (chapters 21-24). So, then, what is a parable? A parable is a teaching Jesus used to tell stories with comparisons and analogies to help declare God's truths. How are they understood? The answer is quite simple, given to us here in chapter 13, verses 1-23 and verse 36. In the parable of the sower and the seed, people will hear Jesus' teaching, but various things keep them from understanding them (the devil, afflictions and persecutions, worries and deceitfulness of riches), which can play a factor in taking away His words and not bearing good fruit (vss.19-22). The person who does receive it in his/her heart, keeps it there, understands it and lives it out and bears good fruit of various proportions (vs.19—in His heart, vs.23—bears fruit; 2:24; 12:50). Those who did not understand, saw what Jesus was doing, but did not "see" Him for who He is (or truly, believe); they were hearing what He said, but did not "hear" with the heart, and so did not understand (vss.13-15). The key for them to understand the parables is revealed to us in vss.16, 36—the disciples came to Him and asked Him to explain the parables to them. Others just left (see 11:7; 12:30) and so, the stories remained in parables, unless they came to Jesus to explain them to them (to turn to Him—vss.10-15; Mk.4:11). This is a very important principle here for us also, to study and understand God's word in its context and ask God to explain His word to us (see also James 1:5). All this with the help of the gift of the Holy Spirit, when we come to believe and receive Jesus into our life (Lk.11:13; Jn.14:16, 17, 26; 16:13-15).

In the mustard see parable (vss.31, 32), the kingdom (God growing His Family, the Church) begins very small (one person at a time, either individually or in crowds), but becomes a huge tree that birds can nest in (the consummation in Rev.21, 22 of the completion of God's Family; see Book 4 of <u>The Family Bible Studies Series</u> called <u>The Theology of the Bible—The Family of God</u>, to see this main theme of the Bible and how God builds His family from the start (Gen.1) to the completed finish—Rev.21,22). Note: Many have said the mustard seed isn't the smallest of all seeds. It was the smallest (as we know, though) to the Palestinian farmer in Jesus' time.

In the parable of the leaven (vs.33), the emphasis is on the dimension of the "hiddeness" of the kingdom. The measure used here is the common household amount for a baking (Vine, for the Greek word, sation). Its "hiddeness" will one day fill the whole earth (Rev.21, 22).

Matthew declares Jesus teaching in parables as a fulfillment of Ps.78:2 (vs.35).

When Jesus went back into the house after teaching in a boat off shore the Sea of Galilee (vss.1, 2, 36), the disciples asked Him to explain the parable of the wheat and the tares (weeds; vss.24-30, 36-43). The parable is similar to Jesus' near-ending of the Sermon on the Mount (7:15-23). Only His Family will be allowed into His everlasting kingdom (vs.43; see the previous 12:46-50), not those who did not produce good fruit (7:15-20; 13:19-22), or those who commit lawlessness (sinful deeds of lifestyle and unrepented—vss.7:23; 13:41, 42); and those who never knew Him (personal salvation—12:46-50; 7:23; Jn.1:12, 13).

The parable of the hidden treasure and the valuable pearl emphasizes the great joy and commitment one expresses when coming into God's kingdom and Family (vs.44-46; 12:46-50; Jn.16:22, 33; 1 Pet.1:3-9; see also Is.33:6).

The parable of the catch of fish reiterates the wheat and the tares; not a lot of difference, but finishes with the same warning at the end of the parable (vss.47-50). Now Jesus says to His disciples that they can take all these great "treasures of truth" and share them with others in His ministry (vss.51, 52; 10:24, 25a).

Matt.13:53-58—Jesus went back to His home town, but was not well received (vss.57, 58; 4:13). As a carpenter's son and His family, they knew, but were bewildered where and how He obtained such miraculous powers and wisdom (vs.54)! They were not connecting His power and words with who He was (the demons sure knew Him—8:29!) and where He was from and who sent Him (10:40). Certainly He was at lease a prophet (vs.57), but more than that (12:41), and greater than Solomon's wisdom for sure (check out their own words—vs.54; 12:42)! And so, the honor was not there (vs.57; Mark in his Gospel expands it some more in 6:4). It was getting difficult for Jesus to find a crowd who would believe and where He could perform His wonderful, miraculous works (vss.54, 57, 58).

Matt.14:1-13—Matthew gives a clear account of how the martyrdom of John the Baptist took place. John had spoken to Herod (Antipas) that it was not right (against the Mosaic law) for him to take his brother Philip's wife (vs.3; unfortunately, things as such were not too uncommon a story with the Roman rulers of that time). So, he was put in prison, known to be a prophet (vs.5). At an overextended grant given by the king to the daughter his wife Herodias, Herodias requested for John to be beheaded and the king regretfully ordered it done (vss.9-11). Verse 13 gives us the response of Jesus once He heard about John. It seems to lean toward a turning point in His ministry. Note: He went away privately to a (literally, in the Greek), desert place, undoubtedly affected by what took place with John the Baptist, especially after such great acclaim was given about John by Jesus shortly ago (11:7-19). With all the previous disbeliefs and now a plot forming against His own life (12:14, 24; 13:57, 58), Jesus knew that His trial would be coming soon, also (16:21).

Matt.14:14-21—In the feeding of the crowd of 5,000, people came from all around neighboring cities to see Jesus; and though Jesus left in a boat, they followed Him on foot to where He was going (vs.13). When Jesus saw them, the first thing He did, when feeling compassion for them, is heal the sick among them (this word "sick" is rare in the New Testament, used only 5 times and can mean "feeble" also—see 1 Cor.11:30). This account of Jesus feeding the 5,000 is written in all four Gospel books of the New Testament. Note vs.15, "…when evening came"—it took some time to heal their sick. The disciples suggested, being this late in the day, for the crowd go to nearby villages to eat. Jesus has a compassionate answer for them—they don't need to (probably a surprise to the disciples—vs.16; John 6:6 says Jesus already knew what He intended to do). Jesus then spoke to the disciples for them to feed the crowd, but with their limited resources available at that time, this would not be possible. But Jesus had a way to make it work (note, already intended). He looked up to heaven first, then, multiplied the fish and bread that the disciples had, and fed the crowd; and they all ate and were satisfied with the food (vss.19, 20). Twelve baskets (large wicker baskets—often used for travel; one might think of a picnic basket today) full, were left over—plenty for all to enjoy (vs.20). A beautiful, miraculous feeding (I have heard or read of similar occurrences happening in our world since the time of Jesus when this took place and in different ways it took place).

Matt.14:22-33—After such a busy day of events, Jesus sent the disciples in a boat to the other side of the lake, and finally gets the moment alone He wanted on the mountain to pray (vss.22, 23). Meanwhile, the disciples were in a wind storm on the sea that was tossing their boat around on the water. Then Jesus came walking on the water to them. They thought it was a spirit or image of something they were seeing and Jesus helped calm them when He said it was Him. Peter wanted to be sure and asked the Lord to call him to Himself. He did and Peter began to walk on the water, but soon began to doubt and to sink into the water (the Greek word, "doubt" occurs only twice in the New Testament, both in Matthew (28:17), and means—to stand in two ways, implying uncertainty which way to take; here for Peter, onward to Jesus or back to the boat). Peter cried out to Jesus to save him and Jesus lifted him back into the boat safely, asking him why he doubted. Those in the boat worshipped Him for who He truly is—the Son of God (vs.33). The wind became calm when Jesus got into the boat (and probably Peter, too).

Matt.14:34-36—They all arrived safely at Gennesaret, a town on the northwest side of the Sea of Galilee. When the people of the town recognized Jesus, they sent word into all the surrounding districts for the ones who were ill to come to Him. They asked

Him earnestly if they could simply touch the fringe of His cloak; and as many did this were completely made well (restored to health—vs.36).

Matt.15:1-20—Matthew now records Jesus having another tangle with the Pharisees, this time over one of their traditions—washing hands before eating bread (to avoid defilement (vss.1, 2). As in the previous battles with the Pharisees concerning casting out demons and about the Sabbath (12:1-14, 25-37), Jesus again breaks down their logic and here shows their lack of a spiritual basis (root) in their traditions. Here He turns the tide on them and asks why they leave the commandment of God and put their tradition in place of it (vss.3, 4)—for children are to honor their father and mother—Ex.20:12; 21:17). The problem is declared in vs.5, what they allowed to take the place of this commandment of God, best stated in its literal meaning by the King James Version—"It is a gift, by whatsoever thou mightiest be profited by me." The problem here is that this is not honorable to the parent, which the parents are responsible to follow as well (the commandment of God—vss.6-9). Jesus clarifies to the crowd what real defilement is, not failing to wash hands but failing to repent of the "defilement of the heart" and what comes from there, needing repentance (quite a list here beginning with evil thoughts—vss.18-20). That is why He came to die and rise again, to free people of these things (see 1 John 3:8; Eph.2:3-6).

Matt.15:21-28—Probably sensing that the Pharisees would not be too receptive to what Jesus just said about "true defilement" (and especially after their previous response in 12:14—remember, His time is not yet ready for His trial, death and resurrection, also),

Jesus heads up north out of His native country to Phoenicia—Syria, to the district of Tyre and Sidon along the Mediterranean Sea coast (vs.21). Jesus now brings "The Hope" to the Gentiles, as prophesied previously in 12:17-21. A lady greets Him as Lord and Son of David—great proclamation and faith statement in a Gentile land (remember, the Jews were still wondering about these proclamations regarding Him (12:23). She was continually crying out to Jesus for mercy to deliver her daughter from a terrible demon-possession (vss.22, 23). Jesus said that He was only sent to the lost sheep of Israel (as a priority first and where He was primarily ministering, to those in Israel (see 10:5, 6), but He did not forget the prophecy in 12:17-21; see John 10:16). She stated in great faith that the outcasts (dogs, Gentiles) will take crumbs that fall from the master's table; i.e., we will take what we can for our hope too, having the same needs as the Jewish people (vss.25-27; 12:17-21). The power of Jesus and her stated great faith healed her daughter at that time (vs.28).

Matt.15:29-39—Jesus left the country up north and went back to the Sea of Galilee, going up to a mountain (more probably, mountainside) to sit. He only now had to observe and watch the crowds come to Him in large numbers and He would begin to minister to them by healing their sick and ailing people. Matthew here not only describes the <u>kind</u> of miraculous healings Jesus did, but the <u>effects</u> (cures) of each kind of healing He did (a great proclamation of the tremendous mighty miracles that Jesus did—vss.29-31; 4:23, 24). The setting is now similar to the feeding of the 5,000 previously (14:13-21). Notes—these had been with Jesus for three days (probably had food initially, but now out;

again, a great sign of the time and need for all the healing Jesus did—vs.32). The disciples stated again to Jesus the similar kind of response and mystery (to them) of how to feed the crowd as previously—vs.33; 14:15-17). Jesus took their seven loaves and few fish, broke them (and multiplied them) and gave them to the disciples to distribute to the people to eat (vss.35, 36). They were all satisfied and seven baskets-full were collected at the end (the word for "baskets" in the Greek refers to a reed basket, plated and can be rather spacious, like a hamper, sometimes large enough to hold a man—Vine, for basket; see Acts 9:25 about the Apostle Paul). Jesus dismissed the crowd and then travelled by boat to the town of Magadan, on the western tip of the Sea of Galilee, after feeding the 4,000 (vss.38, 39).

Matt.16:1-12—The Pharisees and Sadducees wasted no time to approach Jesus and test Him again, asking Him <u>again</u> for a sign from heaven (vs.1; for the word "test" see the explanation of the word back in Matt.4:1). They must have forgotten Jesus' answer previously to this same question (12:38-45)! Jesus is kind and patient in His answer and could have given the same answer to them (and does, in part). But instead, gives them an analogy of predicting the weather—couldn't they "see" who was standing in their midst doing all those miraculous, powerful works (signs) of God and the time of His (the Messiah's) coming? So Jesus warned His disciples to beware of the teaching of the Pharisees and Sadducees (vss.5-12); see previous warning in 15:14; always live by God's word, an important principle for parents teaching their children, as Jesus does here.

Matt.16:13-20—Jesus again briefly headed up north to Caesarea Philippi, about 25 miles north of the Sea of Galilee. It is at the base of Mt. Hermon (9,101 feet high), where many think that the Transfiguration took place (17:1-8). Here Jesus asks his disciples who they think that He is (vs.15). Peter gives his great proclamation answer—"You are the Christ (i.e., the Messiah), the Son of the living God" (vs.16). Jesus affirms to him that it was the Father in heaven who made this known to him (vs.17; see 14:33). Jesus, with this declaration by Peter, changes his name at this time to Peter (Greek for "rock," a large or mass of rock compared to a stone—Vine, for rock), for his rock-solid faith. Keys to the kingdom will be given to him (probably after Jesus' ascension; see how the "keys" began the church in Peter's great messages and miracles in Acts 2-5). The keys and the authority given by Jesus to bind and loose (simply put, handcuff and remain, or set free— see 10:1-8; Lk.10:17-20; Jn.20:23) refer back to Is.22:22, where Eliakim was given the "key of the house of David," managing his affairs while David ruled and fought his battles. He had the authority (and watch) who was allowed in and who (and what) was allowed to go out, the analogy of Peter's authority given by Jesus to proclaim the Gospel message and carry it out in his ministry for the Lord (vss:18,19; compare the opposition in 23:13). Note— Hades (i.e., death, the place of those unbelieving who have died await final judgment—see Lk.16:19-31), shall not prevail over the church—God's family; see John 1:5; 3:16; 10:27-30; Rev.21 and 22). Jesus did not want the disciples to declare Him specifically (yet) as the Messiah, so others would discover it by faith for themselves; plus, to avoid over extended and distracting publicity from His ministry (vs.20).

Matt.16:21-28—Jesus now for the first time announces to His disciples that He is soon to go to Jerusalem and take on the cross of His death. As difficult as this is to hear for the disciples, the word comes to the disciples that they will need to take up their cross and follow Jesus in their ministry for Him, too (vs.24). While Peter, just given a great commissioning by Jesus, tries to prohibit this done to Jesus, Jesus explains why it is necessary for Him to do this in His ministry on earth (see back to the beginning of His ministry at 3:15-17). Jesus' rebuke, I believe, is completely toward Satan in this spiritual battle (best literal translation of the Greek in vs.23—"Get behind me, Satan! You are a stumbling block to Me, for you are thinking not about the things of God but the things of men"). Jesus then stresses, with the meaning of all that is taking place, what it means to gain their life and preserve their own soul (vss.24-26). It all comes out to following Him. Note—see in vs.27, when Jesus comes back to earth, He comes with His angels, in the glory of the Father, to judge and give out His rewards (see 1 Cor.3:10-15). Verse 28 appears to refer to His upcoming Transfiguration, so those with Him may see a glimpse of His glory (truly amazing in light of Ex.33:17-23)...and so it will be in His second coming to earth, to establish and reign in His kingdom—Matt.24:30, 31; Dan.7:13, 14).

Matt.17:1-8—Up on the mountain with Peter, James and John, Jesus is transfigured before them (literally, changed into another form in the Greek word meaning—vs.1, 2). His face then shined like the sun (see Moses in Ex.34:34, 35) and His garments were as white as light (vs.2; Rev.1:16). Moses and Elijah appeared and were talking with Jesus (Luke adds in his account that Moses and Elijah appeared in glory (their glorified bodies) and talked to Jesus about His departure coming up—Lk.9:31). Peter wanted to make three tabernacles, probably indicating the hope that this was the deliverance for Israel (Lev.23:34, 42, 43). Then, out of the cloud over shadowing them, a voice appeared, similar to the start of Jesus ministry at His baptism (3:17), saying, "This is My beloved Son, with whom I am well-pleased; listen to Him" (vs.5). When the disciples became afraid, Jesus touched them and encouraged them not to be frightened; and when they looked up, they were the only ones left with Jesus (vss.6-8).

Matt.17:9-13—Jesus mentions to the disciples who saw His transfiguration, not to tell anyone about it till after He rose from the dead (vs.9; see 2 Pet.1:16-18). Jesus then clarifies the subject of Elijah coming back (Mal.4:5, 6). He speaks to them confirming that he will (vs.11), but John the Baptist came "like" Elijah (i.e. in his spirit and power—Lk.1:17), and even similar ministry to what Elijah will do (Lk.1:17; Mal.4:5, 6); but they rejected him and did whatever they wished to him (vss.12, 13). So, Jesus says for the second time, He will suffer at the hands of men soon coming (vs.12; 16:21—but rise from the dead!). He says this to them for the third time, with all these truths in mind, again in vss.22, 23.

Matt.17:14-23—Matthew records a more brief account of the epileptic boy being healed (Marks account is more extensive—Mk.9:14-29). The complexity with where the boy could fall certainly brings out the urgency of his dad (vs.15). Jesus is disappointed to hear the dad say that the disciples could not cure him (vs.16, in light of the commissioning of 10:1, 8). The rebuke by Jesus, I believe, is not aimed at the disciples, though, because He spoke (in general) to an "unbelieving and perverted generation" (Greek, turned aside, twisted, for the word perverted), certainly the battle of continued ministry in the world…"how long shall I put up with you?" (vs.17; compare 16:15, 16; John 15:3). This particular boy's illness was associated with a demon, and Jesus casted it out and the boy was healed (vs.18). When the disciples asked Jesus why they couldn't cast the demon out, Jesus said because of their "smallness of faith" (vs.20). Mark adds (which may have been added later in Matthew), that this kind can come out only by prayer (i.e., they possibly needed to pray more first (and continue as needed) to accomplish this; God must receive the glory in the healing; careful also, not to get caught up in the excitement itself of the moment at hand; Mk. 9:29).

Matt.17:24-27—This brief passage of paying a tax for Jesus and Peter is more than about paying the tax. So that it does not become a stumbling block to the tax collectors, Jesus has Peter catch a fish and pay it for both of them (quite a miracle in itself here). Peter's answer of telling them that Jesus pays His taxes may have been a little too quick in the immediate answer. The second tax mentioned in vs.25 is a fixed amount per person that is levied on adults. Can't imagine what else Jesus would even have a tax to pay in the life He led on earth. So, He would need to pay this one. Yet, we know He would be consistent paying taxes anyway (22:17-21). Yet, this could have been an opportunity for Peter to declare (as he did in 16:16) that he is walking with and serving "the Son of the living God." He would later write to the church to be ready to give a good answer, as such, to those who ask about the hope that is in you (1 Pet.3:15). Note—Jesus paid not only the tax for Himself, but Peter's also (the coin Peter caught was enough to pay for two).

Matt.18:1-35—Matthew devotes this whole chapter to quite a few discipleship principles Jesus wants the Apostles and the church to know and follow. The question of who is the "greatest" in the kingdom of heaven appears to come about in a discussion about "themselves" (so brought out in Mark's account in 9:34). They may have been looking to ultimate rewards or possibly misunderstanding the statement that was previously given to Peter (16:17-19; see also John 21:2, 3). Jesus wanted to be sure that they were not getting beyond themselves because of their position with Him, so He brings them back to a lesson in humility, as a very important characteristic in their service of ministry for Him (see previous in 11:11, 28-30). Jesus gives the illustration of a child to them (vss.2-4), reminding them of the humble dependence of a child's position. When one becomes a Christian and comes into the Family of God, that person enters as a child, totally dependent on our Father in heaven (John 1:12, 13), as a child depends on his/her earthly parents. Christians are to grow and mature to become men and women of God (Rm.8:14-17; Eph.4:11-13). Humility and dependence on God leads the way in His ministry, which is what Jesus was developing with His Apostles and disciples, to become strong men and women of God in their ministry for Him. They were also to be sure not to cause any stumbling blocks to the little children, as their Father in heaven along with their angel (see also Acts 12:15), who sees the face of God, see them also, as well

(18:5-14; note the great love of the Father here for the children and 1 John 3:1,2; see other related verses of Jesus' lesson being taught here—Eccl.4:4; 2 Cor.10:11-14; Matt.19:13-15). Jesus stresses some more important principles of discipleship in the rest of this chapter. The next issue Jesus teaches is reproving (see this verb in John 16:8 through vs.11) a brother (or sister) when they have sinned (vs.15; see a preliminary of doing this in Gal.6:1, in a spirit of meekness (Greek), for which see back to Matt.5:5 and James 3:13). In a series of steps, Jesus says to start out one on one in the reproof, and only if needed further, then with two or three witnesses; and only then, if still necessary, to take the matter before the church at large (vss.16, 17). Note the careful and respectful progression here. If the one who has sinned still then refuses to listen, they can be treated as a Gentile (outcast) or tax-gatherer (outcast, till proven to do the right thing—vs.17). In this process, Jesus says to them the same "binding and loosing" words that He said previously to Peter in building the church (16:19). Here, whatever things (plural) they bind on earth (context there, sin related issues) shall have been bound in heaven; and whatever things (plural) you loosed, shall have been in heaven. In short, with the help of the Greek verbs here, whatever is bound (not corrected) stays bound; whatever is loosed (set free) is loosed (unbound) in heaven (i.e., the issue has been corrected, vs.18); one can see good Biblical principles here for home life as well; see their commissioning in John 20:23. The next important principle Jesus shares is the importance of agreeing together in prayer to God, and here, in the context, of the related issue(s) at hand (vss.19, 20); the word "agree" here is where, in English, we get the word "symphony." Note that this is the goal from the beginning here (vs.15; let the Bible in its context be our guideline). When people agree on God's word, they can pray accordingly with confidence (see previous 7:7-11; 6:32, 33; also 1 John 5:14, 15). Peter then asks Jesus how many times does a person forgive someone who sins (vs.21). Jesus says not just seven times but seventy-seven times (7 being the number of perfection; and so, however many times are necessary). To the end of this chapter Jesus continues on with the importance of this point by sharing the story (parable) of a servant who was forgiven by the king a large amount of money and the servant did not forgive a fellowman for even a lot less. Jesus said not only to forgive, but to forgive from the heart (vss.21-35, vs.35; see Eph.4:29-32). Note on Jesus' answer to Peter to forgive seventy-seven times, this was not based on the person who sinned asking forgiveness first—it is a way of life in expressing God's mercy, first, to the benefit of His children, and then (hopefully), also received by the recipient (see the Lord's prayer for His children in Matt.6:14, 15; also Gal.6:1 in mind).

Matt.19:1-15—Jesus now leaves the Galilee area and puts Himself in a position to soon enter Jerusalem by going across the Jordan River, east of Judea (vs.1). Great crowds came to Him once again and, as was His ministry, He healed them there (vs.2). The Pharisees had heard also and came to test Him again (see the word "test" again in Matt.4:1, 3), this time on the topic of "lawful divorce" (vs.3). Jesus answers them with God's standard from the very beginning of time, given to Adam and Eve in Gen.1:27; 2:24; 5:2. God made them male and female and when a man leaves his parents and cleaves to his wife in marriage (the Greek word for "cleave" is glue, cement, used with metals and other materials (Vine, for cleave), they become one flesh (as exemplified in their offspring of this true relationship in marriage) and no man is to separate this, as it is God's design (vss.4-6; see the Mark passage in Mk.10:6-9; also, the spiritual representation of marriage of Christ and the church in Eph. 5:22-33). As the Pharisees tried to test Jesus even further by saying that Moses allowed a divorce (Dt.24:1-4), Jesus said to them it was because of "your hardness of heart" and this is not the way it was from the beginning of God's purpose and design (vs.8). He goes on to say that except for immorality (sexual), if one divorces his wife and marries another, that person commits adultery (vs.9; Dt.5:18). Note here even if immorality takes place, as bad as that is, it does not mean that the relationship needs to separate; it is not the unpardonable sin (Matt.12:31, 32). Remember God's design stated here in vss.5, 6; also see The Lord's prayer in 6:12-15. When people marry they need to remember their commitment and God's full design for marriage, and simple, but precise principles (vss.10-12). Love for one another and the family all go together as Jesus exemplifies by letting the little children come to Him in vss.13-15. The disciples began to rebuke them (and needed to take to heart what Jesus said about love for the children just a short time ago in Matt.18:10-14), and so, Jesus said not to hinder them from coming to Him, as stated previously in 18:1-14—the kingdom of God belongs to such as these. There is always a lot to learn from children in God's design.

Matt.19:16-30—Matthew then records the story of one coming to Jesus and asking how He can obtain eternal life. Instead of showing Him the direct path (John 3:16), Jesus shows this particular person his shortcomings—two specific ones. The first is a list from the Ten Commandments for Him to follow. His response (amazingly) is that He kept them all (remarkable; even honoring his parents completely? –vs.9; may have to check with dad and mom first on this one). These are shortcomings for all of us, of course, since the law was brought to reveal the sins of mankind—Rom.7:7-12. The second battle was that he owned much property (vs.22). This is not a problem within itself, of course (all good things come from God—James 1:17), but can be if it stands in the way of receiving God's gift of eternal life (by technical definition, one cannot buy a gift, and so here for sure). Camels would often have to get down on their knees and crawl through a small opening to their cities, owner's property, etc. wherever an entrance like this was required. Indeed, a difficult thing for them to do, especially considering their size and structure (vs.24). So this can be, as Jesus uses this illustration for the rich man. Not admitting one's shortcomings (sins) before God and being over protective (and possessive) of one's material goods and riches can make it difficult to enter into the kingdom of Heaven. But these shortcomings can apply, actually, to anyone. The answer comes when the disciples ask Jesus, "Who, then, can be saved" (vs.25)? His answer? Good news here—impossible with man (to be earned or achieved on one's own merits), but all things (including God's gift of salvation) are possible with God (vs.26; John 1:12, 13; 3:16; Rm.6:23). Peter, wondering about future rewards for them following Jesus, asks Jesus about this. Jesus replies that when He sits on His glorious throne, those who have followed Him (traditionally understood as the twelve apostles here) will judge the twelve tribes of Israel (vs.28; see also Dan.7:9-14). Jesus adds their rewards will be great, not only eternal life, but far outlasting rewards to come (Mark also adds "persecutions" in 10:30, while Mark and Luke bring out in their passages of this verse "many times as much at this time" (Lk.18:29, 30), God's giving, His provision and discretion for gifts and rewards). Many, though, (notice not all, but many) who have had the enjoyment and comforts of the "first" things (regarded as important) of this world (and not building up "greater" rewards to come—6:19-21), will be last (on reward giving); but those last, who have not built their treasures on earth and have been "rich toward God" (Lk.12:16-21), will be first (vs.30); the sowing and reaping principle—Gal.6:7; 2 Cor.9:6, in life living and materials.

Matt.20:1-16—Jesus goes on to share another story with the disciples about rewards, since they were asking about that. He concludes at the end of the story with the same statement He made about rewards previously—that the first will be last, and the last first. But, this one has a different meaning to it. Notice that no matter how long the laborers worked, they all got paid the same (as agreed to with the owner previously to their work, vs.13). So, the first got paid the same as the last, the last the same as the first (vss.14-16). So there (obviously) is a standard of rewards (16:27; Ps.62:12; Prov.12:14); and God is generous (vs.15; Lk.12:32-34).

Matt.20:7-19—Jesus declares to the disciples (for actually, the fourth time—16:2; 17:12, 22, 23) that He is going to be handed over to chief priest and scribes (and into the hands of men) to be scourged and crucified; yet, on the third day, will rise from the dead.

Matt.20:20-28—This statement and request by the mother of the sons of Zebedee (James and John; 4:21) usually receives (as some took it back then) quite a bit of negative review. On the one hand, though, it may not be that much out of line, since Jesus had just mentioned that they will help Him in the future with some of His judgment procedures (i.e., concerning the twelve tribes of Israel (19:28). Yet, it was trying to put them in a personal advantageous position (carrying out this responsibility—vs.21). The other ten (apostles) certainly did not take this in a positive way (vs.24). So keeping on the topic of rewards just mentioned, Jesus exhorts them that if they really desire to be great (vs.26, as asking for such a position), they will need to become a "servant" (quite opposite of the rulers of their time—vs.25), and that it starts with serving each other (vss.26, 27). Jesus was their example (vs.28; and look to the extent He was our example in His life)!

Matt.20:29-34—As Jesus went out from Jericho (about 15 mi. from Jerusalem) He healed two blind men along the roadside. Mark's gospel refers to only one man, named Bartimaeus, who sought Jesus for healing (10:46). But as we see in 9:27-31 of two men Jesus previously healed, it is not surprising that with this kind of handicap that they would have a faithful companion in their travels, and that one would be the primary spokesman, as we see in these cases of Jesus' healings. What is interesting once again here is that while the Jews were still trying to figure out if Jesus was the prophesied Son of David (the Messiah; 12:23), the blind men that Jesus healed had Him figured out all along; and here, calling out for mercy and healing, proclaimed Him twice as the Son of David (vss.30, 31). Such faith brought immediate compassion from Jesus and healing to the blind men, who then followed Jesus (vs.34; 8:22, 23).

Matt. 21:1-11—The Triumphal Entry of Jesus into Jerusalem is covered also in Mark and Luke's Gospel. Two noted prophecies are fulfilled here. The first is from Zech.9:9. Jesus was coming from the Mount of Olives, from where the Jews expected their King to come (Zech.14:4). Some must have noted this prophecy, that Jesus (once again, after the blind men declared on the road) is the Son of David (the Messiah, vs.9). Others, undoubtedly, wondered how a king could come riding on a donkey with the colt, since king's would usually ride a white victory horse (Rev.6:2; but He certainly will—Rev.19:11-16!). And this king, all along, came peacefully and in (literal Greek) meekness (see 5:5; 11:28-30; Zech.9: 9, 10). The next prophecy is from Ps.128:26, praising Jesus who comes in the name of the Lord. Hosanna means for the people a cry for salvation, as they were waiting for their kingdom to be restored (see Acts 1:6) and undoubtedly hoped that was the time. But the city was not all ready, as some asked who this was riding into town (vs.10). The Greek verb helps us here as the crowd answered (imperfect tense, i.e., continuous action in the past) that (as they had been declaring following Him) this is the prophet Jesus of Nazareth of Galilee (the Greek does have the article before the word prophet, and so, most likely, declared here as The Prophet of Dt.18:18, prophesied by Moses). As a result, Jesus gets the acclamation He rightfully deserves going into the city. He will one day reign from Jerusalem as the Prophet and

Messiah and King (and Priest—see Book 4 of <u>The Family Bible Studies Series</u>-The main theme of the Bible, <u>The Family of God</u>) over all the earth (vs.5; Zech 9:9, 10); Zeph.3:14-20; Mt.1:1, 16; Rev.19: 11-16).

Matt.21:12-17—Jesus proceeded to enter the temple and cast out all those buying and selling there (for their sacrifices). This had turned the temple into a place of commercial business, thus robbing God of His intent for prayer and for seeking God foremost. The purchases were to be made outside the temple (see 5:23, 24). The quote here from Jer.7:11 about "robbing God" had to do with mixing worship of false gods with God Almighty in the time of Jeremiah (Jer.7:8-12). Those with handicaps still followed Jesus and He healed them there, a beautiful place to declare the mighty miracles and love of God (vs.14; see also 12:9-13). The children pick up the declaration from the crowd in vs.9 and likewise proclaim hosanna to Jesus, the Son of David (vs.15). When the chief priests and scribes heard this, they expressed anger and asked Jesus if He heard what they said. Matthew records Jesus saying that this fulfills Ps.8:2, where even infants and babes will declare praise to God (vs.16). As the initial design of God, what a great thing for all His family members to do (see the effects of such in the complete verse of Ps.8:2).

Matt.21:18-22—The prophecy of the fig tree refers to Israel and gives the impression that no more harvest was there for Jesus to reap (i.e., the city at large; yet, see Lk.23:41-43). With the fig tree withering, the disciples were amazed and asked Jesus how this happened (vs.20). Jesus uses this example as an opportunity to build their faith in prayer. He said believe what you ask for and you will receive (vs.22; so, asking, believing, (in the Greek, an ongoing participle) and receiving go together; see 7:7-11; also, John 1:50, 51; 5:20; 14:12).

Matt.21:23-32—Demonstrating the difficulty in harvesting at this point in Jesus ministry, the chief priests and elders of the people asked Him where He got this authority to do these things (vs.23). This has been somewhat answered in a previous battle with the Pharisees (12:28-30). But Jesus turns the request right back to them with a question of His own for them, having them acknowledge where John the Baptist's ministry was from—God or man. Choosing not to answer Jesus' question, He did not answer theirs as well (vs.27). Not leaving the question closed though Jesus goes on to speak a family story of a father and two sons. One son said he would do what his father asked but didn't do it; the other said no, but changed his mind and then did it (vss.28-30). Jesus asked them which son did the will of his father (vs.31) and they said rightfully the second. Jesus uses their answer to declare John the Baptist's ministry was done in righteousness (thus choosing to answer the question He asked them), and tax-gathers and harlots are entering into God's kingdom before them as a result (notice Jesus' words let them know they can still change their minds, too—vs.31), because they (tax-gathers and harlots) had received John's ministry (3:5-8).

Matt.21:33-46—Jesus now exposes the plot of the chief priests and Pharisees to kill Him with the parable of the vineyard (see also Is.5:1-7; Matt.12:14). Other slaves in the story could refer to the prophets before from Him (17:12). He predicts its destruction, unless they repent (vs.41). Peter explains the chief corner stone in Acts 4:10-12 (from Ps.118:22). Thus, the prophecy that God's kingdom will be taken away from them and given to another who will produce God's fruit is given (the Church, vs.43). Jesus warned to watch that people would not stumble over Him but accept Him for who He is—the Son of David (Messiah) and the Son of God (1:1, 16; 14:32, 33).

Matt.22:1-14—Jesus continued to speak to them another parable (see Matt. 13 for the definition of a parable). This is a story of a king inviting people to his wedding feast (Rev.19:7-9). Many were being invited, but not accepting the invitation (vs.5). His slaves were even mistreated and killed (vs.6). The king sent his army to destroy the murderers and their city (allusions to Jerusalem in 70 AD; vs.7). His slaves then went out into the streets and highways, and invited guests to come, both good and bad, whoever would accept the invitation (vss.9, 10). His wedding hall was then filled with guests (vs.10). But the king found one not dressed in wedding clothes for his invitation to be there (see Rev.19:7-9). By the king's response, everyone had to have wedding cloths to be there (vs.12; see John 1:12, 13; 3:16 for accepting the King's invitation to His wedding feast and into His family; then, the clothes awarded to them for living a righteous life for Him for His wedding feast—Rev.19:7-9). The chosen ones are those who do this (vs.14), but those who don't (i.e., who don't meet the qualifications see vs.8) are casted into outer darkness (vs.13; see 4:16; 6:22-24; especially 8:11, 12; 25:14-30).

Matt.22:15-46—Jesus receives more testing and "attempted traps" (vss.15, 18, 35) given to Him by the Pharisees and Sadducees now throughout this chapter. Their first question was about paying taxes to Caesar, the Roman Emperor (vs.17). Jesus, taking a coin of that time with the Emperor's engraving on it, said to pay their taxes to the government and then to give to God the things that are God's (vs.21; for them, temple taxes, tithes, festival costs, etc; Deut.14:22-29; 26:1-15; Rom.13:1-10).

The Sadducees then asked Jesus a question on marriage and marriage rights. The issue at hand is that in the Old Testament law, when a wife dies and they have no son for their offspring, a brother in the family of the deceased man was to play his role to the widowed wife and raise up a son for them, so that their name would not die out (vs.24; see Deut.25:5-10). After 7 marriages, who gets the wife? What a question to ask! Jesus, though, patient and even recognizing their evil intent to trap Him in something He says (vs.18), gives them wisdom from God and great insight for us (something to keep in mind when one goes through difficult times and how what we do and say can positively go beyond a trying moment). Jesus says that there is no longer marriage between man and wife in heaven (vs.30); and regarding the assurance of the resurrection, God is the God of Abraham, Isaac and Jacob, and so, the God of the living, not the dead (vs.32; see this statement originally given to Moses in Ex.3:6, 14, 15). Jesus' answers were amazing to the crowds (vss.22, 33, and us, too).

Matt.22:34-40—The testing (see Matt.4:1) continued toward Jesus, this next one from a Jewish lawyer (vs.35). He asked Jesus of all the commandments in the Old Testament Law (Gen.-Deut.), which is the greatest (vs.36)? With a lot to choose from, Jesus gives a 'great' answer—to love God with all your heart, soul and mind (Mark's Gospel adds "strength," also—Mk.12:30); and love your neighbor as yourself (Deut.6:5; Lev.19:18; Matt.5:43-48; 7:12). The whole Law and the Prophets rests on this kind of love (vs.40).

Matt.22:41-46—While the Pharisees had gathered together (vss.15, 34, 41), Jesus decides to ask them a question (vs.41; see previous 21:24). He asks them about the Messiah and whose son is He (vs.42). They answered Him—"The Son of David" (vs.42). The answer, of course, is partly correct (see comments on 21:33-46). Jesus shows a closer connection in His quote from Ps.110:1 in vs.44. A way to better understand this passage and stay in the context is to start from the end and work back to the beginning. David's son is the Lord (vss.43, 44), whom God will have sit by His side to put His enemies beneath Thy feet (vs.44). He is the Son of David, the Messiah (vs.42). While trying to open their eyes (the Pharisees) one more time to who He is, the main message here that Jesus gives them is a stern one—one does not want to be an enemy of the Messiah, with this judgment coming (vs.44; Ps.2:11, 12), instead of accepting the King's invitation to His wedding feast (stated just previously to them in 21:45-22:14).

Matt.23:1-39—Jesus now turns to speak to His disciples and the crowds (vs. 1). The topic is—publicly denouncing the scribes and Pharisees for their religious practices, mainly, saying things to do and not doing them themselves (vs.3; the "chair of Moses" in vs.2 is the teacher's chair). Jesus gives an early list of them in vss.4-7, and then pronounces 7 woes (i.e. denunciations) about them in the rest of this chapter (vs.14 contains an 8th woe, but most scholars say this was a later addition to Matthew, taken from either Mark 12:40 or Luke 20:47 in their Gospel accounts). Jesus reminds His disciples that they have one Teacher, one Father and one leader, who is the Christ (Messiah—vss.8-10). He recalls once again to them that in God's design and priority, being a servant is how one becomes "great" (vs.11; 20:26); and the humble will be the one's exalted (vs.12; see a helpful definition of humility in 11:29, along with Jesus example there). Here are the denunciations Jesus speaks out against—1. Do not prohibit people from entering in God's Family and Kingdom—including oneself! (vs.13, see Rom.6:23); 2. Do not be pretentious in prayers or religious practices; or take advantage of widows for personal gain (vs.14, the 8th added "woe"); 3. To travel long distances to gain one convert does not benefit at all either one, unless brought into God's Family and kingdom (vss.13,15); 4. What is most important is God, and where <u>He</u> lives, not the material things that go with the earthly practices involved in worshipping Him (temple, sacrifices, etc.; see 5:23, 24; 23:16-22; see John 14:16, 17, 23); 5. This is an extension of #4—focusing on the character of God and His work and practices foremost (justice, mercy and faithfulness, vs.23; see Prov.2:6-9; also, Book 3 of <u>The Family Bible Studies Series, Growing in God's Wisdom</u>). The result, otherwise, can be people overstraining themselves on the lesser things, while neglecting the simpler, more important matters of life (vs.24); 6. Jesus came to bring cleansing to the inside of mankind (sins) first and foremost; then, the outside can secondarily follow (vss.25, 26; 15:17-20; Heb.9:13, 14; 1 John 1:9); 7. Again, pretense here (as in #2), appearing to "look" (the outside; see Lk.20:46), but not being "cleansed" from the "inside" first (#6)—vss.27, 28; 8. Finally, Jesus says that they build tombs of the prophets and "decorate" monuments of righteous people of the past, and thus, admit that they are sons of those who murdered so many of them (vss.29-31). Some of their people will continue to do this (vs.34, the Book of Acts, etc.), so the guilt of those of that day who now know better and refuse to repent, falls, along with judgment, upon them (vss.33-36); Abel—Gen.4:8-11; Zechariah the priest (not the prophet Zechariah)—2 Chr.24:20-22). Jesus closes with a heartfelt sigh and disappointment of a "woe" of Jerusalem itself. Its doom is now confirmed and prophesied until Jesus comes back to reign there and they bless Him at large, like some did at the Triumphal Entry into Jerusalem previously (vss.37-39; 21:1-11, 19).

Matt.24:1-14—With the coming soon of Jesus' crucifixion (20:17-19; 26:2), and now hearing from Jesus that the temple will in sometime be torn down (as beautiful as it appeared—vss. 1, 2), the disciples now seem to be aware that there may be a delay in praying "Thy kingdom come" (6:10) as Jesus said for them to do. So they asked Him when will His coming be and the end of the age (vs. 3)? This "end times" discourse by Jesus can be summarized in four individual, yet collective parts: 1) The Gospel proclaimed to the whole world (3-14); 2) Instructions and information about Israel and specifics on what to look for in Jesus' return to earth (vss.15-36); 3) The rapture—like the days of Noah (vss.37-44); 4) Faithful and unfaithful servants (examples; vss.45-51).

Part 1 (vss.1-14)—Jesus says to watch for "birth pangs" that lead to further development in His return to earth (vs.8; note, these are "beginnings" of birth pangs; see John 16:21, 22 for a literal illustration of "birth pangs"). He begins by saying for them not to be misled about His return (i.e., by false prophets—vss.5,

11, 23-26); see previous warnings by Jesus on false prophets, 7:13-23; <u>important note</u>-where they say, "Here He is "(vs.23), or "see <u>their</u> miracles" (vs.24), or "He is out in the wilderness" (like Jesus use to be), or "He is in the inner (private) rooms" (vss.25,26)—note, He is <u>not</u> on the earth—He comes like <u>lightning, on the clouds of the sky, from heaven,</u> <u>for everyone to see</u> (vss.27, 30; Rev.1:7). Other indications are—wars and rumors of wars, along with famines and earthquakes (vss.6-8); tribulation to the saints and hatred toward them, and murders (vss.9-11, Jesus said on account of His name—see John 15:16-27); lawlessness increased and people's love growing cold (vss.12, 13; see again Jn.15:16-19; 13:34, 35; Matt.7:21-23); yet, through it all, the Gospel will be preached in the whole world as a witness to all the nations (vs.14; see Acts 1:8), and then the end shall come.

Part 2 (vss.15-36)—Jesus next addresses concerns for Israel and the "sign" of His coming back to earth to reign (vs.30). The "abomination of desolation" is the prophecy from Dan.9:27. In the middle of the Great Tribulation (vs.21), the "prince of the people" (Dan.9:26) will put an end to sacrifice and grain offering (Dan.9:27, the antichrist; see also 2 Thess.2:3, 4). But not long after it, Daniel 9:27 says he will meet his (the antichrist) desolation. Those in Judea are told to flee to the mountains and how to pray during those times (vss.16-22). Because of the severity of that time and for God's people, those days will be cut short (meaning, most likely, that the days of that time frame will not be that long, i.e., the total number of days, vss.21, 22); see also, Rom.9:27, 28). Corpses gather at the end of these wars in the Great Tribulation and at Armageddon (vs.28; Rev.16:16). Signs in the heavens will accompany the coming of the Lord before His return (vs.29; prophecies from Joel 2:10, 11; 3:14-17; and Is.34:1-4; Zeph.1:15; and Amos 5:20). Then His return, for all to see in great glory (vs.30; see previous Part 1; Dan.7:13, 14; Rev.1:7). The Lord will then send forth His angels (see 16:27; 25:31) to gather His people on earth (vs.31) to begin His wonderful and eagerly awaited millennial reign as conquering Ruler and King (Zeph.3:14-20; Zech.14:9, 16; see also, Mt.5:35; Ps.2:6; Ps.47; 48:1-3; Rev.19:11-18; 17:14; 20:1-6) and Lord of all the earth (Ps.24:1,2; 48:1-3; 50:12; Micah 4:13; Rev.5:9, 10; 11:17).

The parable of the fig tree goes back to Matt.21:19. Referring to Jerusalem and Israel having their country taken away, Jesus said that they would no longer bear fruit (21:19). In Matt.23:38 Jesus declared that it would now become desolate (which took place in 70 AD when the Romans destroyed Jerusalem and took over the country). But in a glimpse of hope, Jesus said they would not see Him again until they declare at large (in His return to earth) what the few had said initially at the triumphal entry from Ps.118:26 (Mt.21:9). So, having rejected their Messiah in His first coming, their city Jerusalem would be left desolate, done to them by the Romans. But here in the fig tree parable, Jesus says it begins to sprout again, branch out, put forth leaves and look forward to summer fruit once again (vs.32). This will be the fulfillment of many Old Testament prophecies of the restoration of Jerusalem and Israel (Ezk.37:24-28; Jer.31:30-34; Dan.9:24; Hos.2:18-23; 3:4, 5; Joel 3:17-21; Amos 9:11-15; Micah 4:6-8; 7:18-20; Zeph.3:11-20; Zech.1:17; 2:12; 8:1-23; 10:6; 14:1-21). God has raised up the Branch for them (Jesus, Jer.23:5, 6; 33:15,

16; Zech.3:8-10; 6:12, 13), who has conquered sin and death, and will come back to rule and reign from Jerusalem—the center of the nations designed by God (Ezk.5:5)—as King forever, in His kingdom that will never end (Dan.7:13, 14; Lk.1:31-33). Verses 33-36 states that the generation who sees these things take place (i.e., all the verses above this) will not pass away until they take place—vs.34 (i.e., they should be the ones knowing and aware of what is going on then, right at their door, vs.33; Greek is plural, doors, probably meaning all the doors of that generation seeing these things). The Greek, also, is emphatic in vs.35, that God's word will not pass away (great comfort here is this statement—see also Ps.119:137-152).

Part 3 (vss.37-44)—These verses about Jesus' discourse concerning "end time" events now focuses on God's judgment in the Great Tribulation and the Rapture for the Church. This is all compared to similarities to "the days of Noah" (vs.37). Verses 38 and 39 compare the judgment in Noah's day to the judgment of the Great Tribulation before Jesus returns to earth. Note in verse 38 Jesus talks about events taking place <u>before</u> the flood occurs, then, Noah and his family enter the ark (see Gen.7:7). Verse 39 says the people of the earth did not understand (what was about to happen), though for many years Noah had been building the ark. Then in the judgment, the flood came and took them away (vs.39), as Noah and his family were not a part of the judgment in the ark. The next two verses are language of the Rapture of the Church—one, (in the literal Greek) is taken, and one is left. There is not in the reading of the Great Tribulation to come where people at large are taken out of it (except the two witnesses of Rev.11:12; note, though, the comfort of the harvest to come of people becoming believers during that time—see Rev.7:13-17). This is the language of 1 Thess.4:13-18 of the Rapture of the Church before God's wrath and judgment come upon the earth (Rev.6-19; similar to Noah and his family taken out of the judgment of the earth at his time, yet in a different way then). In the Old Testament, similar language is used with Elijah and Enoch. Elijah was caught up to heaven to the Lord in 2 Kings 2:11; and Enoch, "walked with God; and he was not, for God took him" (Gen.5:24; see further of Enoch in Heb. 11:5—"he did not see death…because God took him up…before his being taken up he was pleasing to God"). Thus, the message here in this Part 3 is a comfort to those who come to know the Lord (come out of judgment, for the last harvest) during the Great Tribulation, and a comfort to the church before the judgment and wrath of God during that time (1 Thess.4:17, 18; Rev.6:16,17) that comes upon the earth, like Noah's day (as Noah, the Church disappears, until the 144,000 from the Lord begin their witness on the earth early in The Great Tribulation, to help bring in the last harvest—Rev.7:1-8; 14:1-5). Jesus' strong encouragement to both is to be alert and ready, for no one knows the day or hour of both His coming for the Church and for His return to earth to reign after the Great Tribulation; (probably similar to Noah not knowing the exact time as well, to enter the ark, till God declares the word to do so; vss.42-44; note—Paul uses this similar language (even the word <u>birth pangs</u>) in 1 Thess.5 to comfort the Church of the Thessalonians that they were not in the Great Tribulation, but could look forward to the

Rapture since they await obtaining God's salvation, not being destined for His wrath—1 Thess.5:8-11; 1:10).

Part 4 (vss.45-51)—This part of Matt.24 closes with examples of a good and an evil servant. The good servant is prudent (practical wisdom; see Book 3 of <u>The Family Bible Studies Series</u>, <u>Growing in God's Wisdom</u> for further discussion on the word "prudent," part of God's ingredients of His wisdom, for us and for what Solomon wanted for his family), and faithful in carrying out responsibilities (so, of parents of a household—vss.45,46). One can look forward to further blessings and responsibilities of God's possessions from Him in the future (vss.46, 47). The evil servant does not serve for his master, but mistreats fellow servants of the Master (see 18:21-35 and the story of the talents coming up) and can expect an unexpected visit from the Master one day, with judgment following those kind of actions (see 8:11, 12; 13:41, 42, 49, 50; 22:1-14).

Matt.25:1-13—Jesus continues His amplification of Part 4 above by pointing out 5 wise virgins and 5 foolish ones in light of His coming back to reign on the earth (vs.2). The wise virgins know their Lord (they meet the Bridegroom with His feast and were ready and had planned to meet the Bridegroom (Jesus in His return). They take plenty of oil for their lamps, so that day or night, whenever the Bridegroom comes, they are ready (vss.4, 9, 13). The foolish ones did not, and were left out when the Bridegroom came; they didn't know the Lord (vss.10-12) and did not prepare for His coming (similar to Noah, when he was building the ark all those years and the people did not prepare for what was coming (vs.8, 11-13; 24:38-44). So, Jesus says, to be prepared and ready for Him to come (vs.13; see the Prayer in the back of the book).

Matt.25:14-30—The story of the talents elaborates some more on Part 4 of chapter 24 about wise and foolish servants. A talent was a sum of money, given to be invested and to be built up for further gain (one might think of his/her "talents" (abilities) as a gift from God and investment to be made for and to Him, as well). This should be a basic norm for children to do for themselves and for their parents (and God the Father), also. Investments should bring further gain, and lead toward blessing others, as well. The reward comes similar to Matt.24:46, 47 (vss.20-23; yet, see Matt.25:29). The servant who did not put his talent to use and investment, was called "evil" (or wicked-vs.26); lazy (or idle—vs.26); and "useless" (vs.30), similar to the evil (wicked) servant of 24:48, and obviously, by behavior and description, like one who did not know the Master he was to be serving; or the Bridegroom he was to be preparing for when He comes (25:10-13). The results are the same as the wicked slave of Matt.24:51 (vss.8-30).

Matt.25:31-46—Jesus finishes His teaching on the "end time" events by sharing the judgment He will perform when He returns and sits on His glorious throne (vs.31). The nations will come before Him and He will separate them, between sheep (His sheep) and the goats (see the difference in 8:11, 12 between those of the kingdom of heaven and those of the kingdom of the world). Shepherds could raise both sheep and/or goats. Jesus said that His sheep know His voice and He knows His sheep by name (John 10:3, 4, 27); He gives them eternal life and they shall never perish (John 10:9, 28); and, as vulnerable as sheep are, no one shall snatch them out of His or the Father's hand (John 10:28,29). His sheep exemplify character of their Shepherd and follow Him (vss.34-40; John 10:3, 4, 14-16). Those who do not know the Good Shepherd, flee (John 10:12-14; Matt.12:30) and scatter. They do not live for or exemplify the Good Shepherd nor believe Him or follow Him (John 10:26, 27). Thus, they do not show the life of the Good Shepherd (vss.41-46; John 10:10-12) and suffer the consequences of eternal punishment (vs.46), while those who did righteous works like and for the Good Shepherd, go into eternal life and the kingdom of their King they follow (vss.34-40; see also Jn.3:16-21). Note—when Jesus returns, He returns in His glory with the angels (vs.31; 16:27; 24:31; Zech.14:5). The eternal fire is for the devil and his angels, and the final judgment, those who have followed like them and their dominion (vss.41, 46; 8:11, 12; 4:8, 9; 13:36-43).

Matt.26:1-5—Jesus now is coming closer to His crucifixion and reveals this once again to His disciples (vss.1, 2). The plot to kill Jesus and send Him to His crucifixion is being arranged in the court of the high priest, with the chief priests and elders of the people present there (vss.2-5). Doing such a thing to the True High Priest (Heb.2:17; 5:1-10) is a terrible contrast to the meaning of this position of the Jews. Jesus, though, knew this had to take place to fulfill the role of the Messiah; (Is.53; Acts 17:2-4; Matt.26:52-54).

Matt.26:6-13—Jesus then went out to the town of Bethany and was anointed by a woman for His upcoming burial. Bethany was about 1 ½ miles east of Jerusalem. It was called "the house of misery" on account of its lonely situation and invalids (people who were ill or disabled) that lived there (Unger's New Bible Dict., under Bethany). It was the home of Lazarus (John 11:1) and here in this passage Jesus is at the home of Simon the leper (vs.6). Jesus went to Bethany to occasionally lodge there (21:17) and this was the sight of His ascension to heaven (Lk.24:50). To be anointed by a woman openly in public was quite unusual for Jewish custom (see also John 4:27), but Jesus permitted this because of something more important at hand—His upcoming crucifixion and burial (vss.2, 12). Plus, what the lady has done will be remembered as a memorial of her and her deed (certainly recorded in the Scriptures is a high honor for this—vs.13). Note—for the complaint about the money and the valued perfume, see John 12:3-8.

Matt.26:14-16—These verses record the betrayal of Judas Iscariot (along with vs.16, see Lk.4:13).

Matt.26:17-29—Jesus celebrates the Passover and Feast of Unleavened Bread (celebrated together—Deut.16:1-8) with the twelve disciples (vss.17-20). It appears that Jesus had made prior arrangements for this, not unusual to be done for this important festival. Here Jesus made the betrayal of Judas known to all those present (vss.20-25). Jesus then gives the institution of communion with the twelve as a practice for the church to maintain and celebrate (vss.26-29; see also Lk.22:14-20; Acts 2:42; 1Cor.11:23-26). Note the purpose of communion and the death and resurrection included here (vss.28, 29; 1 Cor.11:26. "I drink it new with you in My Father's kingdom" is usually taken to refer to the Marriage Supper of the Lamb in Rev.19:7-9).

Matt.26:30-35—Jesus goes to the Mount of Olives (just east of Jerusalem) and predicts from Zech.13:7 that the disciples will scatter about, as His arrest and trial are about to begin (vss.30, 31, 56). However, in the midst of this grief comes the joy of His resurrection and seeing them again in Galilee after it (vss.31, 32; see also John 16:20-22). The commitment remains strong with Peter's declaration and the others, but Jesus gives Peter the announced denial of Jesus that is soon coming up (though Peter will recover with his strong faith (vss.32-35; see John 21).

Matt.26:36-46—In the Garden of Gethsemane (at the foot of the Mount of Olives), Jesus seeks the Father in prayer before going to His trial and crucifixion. Here we see the strong will of Jesus, physically, spiritually, mentally and emotionally committed to do the Father's will of why He came to earth, to die for the sins of mankind and rise from the dead, before returning back to the Father (see 2 Cor.5:20, 21). Note the tremendous emotional grief experienced by Jesus (vss.37, 38). While the others sat a distance away, Peter, James and John are close to where He prayed (vss.36, 37, 40-43). Though tired then, I think this helped Peter's recovery later on. Note the physical and spiritual battle—Jesus prayed (strengthening Him) three times for the Father's will to be done (vss.39, 42, 44). Then, He knew and said His betrayer had arrived (vss.45, 46), while He was still speaking.

Matt.26:47-56—The actual betrayal of Judas and the process of the arrest by the crowd, with swords and clubs, sent by the chief priests and elders of the people, now begins to unfold (vs.47). Judas had arranged for a sign to betray Jesus with a kiss (vss.48, 49). Peter, in his zealous intention, takes out a sword, thinking to protect Jesus (John 18:10 reveals to us that it is Peter who did this). Jesus instructs Peter to put it away (after cutting off the slave of the high priest's ear, which Luke records that Jesus healed—Lk.22:51). They do not understand yet that Jesus, the Messiah, had to suffer and die, and also rise from the dead (Mt.20:17-19). Note the zeal of Jesus—the Scriptures must be fulfilled (vss.52-56). Verse 56 fulfills verse 31.

Matt.26:57-68—Jesus is taken before the high priest, where the scribes and the elders had already assembled together (vs.57). They gave "false testimony" against Him (since He had done nothing wrong; see 27:4) and so, no evidence was found (vss.59, 60). They continued His trial with someone saying that He would destroy the temple of God and rebuild it (reference to John 2:19; note Jesus did not say that there; technically in the Greek, the verb is 2nd person plural there, referring to the people He was speaking to who would be responsible for the temple coming down because of their denial of Him, the Messiah; He would rebuild it with His death and resurrection and the Church (see Matt.23:37-39; 1 Pet.2:4-10; Eph.2:19-22). Finally, the issue of Jesus being the Son of God comes out and Jesus is put under oath to declare it (vs.63). Jesus, without reservation, speaks His answer as trying to build faith in them by their very own words (two words in the Greek says in English—"You said it"—vs.64). Note the combination of Scriptures Jesus uses for His declared answer—Dan.7:13 and previously quoted Ps.110:1, in 22:44 (vs.64). Not only does Jesus affirm His "kingdom to come" (Matt.6:10; 8:11), but declares He is "the Lord" who will be at God's right hand to judge them in Psalm 110:1 (see also, 25:31). Not willing to face these truths, they decided instead to proceed with His death, on false pretenses of "blasphemy" (speaking an evil toward God, vss.65, 66). They continued on to mock Him after that (vss.67, 68; 20:19).

Matt.26:69-75—Matthew records after this Peter's denial of Jesus, as he followed Jesus and sat in the courtyard of the high priest, awaiting the outcome of this development (vss.58, 69). There seems to be an element of surprise here to Peter as all these people approach him about his allegiance to Jesus. As he denies it the first two times (wondering about what is going on about the trial and the outcome of all this), Peter cannot escape his accent spoken to the people (similar to many of our experiences—vs.73, more specific in Mark 14:70). When the cock crowed, Peter remembered Jesus' word spoken to him about this (vs.34) and had himself a tremendously bitter grief to experience (vs.75).

Matt.27:1-10—The chief priests and elders took Jesus to Pilate, the Roman governor, to proceed with putting Jesus to death, since they are under Roman rule and could not do it themselves (vss.1,2). Judas' betrayal of "innocent blood" leads to his own death, chosen to have done to himself (vss.3-5). Matthew includes here the price and purchase of the Potter's Field as an allusion to the prophet Zechariah's experience in Zech.11:7-14 (vss.5-10). The field was used as a burial place for strangers (vs.7).

Matt.27:11-31—Pilate, the Roman governor, finds himself right in the middle of the battle of the Jews persecuting Jesus. He asks Jesus if He is the King of the Jews. Jesus answered as He did the high priests in 26:64 with two words (in Greek)—You are saying it (with the emphasis on the pronoun added in the Greek) or, "You say (said) it" (vs.11). When Jesus didn't answer anymore questions by Pilate, Pilate went back to the Jews. As the governor was accustomed to releasing a prisoner for the Jews during their Passover feast, they asked for Barabbas, a prisoner who was involved in a riotous rebellion and had committed murder in it (Mark 15:7). Pilate's wife also declared that Jesus was a righteous man in a disturbing dream she had (vs.19). The chief priests and elders said to have Jesus crucified (vss.22, 23), though stating no charge to do this to Jesus (vs.23). Pilate gave in to their demand (vs.26). Notice Pilate's attempt to be innocent (vs.24) and the Jews accepting the blame (and guilt—see Jesus' prophecy of them in 23:29-36). The Roman soldiers joined in with their mockery, after Jesus had predicted this in 20:17-19; then, led Him away to be crucified (vss.27-31).

Matt.27:32-56—As Simon of Cyrene (located at the upper most point of Libya today) helps Jesus to carry His cross, a number of prophecies now begin to be fulfilled in Jesus' crucifixion. The first is in vs.34 from Ps.69:21, when Jesus was given gall to drink (usually known as a bitter herb), probably to lessen His pain. The next was when the soldiers divided up His garments among them from Ps.22:18 (a common custom of the soldiers of that time; vs.35). Pilate also had put on the inscription above Jesus on the cross who He said He was—The King of the Jews (vss.11, 37; 2:2). Matthew states that the next prophecy fulfilled was from Ps.22:7, 8, seen here in part in vs.39 and the rest in vss.41-44 (they not understanding that He was dying for their sins, too). Darkness then fell upon the land during the day (noon till 3 pm—vs.45) and Jesus spoke out the first verse of Ps.22. Jesus feels the forsakenness from God, bearing the sins of the world (read also the remaining part of the verse in Ps.22:1; vs.46). The sour wine in vs.48 may have been for the soldiers, with a continued mockery in mind (see Luke 23:36; Matt.27:47-49). Jesus then, having fulfilled these Scriptures, gave up His spirit (vs.50; see John 19:30 also). Some amazing miracles of God took place when Jesus died—the veil in the temple (opening up now the way to God—see Heb.4:14-16; Eph.2:18) was split from top to bottom (vs.51); an earthquake took place and rocks split apart (vss.51, 54); a resurrection took place of some of the saints and they entered the holy city appearing to many (vss.52,53); and it was a great testimony to the centurion and those with him keeping guard over Jesus, that they declared who He is—truly, the Son of God (vs.54; see vs.43; 14:33). Many of the women who followed and ministered to Jesus, watched from a distance, and received the benefit of witnessing these remarkable occurrences (vss.55,56); and some of these would go on to witness the empty tomb and even see Jesus after His resurrection.

Matt.27:57-61—It is interesting how God provides for an honorable burial for His Son Jesus (see Eccl.6:3). Joseph of Arimathea (located northwest of Jerusalem) was a member of the Jewish Council Sanhedrin (Mk.15:43) and had become a disciple of Jesus (vs.57). Burial customs being so important in Jewish law and traditions (Dt.21:22, 23), he asked Pilate to take Jesus' body down from the cross (and before the Sabbath day (Mk.15:42) and gained his permission (vs.58). He wrapped Him in clean linen cloth and placed Jesus in his own tomb, rolling a large stone then across the entrance of it to seal it closed (vs.60). Two Marys were sitting there opposite the grave (vss.56, 61).

Matt.27:62-66—The Jews, remembering Jesus declaring His resurrection from the dead, wanted Pilate to make His grave more secure to prevent His disciples from stealing the body of Jesus (vss.62-64). Pilate had it more secured, gave them a guard for the tomb and provided his (governor's) seal on the stone (see Dan.6:17).

Matt.28:1-10—The resurrection of Jesus from the dead, as Jesus said would take place (20:17-19), is recorded in all four Gospel accounts. Matthew records what happened first off and John, written later, records more of the end of the occurrence how things took place. After much study and review of the Gospel passages, here is a summary (harmony) of the sequence of events that I have found in the four Gospel books (Matt.-John): Mary Magdalene and the other Mary (27:61; Mk.16:1) came to see the grave (Matt.28:1); an angel had rolled away the stone and sat upon it (Matt.28:2), saying, "He has risen," and they would see Jesus in Galilee; and then the angel said to them, "I have told you" (Matt.28:6,7). Mark then says when they entered the tomb, they saw a "young man (angel) sitting at the right," and gave a little more information to them than they previously had in the Matthew angelic revelation, and restated that they would see Him in Galilee (Mk.16:4-7; Matt.26:32). Luke then records that when they looked into the tomb, they did not find the body of Jesus, and were perplexed (Lk.24:1-4). Luke 24:4 goes on to say that "suddenly" (NASB; NIV, translation of the word "behold" (KJ), meaning "Look" or "see this"), two men stood near them in shining clothing. The angels greeted them with a question of why they seek the living among the dead (Lk.24:5), and then reminded them with more elaborate information, stimulating their memory to recall what Jesus had said would take place about His suffering, dying, and resurrection (Lk.24:6, 7; Mk.9:30-32). Luke goes on to say, then they remember those words He had spoken, thus, satisfying their perplexity (Lk.24:4, 6-8; see Mk.9:32 about how they did not understand this beforehand). Then they went to report all this to the disciples (Lk.24:9-11—see their response in vs.11; also John 20:9, and still not believing the report). John then records Peter and John's visit to the tomb (John 20:2-10). Peter and John take off running to the tomb. John arrived first, but only looked in (John 20:5). Peter went in and saw the wrappings and face cloth lying in the tomb (see John 20:7, 8 for more detail and importance of the wrappings and the face cloth)—John 20:4-9. John then goes into the tomb and believed (John 20:8); and then they went home (see Luke 24:12 for Peter's response).

Mary Magdalene is the one who leads—from the beginning to the finish of the resurrection day events—this march of faith, to the belief and the discovery of Jesus rising from the dead. She was at the grave where they buried Jesus (Matt.27:61, sitting opposite the grave); she came to the grave at sunrise the next morning (Matt.28:1; Mk.16:1,2) and was at the tomb for the first angelic witness, this one outside the tomb (Matt.28:2-7); she was there for the next angelic witness, this one inside the tomb, receiving a similar message as before (Mk.16:4-7); then, still perplexed about where Jesus was, another appearance of two angels occurs. They explained how Jesus had to suffer and die and be raised from the dead, as Jesus said would happen (Lk.24:3-8). Then, they (the women) remembered these words spoken by Jesus previously and went to tell the other disciples. Mary then goes back to the tomb again, weeping and still seeking for Jesus. Once again, she is greeted by two angels, as she again looks into the empty tomb—one sitting at the head and one at the feet where Jesus was laid in the tomb. They ask her only one question— "Why are you weeping?" as she continues to look for Jesus. Then she turns around and sees Jesus, but did not recognize Him. Jesus called out her name and then asked her the same question that the angels did. She recognized Jesus then, and finally saw Him and found Him, now raised from the dead. She did not want to let Him go, but Jesus said for her to go tell the brethren that now she found Him and that He will be ascending back to the Father (John 20:11-18).

In summary about the resurrection accounts in the Gospels, each account is not a complete report of what happens in Jesus' resurrection. Instead, from God's vantage point and intention, each one of the accounts offers a "glimpse" of something that took place on that very important day in the history of mankind and God's intervening mighty works accomplished on earth for the purpose of building His Family, The Family of God, on that glorious resurrection day of Jesus Christ. Each of these "glimpses" gives us another detail of what took place on that one historic day. As a result, we can see a sequence of events that then took place and how it all fit together to accomplish the purposes of God and fulfill the prophesies of the past—preordained and appointed by God—for the coming of the One and Only, our Messiah, the Lord Jesus Christ (Acts 3:18-26).

Matt.28:11-15—When hearing of all that had happened, the Jewish chief priests and their elders at that time paid the soldiers a large sum of money with a fake story to try and cover up the resurrection of Jesus. But as God is always a step ahead of evil schemes, though their fake story had spread among the Jews, it was too late—Jesus, with all the given witnesses and testimonies, had already risen from the dead, (the Gospel account eyewitnesses; (see also 1 Cor.15:3-8), as other eye witnesses, had made it known, also).

Matt.28:16-20—Matthew concludes his great Gospel writing with the words Jesus left with the eleven disciples, and their "great commission" to carry on Jesus' work and ministry to the world. Jesus reminds them that the Father has given Him all authority over heaven and earth (see Matt.11:27; Dan.7:13, 14; Luke 1:26-33; John 1:3, 18; 5:22, 23). Key ingredients of the commission—all nations will hear the Gospel and can come into God's Family believing in Jesus (Matt.24:14; John 1:12,13; 3:16; 10:16; Eph.2:13-22); the importance of baptism with the conversion experience (Mk.16:15; Acts 2:41,42); baptizing in the name of the Father, Son and Holy Spirit (the Eternal Family of God—see Book 1 of The Family Bible Studies Series, The Family of God—Foundation, for further insights on the Trinity, their functions and their character); teaching all to observe all His commands; and He assures them that He will be with them (the Church) till the end of the age (end means, in the Greek, heading up of events to the appointed climax—Vine; see the commission and promise given to Peter in Matt.16:18; also, John 1:5; Rev.1:17,18; 1 Tim.3:15,16).

The Gospel of Mark

Most of the Gospel of Mark is found in the similar passages in the Gospel of Matthew. So I will refer those appropriate passages and comments back to Matthew and simply add any significant differences to this Gospel here in Mark. They will usually be listed with the word "note," as was done in the commentary of the Gospel of Matthew.

Mk.1:1-8—Mark begins his Gospel writing with the title that this is the "beginning of the Gospel of Jesus Christ," and follows along that it "begins" with the appearing of John the Baptist (see Matt.3:1-12). Jesus' proclamation of His relationship with the Father (as the Son of God) was the main issue at His trial (Matt.26:63-65; Mk.14:61-65). Here in Mark's Gospel, this is proclaimed and established early, in the title of his Gospel writing (see also 1:11; 3:11; 5:7). Note—Mark quotes from Micah and Isaiah about John the Baptist, but says written in Isaiah the prophet (vss.2, 3). Both apply to John's coming and Mark simply quotes Isaiah specifically since he uses his verse last and it is the most descriptive (some commentators think similarly for Matt.24:9, 10 combining passages from Jeremiah and Zechariah). In verse 8,

Jesus baptizes with the Holy Spirit, since He does the baptizing, as the verse says.

Mk.1:9-11—See Matt.3:13-17.

Mk.1:12, 13—See Matt.4:1-11. Note—The word for the Holy Spirit's "impelling" Jesus into the wilderness, in the Greek means" to lead or bring out, as a shepherd would his sheep" (BAGD).

Mk.1:14, 15—See Matt.4:12-17.

Note—In verse 15, Jesus says that the time is fulfilled (time—a fixed or definite period; a season (Vine); see Matt.11:13; Heb.1:1, 2; Gal.4:4.

Mk.1:16-20—See Matt.4:18-22.

Mk.1:21-28—Jesus went with His recently called Apostles into a synagogue in His home town of Capernaum (see Matt.4:13). He was teaching in the synagogue and casted an unclean spirit out of a man (vss.22-26). Note the evil spirit knew who Jesus was and yet spoke on behalf of the larger group of evil spirits, also—(vss.24, 34). Jesus not only taught in God's authority (the Father) but acted in God's authority (vss.22, 25). Jesus came to set the prisoners free (Is.61:1-3; Lk.4:18-19).

Mk.1:29-34—See Matt.14-17.

Mk.1:35-39—Jesus was fond of getting away (when He possibly could) to go to a mountainside alone and pray (vs.35; 6:46; Matt.14:13, 23; Lk.6:12). Note the contrast in vs.37 and 38 here—see what the crowds were looking for (in vss.32-34, 37) and see what Jesus was looking for (vs.38).

Mk.1:40-45—See Matt.8:2-4.

Notes—Mark adds that it was the compassion of Jesus that moved Him to heal the leper (vs.41). Jesus' command to fulfill the

Levitical cleansing (Lev.14) was for the testimony to the priest(s) that He healed him (vs.44). As quiet as Jesus wanted the leper to remain, he spread it all the more, limiting Jesus' range of ministry, as people came to him now (literally in the Greek)" from all directions" (vs.45).

Mk.2:1-12—See Matt.9:1-8. Note here the effort it took by the paralytic and his friends to even get to Jesus (vs.4—great physical work and faith combined). Note also the discerning spirit of Jesus in vs.8—perceiving in His spirit what they were thinking (reasoning) within themselves.

Mk.2:13-17—See Matt.9:10-13.

Mk.2:18-22—See Matt.9:14-17.

Mk.2:23-28—See Matt.12:1-8. Note there is no Old Testament law forbidding this to be done on a Sabbath (Dt.23:24, 25). The Pharisee labeled this as work, and so their law became more important than the need of the disciples, necessitating Jesus' answer (vss.27, 28; thus, the need of "new wine and wineskins;"— vs.22; see also 3:4).

Mk.3:1-6—See Matt.12:9-14. Note Jesus' response to the lack of compassion for the man by the people in the synagogue (vs.5).

Mk.3:7-12—Mark has a more expanded writing compared to Matthew's brief summary in Matt.12:15, 16. Mark details all the country sides from all over that were new coming to Jesus (north, south and east (vss.7, 8). Also, the result of all His healings brought a "crowding all round Jesus" for the need of more of the same (vs.10). Note the contrast here in vss.11, 12.

Mk.3:13-19—See Matthew's great expansion of the calling of the Apostles in the full chapter of Matt.10.

Mk.3:20-30—See Matt.12:24-32. Note that the crowds were now pressing so hard on Jesus and the disciples that they could not even get into the house to eat (vs.20). So, his own people (probably friends and followers—see later vs.31) came to "rescue" Him from the crowd, for some of the crowd was saying that He was "beside Himself" (i.e., losing His senses, NASB, vs.21).

Mk.3:31-35—See Matt.12:46-50.

Mk.4:1-34—See Matt.13:1-52. Note here in Mark that the parables are not meant to remain secret (vss.21-25), but to be understood and shared (vss.33, 34; Matt.13:52).

Mk.4:35-41—See Matt.8:23-27. Mark's description of this storm is "a great storm of wind" (vs.37, KJ).

Mk.5:1-20—See Matt.8:28-34 and Lk.8:26-39. Mark's details here are the longest account of this incident in the recordings of the three Gospels. Some noteworthy observations: See the strength and paralyzing trauma this man had in vss.2-6 (Lk.8:27-29 adds a bit more). One speaks for the demons (Legion) initially, but all plead to Jesus in vs.12, that this is would not be their final judgment (verses 7, 12, 13; Lk.8:31). They do not want to go out of the country (vs.10), but look what they were doing to this man (Lk.8:29)! Jesus was continuing to speak (ongoing past action in the Greek—Mk.5:8; Lk.8:29) to the unclean spirit to come out of the man (Matt.8:32), yet gave them permission to go into the pigs (vs.13). The town earnestly asked Him to leave (see their response—vs.15; Luke 8:35-37). "Earnestly" is the same word used by the demons plea in vs.10. While the man could not be conquered by human strength (vs.4), only by the power of the Spirit of God through Jesus was the man delivered of his agony (Matt.8:32; 12:28) and his life a great testimony to many, including the large country east of the Jordan River—the Decapolis (vss.15,16,19,20; Lk.8:35-39).

Mk.5:21-43—See Matt.9:18-26. Note in verse 29 that the woman who had the flow of blood felt in her body that she was healed of her affliction, before she told Jesus the whole truth (vs.33). Jesus had great affirmation for her (vs.34). Jesus also had great compassion and comfort (during this slight distraction) for the synagogue official, even though his daughter had died (vs.35). He said not to be afraid, but only to keep on believing (present imperative in the Greek—vs.36). Him and his wife then saw Jesus raise their daughter from the dead (vss.40-42).

Mk.6:1-6—See Matt.13:54-58. Note vs.4 is expanded some compared to Matthew 13:57.

Mk.6:7-13—See Matt.10:1-14. Note Mark includes the success the Apostles had with the authority Jesus gave them to perform in His ministry as He had been doing (vss.7, 12, 13, 30).

Mk.6:14-29—See Matt.14:1-12. Note that Mark gives a few more details of this account—Herod's wife held a grudge against John (vs.1); Herod used to enjoy listening to John and protected him (vs.20); Herodias' daughter asked her mom (Herodias) what to ask the king for in his promise to grant her any request she would like (vss.23, 24); the daughter then quickly ran back to the king and demanded the request at once (vs.25).

Mk.6:30-44—The feeding of the 5,000 is an account that is covered in all four Gospel writings (Matt.14:13-21; Lk.9:10-17; John 6:1-14). Mark, Luke and John record at their beginning that the Apostles were with Jesus (Matthew emphasizes the disturbance

Jesus had hearing about John the Baptist's death, Matt.14:13; see the Matthew commentary on Matt.14:13-21). John records that Jesus distributed the food to the crowd, which could mean He helped the Apostles in the process or it was through the Apostles that this was done (Jn.6:11; compare Lk.9:16). John alone records the people's response to this that certainly this must be the Prophet whom Moses prophesied to come (Jn.6:14; Dt.18:18; Matt.21:11). John also states the words that the people ate as much as they wished (Jn.6:11; compare Mk.6:37).

Mk.6:45-52—See Matt.14:22-33. Note here at the ending of feeding the 5,000, Jesus didn't just get up and leave them— He dismissed them and said good-bye to them (vss.45, 46, 34; Matt.9:35, 36; John 10:11). Mark alone records that Jesus intended to pass by them (possibly to meet them on land at shore; see John 6:21). They did not yet understand who the Almighty Lord was, who was with them in the boat (vss.52; 4:35-41; 8:17-21; hardened heart, i.e., they still were not seeking Jesus for whatever their need may be, in spite of all the miracles they were seeing).

Mk.6:53-56—See Matt.14:34-36. The crowds were "earnestly asking Him" (past continuous tense in the Greek) that they could touch the fringe of His garment to be healed (vs.56).

Mk.7:1-23—See Matt.15:1-20. Corban, in vs.11, is "a name common to any sacred gift...things or persons consecrated (or vowed) for religious purposes" (Unger). Note 3 times in six verses Jesus says they left the commandment of God for their own tradition (vss.8-13). "All foods clean" comes out of Jesus' explanation of "defiled" things in vss.15-23. Food is no longer one of them, but His list in vss.20-23 includes the things that <u>do</u> defile a person (see also Acts 10:15; 11:8, 9). Verse 16 is absent from the earlier, most testified manuscripts of the New Testament, possibly carried over from verses 4:9, 23).

Mk.7:24-30—see Matt.15:21-28. Note up in this country Jesus was hoping to escape notice of the crowd, but couldn't do it, even being out of His native country (vs.24). Mark elaborates on the recovery of the daughter (vs.30).

Mk.7:31-37—Mark records a story of Jesus healing a man who was deaf and had trouble speaking (vs.32). Some people approached Him and earnestly asked Jesus to heal the man (vs.32). Mark states Jesus travelled up to Sidon first (above Tyre on the seacoast) then to the Decapolis (where the demoniac was healed—5:1-20; this was east of the Sea of Galilee, so quite a walk indeed!). Verse 34 says that Jesus looked up to heaven with a deep sigh (an inward, unexpressed feeling of sorrow—Vine, under the word grieve), which Jesus probably felt for this man (not hard for us to do, either; see 8:2 upcoming). The man's bond(age) was removed and he spoke plainly (correctly, vs.35).

Mk.8:1-10—See Matt.15:29-39. The feeding of the 4,000. Dalmanutha in Mark is the same place as Magadan in Matt.15:39, the birthplace of Mary Magdalene (Jn.19:25; 20:1, 18), on the western tip of the Sea of Galilee.

Mk.8:11-21—See Matt.16:1-12. Once again we see Jesus expressing a "sigh," same root word here, but with a prefix for a stronger emphasis; not surprising of this from Jesus, as they had already asked this before (Matt.13:38-40; compare how the disciples rightly ask this of Jesus—13:4).

Mk.8:22-26—Now at the far NE part of the Sea of Galilee, Jesus heals a blind man at Bethsaida (means, house or place of fishing—Unger). A discussion of why Jesus spit once again (7:33) to bring about a healing would probably not lead us to much productive conclusion to help in discovering this. What is important, though, is Jesus' persistence in pursuit of the man's healing, as twice He laid His hands upon him (similar persistence with the demoniac –5:8). Such great miracles were still going to be difficult to keep quiet about (vss.26 and 30).

Mk.8:27-30—See Matt.16:13-20.

Mk.8:31-38—See Matt.16:21-28. Note here as in Matt.16:27, Jesus returns with the holy angels, who will be used to carry out His judgments then (Matt.13: 41, 42) and to gather His elect on the earth for His millennial reign (Matt.24:31; Mk.13:27).

Mk.9:1-8—See Matt.16:28-17:8.

Mk.9:9-13—See Matt.17:9-13.

Mk.9:14-29—See Matt.17:14-21. Mark goes into some detail here on the healing of the epileptic boy. He explains what kind of demon was causing this (vs.25; we are not led to think here that demons are the cause of this all the time; (Matt.4:24); note how specific Jesus was here to the demon in vs.25). Mark says after a terrible convulsion, the boy looked dead (not uncommon of a seizure aftermath—vs.26). Mark includes much of the discussion Jesus had with the boy's father; always building faith, with all involved (vss.21-24, with a loud cry from the dad—vs.24).

Mk.9:30-32—See Matt.17:22, 23 and Lk.9:43-45.

Mk.9:33-37—See Matt.18:1-35. While Matthew has the expanded version here, the discussion of "the greatest" may have come (unintentionally) from the three Apostles going up with Jesus in the Transfiguration (9:2, tough things for parents at times to avoid any signs of partiality). But the Matthew account covers this well.

Mk.9:38-50—Jesus is more concerned here for the disciples with the character of a "true" disciple of His in lifestyle, not their topic of concern (vss.34, 35, 50). Note doing "true" miracles in "His name," compared to "false prophets' (vs.39; Matt.24:24). The quote from Is.66:24 refers to eternal judgment (vs.48). These are some examples how God's Family are to exemplify God's character (so different from the world we live in—see Matt.24:11-14) and to be at peace with one another and, when possible, with all men (vs.50—salt is a preservative; Rom.12:17-21; Prov.16:7; Col.3:15).

Mk.10:1-12—See Matt.19:1-12.

Mk.10:13-16—See Matt.19:13-15.

Mk.10:17-31—See Matt.19:16-30. Note in this passage Mark says that Jesus felt a love for this man for keeping (trying to keep) the commandments of God (vss.19-21). Jesus mentions the difficulty with wealth and riches to enter the kingdom of God three times in three verses (vss.23-25; 4:18, 19; but, of course, not impossible with God—vs.27).

Mk.10:32-34—See Matt.20:17-19.

Mk.10:35-45—See Matt.20:20-28.

Mk.10:46-52—See Matt.20:29-34. Mark records the blind man (men's) response after crying out to Jesus on the roadside and He called him (them) to come to Him with their request to receive his (their) sight (vss.49-52).

Mk.11:1-10—See Matt.21:1-11.

Mk.11:11-14—See Matt.21:18-22.

Mk.11:15-19—See Matt.21:12-17. With the fig tree (Israel) now prophesied as withered (vss.14, 20), Mark quotes the full verse recording of Is.56:7, that Gentiles will now be welcomed into God's Family for salvation and worship to God. Read the full context of Is.56:6-8 for a broader understanding of this message and prophecy fulfillment (vs.17).

Mk.11:20-26—See Matt.21:19-22. Of these events in chapter eleven of Mark, as the writer of this Gospel, Mark seems to follow more of a chronological theme of Jesus events, while Matthew takes more of a theme of the Messiah approach to his writings of the Gospel of Jesus Christ of His experiences (the Triumphal Entry, the fig tree and clearing the temple). Matthew combines the fig tree discourses in Mark (Matt.21:19-22) and Mark elaborates more on the prayer lesson that Jesus teaches the disciples about the fig tree (vss.21-26). This prayer lesson is very similar to Matt.7:7-12 (see this commentary in Matt.7). Note in vs.24 Jesus says regarding all the things which we pray and ask for…makes me think that sometimes we pray, but forget to ask…or sometimes just don't ask God for what we are requesting; example, "Lord we really need a new car" (but forgot to ask Him for it), or "Lord, bless this person for what they need" (but did not ask or be specific about it). See James 1:5 and Book 3 of the <u>Family Bible Study Series</u>, <u>Growing in God's Wisdom</u> about more of God's "ingredients" of wisdom in being more specific of what we are asking Him for…or need to ask Him for, more specifically. Also note the importance of forgiveness in our prayers (vs.25; Matt.6:12-15; no conditions here and does not even need to directly relate to the prayer request made).

Mk.11:27-33—See Matt.21:23-32.

Mk.12:1-12—See Matt.21:33-46.

Mk.12:13-17—See Matt.22:15-22. Little is known about the Herodians. May possibly been formed by Herod the Great, in fear toward Jesus developing His kingship (Unger).

Mk.12:18-27—See Matt.22:23-33.

Mk.12:28-34—See Matt.22:34-40. Note Mark's extended proclamation of Jesus on the Greatest Commandment (vss.29-31). He begins by quoting Dt. 6:4. "The Lord our God is one Lord." (Note that this context is about parents teaching their children God's word—Dt.6:4-7). The word "one" here in Dt.6:4 does not have a numerical emphasis but means "united" (ordinal emphasis, and so, importance or most important; thus, the first and most important part of the Greatest Commandment; see Jn.10:30 with this in mind; Strong's Exhaustive Concordance). It is hard to say what the scribe had in mind for sure in vs.32 about God being one; if the Hebrew understanding was there, that was correct; if he meant a numerical response (as the Jews were monotheistic), then the understanding of the Trinity was yet to come, as Jesus came to reveal the Father (John 1:18) and give the gift of the Holy Spirit to those who believed in Him (Mk.1:8, John 14:15-18; 16:13-15; Acts 2:38,39; see Book 1 of the Family Bible Studies Series, The Family of God—Foundation for further understanding of the Trinity, Their functions and character). And so, Jesus said He was not far from the kingdom of God (vs.34).

Mk.12:35-37—See Matt.22:41-46.

Mk.12:38-40—See Matt.23:1-7; Lk.20:45-47.

Mk.12:41-44—Jesus sights a great example of giving to God in the temple treasury. The amount the poor widow gave was equivalent to one-eighth of an hour of work (based on an 8 hour work day). Jesus said she put in more than all the contributors did (proportionately—all she owned and had to live on—vss.42-44; Lk.21:1-4; 12:16-21).

Mk.13:1-37—See Matt.24:1-51. In Matthew I divided this "end times" passage into 4 sections for clearer understanding. Mark has all the sections of Matthew except the Rapture verse 37-44 of part three. Read Matt.24, also, for the expanded and more inclusive information about the end times.

Mk.14:1-72—See Matt.26:1-75. The only inclusion of different verses here other than what Matthew contains is in Mark's verses 51 and 52. While the young man's identification is ambiguous, a number of commentators think this may have been Mark himself, especially since the word order follows like Matthew records, except for these two verses.

Mk.15:1-47—See Mt.27:1-61. Note Mark elaborates on the crimes of Barabbas in vs.7. Matthew includes the plot of the Jews to try and make the tomb more secure before writing on the resurrection of Jesus (Mt.27:62-66).

Mark 16:1-8—For the harmony of the resurrection accounts in the Gospels, see Matt.28. The conjecture about the ending of Mark continues to the day of this writing—did Mark intend to finish his Gospel at 16:8 or did the leaf to his writing get lost somewhere in time? Most would go with the second view, since verse eight and its wording appears uncharacteristic for the closing of this event. Quite a few other endings have appeared as well, but the most traditional one down through the time is the one we have in our translations today. One can see, though, as most scholars agree, that it is an addition by another author, with wording like an Acts of the Apostles or post-Acts period of writing.

The Gospel of Luke

Lk.1:1-4—In his introduction, Luke addresses his book to one named Theophilus. His name means "friend of God" and may have been one having a rank or "seat of government" in Antioch of that time (Unger). He also may have become a Christian there (previously instructed; the Greek means oral teaching), possibly even by the Apostle Paul, though this point remains uncertain. The accuracy in Luke's research is brought out in the words he uses—"eyewitnesses and servants" of the Lord (vs.2); tracing all things out by their course of the events accurately (vs.3); so that Theophilus (and us now) could know the "certainty" of the things he was taught (and now recorded for us by God from His servants in the Bible (vss.2-4).

Lk.1:5-25—Luke records in a detailed fashion the birth of John the Baptist, given through his father Zacharias and to his mother Elizabeth, who had been wanting a child (vs.25). It came to his dad while doing his priestly duty in the temple through angelic revelation. The child's commitment will be strong to the Lord (vs.15), as a forerunner to the Lord in the "spirit and power of Elijah," to turn many sons of Israel back to Lord their God (vss.16, 17). Because of their age (of the parents), he disbelieved in the angel Gabriel's words and, as result, remained, unable to speak until the birth of his son (vss.18-20,64).

Lk.1:26-56—Luke now declares the prophecy given to Mary by the angel Gabriel and that she would be the recipient of the King of the descendant of David (1 Chron.17:11-14), the Son of the Most High, who will reign over the house of Jacob and never have an end to His kingdom (vss.32,33). His name will be Jesus (which means "Savior,"—Mt.1:21; Lk.1:31; 2:11). Note assuredly the virgin birth mentioned often in this announcement to Mary—twice the word "virgin" used in vs.27 about Mary (God knew and her husband knew for sure—vss.26,27); Mary declares herself a virgin, using the word in verse 34; and the angel Gabriel proclaims how this will take place, by the birthing of the Holy Spirit (vs.35—note here that God birthed His Son, and so, who He is, the Son of God—not difficult for God to do—vs.37).

The prophecy of vs.15 becomes real to Elizabeth when Mary visits her (vss.41-44). Mary gives praise to God, exalting Him as her Savior; acknowledging her humble state and what the Mighty One has done for her; and remembering His promises to Abraham and Israel and their offspring (vss.46-55).

Lk.1:57-80—The time now came for Elizabeth to give birth to their son, John the Baptist (vs.57). Everyone was happy, as it was said would be (vss.13, 14). But Zacharias his Dad was still waiting to start speaking again. Finally, at the event of their son's circumcision, Zacharias wrote that his name will be John and he began to speak again (vss.59-66). He then began to prophesy by the Holy Spirit, thanking God for raising up their prophesied King ("horn of salvation"—vs.69; see Ps.89:19-29) through the house (lineage) of David (see 3:23, 31, 38); and remembering His covenant with Abraham (vss.72, 73), and to be delivered from their enemies (vs.74). John's ministry will be one of a prophet (vs.76), to prepare the way of the Lord (vs.76; Mal.3:1), and knowledge of salvation through the forgiveness of sins (vs.77; Matt.3:3-6); as the Savior comes to shine His light in the darkness and guide us into the way of peace (vss.78, 79; Mal.4:2; Is.9:1, 2, 6, 7).

Lk.2:1-20—Jesus' birth took place in Bethlehem, the city of David (1 Sam. 16:1). Mary and Joseph were there as a result of a census being taken at that time (vss.1-5). Then the time came for Mary to give birth (vss.6, 7). The revelation of the Savior's birth was made known also to some shepherds in near-by fields (vs.8). The shepherds were given quite a greeting from God indeed! An angel first appeared and the glory of God had shown around them (vs.9); the angel gave a proclamation message of the birth of Jesus to them (vss.19-14); and then a multitude of angel's joined in praising God on high and His bringing peace to men on earth (vs.14). The angel's message to them was "good news of great joy" (vs.10, no holding back here); for look Who is born—God's Savior (1:31-33;2:21), the Christ (the Messiah; Acts 3:20), the Lord (Acts 2:36;10:36—of all; vs.11); yet, He comes humbly, being born in a manger (vs.12), while a multitude of heavenly hosts (angels) proclaim to the shepherds, "Glory to God" and peace on earth to men of goodwill (descriptive genitive here in Greek, as God's peace reaches out to men of goodwill, a qualifying factor (in whatever degree) for mankind to receive peace (salvation) from and with God (Rom. 5:1,2; Eph.2:11-22)—vss.13,14. After visiting the manager and seeing the baby Jesus, the shepherds left, giving glory and praise to God (as the angels were) for what God had revealed to them and seeing God's Savior, Messiah and Lord sent to earth (vs.20).

Lk.2:21-38—During Jesus' time of circumcision and presentation in the temple (Gen.17:12; Ex.13:2, 12), two great testimonies came forth about Him. The first was to Simeon, whom God had revealed that he would not die until he saw God's Messiah (vs.26). He receives God's message of peace (vss.29-32, 14), now seeing God's salvation (vss.30, 69, 77), who will be a light to the Gentiles and glory to his people Israel (vs.32; Is.9:1, 2; 49:6), and also for the rising up (word also used for resurrection here) and fall of many (Matt.21:43, 44; 1 Pet.2:6-8). Then, the prophetess Anna, who was looking forward to the redemption of Israel, began at that time to give thanks to God and to speak to others about Him, who were also looking for God's redemption, as she was continually devoting herself to God (vss.37, 38).

Lk.2:39-52—Two great positive descriptions are given about Jesus here in summary in verses 40 and 52. Both contain growing in God's wisdom (a great emphasis and goal here for individuals and parents for their family; see Book 3 of <u>The Family Bible Studies Series—Growing In God's Wisdom</u>, for a listing from Prov.1:1-7 of "ingredients" of and praying more specifically for God's wisdom). In vs.40 about Jesus becoming strong, the word is "manifested strength," more than a physical strength (different Greek word for that), meaning more, in this context, His growing in God (strength and obedience; see Heb.5:7-10). His growing in moral stature found favor with God and man (vs.52). His town to grow up in would now be Nazareth (vs.39). As He was attending a

Passover Feast in Jerusalem at age twelve, He stayed in the temple as His parents left town to go home (not too uncommon at that time as people were often with friends or relatives for such the occasions). Coming back and finding Jesus in the temple, Jesus' response was one of surprise about why they were looking for Him, since He needed to be about (concerned with) the affairs of His Father (vss.48,49; 1:35,3:38). Though not understanding this, Mary treasured these things in her heart (vss.51, 19, 28-33; 1:30-33; see also Is.33:5, 6).

Lk.3:1-20—Luke gives his account here of the calling and early ministry of John the Baptist, and up to his imprisonment. See Matt.3:1-12. Notes—Tetrarchs were governors over a certain land or country (tetra means four, arche is rule, so, four rulers over this district—Judea, Galilee, Ituraea and Trachonitus (above Galilee) and Abilene (above Ituraea). In Luke's expanded quote from Is.40:3-5, the language of vs.4 sounds like Jesus' first coming, and verse 5, has language sounding like His second coming (Matt.24:30; Rev.1:7;16:20). Luke also includes here three exhortations to three groups (the crowds, tax-gathers and soldiers) about "how to produce "fruits with their repentance" (vs.8—fruits is plural; vss.10-14). In verse 18, the word for preached is "evangelized" (where we get the word Gospel); so preaching the Gospel here is what John was doing for the people.

Lk.3:21, 22—See Matt.3:13-17.

Lk.3:23-38—See Matt.1:1-16.

Lk.4:1-13—See Matt.4:1-11. Note, Jesus saw right through the devil's scheme and temptation (vss.2, 12, 13).

Lk.4:14-30—Jesus returned to Nazareth where He grew up and went into a synagogue on the Sabbath. He read Is.61:1, 2a, and said that this Scripture has been fulfilled in their midst (in Him—vs.21). People were amazed at the gracious words He was saying (vs.22). Anticipating them demanding a sign, Jesus gave two examples of healing from two of their great prophets—Elijah and Elisha. Both of these two healings were performed outside Israel. Enraged, they tried to kill Jesus but He slipped outside of their midst (vss.29, 30). Note Jesus foresees them saying to Him to heal Himself, i.e., shows us you can do here what you did there (derogatorily, get yourself together and prove yourself to us too!—compare Mt.13:54-58; 27:40). In verse 19, the year of the Lord's favor, see 2 Cor.6:2.

Lk.4:31-37—See Mark 1:21-28.

Lk.4:38-41—See Matt.8:14-17. Note how demons tried to proclaim who Jesus was to disrupt His ministry, thus causing some to demand what Jesus said in 4:23 (vs.41).

Lk.4:42-44—See Mark 1:35-38.

Lk.5:1-11—See Matt.4:18-22. Note here in this expanded version the faith building for Peter, with the hard work demanded of being a fisherman—no catch all night (vs.5), then, two boats full of fish at the word of Jesus spoken (vss.5-7). Enough seen for them to leave it all there and follow Jesus, and go out and start catching men for the Family of God (vss.10, 11). Lake Gennesaret is the Sea of Galilee (vs.1).

Lk.5:12-16—See Matt.8:2-4; 4:23-25; Mk.1:40-44. Note how Luke has an important emphasis on Jesus spending time in prayer (vs.16; 3:21; 6:12; 9:18, 28, 29; 21:36; 22:40, 41).

Lk.5:17-26—See Matt.9:2-8; Mk.2:3-12. Note Luke has a bit more emphasis and drama presented on the effort it took to work through the roof of the house and lower the paralytic right in front of Jesus (vss.18, 19).

Lk.5:27-32—See Matt.9:9-13.

Lk.5:33-39—Compare Matt.9:14-17.

Lk.6:1-5—See Matt.12:1-8; Mk.2:23-28.

Lk.6:6-11—See Matt.12:9-14. Note the motive in vs.7 and concluded decision in vs.11.

Lk.6:12-19—See Matt.10:1-4; Mk.3:13-19.

Luke gives a good description of the crowd waiting to see Jesus after calling His Apostles on the mountain and the healing He performed on them all (vss.17-19).

Lk.6:20-49—This is Luke's more summarized version of the Sermon on the Mount (see Matt.5-7). Most of the verses are found in the Matthew account, but a few are found in other chapters of Matthew as well (example, vs.39 in Matt.15:14; and vs.45 in Matt.12:35; vs.36 is not found directly in Matthew, but the Beatitudes bring it out in another way—Matt.5:7; also Rom.9:15 and Heb.2:17). Verse 20 about the poor (along with Matt.5:3, poor in spirit) covers all mankind, because without the Lord in our life, we are all poor in spirit; and so, the Gospel reaches out to us all—Lk.7:22; Matt.24:14.

Lk.7:1-10—See Matt.8:5-13. Luke brings out the benefit of this centurion to the Jewish people and what he had done for them (vss.4, 5).

Lk.7:11-17—This is a great passage of Jesus raising a young boy from the dead out of his coffin of a widow lady in the city of Nain.

Nain was located SW of the Sea of Galilee, and on the travel and trade route to Samaria and Jerusalem. This boy was the widow's one and only son (same word used of Jesus in John 3:16; vs.12). Jesus knows that kind of relationship and felt compassion for her (vs.13). With a large crowd at hand, he raised the young boy from the dead and gave him back to his mother (vs.15). Fear gripped the people and while the news about this spread through Judea and the surrounding district, they declared Him as a "great prophet" (vss.16, 17).

Lk.7:18-35—See Matt.11:2-19. Note Luke records that at that very moment Jesus had just performed many miraculous healings (vs.21). Luke also brings out the effectiveness of John the Baptist's ministry with the people and tax-collectors acknowledging God's justice in Jesus' ministry, while the lawyers and Pharisees had rejected both of them (vss.29,30; the wisdom of God was shown right by those who responded to Jesus' message—vss.29,35).

Lk.7:36-50—Luke records the story of an immoral woman expressing great love for Jesus in being forgiven of her sins and receiving salvation from Jesus from her faith. Because she was forgiven much, she loved much (vs.47). Jesus shared a similar response to the paralytic (5:20). Jesus' willingness to forgive is stated to the Pharisee in His story to him, whether it be little or much (vss.41, 42).

Lk.8:1-3—See Matt.27:55, 56.

Lk.8:4-18—See Matt.13:10-23. Note Luke's description of those who are of "good ground" and receive the seed (God's word) with "an honest and good heart" and go on to bear good fruit with perseverance (vs.15).

Lk.8:19-21—See Matt.12:46-50.

Lk.8:22-25—See Matt.8:23-27.

Lk.8:26-39—See Matt.8:28-34; Mk.5:1-20.

Note in verse 31 the demons were asking Jesus not to send them into the abyss (the abode of imprisoned demons—Unger; Rev.9:1, 2; 17:8; 20:1, 3). See in irony how the people were gripped with great fear (on-going past tense in the Greek) after Jesus healed the demoniac from his problems and great fear (vss.28, 29, 35-37).

Lk.8:40-56—See Matt.9:19-26; Mk.5:22-43. Luke adds that Jesus knew when the lady was healed because power had gone out from Him to heal her (vs.46).

Lk.9:1-6—See Matt.10:1, 5-15.

Lk.9:7-9—See Matt.14:1, 2.

Lk.9:10-17—See Matt.14:13-21; Mk.6:32-44; John 6:5-14.

Lk.9:18-27—See Matt.16:13-28. Note Luke adds the word "daily" for one taking up his cross and following Jesus (vs.23). Note also when Jesus returns He comes in the glory of the Father and with the holy angels (vs.26; Matt.16:27; 25:31; 1 Thess.3:13—the word there is "holy ones)."

Lk.9:28-36—See Matt.17:1-9; Mk.9:2-8. Luke adds in the transfiguration in his passage that Moses and Elijah appear with Jesus (who appears in His glory, vss. 29, 32) in their glory also (i.e., glorified bodies, vs.31), as they talked with Him about His upcoming departure in Jerusalem in vs.31 (see 1 Pet.1:16-18; Lk.9:51).

Lk.9:37-45—See Matt.17:14-23; Mk.9:14-29. Note in vs.45 as Jesus declares again about His upcoming suffering (see vs.22), this understanding was concealed to the disciples (passive participle in the Greek—see vs.36; Matt.17:9; John 2:22).

Lk.9:46-48—See Matt.18:1-6.

Lk.9:49, 50—See Mk.9:38-40.

Lk.9:51-56—Knowing the division that still existed between the Jews and Samaritans, the disciples should have remembered the miraculous visit Jesus had with the woman at the well, and the great harvest Jesus accomplished with His time spent with the Samaritans recorded in John 4:3-42 (assuming that was done before this event).

Lk.9:57-62—See Matt.8:19-22. Luke adds one more example in the desire of these people to follow Jesus (vss.61, 62). The example of Elisha to follow Elijah is often referred to regarding this passage in 1 Kings 19:19-21. In the passage recorded in 1 Kings, Elisha was prepared and ready and began ministering to Elijah. Here in Luke, the man does not say how long this departure may take with his family (see Lk.14:26). When one begins to plow, the sight ahead always looks straight, but looking behind it is crooked. So with following Jesus, the path must be straight to Him.

Lk.10:1-16—See Matt.9:37-10:15, 40. Note whether it was 70 or 72 Jesus sent out has about equal evidence in historical background either way. Only one slight difference found is that the number 70 is used a lot more in the Old Testament than the number seventy-two (in NASB, only here possibly and Rev.21:17).

Lk.10:17-20—As exciting it was for the disciples to return and share the submission of demons in Jesus name in their ministry, it is always more exciting to rejoice in what the Lord has done for us (vs.20). The NASB properly translates the Greek word in vs.19 as "injure" you.

Lk.10:21-24—See Matt.11:25-27; 13:16, 17. Here, in this context, this prayer of Jesus is beautifully attached to the newly-appointed disciples Jesus sent out as "lambs in the midst of wolves" (vs.3). Think of their advancement in such a short time—they have heard Jesus' message, have responded to His message, have received His word (vss.23, 24), and now, as disciples, are sent out with the Gospel ahead of Him to where He would be going (vs.1, similar to John the Baptist's ministry—3:4). And yet, the next passage shares with us of one who specialized in knowing the Jewish law given by Moses, and how he was still struggling with all these things (vs.25).

Lk.10:25-37—See Matt.22:34-40. Note in the story of the Good Samaritan the lawyer did not want to pronounce the word Samaritan, but Jesus wanted him to learn from the Samaritan's example (vs.37). One might wonder if Jesus may have actually seen such an occurrence in His great harvest and stay He had with the Samaritans or somewhere in His travels along the road (John 4:40-42).

Lk.10:38-42—This is a good learning interaction between Jesus, Mary and Martha. Martha is a good example (overall) of hospitality. However, she was distracted in various directions (Gk. meaning for anxious or worried in vs.41 (Vine); see Ps.86:11). Mary, from the time Jesus came, was sitting with Him listening to

His word (vs.39). One was busy and over occupied (vs.40) and one was actively listening to their Special Guest (vs.39; note Martha did not give Jesus a chance to answer the question she asked Him (vs.40). However, Jesus did answer the question, and Mary chose the right thing available for them to do—and much more long-lasting (vs.42).

Lk.11:1-13—In Luke's shorter version of the Our Father Prayer, the essence of these verses is to persist in prayer and depend on God for all the good things we ask of Him (and all the good gifts He is willing to give to His children—vs.13). Note in vs.4 how we are to forgive everyone indebted (including sinning) against us (see 6:37; Matt.6:12-15). For vss.9-13, see Matt.7:6-11. See in verse 13 how our heavenly Father gives us His very best—His kingdom and meeting our needs (vss.2-4; 12:32); His Son (9:48; John 3:16); and the Holy Spirit to live within us (vs.13; John 14:16, 17).

Lk.11:14-32—See Matt.12:22-50.

Lk.11:33-36—See Matt.5:15; 6:22, 23.

Lk.11:37-54—The principle begins here similar to the Matt.15:1-9 passage and Luke then follows this with many of the "woes" given by Jesus to the scribes and Pharisees in Matt.23:25-36, plus verses 2-4, 13 from Matt.23 (see Matt.23). Note vs.41 where Jesus says to give from within as charity is followed up in the next verse with justice and love of God (vs.42; see back to 10:27, 28).

Lk.12:1-12—See Matt.10:17-33; for Lk.12:10, see Matt.12:31, 32.

Lk.12:13-21—The lesson in Jesus' story here is the mistake of hoarding (storing up) one's goods they have and not being rich toward God, who is the One who gives us all good things (vs.21; James 1:17). The

Tenth Commandment is also the warning (Dt.5:21). Other Bible passages give similar instruction (vss.34; Prov.3:7-10; 1 Tim.6:6-10; Matt.6:19-21). Note how God still speaks to people in their own thinking and reasoning here (vss.19, 20; Prov.3:5-12).

Lk.12:22-34—See Matt.6:25-33. Luke adds the gracious generosity of the Father in giving His kingdom to His children in vs.32. They are encouraged to be contributors to this in the following vs.33 and to seek the kingdom's coming in vs.31, which, in bringing this all together, is amazing how our needs are met by our Father in Heaven in the world we live in now (vss.29-34). Note the word not to be "anxious" is mentioned three times in five verses (vss.22-26). The word "worry" in vs.29 occurs only once in the New Testament and means "distracted, wavering between hope and fear (Vine, under doubt). But Jesus encourages us that the Father knows this before we do and simply instructs us to seek the Father and His Kingdom for all we need (vss.29-32; 1 John 3:19-22).

Lk.12:35-48—With Jesus now heading toward Jerusalem (9:53), He continues to speak first to His disciples (vs.1). He wants His disciples to be alert and ready for His return (see Matt.24 and 25:1-13). His girding Himself and serving them is thought to be the gathering of the marriage supper of the Lamb (vss.36, 37; Rev.19:7-9). For vss.42-46 here in Luke, see Matt.24:45-51. Verses 47 and 48 declare to us by Jesus that it is more punishable to know God's will and not do it then to not know it and not do it (common sense here on responsibility). And so, those who have more will have more required of them (example, Lk.12:16); and those entrusted with more (example, authorities and positions) will have more asked of them (vs.48).

Lk.12:49-53—See Matt.10:34-36. Jesus' baptism in vs.50 is His upcoming trial and crucifixion.

Lk.12:54-59—See Matt.16:2, 3 and Matt.5:25, 26. Here Luke uses these passages that were recorded in Matthew to speak to the crowds about the coming judgment, if they do not repent and believe in Him, the Messiah, the Son of God, as God has given all judgment to be executed by His Son (vs.58; 13:2, 3; Jn.3:16-18; 5:26, 27).

Lk.13:1-5—Jesus continues on with the theme of the necessity to make right (repent) to the Judge before a final sentence is pronounce (12:57-59). The "blood" referred to in vs.1 appears to be the killing by Pilate of certain Galileans who were offering their sacrifices in the Temple (Unger, under Pilate). The "tower of Siloam" was thought to either be part of the old wall of Jerusalem or connected in some way with the "pool of Siloam" (John 9:7, 11).

Lk.13:6-9—With the similar emphasis as the previous passage, the fig tree here can have the general meaning of what happens if it does not produce fruit, or, more likely, can be pointing to (as often does) the nation Israel and its upcoming doom done to it by the Romans in 70 AD (see vss.34, 35, and Is.5:1-7). See Matt.13 for the meaning of a parable.

Lk.13:10-17—This passage is similar to Mark 3:1-5 of Jesus healing on the Sabbath. Note the various contrasts occurring here of Jesus healing the lady bent over for 18 years: Jesus healed on the Sabbath and they would not allow it (vss.14, 15); the synagogue official's response and the lady who was healed (vss. 13, 14; her "glorifying God" in the Greek is a continual, ongoing verb in the past tense); and the opponents reaction to Jesus compared to the "entire multitudes" response (vs.17). God will always receive the glory for His good works (Rev.15:3, 4).

Lk.13:18-21—See Matt.13:31-33.

Lk.13:22-30—As Jesus proceeds onward to Jerusalem, the urgency to respond and receive His message increases. He is "the Door" that people must enter to be saved (vss.24-29; Jn.10:9; Matt.7:13, 14, 27; 25:11, 12; 8:11, 12; Acts 4:12). For "the last, first and the first, last, in vs.30, see vss.24 and 27-29.

Lk.13:31-35—Note the probable slyness of the Pharisees wanting Jesus to leave here (see Mk.3:1-6). A fox digs holes for their prey to fall in for their capture. He knew His purpose and already had His destination, purpose and goal in mind (vss.32, 33; 9:31; 13:22; John 13:1; 17:4, 5). See Matt.23:37-39 for Jesus' heart cry for Jerusalem. The end quote of Ps.118:26 will be a full response from the people then; for now, it would only be a partial response (Lk.19:37, 38).

Lk.14:1-6—See Lk.13:10-17.

Lk.14:7-14—The key understanding of this parable that Jesus teaches is that honor (i.e., respect or fame) cannot be presented or given to oneself by oneself, but only comes from a worthy life of such given by the Lord (vs.10). It is brought about by the One who extends such an invitation to the one worthy to receive it (vs.10). And when putting on receptions, invite those who cannot pay you back for such a kind deed (vs.13). Similarly with the passage before this, let the Lord be the One who does the repaying (vs.14).

Lk.14:15-24—Jesus now tells a story about how this is worked out (vs.13). People invited made excuses of why they could not receive this (God's) invitation to His great dinner (vss.18-20, using their land, business or marriage as an excuse). So, the people of vs.13 are invited, and implied, accepted the invitation, or, at least, were better receptive as a whole—vss. 21, 22. Others out on the highways and hedges (walled in or fenced in) were compelled to come to the dinner. There is a sense of urgency here as Jesus said that those who rejected the invitation shall not taste of His dinner (vs.24; see also 13:28-30).

Lk.14:25-35—Jesus here in this passage gives five distinct characteristics of being His disciple. Note here Jesus is talking to large crowds who were following Him around and going along with Him (vs.25). First, one must love the Lord first and foremost above all other relations (vs.26). Second, one must carry his own cross (remembering what that represents) and follow after Jesus (vs.27). Third, being His disciple is a lifetime commitment (i.e., to complete it with one's life (vss.28-30). Fourth, being Jesus' disciple is a total commitment ("strong enough" (with the Lord's strength) to face and work through whatever one encounters—vss.30-32), with one's life (own cross) and with one's possessions—vs.33 (see vss.18, 19; 2 Cor.12:9, 10; Lk.12:30-34). Fifth, a disciple of Jesus is salt (remember its various uses in the world for Him—see Mt.5:13-16. Carrying one's cross comes with being His disciple (vss.34, 35; 13:26-30; vs.27).

Lk.15:1-32—These three stories shared by Jesus—The Lost Sheep, The Lost Coin and the Prodigal Son—are all about how people come into the Family of God. The lesson about the Prodigal Son is one of the most tender and compassionate stories we have about the love for a father (Father) toward his son(s), and how God miraculously works out "the lost and found" here on earth and brings His sheep into His Family (see also Jn.10:10-18; 27-30). Note in vss.1 and 2 the great contrast of two different groups of people and their response to Jesus. This sets up the stories to follow. The key point in the Lost Sheep (vss.4-7) is that Jesus goes after the lost, until He finds them (vs.4, and still does!). In the lost coin, the emphasis here is the diligent search that the Lord does to find them (vs.8). Note how heaven and the angels rejoice over each one coming into God's Family (vss.7, 10). Notice how repentance from sins is necessary to come into God's Family in all these stories, also (vss.7, 10, 18, 21). The Prodigal Son stresses the great joy and compassion of <u>the Father</u>, when one repents and comes into the Family of God (vss.20-24). Note this emphasis in vs.20—the Father saw him a distance (implying a longing to see him again), felt compassion for him, <u>ran</u> to see him (one would think the other way around), <u>embraced</u> him and <u>kissed</u> him (NASB in the margin puts—"kissed him again and again;" the Greek word stresses the fervency of the action taking place here). Note the sons rather mature confession, realizing his sins have been against both heaven and his family (vs.21). His gifts of clothes and a ring, reinstate him into his family (vs.22). His brother should have rejoiced for him, too, for making the right decision to return; plus, all the remaining inheritance was his (vs.31). His father explained that it was necessary (the Greek word here) to be merry and rejoice, because his brother "has come to life" (Greek past tense and middle voice, meaning this was done as an advantage to the subject—his brother—who made the right decision for himself); for he was dead (spiritually) and now came to life; he was lost, and now found (vs.32).

Lk.16:1-13—The story of the unrighteous steward emphasizes the importance of serving God rather than money (so then, using our money to serve God—vss.9, 13; Note: How Jesus is now speaking to His disciples). The steward received a strong verbal complaint that he had squandered (scattered about) his master's possessions (vs.1; see 15:13 for the same word with the Prodigal Son). Before being let go, though, he settles very wisely some accounts for his master, in hope to make friends with the debtors (vss.3-7; the amounts settle were both in line for the value of those goods at that time). He was praised for acting so wisely in bring this about (Jesus says the "sons of light" should take note here and learn to act as well with each other—vs.8). Use money on earth to work for eternal purposes (vss.9-12). In vs.11, what are the true riches that Jesus speaks about here? This is a great topic for discussion. Spiritual compared to physical or earthly things is a good start here (see 2 Cor.4:16-18 for better understanding in this comparison; hint—the true riches will center on the things specifically of God and His character. See Book 3 of <u>The Family Bible Studies Series</u> called <u>Growing in God's Wisdom</u> for a great help and aid on this topic, for personal and practical daily application).

Lk.16:14-18—Jesus now speaks in a response of the Pharisees about Him (vs.14; see 15:2). In vs.15, Jesus just emphasized that there are true riches of God that man are to seek (vss.11, 12). In vss.16, remember the story just shared on the Prodigal Son and also see Mt.11:12, 13. For God's eternal word, see Mt.5:17, 18; 24:35. And on marriage and divorce, see Mt.5:27-32; Ex.20:14.

Lk.16:19-31—This passage about the rich man and Lazarus is an important passage that gives us here on earth a glimpse of some of the features of life after death. It is also significant to point out the principle in Bible study of staying in the context, so as not to extract from the verses more than what they are saying. Note that here Jesus is continuing to speak to the Pharisees (vss.14, 15) and the connection to them is seen at the end of this passage of Scripture. Note that it is also important to say that this is a passage with spiritual reality and not a parable (as this word is also not used by Jesus to introduce this, as He does when speaking in parables (5:36; 6:39, 8:4, etc.; see Matt.13 for the definition). Significant notes—the rich man is in Hades (for which see the commentary of Mt.16:18) and Lazarus is at Abraham's bosom (vss.22, 23). Notice that Lazarus is at Abraham's bosom, not at a stated place. In my own studies of the Bible I believe this is so because Abraham is in heaven and he was the closest association for a Jew to relate to (the father of their nation—vss.27, 30) before the resurrection of Jesus. These combined Scriptures will also help in seeing this insight (Ex.3:13-15; Mt.22:32; Lk.9:29-31; Jn.8:56). Regarding the rich man, see previously in Lk.12:16-21, a parable, and Lk.14:18, 19; Lazarus desired just some crumbs that would fall from the rich man's table (vs.21). No one can cross the great chasm (compare on earth 2 Sam. 18:17). Why wouldn't resurrecting from the dead be persuasive enough? See ahead in Lk.24:11, 27, 44, 45, instead of believing God's eternal word (vss.29, 31; 24:44; Matt.24:35); and this is what relates back to the Pharisees (vss.16, 17).

Lk.17:1-10—Luke records Jesus speaking back to His disciples and here about the ministry of forgiveness to one another. Since he doesn't mention children in verse 2, I believe Doctor Luke is referring this to children and adults (vss.2, 3). Good family practice here. This is all part of doing what we are to do as faithful servants of the Lord (vs.10; Eph.4:31, 32; Mt.6:12-15). The extent and balance of discipleship is brought out also in vss.8-10, in doing the proper thing to be done—another good family practice.

Lk.17:11-19—The healing of the ten lepers reminds us of an earlier healing of a leper in Jesus' ministry (Mt.8:1-4). Also, about the Good Samaritan (esp. since Jesus was near their territory here again; vs.11; 10:25-37; Jn.4:39-42). For the testimony to the Jews, Jesus had to fulfill their Levitical duty (vss.14, 19; Mt.8:4; Lev.14).

Lk.17:20-37—Jesus now answers questions about the Kingdom of God to the Pharisees and teaches about His second coming and the rapture to come for His disciples. Speaking to the Pharisees, the kingdom is right before them (the King and the building of His kingdom—16:16, 17; 19:38). They needed to receive His message (8:10; 15:1, 2, 21). For His second coming and the rapture, see commentary on Matt.24:37-44, 28.

Lk.18:1-8—After sharing about end times events with the disciples, Jesus encourages them with this story to always be praying and not "lose heart" (vs.1; always remember Jesus' example—5:16; 6:12, 28; 9:18, 28, 29; 21:36; 22:44). Note the widow's determination in Jesus' story (vss.3-5). "Faith on the earth"—faith has an article with it in the Greek, and so can be "the faith" or "faith (vs.8; for its understanding, see the previous context—17:26-18:1).

Lk.18:9-17—Jesus simply warns here with another parable against having a self-righteous attitude—toward oneself and others. Note the list of terrible sins used here (as some may say, "I've never done anything like that before!"); and even admirable religious practices in vs.11, 12 (but see likewise in a different situation—2:36-38). When approaching God, one must come humbly as the attitude of the tax collector (note Jesus' previous messages—13:1-9; 15:21; and so here in vs.14), as also the example given here of the little children (vss.16, 17).

Lk.18:18-30—See Matt.19:16-29.

Lk.18:31-34—See Matt.20:17-19.

Lk.18:35-43—See Matt.20:29-34; Mk.10:46-52.

Lk.19:1-10—A good number of the tax collectors were favorable to the message of Jesus (3:12; 5:27-30; 7:29, 34). Zaccheus was one of them (a chief tax collector, who was rich—vs.2). He was trying to see Jesus and seems to have heard about Him previously, and so God was already working on (in) his heart (vss.3, 4). Compare those grumbling about Jesus (vs.7) to Zaccheus' confession and hurried manor with a rejoicing heart to be with Jesus (vs.6), bringing the declaration that salvation has come to this descendant of Abraham (vs.9). This is another great story of how Jesus came to go after the lost sheep until He finds them (vs.10; see 15:3-7).

Lk.19:11-27—As the Pharisees had asked previously about the coming of Jesus' kingdom and now, with Him about to enter Jerusalem, some thought the kingdom would appear at any moment. Jesus answers with another parable about the delay of the kingdom being completed and two different kinds of people responding to His message and authority. The first group are those who receive His message and do business for Him with the things given to them. They are faithful servants in His service awaiting His return (vss.13-19; see also 12:42-44). The other group do not receive His message (vss.14, 20, 21) and do not put to good use and profit what they have or want Him to reign over them. They reap the results of their decision (vs.27; see similar in 12:45, 46; 17:26-30). The faithful servants were awarded with more authority, taking care of their Master's goods and possessions (vss.17-19; 12:42-44).

Lk.19:28-44—See Matt.21:1-11; Mk. 11:1-10. Note how the large crowd of disciples praise God, loudly and joyfully, for all the miracles Jesus had done—a great, well-deserved tribute for all Jesus had done in His ministry (vs.37; Rev.5:9-14; 15:3, 4). For the declaration of Jesus their King, see also 13:35; and for the acclamation of peace and glory in the highest (vs.38), see the similar testimony given to Jesus at His birth (2:13, 14; and the ever ongoing proclamation in heaven—Rev.4:8-11!). Since His declaration as king is only partial in the city then and awaits the fulfillment (13:35), Jesus wept over the city and pronounced its upcoming destruction, not wanting their King to rule over them (vs.14; note here their statement about Him "after" He came).

Lk.19:45-48—See Matt.21:12-16; Mk.11:15-18; John 2:14-17.

Lk.20:1-8—See Matt.21:23-27.

Lk.20:9-20—See Matt.21:33-46.

Lk.20:21-47—See Matt.22:15-23:7.

Lk.21:1-4—See Mark 12:41-44.

Lk.21:5-38—See Matt.24 for the bigger picture and summary of the end time events. Here in Luke's passage is also the destruction of Jerusalem and the captivity of the Jews carried off to other nations, called "the time of the Gentiles" (see Rom.11 for a more complete explanation about this time frame), until the Lord returns to rule in His millennial reign (vss.20-24; 13:35; Rev.20:1-6). Other notes and additions—in vs.9, disturbances (tumults, uproars, confusions, noisy commotions) take place first; Luke adds pestilences (deadly infectious diseases) and "fearful sights" (KJ; objects or instruments of terror) will occur, vs.11; probably goes with the signs in the heavens following this word). God gives the words to say in defense of His work (vss.12-15). With signs in the heavens will come distress among nations and perplexity (uncertainty, confusion) about the roaring of the sea and waves on earth (vs.25), causing fear and fainting on some with the expectation of things taking place (vs.26). Luke adds a beautiful prayer stated by Jesus regarding end time events in vss.34-36. Jesus says not to be weighted down in one's heart with (literally) drunkenness and the anxieties of life (see Matt.6:25-34), so that these things will not come as a surprise or trap (vss.34, 35). Instead, praying at all time to be able (be in a position—BAGD for the Greek word here) to escape out of (Greek word meaning here) all the things mention and stand before the Son of Man (see, like the times of Noah—Matt.24:37-44 commentary).

Lk.22:1, 2—See Matt.26:1-5; 21:46.

Lk.22:3-6—See Matt.26:14-16.

Lk.22:7-13—See Matt.26:17-19; Mk.14:12-16.

Lk.22:14-23—See Matt.26:26-29.

Lk.22:24-30—See Matt.20:25-28; 19:28.

Lk.22:31-34—See Matt.26:33-36. Jesus shows the great support for His people by praying for Peter here and understanding what he was about to go through; and once he was strengthened, to then strengthen his brothers also (vss.31, 32; to sift wheat was to throw it in the air to separate it from the chaff; see Mt.3:12).

Lk.22:35-38—Jesus now prepares the Apostles for His departure from earth and back to heaven. They would now need a certain amount of travel supplies for their ministry (vs.36). A sword is mentioned, but even though He was going to be numbered as a criminal (vs.37; Is.53:12 prophesied), He did not carry a sword (to fulfill the prophecy in Isaiah, stated to the Apostles). Yet, He would be their intercessor (vs.32; Rm.8:27, 34) and they would learn to do likewise and wage war with the weapons of God (vss.38, 51; Eph.6:10-20; 2 Cor.10:3-5; Mt.26:51-56).

Lk.22:39-53—See Matt.26:36-56. In verse 42, as Jesus taught His disciples, so He carried out (Mt.6:10; Heb.5:7-10). Luke records His sweat became "like drops of blood" (vs.44). In agony He prayed very fervently, experiencing deep grief to the point of death (vs.44; Mt.26:37-39), something quite remarkable for us to understand, for the One who knew no sin and died in our place for our sins (2 Cor.5:20, 21; Heb.4; 14-16). So then, Luke records the disciples sleeping from sorrow (vs.45), which began in part (the sorrow) back at the Passover dinner (Mt.26:21, 22). Luke records Jesus healing the right ear of the high priest's slave (vs.51), that John records was Peter's action (Jn.18:10, 11).

Lk.22:54-62—See Matt.26:69-75; Mk.14:66-72; Jn.18:16-18, 25-27. John adds that it was a relative of the slave of the high priest being one of the one's recognizing Peter warming himself in the courtyard (Jn. 18:10, 26).

Lk.22:63-65—See Matt.26:67, 68.

Lk.22:66-71—See Matt.26:63-66.

Lk.23:1-7—See Matt.27:1, 2; 11-14.

Lk.23:8-12—Luke records Jesus being sent to Herod by Pilate, since Jesus was from the Galilee area (vs.6, 7), which was Herod's district of governing. Jesus was accustomed to some people wanting to see a sign from Him, not understanding what His ministry was about in service to God the Father (see Lk.11:16). So even after much questioning, Jesus was silent before Herod, as He was to Pilate (vs.9; Mt.27:14; Is.53:7). After the Jews tried to accuse Him (vs.10) and Herod and his soldiers despised and mocked Him, Jesus was sent back to Pilate (vs.11).

Lk.23:13-25—Matt.27:15-26. Noteworthy in Luke's account of the trial of Jesus is that three times Pilate is recorded as saying "I find no guilt in this man" (vss.4, 14, 22; and Herod also –vss.14, 15).

Lk.23:26-31—On His way to the cross, Jesus instructs the women lamenting and mourning over Him to weep instead for themselves and their children because of the upcoming judgment on Jerusalem (vs.28). There will be judgment coming in the Great Tribulation before the Lord's return (vs.30; Rev.6:16; Is.2:21; Lk.21:20-24; Mt.24:15-21). Verse 31, I believe, is referring to the Roman army, about to take over Jerusalem (vs.29; 21:20-24). If they do this to Jerusalem (and others) in their prosperous "green" time, who will help them in their "dry" time? Western Roman Empire and Rome were taken over during a declining time in their part of the western empire by German generals in 476 AD.

Lk.23:32-43—See Matt.27:33-44. Luke records Jesus forgiving those crucifying Him (vs.34, a tremendous prayer for all the agony and pain He endured—see also Acts 7:60). Luke alone records the faith of and the promise given to the thief on a cross next to Jesus (vss.39-43; Matt.27:38).

Lk.23:44-49—See Matt.27:45-56.

Lk.23:50-56—See Matt.27:57-61; Mk.15:42-47; John 19:38-42.

Lk.24:1-12—See Matt.28 for the harmony accounts of the resurrection of Jesus.

Lk.24:13-35—Jesus appeared to two who were going to Emmaus but they at first did not recognized Him and were prevented at first from doing so (vs.16; see Mary Magdalene's experience in John 20:15, 16). Jesus explained about Himself to them from all the prophets and in all the Scriptures (vss.27, 32). When Jesus broke bread with them, their eyes were then opened (vss.30, 31, 35). In returning to the eleven in Jerusalem (vs.33), they related their story and heard that the Lord had appeared to Simon, also (generally accepted to be Simon Peter along with 1 Cor.15:5).

Lk.24:36-49—Jesus then appears to them (vs.33) in Jerusalem. While they thought they were seeing a spirit (vs.37), He was appearing to them in His new resurrected body and encouraged them to touch it and see His hands and feet (vs.39; see also Jesus with Thomas in John 20:26-28). He demonstrates this again by asking for something to eat and He ate the fish they gave Him (vss.41-43). Jesus says to them, as He did previously to the two on the road to Emmaus, that all the things written about Him in the Law, Prophets and Psalms had to be fulfilled (vss.6, 7, 44-46). As He did throughout His ministry, the disciples as His witnesses were to go out to the nations and proclaim repentance for forgiveness of sins in His name and make the Gospel (Mt.28:19,20) known, so people can come into the Family of God (vss.46-48; John 1:12, 13—to be born into His Family—the Church, John 3:16). They were instructed to wait for the Promise from the Father, the Holy Spirit, and to be clothed with power from on high to go out on their mission, which took place at Pentecost (vs.49; Acts 1:1-5; 2:1-47).

Lk.24:50-53—Jesus blessed them and then ascended back to the Father in their midst; and they continually went out praising God with great joy in the temple (vss.50-53; Acts 1:9-11; Heb.1:1-3).

The Gospel of John

Jn.1:1-18—The introduction to the Gospel of John follows a very similar pattern to Jewish poetry—the author states an important topic at the beginning and finishes the writing with the same topic or point to be made at the end. Here in John's introduction he continues this pattern two more times after his first topic he introduced—i.e., the next subject after the first occurs again just before his ending and his next point follows the same thing, occuring after point two is made and the third point (repeated) from the ending. In the very middle, all by itself, is the main theme (or purpose) John is emphasizing, which turns out to be the theme of his Gospel writing.

So, John's poetic pattern follows out like this-A-B-C-D-C-B-A. Let's take a look how it works out and the topics John emphasizes in his introduction to the Gospel of John.

The main topic John brings out in point A of his beginning (vss.1-3) and at the end (vss.14-18) is that Jesus is God (the second person of the Trinity), who came to earth, as one of His main purposes, to reveal the Father (vs.18). The long and the short and in between of John 1:1 translates that the Word (Jesus) is God. He was with God in the beginning (vss.2,3) and so, in the early manuscripts we have available, vs.18 translates that Jesus is the <u>only begotten God</u>, a word that John uses four times (only begotten) in his Gospel writing (out of 9 in the New Testament) to show that Jesus is the Son of God (see vs.14 and 3:16 and 18).

Next, point B that John declares is that in Him (Jesus) was life (eternal life) and His life was (is) the light of men (vss.4, 5; 3:19-21; 8:12). It shines out in such a way that the darkness does not overcome it (vs.5; 1 Jn.3:8; Jn.16:33; 1 Jn.5:3-5). Verses 9-13 are the corollary of Point B, coming just before the ending in vss.14-18. Verse 9 emphasizes that Jesus is the True Light and vss.10-13 shows how He brings His life (eternal) to mankind. This comes through the spiritual birth, when one believes in Jesus and receives Him into their life and comes into the Family of God as God's child (vss.12, 13; 3:1-16; 10:9; see the Prayer at the end of the book). Thus, His life becomes the light of men (vs.4). The next segment, topic C, focuses on John the Baptist and His ministry (vss.6, 7a). John came to bear witness of the Light (vs.7; 1:19-36; 3:27-36). The second part of topic C, vs.8, essentially makes the same point and comes right before topic B at the end (vss.10-13). Then, topic D in the outline, comes by itself and right in the middle of John's introduction and right between the C parts, and is the main theme and purpose of his Gospel writing—"that all might believe through Him" (i.e., all God's revelation of His Son in the A-C parts, stated here in the beginning of his Gospel writing, vs.7b; (see this restated and elaborated on in the finishing of John's writing—in Jn.20:31, his purpose of writing the Gospel of John). Note the new birth is the work of God (vs.13), not of bloods (ancestry), not of the flesh (not a physical, but here the spiritual birth) and not of man's will (man cannot counterfeit this or "try" to make it happen; from beginning to end, it is all God's work to bring about the birth of the believer into His family, as God their father; thus, born of God; vss.12,13; 3:16-21; 6:44; 14:15-24).

Jn.1:19-36—The Apostle John now gives some specific statements about the ministry (witness, vss.19, 34; 3:33) of John the Baptist. People wanted to know who he was and he said he was the one preparing the way of the Lord from Is.40:3 (vs.23). Then they were asking him why he was baptizing people (vs.25). John the Baptist put the emphasis on the Lord coming after him, for He is more important than him (i.e., John the Baptist; vss.26,27,30; 3:28-30; we know from the other Gospel books that John's ministry was preaching baptism for the forgiveness of sins—Mt.3:5; Mk.1:2-4), to point to Jesus who was the One who would take away the sin of the world—vs.29; Mt.1:21; 2 Cor.5:21; Is.53:10-12). John referred to Jesus as the Lamb of God who would do this (vss.29, 36; Is.53:4-9). When John saw the Holy Spirit descend on Him, he knew Jesus was the one (vss.32-34) and declared Him to be the Son of God (vs.34; see also Mt.3:16, 17).

Jn.1:37-51—John now records some of the disciples who acknowledged Jesus and began to follow Him. John writes that Andrew, Simon Peter's brother declares first a very noteworthy proclamation as Jesus being the Messiah (vs.41) and that they had found Him. Philip's declaration connects Jesus as "the Prophet" (Dt.18:18) Moses wrote about, who was from Nazareth and the Son of Joseph (vs.45). When Jesus makes known to Nathanael that He knows him (not having any slyness or deceit—vss.47,48),

Nathanael proclaims in his response back to Jesus that He is "the Son of God," the "King of Israel" (this probably has the help of Almighty God here, similar to Simon Peter's declaration of Jesus later in Mt.16:16,17; Jn.1:49; 3:27). The "greater things' Jesus referred to in speaking to Nathanael, refer back to Gen.28:12-17, often stated as "Jacob's ladder," in his dream of angels ascending and descending in the place where he was that night (calling it Bethel—the house of God, and that this was the "gate of heaven"—Gen. 28:17). Nathanael will see "greater things" coming up done by Jesus the Messiah and will see that He is the "Gate of Heaven" (Jn.3:16; 10:9); for as Peter testifies coming up in chapter six, only Jesus has the "words of eternal life" (6:68, 69).

Jn.2:1-12—At the wedding in Cana (west of the Sea of Galilee), Jesus revealed His glory (miraculous power) and His disciples believed in Him (vs.11). Mary His mother had the right faith at the wedding (vs.5), though Jesus had said His hour had not come yet (i.e., His purpose for coming to earth—7:6, 8, 30; 8:20; 13:1; 1:29). His "new wine" was better than the previous (vs.10; see also Mt.9:17).

Jn.2:13-25—The Apostle John now writes about Jesus cleansing the temple, placed very early here in Jesus' ministry events, while the other Gospel writers include it much later, just a short time before His trial began (Mt.21; Mk.11; Lk.19). Many ask why this was so and we see that John has a different concluding emphasis here compared with the other Gospel writers. John writes early in his passage account here with the similar declaration of the previous Gospel writers that Jesus did not want His Father's house to be a "house of merchandise" (vs.16; see the commentary of this in Mt.21:12-17). But John has a different concluding proclamation here that Jesus makes about the temple. The prophecy about this was given by God through the prophet Nathan to David in 1 Chr.17:4-15. With David wanting to build a temple for God (Solomon completed it), God said to David that He would build a house for him (1 Chr.7:10). This would occur after David had died and gone on to be with his fathers (1 Chr.17:11, 12—note Solomon had already been declared king before He died and immediately sat on the throne when David died—1 Kg.2). So, One was then yet to come, who would be a Son and His kingdom would last forever (1 Chr.17:12-14; see also 2 Sam.7:11-13; Lk.1:31-33). In vs.19 in John chapter two, the word "destroy" (of the temple) is a second person plural verb, referring back to the Jews in Jesus' statement to them. Their lack of receiving their Savior and Messiah brought the destruction of the temple and Jerusalem in 70 AD by the Romans (Mt.23:37-39; Lk.19:43, 44; 21:20-24). This statement by Jesus was twisted and unfairly stated by the Jews about Him in His trail (Mk.14:58, 59). So here in this passage John is stating that Jesus is the One who has come from God to fulfill these Old Testament prophecies, that He is the one who will build the Temple of God. After Jesus rose from the dead, His disciples remembered this and believed what He had said (vs.22; see also 1 Cor.6:17-20; Eph.2:19-22; 1 Pet.2:4-10).

Many believed in Him seeing the miracles He performed (vs.23); yet, He knew the condition of mankind and what He had come to earth to do (vss.24, 25; 1:29, 36).

Jn.3:1-21—With the main theme of the Gospel of John being written previously in John's introduction (1:7), John now records this great passage and event of the spiritual birth (1:12,13) with Nicodemus talking with Jesus about this. Some very noteworthy points are good to mention in this wonderful writing of Scripture. Nicodemus was present with Joseph of Arimathea to help in the burial of Jesus (19:39). He may have become a believer (or was becoming one) due to the great miracles Jesus was doing (2:23; 3:2). The word in the Greek for being born "again" (or from above) can have either meaning, and may have been intentionally used by Jesus for both meanings (BAGD; 1:12, 13) in the spiritual birth experience (vss.3, 7). Jesus goes on to explain the difference between physical and spiritual births (vss.5-8). The words "water and spirit" in verse five are jointed together in the Greek language and so they go together as a unity (the new spiritual birth, a baptism of water and a baptism of the Spirit). While it in only the spiritual baptism (the Holy Spirit coming into the life of the believer—14:15-17) that saves a person (see Peter's written distinction in 1 Pet.3:21; thus, also, the Apostle Paul—one baptism—Eph.4:4-6; Tit.3:5,6), the apostles considered it very important to also carry out Jesus' command of the Great Commission of water baptism with the believer's experience of the spiritual birth (Mt.28:19,20; Mk.16:15,16), which is found in every case in the Acts of the Apostles when the spiritual birth of coming into the Church occurs (some examples—Acts 2:41;8:12,13; note the fulfillment needed in Acts 8:14-17 to receive the Holy Spirit with their believing; 16:15,33). So, two separate actions take place, one that brings salvation to the believer (the spiritual birth) and the other became a regular church practice (the outward expression and testimony, declaring the "new life" inward experience (1:4, 9, 12,

13; 1 Pet.1:8,9; see Rom.6:3-11 for the meaning of water baptism and the working of the spiritual baptism; also see John 16:7-15, the work the Holy Spirit does, given some testimony by Jesus here in this passage of John 3:6-8). Note Jesus predicting His ascension in vs.13, same word used as in 1:51; and His kind of death He would experience in vs.14 and says it is necessary (Greek word in this verse) for us (mankind) to receive eternal life (vs.15;1:4, 12, 13). All this is prompted by God's love (The Father, Son and Holy Spirit) for mankind to be saved (vs.16). Here again, Jesus, God's Son, is made known (vss.16, 18; 1:14, 18) for who He is. The word "perish" in vs.16 is in the Greek aorist tense verb, showing a point in time (one time past tense) event in the spiritual birth of the believer, while the" believing" here is a present participle, on-going lifetime verb in the believer's spiritual birth and life. The necessity of believing and receive Jesus and the Gospel message in brought out in the next verses (vss.17-21; 1:10-13). Because of mankind loving darkness and not wanted to be reproved (same word of the Holy Spirit's work John 16:8), it is necessary for mankind to receive the True Light (Jesus) to be saved (vs.21; 1:4, 9; 8:12; 14:6), and then to display His good works in one's life (vs.21; Mt.5:13-16; Phil.2:12,13.

Jn.3:22-36—John continues his witness about Jesus, saying how joyful he is to hear the Bridegroom's voice (vs.29), and from here on He must increase while John decreases (finishing his ministry—vs.30). One who receives Jesus' message and ministry will set his seal (stamp) regarding Him that God is true (vs.33). Giving the Spirit without measure means unlimited and unreserved, referring to the words and ministry of Jesus (vs.34; shown in vs.35

of all things given into His hands; total freedom and self-control operable at all times, the work of the Holy Spirit—1 Cor.3:17; Gal.5:22,23). Verse 36 restates Jesus' words in vss.16-18.

Jn.4:1-42—The woman at the well (a Samaritan) is one of the most beautiful passages about how God can break down cultural and religious barriers to win people into His Family. Both the cultural and religious differences here are quite difficult and significant. Note the cultural barriers here that Jesus breaks down with the love of God—a man taking the initiative talking to a woman (and yet, with a command—vss.27,7); a Jew talking with a Samaritan (vs.9); Jesus was at the well and without a bucket to draw water (vss.6,11); a man (even a Jew) talking with a lady who is living with one not her husband (and having had five husbands—vss.16-18); and going back to her village and saying she talked to a male Jew, who may be a prophet or the Messiah (vss.28, 29, 39). Quite a hand full of cultural differences here. Religious barriers are obvious here too—Jews relating to Samaritans (vs.9); the mountains of where to worship God are not the main emphasis now (as was important with their past—vss.20,21); the Jews maintained their worship of the monotheistic God who has revealed Himself to them (example, through Moses); Samaritans, from the start with Jeroboam, worshipped false gods (vs.12;1 Kg.12); the result is that salvation is from the Jews (vs.22); and true worship is knowing the Father and worshipping Him in spirit and truth (vss.23-25).

Jesus' topic of discussion with her follows as such—from drinking water (vss.10,11); to receiving water welling up to eternal life (vss.10-15; 7:38,39); to revealing her current living situation and past husbands (vss.16-19); to the importance to know the Heavenly Father and worshipping Him in spirit and truth (vss.20-26; 1:18—possibly another cultural barrier to help her overcome, depending on her family upbringing, i.e., relating to her father—vss.16-19).

The doors were not always open to ministering to the Samaritans (see Lk.9:51-56; yet, see Acts 8:14-17), but this one was open to Jesus. And so, knowing His mission, He knew ahead of this that He had to go this way (Greek word "necessary in vs.4); and the result was a great harvest and a two day stay with the Samaritans (vss.39-42) and great joy among them. It was also a great lesson for the disciples to know the "food" Jesus fed on and how to follow His example—"to do the will of Him who sent Me" (vss.32-38).

Jn.4:43-54—The healing here of the royal official's son appears similar to the centurion's slave in Matt.8:5-13 and because of these differences most think these are separate events in Jesus' ministry. First note, though, the distinction like night and day, of how the Galileans received Jesus, compared to Nicodemus coming to Jesus at night (vss.43-45; 3:1, 2). Seeing or hearing of the great miracles Jesus was doing, it was not uncommon for people to request the same when He visited there city (vss.45, 48; Lk.4:23). But this man (an officer in the king's service) not only believed the word Jesus spoke to him, but also believed in Jesus along with his household (vss.50,53)—and that is the Apostle John's theme of this Gospel writing, and recording the testimonies of those who came to believe in Jesus the Messiah (1:7; 4:39-42; the word Messiah is only recorded twice in the New Testament, both in John's Gospel, statements made by people (Andrew in 1:41 and the woman at the well in 4:25; the Greek equivalent is <u>Christos</u>, which is the more frequent term used of Jesus in the New Testament).

Jn.5:1-29—John begins this chapter and vs.14, along with the start of chapters 6 and 7 with the words "after these things"—a common statement of John used regularly in his writing in the book of Revelation to note the sequence of events, that take place. The healing of the man at the Bethesda (meaning, "house of grace"—Unger) pool is significant, not only for Jesus' miraculous healing (on a Sabbath), but now He amplifies in His teaching what His ministry is about, and the "many witnesses" backing it up. It may have not been lawful because of this law the Jews made for the man to pick up his pallet (portable bed) and walk with it after Jesus healed him (vs.10), but it was for Jesus, certainly to demonstrate God's mercy and power to him and to the Jews of God's great healing grace to this man. He (the man made well) becomes Jesus' first witness here of His ministry and mercy and grace to mankind at this event (vss.10-16). Next is the witness of the Father, mentioned quite often throughout this chapter (vss.17-21; "greater works" in vs.20 is exemplified in the next verse and vss.24-29). Verse 17 is Jesus' verbal declaration of John 1:1, as the Jews clearly understood it (vs.18). Verses 24-26 show the witness of God's grace and mercy to mankind when one receives eternal life from Him (1:4, 5, 12, 13) and the resurrection from the dead to come to experience it with Him forever (see the Prayer in back of the book; vs.24 is the word "passover," from death to life, which without a doubt, many in that crowd pick this up from Him at that time—a "greater one (work) now at hand—vs.20). Jesus also has been given by the Father to execute His judgment, amplifying the choice mankind has to make about Him, mercy and grace or judgment (vss.21-29).

Jn.5:30-47—Jesus continues on in this chapter of John to amplify His witnesses and to declare more of them here. Verses 30-32 emphasize the Father once again as Jesus' primary witness, working with the Father (as first stated in vs.17). John the Baptist is another one (his primary witness was to Jesus—and Jesus is now "increasing" in God's work—vss.33-38; 3:30). The Scriptures also testify and witness about Jesus (vss.38-40; see also Lk.24:44). The next verses testify that Jesus does His ministry in the love of God—something that should have been evident to all who saw it (and now read it, also—vss.41-44), making this another witness of Jesus' great works. Finally, Moses specifically was Jesus' witness, also, writing about Him, which they needed to also read and believe about Him (vss.45-47; Dt.18:18; Lk.24:44; Jn.6:14).

Jn.6:1-15—This account of the feeding of the 5000 is recorded in all the Gospel writings. See the Mt.14:13-21 commentary. Here we see Jesus developing in His disciples a dependent heart on God as well as a servant's heart in His work for Him. This leads up to His speaking to the crowd that He is the Bread of Life.

Jn.6:16-21—See Mt.14:22-33.

Jn.6:22-71—Crowds were now seeking Jesus because of His performing miracles and also, for feeding them (as much as they wanted to eat at that time, too—vss.11, 2, 26). They even appeared saying that they were ready for another meal (vss.30-31)! Jesus teaches them that <u>He is the Bread of Life</u> (vss.35, 48, 51). The "food" Jesus wants to give them is eternal life (vss.27, 29,

40, 54, 68). God has set His "seal" on His Son (vs.27, for which see 3:33; Mt.3:17). With their apparent request for another meal (vs.31) and God feeding their fathers with the bread (manna) from heaven, Jesus turns to the spiritual bread from heaven, namely Himself, and that He came to give them life (not just a meal), but life eternal (vss.31-33). He is the <u>Bread of Life</u>, who came down out of heaven. Coming to Him involves doing the will of the Father, as Jesus did; and coming to Jesus and believing in Him, one would look forward to Him raising him from the dead on that glorious day to come (as He would soon raise from the dead—vss.34-40; 5:26). They wondered what Jesus meant by "coming down from heaven" (vss.38, 41), since He was from the family of Joseph and Mary (vs.42; but see 1:45, Philip's declaration). Jesus said if one hears and learns from the Father, they come to Him (vs.45; see all the previous witnesses in chapter five). He is the One whom the Father sent to earth (5:36; 6:29, 38, 39, 44, 57), the One being (a present participle in the Greek) with the Father (vs.46). The Great News in vss.50, 51—whoever receives <u>this Bread</u> (Himself) coming down from heaven shall live forever (vss.47-51, 58). Jesus gave His flesh (on crucifixion day) for the life of the world (vss.51, 38). To have eternal life in oneself, one needs the spiritual birth (1:12, 13; 3:3-8), by receiving Jesus into their life (1:12, 13). Asking Him into one's life then receives His life into theirs, thus taking part with Him in His life (His flesh and blood and ministry). This true food is true life indeed (eternal), and thus lived out in the life of the believer, vss.55-58 (vss.53-59, 27).

Jesus' words spoken were spiritual words and true words of life (vss.64, 64). Some, not comprehending His words, chose to no longer follow Him (vs.66; see, though, Mt.13:10-17, 36). Peter's proclamation demonstrates those whom God had drawn to Jesus (vss.68-70, 44, 64, 65). As in vs.62, Jesus words and works all speak for themselves (i.e., Himself, for who He is—5:18; 6:29).

Jn.7:1-53—Jesus appears at the Feast of Tabernacles and presents His public teaching there. Because the Jews were looking to kill Him (vs.1; 5:18), He went to the Feast secretly at first (i.e., not publicly, vs.10), waiting, at first, against the advice of His brothers, who did not believe in Him at that time (vss.3-10). The crowds were still wondering if He would come and who He really was (vss.10-15). Jesus continued to emphasize that He was sent by the Father with the Father's teaching that He was sharing to the people (vss.14-18, 28, 29). He reveals the Jews plot of trying to kill Him and that they should not be angry about His healing in making a man well on the Sabbath. They needed to hear His injunction to make righteous judgments (vs.24; see 1 Sam.16:7; Is.11:1-5). As the Apostle John continues to work out is theme (1:7; 20:31) in writing this Gospel book, many in the crowd believed in Jesus because of His message and great miracles performed (vs.31; 6:68, 69). He mentioned He would not be much longer with them (the unbelieving crowd) and where He was going, they (in their current unbelieving condition) could not come (vss.32-36). Yet, His message, while it could be presented, was to come to Him to find true living water, so one would not thirst again (i.e. receiving eternal life and the Holy Spirit to soon come at Pentecost—vss.37-39; 1:12,13; 3:16). Many came to believe in Him as the Messiah (vs.31), yet many others still wondered Him (vss.41, 42). Some were thinking He may be the Prophet Moses prophesied about in Dt.18:18 (vs.40). But since He was from the Galilee area, those doubting still continued to do so (vs.52; see Mt.2:1, 2). Those who believed in Him believed because of His words of life (vss.37, 38; 6:40, 46-51; 3:16) and the miraculous works He performed, that only God can do (vs.31; 2:23; 3:2; 6:2; 20:30, 31).

John 8:1-11—In keeping with the theme of the Gospel of John (1:7; 19:35; 20:31), we see in the next two chapters Jesus winning as many as He can when speaking to the multitudes (8:30), while also reaching out to win into the Family of God the individual ones, here, neglected, being blind and man not having a solution to help him (9:6, 7, 35-38).

The passage of the woman caught in adultery (8:1-11) is not found in the early manuscripts we have of the New Testament. But this passage does contain the benchmarks of being an actual historical occurrence in Jesus' ministry (possibly added in a short time after John wrote this Gospel—see 20:30). The account has great benefit for us by the message it teaches. At least three strong compelling points stand out here for us to learn—1) Note clearly the evil intent to once again try and "trap" Jesus in something He would say—here, even to accuse Him (vs.6), by the scribes and Pharisees; 2) they tried to get Jesus to be the Judge of this woman (vs.5, 7—persisting in doing it). Jesus already had declared that He came not into the world to condemn it, but to save mankind from their sins (3:16-21; and declaring again in 8:15, 16; 12:46-50). 3) Note carefully the lack of witnesses here in making this known to others—at least 2 or 3 were needed to proceed with this (Mt. 18:16; Dt.19:15; 8:17; note the proper procedure that Jesus instructs for the church (and even legally) to take in Mt.18:15-20). If more than one actually witnessed this event, the whole set up could be highly suspect from the beginning (not uncommon even in other domestic disputes; see the commentary in Mt.19:1-12 in the importance of what Jesus is teaching here, remembering that this is not the unpardonable sin). Since Jesus did not witness this either, He said for her to go on her way and sin no more (vs.11).

Jn.8:12-59—Jesus is probably continuing on with the discourse He begins in 7:14 here. In a hostile environment (vss.37, 59), still many came to believe in Him (vs.30). He came as The Light into the world (vs.12; 9:5) so people would be saved from their sins (3:16-21) and have His "life" as their "light" and life (vs.12; 1:4; 3:20,21), and so mankind would no longer live in darkness (3:19-21;12:46—"darkness" has the article before it in the Greek here; 1:4-9; 1 Jn.3:8). Unless they did, they could not go where He was going (back to heaven—vss.21-30; note in vs.29 that Jesus always did the things that are pleasing (present tense) to the Father).

The dialogue and tension progresses as Jesus proclaims their motive to kill Him (vs.37), while He continues to reveal the Father to them (vss.27-47; 1:18). The Jews remained in their own dilemma, trying to declare who their Father was (vss.39-41). Their intent and eventual actions lead to only one answer—the devil and his works (vs.44). They then come to the threshold of committing the impardonable sin (vss.48, 52; see Mt.12:22-37). Jesus kindly reminds them that whoever keeps His word will never see death (spiritual death—vs.51). They still greatly struggled about who Jesus was (vs.53). Jesus reveals that Abraham saw His day and rejoiced (vs.56) and declared that He existed before Abraham was born (vs.58; the proclamation of Jesus being the great "I am" refers back to Ex.3:14, 15, of God's eternal existence, and so, John 1:1, 2, 18; 8:24). Jesus once again eluded their taking a hold of Him, for His time was not yet at hand to be delivered up to them (vss.20, 59).

Jn.9:1-41—This marvelous healing of Jesus of the blind man (see vss.32, 33) eventually leads to the man previously blind to testify to the Pharisees and then his being put out of the synagogue (vs.34). However, it furthers the testimony of Jesus' healing the man previously blind to others and his subsequent becoming a believer (vs.38). The resulting response of the Pharisees asked Jesus if they were blind too (vs.40). Jesus said that if they would come to know Him like the blind man did (8:51), they would no longer be blind (of spiritual truth and about Him); not doing so leaves their sins remaining with them (and spiritual blindness, vs.41). Note in vss.1-4 we have the warning to not always look for the cause of physical ailment (which can be allowed for the glory of God and the person here became a believer—vss.3, 35-38). Jesus also declares that we all should be participating in doing God's work while we can (vs.4).

Jn.10:1-42—Once again, Jesus proclaims His salvation message to the antagonistic crowd and has to flee from them at the end; but many follow Him and come to believe in Him beyond the Jordan River (vss.32, 39, 40). His tender and very real analogy of sheep needing Him, the Great Shepherd of the sheep, surely caught the hearts and minds of the crowd (vss.1-18, 42; see also Mt.9:36; Heb.13:20; 1 Pet.2:25; 5:4). Sheep pens usually have just one entrance, allowing only the shepherd (or one appointed) to go in to the sheep (vss.1, 2). Note the simplicity of vs.5—they only know the Shepherd's voice and not strangers (plural); and so, they follow Him (vss.4, 27; note vs.28 where Jesus gives His sheep eternal life and they shall never perish, same word here as in John 3:16; the Greek uses an emphatic negative here said by Jesus, showing the strongest way in the language that something would not take place). The word "snatch" or "seize" out of Jesus' hand and the Father's hand is the same word for "rapture" in 1 Thess.4:17, as going against the forces of nature there by the power of God, so no one has the "force" to take His sheep from Them—vss.27-29. In declaring that Jesus and the Father are "one," Jesus is stating His unity with the Father, along with having the nature and character of the Father, which the Jews picked up loud and clear spoken to them (vss.30-33, 38; 17:21,22; 8:58; 1:29,34; see Book 1, The Family of God—Foundation, for further discussion about the Trinity). The Feast of the Dedication is the Feast of Lights, which is the renewing of the Temple under Judas Maccabaeus (vs.22). Jesus quotes Ps.82 to the Jews to help them understand Him being the Son of God. The context of Ps.82 is referring to leaders in the world, at times being given some kind of declaration of divinity by the people in the world (so-called, gods—Ps.82:6; see example in Acts 12:20-23). If they could recognized so-called "greatness" in man, why could they not recognized God's Son doing the great works of God (vss.34-38)? But still, some were unwilling (8:27), yet many came to believe in Him for who He is and what He did in performing God's mighty miracles in their midst (vs.40-42;2:23).

Jn.11:1-57—John includes this very moving and powerful event of Jesus raising Lazarus from the dead because of the great testimonies proclaimed here and in keeping with the theme of the book (1:7; 20:31), as many of the Jews witnessed this and came to believe in Him (vs.45). During His ministry on earth Jesus used to go out to Bethany and lodge there (Mt.21:17; 26:6). Once more, Jesus declares that this sequence of events is for the glory of God (vss.4, 40), with others coming into the Family of God through Jesus' ministry (vss.42, 45, 51, 52). Mary's experience is mentioned in 12:3 (vs.2). Note Martha's faith initiative here and strong proclamation about who Jesus is in vss.20-29. The first part of Jesus declaration of who He is applies first to Lazarus in the prophecy about him in vss.25; then, to him and all believers who receive His gift of eternal life (vs.26). Here, emotionally, we see Jesus felt their grief, and expressed it with tears (vss.33-38). God even used the statement by the Jewish high priest (involved in the plot and scheme to put Jesus to death—Mt.26:3, 4, 57-68; 27:1, 2), that Jesus would die for the nation and all those who would come to believe in Him (vss.47-53). Jesus left and stayed at Ephraim (Northeast of Jerusalem), as now the word was put out to bring Him to the Jewish authorities if anyone should find Him (vss.54-57).

Jn.12:1-11—The occasion of Mary, Martha and Lazarus was truly a great celebration for them with Jesus. Part of the celebration, though, involved preparing Jesus for His upcoming burial. Note the role Judas was already playing out (vss.1-9). As a result of Lazarus being raised from the dead, many of the Jews were continuing to believe in Jesus (vs.11).

Jn.12:12-19—For the Triumphal Entry into Jerusalem, see Mt.21:1-11.

Jn.12:20-36—Jesus now declares that the time had now come to fulfill His coming of crucifixion and resurrection. This came at the time the Greeks were seeking Him in coming to the Passover, whom their countries would be reached through the Apostles and those coming into the Church after Pentecost (vss.20-26; Acts1:8). As the Light of the world, Jesus would be with then only a little while longer, then the Church would take over His ministry (vss.35, 36, 46; 1:4-9; 8:12; 9:5). With Jesus' triumph over sin and death coming up, the ruler of this world would be defeated and judged (vs.31; 8:44; 1Jn.3:8) and Jesus would draw all people to Himself—as Lord and Savior or as Judge (3:13-21; 5:21-29; 8:28; 12:28, 35, 36).

Jn.12:37-50—Inspite of the predicted unbelief declared by the prophet Isaiah (vs.38-40), still, miraculously, even rulers were coming to believe in Jesus (vss.42,11). Isaiah saw the Lord's glory (vs.41; Is.6:1-5) and those witnessing His great works were seeing the Lord's glory, too (11:4, 40; 1:14; 17:4, 6), and His great resurrection coming up (vs.28; 20:1-10). See the commentary on Mt.13 for the passage about their unbelief from Is.6:10 (vs.40). Jesus reminds them again that He came to save mankind from their sins in His coming to earth and not to condemn them (vss.46-48, 50; see also Rm.11:30-32; Jn.3:16-18). As He has been declaring to them, the Father teaches Him what to say to them (what to say and speak, i.e., "go and proclaim the Gospel and say this to them (the general and the specifics—vs.49; see 3:34); and His commandment is to believe in Him, whom God sent to save the world, and receive His gift of eternal life (vss.46, 50; 3:14-17; 6:29; 17:1-3).

Jn.13:1-20—Jesus now realizing that the time had come for His glorification (trial, crucifixion, resurrection and ascension—12:23, 24; 13:31, 32), He spends in the next five chapters, including the prayer in Chapter 17, in the final teaching and discourses with the Apostles. The supper Jesus shares with the Apostles to begin Chapter 13 is certainly, according to the context of the Gospel of John, before the Passover (11:55; 12:1; 13:1,29; 18:28; 19:14). As we know in the Gospel of John, John's emphasis is often more theological than strictly a narrative account (example, chapter two of the temple cleansing). The emphasis on this supper is more on servanthood and the revealing of the betrayer.

Jesus' example of servanthood in washing the Apostle's feet is similar to other teachings He shared with them about being a servant to one another (Mt.23:11, 12; 24:45-47; Lk.22:24-27). Here, He showed them that example, so they would continue it with one another (vss.14, 15, 34, 35), reminding them that a slave (or servant) is not above their Master (vss.16, 17).

Jn.13:21-30—John devotes a good length of writing to show the development of Jesus' betrayer—Judas Iscariot. Understandably troubled in His spirit to reveal this (vs.21), Jesus knew the one from the beginning who would betray Him (vss.11, 26; 6:64, 70, 71; see also Lk.4:13; 22:52, 53).

Jn.13:31-38—Jesus now gives His disciples a new commandment—to love one another. New, because it is for the

Church; and new, because it follows His example (vss.34, 35), and demonstrates to the world that we are his disciples (vs.35; 15:12, 13). For Peter's following Jesus later, see 10:27-30; see also Mt.26:33-35 for more on Pete's denial.

Jn.14:1-31—In beautiful teaching and recorded dialogue, Jesus now comforts His Apostles with many great and needed promises and prophecies for their days and ministry ahead after His departure. They are going through a great time of grief hearing He is about to suffer and then leave them, especially hoping that possibly at this time, the kingdom would return to Israel (16:6, 20, 22; Acts1:6). But when they see Him after His resurrection and with the coming of the Holy Spirit at Pentecost, their grief would turn to joy—a joy no one would ever be able to take away from them (16:20-22).

With His soon leaving them (13:1), Jesus begins His instructions to believe in Him as they believe in God (vs.1; 10:30). Then He assures them that He will come back for them (vss.2, 3). The Father has many "dwelling places" and Jesus is going to prepare a place for them (The Church, since this is yet to occur), so that they may be with Him (vs.3). Since this yet to take place, this refers to the Rapture of the Church at large, with the key words here being "receive you to Myself" (something not occurring this way at His second coming, but right in line with the Rapture of the Church; the second coming involves the "in-gathering" after Armageddon—Mt.24:31; Rev.16:16). The Rapture of the Church is when Jesus presents His Bride (the Church) before the throne to the Father (2 Cor.4:14; Jn.5:24, 25) and occurs before the Great Tribulation (since Jesus comes back to earth for His millennial reign on earth after the Great Tribulation), and then to enjoy their home in heaven with Him forever (14:2,3; 1 Thess.4:17; see 1 Thess. 4:13-18 for further explanation of the Rapture of the Church). They know the way to heaven because He is "the Way, the Truth and the Life" (vs.6). Next, the Apostles want to see the Father and Jesus says that they already have, by seeing Him (vs.9; 10:30). The Father's works speak for that through Jesus (vss.10, 11), that the Father abides in Him (vs.11). The "greater works" in vs.12 are the "greater works of faith", by and through them, since Jesus will not physically be with them, that God will do; plus, reaping in a harvest (and outside to the nations) by what He has initiated and begun to sow (4:35-38; 5:20); and comes through faith and prayer (vss.12-14). The initial promise and comfort of not leaving the Apostles as orphans and coming to them is first established through the coming of Holy Spirit (vss.15-20; see vss.20, 23) at Pentecost, Acts 2). The Holy Spirit will come to abide (dwell) in them (also all believers, and be with them forever (and so, no longer being orphans—vss.16, 17; the word "another" in verse 16 means "another of the same kind" –Vine). His coming for the church at large comes at the Rapture of the Church in vss.2, 3 (see the previous discussion on this), and thus, the Church always has that "expected Hope." Mentioned several times in these verses is that those who love the Lord Jesus will keep His commandments (vss.15, 21, 23, 31), with the presence of the Living God being with them (vs.23). The coming of the Holy Spirit will pick up where Jesus left off, reminding them of the things He said while on earth; also, with the great promise to "teach us all things," (vs.26). Jesus' peace is not like the world's because His peace first comes inside a person (vs.27; 16:33; Lk.2:14; Rom.5:1, 2), and so, not to be greatly disturbed by <u>outward</u> circumstances ("fearful"—vs.27). The Father being "greater than I "refers to Jesus fulfilling the Father's commands (vs.31) and completing the work the Father had sent Him to do (15:1; 17:4); see also 1 Cor.15:20-28; His subjection to the Father in His ministry on earth and to accomplish His work—Jn.10:29 Mt.6:10).

Jn.15:1-27—As Jesus continues His discourse and instructions with the Apostles, chapter 15 can be summarized with three particular topics being discussed—1) the character and benefits of being a disciple of Jesus and one who is not a disciple; 2) the vast expansions and dimensions of God's love; and 3) persecutions may come in Jesus' name being His witness.

In part one (vss.1-8), Jesus begins by stating that He is the True Vine (from Whom we get our life sustenance and nourishment for life (physical and spiritual—1:4; 6:51; 14:6). The Father is the Vinedresser (the Caretaker and Pruner of the Vineyard—vss.1, 2). The Apostles and His disciples are those who know Him and produce His fruit (character and works displayed—3:21) and gain the benefits through prayer of their necessities, requests and provisions met (vss.3-5, 7, 8, 16), thus, proving they are His disciples (vs.8). Those not producing His fruit (vs.2, even up to the claim of being a "follower" (see 6:60-71) and not knowing the Lord personally in the spiritual birth (abiding—knowing Him—vs.6; 1:12,13) are dry and casted out to be burned as dry branches (not producing His character fruit, thus, not His disciples (vs.6; Mt.7:15-27). As in Jesus' life, the Father is glorified by the disciples producing much fruit (vss.8, 16).

In part two (vss.9-17), we see the vast expansions of God's love, reaching the world through Jesus in which we live (see also Eph.1:4-7; 3:17-19). Jesus' love for us is a direct carry over from how the Father loves Him and disciples are to live in His love (vs.9). By following His commands, one abides (lives) in His love (vss.10-17). Loving one another was His new command to His disciples (see 13:34, 35; 15:12, 17). "Fruit that will remain" (or last) contains at least two important dimensions—works that endure with God's eternal results (4:34-36; 6:27-29); and the continual "fruit of the Spirit" expressed in one's life (Gal.5:22, 23).

In part three Jesus expresses the hard declaration that persecutions can come from being His witness (vss.18-27), as happened to Him (vss.20,24,25). Others, though, who have kept His word, will keep theirs, too (vs.20). Note some do this out of hatred for God (vs.24) and without a cause (undeserved, without reason—BAGD; vs.25). The work of witnessing for Jesus is the working with the Holy Spirit (vss.26, 27; see also John 8:42).

Jn.16:1-33—The main central point of this chapter is now the Apostles learn clearly that Jesus came from the Father and was now going back to Him (vss.28-30). This was one of the main reasons why Jesus came to earth (to make the Father known—1:18; 3:16) and the main topic the Apostles were trying to understand in these chapters of Jesus' discussion and teaching (chapters 14-16; 14:7-11).

He begins this chapter saying to them that these things were shared with them in advance to keep them from stumbling (falling aside or into sin, vss.1, 4). For an example of vs.2, see Acts 26:9-18 (those not knowing the Father or Jesus—vs.3). Their grief of Jesus leaving them will be comforted by the coming of the Holy Spirit (vs.7, 14:16-18, The Comforter). The Holy Spirit will continue the work of Jesus, but now, in the continued completion of His ministry (vs.11; 17:4). Note one of the works of the Holy Spirit is to "guide us into all truth" (vs.13—the word "guide" is a path, a road to take to a destination). He also reveals the things to come (vss.13-15; examples are 1 Thess.4:13-18—note the word "comfort" here at the end of the chapter, same word as the comforter, the Holy Spirit—14:16; 16:7; also, the book of Revelation—four times John states he was "in the Spirit" when writing the Revelation—1:10; 4:2; 17:3; 21:10). Then, in one of the greatest declarations that God has given to us of His everlasting joy, Jesus announces to them that their grief will be changed to joy within them and that no one will be able to take it away from them (vss.20-22; 17:13)—when they see Him after His resurrection and the coming of the Holy Spirit at Pentecost (see 14:16-19; 1 Pet.1:3-9). As a result, they will be able to pray to God directly for their needs in Jesus name (vss.23, 24, a continuation and building of the joy they have already). The "scattering" (vs.32) occurred at Jesus' arrest (Mk.14:27, 49, 50). Jesus spoke these things to them (us) so that we may have His peace (vs.33; see 14:27); and in His great proclamation of "overcoming the world" (1:5; 17:4; 1 Jn.3:8; Jn.5:24, 25), Jesus says to "have courage," knowing whatever we encounter in life, in our trust in Him, that He has overcome it (vs.33; Heb.4:14-16).

Jn.17:1-26—This beautiful prayer from the heart of Jesus records Jesus praying for three subjects of His concern—Himself, the Apostles and the Church at large. Jesus begins by praying to the Father (once again—12:23, 27, 28; 13:31, 32) that He will glorify the Father in the finishing work of his trial, crucifixion, resurrection and ascension (vs.1). Eternal life is defined here by knowing the Only True God and Jesus Christ whom God had sent into the world, to save mankind from their sins through the spiritual birth (1:12-18; 3:13-21; Mt.1:21-25; see Book 1 of The Family Bible Series called The Family of God—Foundation, for more discussion and understanding on the Trinity, Their character and functions). Having completed His ministry message and works on earth, He would now bring it to completion (vs.4) and look forward to His returned glory with the Father in heaven, before the world was ever created (vs.5; 1:1, 2, 10). Jesus then prays for His Apostles (vss.6-19). They have come to know the Lord for Who He is (vss.8, 26; 6:68, 69; 16:30). He has protected them in the world (vs.12; 18:8, 9) and asks the Father to continue the same for them (vss.9-12, 15-19) through the name of Jesus (vs.11). Jesus prays that they be unified with Him and the Father (vs.11). He prays that they will have His joy fulfilled in themselves (vs.13; 16:22). Part of the protection is spiritual, as well as physical (set apart in truth for God's service—vss.17-19), as they, as their Lord, are not of this world and it's ways (vss.14, 16; Phil.3:20, 21).

The last part of Jesus' prayer is for the church at large (vs.20). Unity with the Father and Son (like the Father and Son) is the first prayer that Jesus makes, so the world may come to see and believe in Him, sent by the Father (vss.21-23); and know His love for them, exemplified by Jesus (vss.23-26). Jesus' desire and prayer is for them to be with Him and see His marvelous glory (vs.24; 14:1-3; 1 Jn.3:1, 2).

Jn.18:1-14—See Mt.26:47-56. John records more emphasis on the betrayal in his account (vss.2, 3); plus, the duplicity in those arresting Him (vss.4-6). John also gives the name of the high priest's servant, whose ear Peter had cut off (and Luke, records that Jesus healed it—Lk.22:51). John records the words stated by Caiaphas, stating Jesus would die for the nation and for those who would come to know Him throughout the world (vss.12-14; 11:49-52).

Jn.18:15-18, 25-27—See Mt.26:69-75. John alone records how Peter was able to enter the courtyard of the high priest (many believe John was the likely person—vs.16).

Jn.18:19-24—John records the brief statement made by Jesus to Annas the high priest. Jesus' statement made here is looking for necessary evidence for further judicial proceedings by any accusers (Jn.8:10, 11; Mt.18:16; Dt.19:15; see Jn.18:29).

Jn.18:28—19:16—See Mt.27:1-31. During Jesus' trial, John concentrates solely on Jesus' appearance before the governor Pilate. Some notable points to make here are: Pilate's threefold declarations of Jesus' innocence—"I find no guilt in Him" (18:38; 19:4, 6) and making efforts to release Him (19:12); Pilate (the governor) asking "What is truth?"—Jesus' answer—14:6; 18:37—Pilate still declared Him as "the Man"—19:5 (see also vs.7; and Jn.1:14, 17); Pilate's repeated attempts to put their demands back into the hands of the Jews (18:31, 39; 19:6, 15) for final decision; and the Jews rejection of their King brings remembrance of 1 Sam.8:4-7, when the Jews rejected God as their King (see Ps.2; Jn.18:37).

Jn.19:17-22—See Mt.27:33-44. John includes the inscription of Jesus being written in the three languages (Hebrew, Greek and Latin—vss.20-22).

Jn.19:23-27—John includes with Jesus on the cross the commitment of Jesus' mother Mary to the Apostle John's care (vss.26, 27). Also, the fulfillment of Ps.22:18 in Jesus' crucifixion (vs.24). For the seamless, one piece garment (vs.23), see Lev.19:19.

Jn.19:28-30—See Mt.27:48-50. John records the fulfillment of Ps.69:21 here at Jesus' crucifixion as the last one before His death. Note Jesus' death is referred to as "giving up His spirit" (vs.30; see Eccl.12:7).

Jn.19:31-37—Sacrifices for the Jews were to be unblemished (Ex.12:5), and so, with Jesus fulfilling this Scripture (Ex.12:46; Num.9:12; Ps.34:20; Heb.9:11-14; 1 Pet.1:18-21). The quote from Zech.12:10 has a double fulfillment—here (with the crowd at the crucifixion—see Mt.27:33-50, 55, 56), and the second fulfillment to come in Rev. 1:7 at Jesus' second coming to earth to reign as Prophet, Priest and King (Rev.19:11-16; Is.9:6, 7; Heb.2:17; Jn.19:37).

Jn.19:38-42—See Mt.27:57-61. John includes Nicodemus' participation in the burial custom of the Jews of Jesus (vs.39; 3:1, 2).

Jn.20:1-18—For the sequential account of the Gospel resurrection writings and the role of Mary Magdalene, see the Mt.28 commentary. Important note on the bodily resurrection that John includes in his Gospel writing of Jesus' resurrection from the dead (vss.6-8)—in vs.6, the wrappings of the burial remained in place where Jesus was laid in the tomb; however, the face cloth (like a handkerchief) was taken off His face and rolled up and put in a place by itself (vs.7), showing and demonstrating the "new" resurrected body that Jesus has. He rose <u>through</u> the linen cloths—and <u>took</u> <u>off</u> the face cloth Himself and put it aside its own place—showing a "spiritual" side of the new body (through the linen cloths) and the "physical" side too (taking off the face cloth Himself). This is the "new" spiritual/physical resurrected body (Lk.24:39), with newer dimensions than what we know of today, that can even appear from the outside into the inside of a closed building or structure (see also vss.19, 26, of Jesus appearing after His resurrection to the disciples). It also demonstrates clearly that Jesus rose physically from the dead (see also Lk.24:36-48; and 1 Jn.3:1, 2).

Jn.20:19-31—In His new resurrected body, Jesus appears two times to the disciples, while they were inside behind closed doors (vss.19, 26). The first occasion is for the purpose of their commissioning to His work and continued ministry (vss. 21-23). They were to wait to receive "the promise of the Father," the Holy Spirit, as He acted out a "breathing upon them" to receive the Holy Spirit coming at Pentecost (note, no change in the Apostles behind closed doors in both visits, vss.19, 26), quite different than immediately following Pentecost!). Their duty (commissioning) will be Gospel presentation and the forgiveness of sins (similar to the one given in Mt.16:17-19). Jesus makes another appearance for Thomas to see Him resurrected from the dead. Thomas had no doubt when he saw Jesus then (vss.27, 28).

John concludes his theme of the book, that he has carried out all the way through, stated in vs.31—so that people may believe that Jesus is the Son of God (see 1:34), and that in believing in Him, one may receive Him and His free gift of eternal life (vs.31; 1:7, 12, 13; 3:16; 5:24; 8:12; 10:9, 10; 17:3; Rom.5:20, 21; 6:23; see the Prayer in the back of the book).

Jn.21:1-25—The vast majority of commentators agree that this chapter was an appendage to the Gospel of John, written by him but added not too long after he wrote the Gospel. Verse 24 points well to this conclusion (some or someone wanted it included). It is a great passage with additional helpful information. Some notable points to be made are as follows—The Sea of Tiberias is another name for the Sea of Galilee (vs.1; 6:1). The first part of the chapter has some similarities to Luke 5:1-11. The whole chapter, though points to Jesus encouraging Peter in his commission to serve the Lord. The charcoal fire, some think, may remind Peter of the past denials and his current encouragement to the Lord's ongoing ministry (vs.9; 18:18). Since no further explanation is given, the 153 catch of fish seems to simply state a careful count by someone on a large catch of fish (vss.6-11). Jesus again shows then that He is the Bread of Life (vss.11-13; 6:1-14, 47-51). The "verbs of love" that Jesus used to show His love to him and the disciples is to demonstrate the vast depth and complete love He has for him (them; both the affectionate love and God's unconditional love used here; each counters the three denials, as well—vss.15-17). Peter's death is also prophesied here; history records Peter choosing to die upside down in crucifixion form, saying he was not worthy to die the same way his Lord did—vss.18, 19). The main emphasis of Jesus' exhortation now to Peter was "to follow Me" (vs.20-23, a good counter once again to the three previous denials). The ending verse (vs.25) may possibly be the group's writing (or intention) in their words what John had said previously in his (20:30), as it seems to read as a continuation of the verse before it (vs.24).

The Book of Acts

Acts 1:1-11—In Luke's writing of the Book of Acts, he records for us early in this chapter the theme of the book—being witnesses for Jesus (1:8). One will see the word "witness" used throughout the book, along with all its various demonstrations. The Apostles knew from Jesus that they would be "His witnesses," when the Holy Spirit would come and dwell within them (John 14:16, 17; 15:26, 27).

For the background of Theophilus, see Lk.1:1-4. Many convincing proofs (BAGD) were given of Jesus' resurrection from the dead (vs.3; see 1 Cor.15:3-11). Jesus taught them that His everlasting kingdom would be called the Kingdom of God (vs. 3; Mt.4:17, Mk.1:15), where barriers between Jew and Gentile would be broken down and peace with God and each other would be established through the Gospel of Jesus (Rom 5:1, 2; Eph.2:4-22). Jesus' instruction to the Apostles was to wait in Jerusalem till they received the "promise of the Father," the Holy Spirit (Lk.24:49; Acts 1:4, 5; Jn.15:26, 27). They would then also receive "His power" to be His witnesses (vs.8) to the world. "Times and seasons" in vs.7 are durations of time and their specific characteristic events (Vine), all set by the Father. The angels made known to them about Jesus' return in the same place His ascension occurred (vss.9-12; see Zech.14:4, 5).

Acts 1:12-26—Peter speaks to the brethren about the replacement for Judas (see Ps.109:8). He had to be one who had been with them for the entirety of Jesus' ministry and (the next use of the word from vs.8) a "witness" of the resurrection of Jesus (vs.22). By "the lot," Matthias was chosen (vs.26; for using the lot, see Num.26:55; 1 Chr.24:7-19; Prov.16:33; 18:18).

Acts 2:1-42—Pentecost was the time and celebration of the Jewish harvest (also known as the Feast of Weeks—Lev.23:15-22). It occurred (as the word means) "50"days after the Passover Feast. It now celebrates for Christians the initial "ingathering" of the Church of Jesus Christ. The Holy Spirit came as a rushing wind and fell upon them at the gathering (1:15) as "tongues of fire" (see Mt.3:11, 16, 17). As they then spoke out in other languages (vs.4), this becomes the "first witness" of their testimony to many people of their own and other countries (see the listing in vss.7-11). Peter then spoke out and gave explanation to what had happened. Peter quotes three Old Testament passages to deliver his message. The first from Joel 2:28-32. For the term "last days," see Heb.1:1, 2. The coming of the Holy Spirit can bring prophecy declarations (the forth-telling of God's word) from even now the most common of everyday folks (vss.17, 18) as His witnesses. The "Day of the Lord" (the Great Tribulation) will conclude with the Lord's glorious return to earth to reign (vs.20; Mt.24:30); and so, all who call on the Lord Jesus for their spiritual birth will be saved (vs.21; Jn.1:12, 13—all who come into the Family of God through this spiritual birth of God; Jn.3:16-18). Note "signs and wonders" will accompany the Lord's return (vs.19; Mt.24:29-31); they were performed in Jesus' ministry (vs.22) and were accomplished through the Apostles, also (vs.43). Note also the coming and ministry of Jesus was the predetermined will and plan of God (vs.23; 1:7; the word for "predetermined" in the Greek is where we get our English word "horizon" and means, to mark out the boundaries of a place or thing—Vine). The resurrection of Jesus put an end to the "chords of death" (BAGD), that is, spiritual death and separation from God, vs.24). Peter then quotes Ps.16:8-11, declaring David telling and prophesying, of what came to be Jesus' resurrection from the dead, which Peter testifies to the crowd that he and the Apostles were "witnesses" of His resurrection (vs.32). Peter's last quote is from Ps.110:1, which Jesus quoted to the Pharisees in the form of a question to them in Mt.22:41-46 (for which see the commentary of the passage). The message here is that the Person that God placed to sit at His right hand until His enemies are place under His feet (that is, defeated) is Jesus (see Heb.1:1-3)—the One they crucified (vs.36). Some present certainly got the message and were "pierced to the heart" (vs.37). Peter said to them to repent of their sins and be baptized in the Name of Jesus (Mt.28:19,20) and to receive the gift of the Holy Spirit, for them and their children (vss.38, 39; note here God's desire to save families; see Acts 3:25; Gen.12:3; see also Book4 of The Family Bible Studies Series—The Theology of the Bible—The Family of God, for God's history of the bigger picture of this—the theme of the Bible—throughout time since His creation of mankind, made in His image). 3,000 were added to the church that day and baptized responding to his message (vs.41).

Acts 2:43-47—Now with such a large number of people coming into the Family of God—the church of Jesus Christ in the New Testament—some of the most important practices for the church were defined and set out for the people to follow. The Apostles' teaching is listed first (vs.42; the Bible; Eph.2:19-22; 2 Tim.3:16, 17); then, the fellowship of Christian believers (the Greek word for fellowship is the word "to share;" consider what God has "shared" to us—2 Pet.1:4; Jn.3:16, 17; 14:16, 17, 23; Lk.12:32; Eph.4:31,32; Rev.21, 22); the "breaking of bread" was the Jewish gathering together at the common meal. The early church practiced the Lord's Supper at this meal—see Acts 20:7; 1 Cor.11:20; then, their devotion to (literally),"the prayers" (The Greek is plural here, referring to the church committing themselves to the prayers of each other (i.e. requests) and other concerns). Note also baptism here with salvation (vss.38, 41), which became a basic practice of the church, as one finds throughout Acts (see Jn.3:1-21 for a more complete understanding of baptism in the church). Worship and praise declaration occurred to God (vs.47) and in the larger gathering was a natural (supernatural) outflow going on (Lk.24:52, 53). Their sharing became natural to help meet the needs of each other (vs.45; 4:34-37). They were glad (literally, rejoicing greatly) and had a singleness of purpose in serving (giving to) God (vss.44-46; 2 Cor.8:1-5). With all this, God added to their number day by day, along with their Gospel proclamations and God doing mighty works through the Apostles (vss.43, 47).

Acts 3:1-26—Luke now begins to record "witnessing" stories that God does directly (example, Paul in Acts 9) to people or through the Apostles and the Church, along with miracles and, at times, persecutions (John 15:16-21). Here, God heals a lame man through the faith and witness of Peter and John at the gate of the temple (see Mt.11:5, 6). Peter said to him to rise and walk in Jesus' name and took hold of him firmly and helped him stand (vs.6). The passage says that the man's feet and ankles were made hard (firm—vs.7) and God gave Him complete soundness in every part ("perfect soundness," KJ, vs.16). The man did not hesitate to demonstrate this, either (vss.8, 9). Peter's message to those in the temple declared this happened not by any power or godliness of their own, but by the Name of Jesus and faith in Him (vs.16). The Living God glorified His servant Jesus (see Mt.22:32)—who is the Holy and Just One, the Author (originator) of Life (vss.14, 15; Jn.1:1-3)—that they rejected and had crucified, but God raised Him from the dead, and Peter again testifies that they are "witnesses" of His resurrection (vss.12-16). In their ignorance of doing this, he exhorts them to repent of their sins and follow what all the prophets had declared—that Jesus was appointed by God to be their Messiah (vs.20; BAGD); and He is the Prophet that Moses spoke about to Israel and for all the world to know (vss.17-26; Dt.18:18, 19), so that in Abraham's seed all the families on earth shall be blessed—vs.25; Gen.22:18) and that times of refreshment may come to them (vs.19; 2:26-28).

Acts 4:1-22—As Peter (and John with him) was giving his message of the Gospel of Jesus to the crowd, many came to believe in Jesus (about 5,000) and come into the Family of God (vs.4; Jn.1:12,13). But some priests, the captain of the temple guard and some Sadducees had them put in jail, being "greatly disturbed" hearing about Jesus and His resurrection from the dead (see Mt.22:23). A large group of Jewish leaders (see vss.5, 6) gathered the next day to question them further about the healing of the man once lame. Peter's answer to them was similar to the one he just gave to the crowd previously—declaring the power in Jesus' name and His resurrection from the dead (vss.8-12; 3:6, 15, 16). He proclaimed that Jesus is the "very cornerstone" (from Ps.118:22) that they rejected (vs.11) and stated confidently that there is salvation in no other person (other, here meaning, of the same kind or sort); for there is no other name (other here meaning even of a different kind or sort) given under heaven among men by which we must be saved (vs.12). Note the "witnesses" now that were there testifying against the Jewish leaders of God's great work—Peter and John; the man healed and once lame; and 5,000 new believers, who were glorifying God for what had just happened (vss.19-22). Quite a testimony of God's works indeed! And so, no basis for punishment here was spoken to them (just the direct opposite was happening!), as Peter and John had to go on speaking of what they have seen and heard (vss.19-21).

Acts 4:23-37—Peter and John went to their own (other believers) upon their release and reported what took place (vs.23). In one accord, the lifted up their voices to God and acknowledged that this was declared to take place from Ps.2:1-3 (yet, notice verse 4 and the rest of Psalm 2), through God's preordained counsel (vss.24-28; 2:22, 23). They prayed to God for continued boldness and that healings and sign and wonders would also continue on through the name of Jesus (vss.29, 30). Their gathering place was shaken and all of them were filled with the Holy Spirit, and spoke the Word of God with boldness (answer to their prayer—vs.31). A major factor in their answer to prayer is having "one heart and soul" together (vss.24, 32), and in their deeds, having their possessions as common to each other (see 20:35). As a result, needs were being met among then (vs.34), even the selling of land and houses and the Apostles distributed the proceeds to those in need (vss.34, 35). Luke notes the commitment of Barnabas as an example in this (vss.36, 37).

Acts 5:1-11—However, after the example of Barnabas (and others), people would not get by the Apostles (possibly trying to make good or look good to them) giving a portion of money of their sale and saying that it was the total price of it (thus, keeping some back for themselves). This was the experience of Ananias and his wife Sapphira. They died as a result, there on the spot. All they had to do was be honest (not trying to make like someone else), which is always the right thing to do before God and man (thus, the result had great fear (reverence for God) on the church and those who heard of this –vss.11, 13).

Acts 5:12-16—In answer to their prayer (4:30), signs and wonders continued through the Apostles (signs appeal to the understanding and wonders to the imagination—Vine; vs.12). Solomon's portico was the outer corridor of the temple (Unger), a covered colonnade (columns along the side of a building) and so a popular walkway (vs.12). The ministry of witnessing (the message of the Gospel of Jesus) and healing was now developing for the apostles as it did for Jesus (see Mt.8:14-17; 9:21; 14:36; Lk.6:19). Many more were coming into the Family of God, as the church continued to grow (vs.14); and large numbers were now coming from the vicinity outside Jerusalem to be healed of sicknesses and from unclean spirits, and all were being healed (vs.16).

Acts 5:17-42—With God's work continuing to increase and grow the Church of Jesus Christ (vss.14-16), the high priest and his associates out of jealousy had the Apostles put in jail (vss.17, 18). But an angel of the Lord came during the night and released them from prison and they returned teaching in the temple the next day about daybreak (vss.19-21). The captain of the temple guard and his officers then brought them back to the Sanhedrin, the ruling counsel of the Jews (vss.26, 27). In difference to being told not to speak any more in Jesus' name as previously (4:17, 18), Peter and the Apostles declared that they must obey God rather than men (vs.29). It was "the God of our fathers" who raised Jesus from the dead, and they were the ones who put Jesus to death, hanging Him on a cross; and God exalted Him to His right hand (see Mt. 22:41-46), to grant repentance to Israel and forgiveness of sins (to the world, also), vss.30, 31; and continuing with the theme of Acts (1:8), they testified that they are "witnesses" of these things, along with the Holy Spirit, Whom God gives to those who obey Jesus (vs.32). The Jewish leaders were cut to the heart in hearing this convicting message and intended to kill the Apostles (vs.33). But Gamaliel, a Jewish teacher of the Law (see also 22:3), convinced them to reconsider such an act, for if this was man's doing, it would be overthrown; but if it is God's work, they don't want to fight against God (vss.38, 39; see Prov.21:30). They were flogged and told again not to speak in the Name of Jesus. Instead, they rejoiced that they were considered worthy to suffer for His Name sake; and kept right on (the Greek verb is in the middle voice, meaning a special advantage for the subject, i.e., the Apostles here in this passage) proclaiming Jesus as the Messiah (vss.40-42; see 3:19-21).

Acts 6:1-7—In this recording, the Apostles help solve a problem in the distribution of food between two Jewish groups—the native Jews and the more Greek cultured, speaking Jews (Hellenistic). Note the Apostles do not solve the problem for them, but direct them to choose godly men, full of the Spirit and wisdom, to handle the difficulty (vss.3-5). The emphasis here actually is seeing that the ministry of God's Word (the Gospel) continues to go forth (vss.2, 4). Note how it does—5:42, teaching and preaching it; and the Apostles and disciples continuing to spread it throughout (vss.4, 7 and Stephen's discourse coming in chapter seven). The result of this was that more people were coming into the Family of God by hearing His word, including many priests becoming obedient to the faith (vs.7).

Acts 6:8—7:60—Stephen now delivers his beautiful address to the Sanhedrin, covering a great historical account of Israel from Abraham to David's desire to build a temple for God. It began with a dispute with the freedmen (considered to be Jewish slaves or prisoners of war released by the Roman government—Unger). They were not able to contest him, by the working of the Holy Spirit and God's wisdom (vs.10). So they accused him and brought false witnesses against him (see as similar to Jesus—see Mt.26:59-61; Jn.2:18-22, and the commentaries of these passages). For the "customs of Moses," see 21:21, 28; 25:8. Having a face "like an angel" (vs.15), Stephen very splendidly covers highlights of Israel's history from Abraham to David. Well studied and knowledgeable in his presentation, he concludes with David's desire to build a temple for God (see that in 2 Sam.7:5-13; 1 Chr.17:1-14). Trying to make known to them (from Is.66:1, 2) that God's dwelling place is in heaven, was something he had been attempting to help them see, even before (6:13) and it was not being understood. But they were convicted by his message (vs.54; same verb here as in the Apostle's witness in 5:33). It is somewhat of a mystery why Stephen stopped that passage going into his exhortation to the Sanhedrin (6:12). As far as Israel's history is concerned, it falls right in conjunction with the prophecy for Israel from Hosea 3:4, 5, as the things regarding a temple and a kingdom would not take place for a long time to come, until they come trembling back to God and David in the in the last days, in their time of restoration (see commentary on Mt.23:37-39; 24:15-36; Ezk.40-48).

Acts 8:1-40—A persecution arose against the church in Jerusalem and except for the Apostles, they were scattered throughout Judea and Samaria. This was how the Word of God began to spread throughout the land (vss.1, 4; witnessing—see 1:8). The first mention of Paul (Saul) occurs in these early verses. This chapter details the work of Philip the evangelist and his contributions to the early development of the Church of Jesus Christ. God did great things through Philip, accompanying the Gospel message he presented with miracles, including healings (the lame and paralyzed) and deliverances from unclean spirits in Samaria (vss.6, 7, 12, 13), bringing much rejoicing in that city (vs.8). Simon a magician (pretender of magic powers, vs.9; Vine), had previously caught the attention of many in that city (vss.9, 10; for the people declaring him to have divine powers, see commentary on John 10:1-42). Note in vss.11, 12, the people "saw" and "were astonished" by his magical acts; but by God's powerful works through Philip, they came to "believe" in Jesus (vs.12). This included Simon himself, but after that Peter declared to him that he had a bitter spirit and bond of unrighteousness, which he needed to seek God for forgiveness and healing (vss.13, 22-24). No explanation is given to us why the Samaritans did not receive the Holy Spirit when they believed (see 19:2-6; and the commentary of Jesus' previous harvest of the Samaritans with the women at the well in John 4:1-42). Peter and John were sent to them, so that they received the Holy Spirit (vss.14-17) and they preached the Gospel (the word witnessing in the Greek) to many Samaritan villages along the way (vs.25). This chapter concludes with Philip ministering the Gospel and baptizing the Ethiopian eunuch, who was in charge of the queen of the country's personal household and possessions (vs.27). Philip explained to him some of the sufferings and trials of Jesus, up to and through His crucifixion, and the outlook, as some may have seen it, in aftermath of His crucifixion (vss.32-38; the eunuch was reading Is.53:7,8). The verb for Philip being "taken away" is the same word for "the Rapture" in 1 Thess.4:17. He was transported by the Holy Spirit to Azotus (almost directly west of Jerusalem, just off the coast of the Mediterranean Sea) and continued northward up the coast to Caesarea (vss.39, 40).

Acts 9:1-31—The conversion of the Apostle Paul is one of the most remarkable miracles of one turning in faith to receive Jesus Christ that has ever been heard. This testimony is a direct "witness" by Jesus to turn the Apostle-to-be Paul from the chords of death to receiving God's gift of eternal life and come into the Family of God (2:24; Jn.1:12, 13; 5:24). Paul, once threatening to kill believers in Jesus (vs.1), now, seeing once again physically (vs.18; and truly for the first time spiritually), went out proclaiming Jesus, the Son of God (vs.20), the Messiah (vs.22), a truly tremendous miracle of God, to turn one from persecuting the Church to serving the Living God and devoting his life to proclaiming the Gospel and giving his life efforts to working for Jesus and His Church. Filled with the Holy Spirit, he immediately went out and proclaimed Jesus the Messiah (vs.22). His strong testimony (vss.20, 27-24) brought opposite reactions from the Jews, who immediately looked to do away with him (vs.23), even then to put him to death (vss.24, 29). Through the faithful servants Ananias (who courageously helped bring Paul to know and receive the Lord Jesus—vss.10-18) and Barnabas (who helped the Apostles and disciples understand his conversion—vss.26-30) and help from the brethren in Jerusalem, he was brought out of Jerusalem safely and sent to Caesarea, and eventually to Tarsus, his birthplace and early residence (the northeastern part of the Mediterranean Sea; the city was a Roman colony). Note—Paul was secretly released safely down an opening in the city wall in Damascus in a large basket (similar to a large hamper basket—vs.25; Vine). The results of these testimonies ("witnessings") brought continued increased numbers into the Family of God, where the Gospel had been going out to (Judea, Galilee and Samaria—1:8). They now enjoyed a time of peace (from the Gospel of Peace—Eph. 6:14, 15; see Is.52:7-10, and about the Prince of Peace—Is.9:6,7), as the church was growing and maturing through the work of the

Comforter—The Holy Spirit (vs.31; Jn.14:16, 17; 15:26; 16:8-15; 1 Cor.2:12, 13).

Acts 9:32-43—As the healing miracles were a testimony in Jesus' ministry to bring people the Gospel and display the great works of God (10:38; Jn. 2:23), so also the Apostles continued on with this work and ministry of Jesus, which brought many to faith in Jesus as a result (see 2 Cor.12:12). As Peter was instrumental in the man formally lame in 3:4-8, The Book of Acts records two more healings that Peter was involved in here in chapter nine. The first was in Lydda, northwest of Jerusalem, involving a man paralyzed (vs.33; see 8:6, 7 with the Apostle Philip). The result of this healing brought many into the Church throughout the fertile coastal plain area (all those who saw him (the man healed) turned to the Lord in the area—vs.35). Similar results took place with the raising of Dorcas from the dead in Joppa (on the sea coast, northwest of Jerusalem). Her craft was making inner and outer garments for the people of her time (vs.39), as Peter had the opportunity to see. After Peter knelt to pray, he then commanded her to rise and he then helped her up. Many there believed in the Lord as a result (vs.42). Peter then remained in the area at Joppa, staying with a tanner (maker of leather materials) named Simon (see Mt.10:10-13).

Acts 10:1-48—The conversion here of Cornelius and those with him have a good number of significant events and works of God's truths occurring among them. In Jesus' ministry, He initiated the truth of His Gospel of Salvation going out and reaching the nations of the Gentiles also (see commentary on Mt.12:15-21). At Pentecost, a small variety of the nations heard it—and here, through Peter, they begin to receive it, and confirmed by the testimony of the Holy Spirit, falling on them as similar to Pentecost (vss.44-46; 11:15; see Mt.16:18, 19). Cornelius is a captain over about 100 soldiers. His devoutness with his soldiers, relatives, close friends, household (11:14), community, along with his charitable giving, demonstrate him as a man of noble character (vss.1-3, 22, 24). Note his wording and readiness to receive Peter's message (vs.33).

Peter is visited with a vision from the Lord with variety of animals on a sheet (while being hungry—vss.10-16) and comes to realize that Gentiles will now be accepted into God's Family who believe in Jesus (vss.28, 34, 35; 11:17, 18; Jn.1:12, 13). With this understanding and vision, a voice said to Peter that now all the things he saw would be considered clean to eat (vs.15; Mk.7:18, 19—all foods; Rom.14:14; 1 Cor.10:25, 26; 1 Tim.4:4, 5). The Holy Spirit then said to Peter that three men were looking for him (from Cornelius—vs.19; 11:11; second recording of the Holy Spirit speaking in Acts –8:29; 11:12; and one more to come—13:2).

Peter uses the theme word "witness" four times in five verses in explaining the Apostle's ministry to Cornelius, all in a slightly different way: they were "witnesses" of Jesus' ministry throughout the country, including Jerusalem, where He was crucified (vs.39); they were chosen by God <u>beforehand</u> to be His "witnesses" (Jn.15:26, 27) and ate and drank with Him <u>after</u> He rose from the dead (vs.41); Jesus gave them the command to proclaim and "witness" that He is the One designated by God (see the same word in 2:23) to be the Judge of the living and the dead (vs.42;

Jn.5:24-30; 12:31-33; Rom.14:9); and all the prophet's "bear witness" to Jesus, that whoever believes in Him receives forgiveness of sins (vs.43; Mt.1:21-23; Acts 4:12). Note the Apostles always in Acts followed through with the importance of baptism with the gift of salvation (the outward testimony of the inward work of God—vss.45-48; see also Jn.3: 1-21; Mt.28:18-20; Mk.16:16).

Acts 11:1-30—In Jerusalem, Peter reports his testimony to the Jewish brethren, as they question him about going into a Gentile home (vss.1-3). Peter adds to the testimony about Cornelius that Cornelius said Peter's message would be one of salvation, for him and his household (vss.13, 14). Peter stated to them also that he recalled the words of Jesus about the coming baptism of the Holy Spirit (vs.16, as Cornelius and his household, so like Pentecost). The brethren then understood that God had given "repentance that leads to life" to the Gentiles, also (vs.18). From the scattering of the Church after Stephen was martyred (Acts 7), the Gospel was also going out to people in the nations, first to the Jews alone (vs.19). But now, some from the island of Cyprus and Cyrene (North Africa, Libya of today) began sharing the Gospel to Greeks (Greek speaking people) also, in Antioch, the northern part of Syria (vs.20). It was a large city for that time and many people believed and came to know the Lord (vs.21). Barnabas was sent from Jerusalem to them and rejoiced, seeing God's grace upon them, and encouraged them to remain devoted to the Lord (vss.22, 23); and he helped bring a considerable number of people into the Family of God, being noted as a good man and full of the Holy Spirit (vs.24). He left briefly to go get Paul to help with the growing ministry needs there and they both began ministering out of the church there at Antioch. Prophets from Jerusalem had gone also to Antioch and one, by the name of Agabus, predicted a famine throughout the world to occur (vs.28), which happened in the Emperor of Rome, Claudius' reign (41-54 AD). A collection for the brethren in Judea was taken and sent to them, by the hands of Paul and Barnabas. Note God's comfort, before the famine took place (vss.27-30; 9:31).

Acts 12:1-25—This passage of Peter's miraculous rescue from prison by the angel sent from the Lord has quite a few practical applications to learn from it. As seen previously in Acts, being arrested and put in prison was not new to Peter (4:3; 5:17, 18). Even miraculously delivered from prison by an angel of the Lord was experienced by Peter and the Apostles before Acts 5:17-21. We see the simple proverb in life of sowing and reaping at the beginning and end of this chapter. Herod Agrippa I, grandson of Herod the Great, had James the brother of John put to death with a sword (vss.2, 3). He soon met his death, giving a speech in Caesarea (vss.18-23). After Peter was put in prison, a contrast is written out in the Greek in vs.5—On the one hand, they were keeping Peter in prison; on the other hand, the church was earnestly praying to God for him. He was well covered by guards in prison—by him outside in front of the door (vs.6), but, quite easy for God to release him from all the barriers he faced (vss.6-11; chains, guards, two passage way exits with guards, and then, the iron gate—which opened up "automatically" (from the Greek word "automatos," 2 times in the New Testament—Mk.4:28). With the church praying for Peter's miraculous release from prison (after the experience of James in vs.2,), it may be difficult to pray for miracles sometimes (yet, pray all the more as the Church did); but when we do, we must believe, also (vss.12-17; God is faithful—see 1 Cor.10:13). James in vs.17 would be the brother of Jesus. As an important point to make here from this chapter and from up to this point in Acts, the Gospel is about to go forth to the nations now and spread quite rapidly (Acts 13 and forward). One cannot help to wonder why the people did not heed the great words of the teacher of the Law, Gamaliel, in Acts 5:38, 39—if man's actions are not good, they by will be overthrown; but if acts are good and found to be done by God (of course, even through man—Jn.3:19-21; Phil.2:13), then one will not be able to overthrow them, and may be found fighting against God. Such a clear and obvious truth as seen throughout history, holding firm and still ringing out true for today (see Jesus' teaching in Mt.22:41-46).

Acts 13:1-12—Over half of the book of Acts covers the conversion and ministry of the Apostle Paul. Immediately after his conversion, the Apostle Paul began to display great courage and boldness in speaking out the Gospel of the Lord Jesus Christ (9:20, 22, 27, 28; 13:46). From the beginning and often throughout his ministry, he was driven by opposition out of cities he preached in and had to flee for his own life (9:23-25; 29, 30; 13:50, 51; 17:10, 11; 23:16, 31); but learned and declared that God would make the "way of escape (1 Cor.10:13; see Mt.10: 23; Jn.15:20). He listed quite a few attacks upon himself and his followers (2 Cor.4:7-14), but instead said that we are "more than conquerors," and found his comfort in the "God of all comfort," who's love for us no one can measure (Rm.8:37; 2 Cor.1:3-7; Eph.3:14-19). He apparently was not known to be an eloquent speaker (Greek word here meaning his speech could be even looked down upon—some or someone must have said—2 Cor.10:10), but learned to be gracious in his speech and kind and forgiving to opposing people (Eph.4:29-32; 2 Cor.2:5-11; Col. 3:12-14). When he wasn't sure where to go, he knew God would show him the way (Acts 16:6-10). When hatred about the Lord's name would come toward him (Jn.15:18-21; 1 Cor.4:9-13), he learned God's love to express even in those difficult times, which are the first two characteristics he listed and described as "longsuffering and kind" about love in 1 Cor.13:4; (see also 1 Thess.2:7-9). And through all the obstacles and battles for the Lord he had to face and overcome (see 2 Cor.11:23-33), he came to see that it was better to boast in one's weaknesses, knowing God could strengthen him (us) regarding any need or situation that occurs (Phil.4:12, 13); and with God being the Captain of the sea (Acts 27, 28) and the Creator, Director, Cultivator and Provider of the land (Acts 14:17; 14:15; 17:24-28; Is.28:23-29; Jn.15:1), He would one day bring him safely to His heavenly kingdom, to be with the Lord forever and ever (2 Tim.4:18; Phil.3:20, 21; Col.3:1-4).

His calling to begin his ministry came at a gathering of prophets in Antioch (vs. 1). In a time of worship and fasting, the Holy Spirit said to set Paul and Barnabas apart (from the group) to the ministry He was calling them to do (vs.2). They were sent out by the group and the Holy Spirit (vss.3, 4). They started out going to the island of Cyprus (still there today). After going through Salamis on the eastern side and through the whole island to the capital Paphos (Barnabas was a native of Cyprus—4:36), Paul had to rebuke a magician (see Acts 8, same word here) for trying to obstruct and prevent the governor there, Sergius Paulus, from become a Christian. Paul gives quite a list of negative statements to the magician about himself (vs.10) and pronounced blindness on him for a time (vs.11). This amazed the governor, who came to believe in the Lord (vs.12; 14:13; see Jn.2:23).

Acts 13:13-52—Paul and Barnabas leave Cyprus and go travelling through the Mediterranean Sea northward to Asia Minor (current day Turkey). They travel through the capital of Pamphylia (far south Asia Minor) to Pisidian Antioch (south central Asia Minor—vss.13,14; note that this is not the Antioch where Paul and Barnabas left to begin their ministry journey in vs.1; that is in northern Syria and this is westward to Asia Minor, modern day Turkey). Pisidian Antioch was the capital city of the territory of Galatia. We see the theme of Acts being carried out here as Paul declares the "witness" of Jesus' resurrection from the dead, now going forth being proclaimed to the world (vs.31); and so, the word of the Lord was spreading throughout the whole region (vs.49).

The Apostle Paul gives a brilliant proclamation of the Gospel to this capitol city in a Jewish synagogue (vss.4, 15). He gives a brief history of Israel up to the time of David (vss.16-23; note vs.18 "put up with them in the wilderness" –the word means to bear another's manners (Vine), so the KJ, "suffered He their manners"); then, Paul states from the descendants of David (vs.23), came Jesus the Savior (vs.23), and presents His suffering, crucifixion and resurrection from the dead (vss.23-37); and so, he shares the "Good News of the Gospel" in a great summary to them in this declaration (note Ps.2:7 connected with the resurrection, from vs.33); and forgiveness of sins was proclaimed to them, by what Jesus did for all mankind (vs.38; 1 Jn.2:2), bringing justification to those who believe and receive it (vs.39; Jn.1:12, 13; Rom.5:1,2). Paul concludes his message with a strong exhortation to heed from Hab.1:5—don't get caught in the judgment of God (vss.40, 41; see Jn.3:16-21; in Habakkuk's time, the judgment coming upon Israel was by the Babylonians—though the Babylon would not escape this either, doing this to Israel—Habakkuk chapter two). As Jesus had said, some would accept the message of the Gospel and some would not (Jn.15:20-25). So here, the Gentiles rejoiced hearing God's word of acceptance being given to them too (vss.46-49); but some of the Jews, jealous of them winning a crowd over, formed a plot and spoke against them, persecuting them and drove them out of the city (vss.45-50; for "shaking the dust off," see Mt.10:14,15 and the commentary). But see the joy of the disciples in this contrast in vs.52.

Acts 14:1-7—Paul and Barnabas went to Iconium (east of Pisidian Antioch) and preached there, bring a great number of both Jews and Greeks into the Family of God (vs.1). Though opposition stirred up again, they spent a long time there "witnessing" to the people God's word of grace (vss.2, 3). The Greek brings out two contrasts in vss.3 and 4—while they continued "witnessing" God's Word (vs.3) the city was divided (vs.4); some on the one hand with Jews, and others with the Apostles (vs.4; see Mt.10:34-39, the result of preaching the word and it's possible effects). When an assault was raised up against them to mistreat (literally, insult) them and to stone them, they fled south to the cities of Lystra and Derbe, continuing to preach the Gospel in those cities (vss.6, 7).

Acts 14:8-28—Arriving at Lystra (18 miles south of Iconium—Unger), they preached the Gospel there. Paul during his message spoke out to a man in the crowd who was lame from birth (vs.8). Paul, seeing he had faith to be made well, called out loudly to him to "stand up." God's word of grace (vss.3, 7) healed the man who leaped up and began to walk (see 3:1-10). Some of the crowd honored Paul and Barnabas as some kind of a god, but Paul sternly makes known that we are all here to honor the God of all creation (vs.15); and He has "witnessed" this by providing food and fruit seasons for us, making our hearts glad by His kindness and care of what He supplies for us (vs.17). Some Jews from Antioch and Iconium came down and stoned Paul, supposing him to be dead (vs.19); but Paul got up and they went to the town of Derbe (vs.20, about 16 miles east of Lystra—Unger). Paul and Barnabas then went back and visited the places that they had shared the Gospel in the towns they visited. They then headed back to Antioch in Syria, completing their first missionary journey and recounted their expeditions and travels with the disciples there and remained a long time with them (vss.21-28).

Acts 15:1-35—The issue at this Jerusalem council is what are the Gentiles, who have become Christians, to obey in respect to, now being justified by faith (see 13:39), the Jewish traditions and laws (vs.5)? Some of the Pharisees who came to believe seemed to get ahead of the answer to this question, and so necessitated this council meeting of the elders (vs.4). With no distinction now between Jew and Gentile (vss.9, 14), the elders decided three things to abstain from—things sacrificed to idols, fornication and things strangled and blood (vss.20, 29). While the passage does not elaborate on how these were concluded, a safe conclusion for consideration may be derived from the context of the writing we have here. The statements made here, directed toward the Gentiles, appears (and I mention again, appears) here to center on idols and things related to their sacrifices (note the rewording in vs.29; fornication and blood and strangled things (animals) were all known to be a part of cultic sacrifices). These injunctions not being a criteria for salvation (vss.10, 11; 13:39) are still a good instruction for the Gentile (and Jew) in living a good life (to abstain from fornication still always applied in the Old Testament Law—see also 1 Thess.4:1-8; Mt.19:4-9; Ex.20:1-17). Anything involving one's practice in addition to this would involve their faith, values and conscience to be applied (Rm.14; 1 Cor.8). When they took these conclusions back to Antioch, they rejoiced hearing this and were encouraged (vs.31).

Acts 15:36-41—Paul and Barnabas had a disagreement about going on their second missionary journey (vss.38, 39). They decide to take different partners this time and begin covering territory from their first mission (vss.36, 41). Note how they now covered more territory going two different directions. The church at Antioch committed them to God's grace in their journeys, as they had previously done (vs.41; 14:26).

Acts 16:1-5—Paul and Silas (15:40) set out together on the second missionary journey and travelled north, going through Galatia once again (Derbe and Lystra). They met Timothy who was well spoken of in the area there (vss.1, 2). His mother, Eunice (2 Tim.1:5) was a believer and his father was a Greek (vs.1). He became a ministry companion with Paul, as the churches there were strengthening and growing in numbers daily (vs.5).

Acts 16:6-40—Paul and Silas then travelled northwestward in Asia Minor (north Turkey today), but the Holy Spirit prevented them from speaking the Lord's word in these areas (Bithynia was quite mountainous and wooded area—Unger). They went as far as Troas (far northwestern seaport in Asia Minor) and there they met up with Luke (notice the" we" pronouns in vs.10) and Paul received the vision to go over across the Aegean Sea to Macedonia, and ended up just inland a little ways at Philippi (vss.6-12). This was a Roman colony and an important military base (vs.12). There, by the riverside on a Sabbath, they met Lydia, and God opened her heart to respond to Paul's message (vs.14). She was a seller of purple fabrics (purple was a dye taken from tiny mollusks and great labor was required to extract it, resulting in only royalty and the wealthy able to afford it—Unger). Note twice in this chapter we find two people becoming believers, and their households were baptized with them, showing God's desire to bring families here on earth into the Family of God (vss.14, 15, 33, 34). Again finding opposition, Paul had to cast out a spirit of divination from a slave girl who brought much profit to her masters by fortune telling (vss.16-19). Her masters had them brought to the officials and they were beaten with the rods and put in prison (vss.19-24). But Paul and Silas were singing hymns to the Lord and an earthquake occurred and everyone's chains fell off (vss.25, 26); and Paul led the jailer and his household into the Family of God (vss.27-33). In a great turnabout, they rejoiced greatly (with Paul and Silas—vs.25) and took care of their needs (vs.34). The chief officials released them the next day, but Paul had them come to him and made known that he was a Roman citizen (beaten without a trial). They continually asked them to leave and so, they visited Lydia again and then left Philippi (vss.35-40).

Acts 17:1-9—Immediately following the Apostle Paul's conversion to Jesus, he began proclaiming Jesus is the Messiah (9:22). When looking for the Messiah's coming in the Old Testament passages, at least seven predominantly important prophecies come into play: 1) The prophet declared by Moses (Dt.18:18; Mt.21:11; Jn.1:1; 6:14; 7:40; 12:49, 50; Acts 3:19-14); 2) the Perfect Priest of God, offering Himself as the unblemished sacrifice to God for the sins of the world, who will also sit at God's right hand to judge the enemies of God (Ps.110:1-7; Is.53:7-12; Heb.2:17; 4:14-16; 9:11-15; 1 Pet.1:13-19; 1 Jn.2:1,2); 3) The Conquering and Ruling King of the world (2 Sam.7:10-14; 1 Chr.17:9-14; Ps.2; Jer.23:5; Is.9:6, 7; Dan.7:13, 14; Zeph.3:14-20; Mt.24:29-31; Lk.1:31-33; Jn.12:12-15; Rev.19:11-16); 4) God's Holy One would not see decay, foreseeing the resurrection of Jesus (Ps.16:7-10; Mt.28:1-10; Acts2:22-32); 5) He will fulfill the Servant passages of Is.42-53—"The Servant of Rulers"—49:7; 6; He will be the Seed of Genesis and Abraham (Gen.3:15; Rom.16:20; Gal.3); and 7) He will be born in the small town of Bethlehem in Judea (Mic.5:2-5; Jn.7:42; Lk.2:1-7). Paul demonstrated that Jesus is the Messiah (Acts 9:22; 17:2, 3; 18:5, 28; 26:22, 23), as did Peter (Acts 3:18-21), Philip (Acts 8:5), the Apostles (Acts 5:42) and Apollos (Acts 18:28). Paul's next stop was in Thessalonica, a seaport south of Philippi (and still there today). As Paul preached in a synagogue there, some were persuaded hearing him and a large number of

God-fearing Greeks and prominent women in the community became disciples (vs.4). But some Jews became jealous and made Jason, the head of the home they were staying at, pledge a bond to the rulers of the city not to house them any longer (vs.9). So, they sent Paul and Silas at night off to Berea (southwest of Thessalonica; for vs.7, see Jn.19:15).

Acts 17:10-15—The Bereans were characterized as being more noble-minded (that is, having higher moral qualities) than the ones in Thessalonica (vs.11). They even received the word proclaimed to them with (literally), "all eagerness" (with emphasis on goodwill and absence of prejudice—BAGD), and examined the Scriptures daily to see if what they were being taught was true (vs.11). Many came to believe in the Lord there, but Jews from Thessalonica came and stirred up the crowds and the brethren put Paul out to sea and he went south to Achaia (Greece) and stayed in the seaport of Athens (vs.15).

Acts 17:16-34—Athens was a great center for the arts (literature, drama, architecture, and other art forms and philosophy—Unger). It was under Roman rule when Paul visited it. He noticed the town was full of idols (vs.16) and began preaching to the people in the market place and the philosophers of that time there (vss.17-21). He was taken to Mars Hill (Latin for the Areopagus) where he proclaimed a great presentation of the Gospel to the people on hand there. He noticed their religiosity and spoke to them about an inscription on one of their altars titled "to an unknown god" (vs.23). He declared to them that God made the world, giving life and breadth and all things to all, and does not dwell in structures made by human hands, since He is Lord of heaven and earth (vss.24, 25). By one man (Gen.1) He made all the nations to live on the earth, determining seasons and boundaries for them to live by (vs.26; see 2:23 for the meaning of "determine and boundaries," same root Greek word here (English, horizon); for seasons, see Gen.1:14; Ps.104:19); that they should seek after God (the word literally used means, to feel or touch the surface of something—Vine), though He is not far from each one of us (vs.27). Because of God, we all live and move and have our being (vs.28), and so one should not think of God's nature in relation to a created thing made of gold, silver, stone, work of art, or the thoughts and imaginations of mankind (vs.29). Instead, God is declaring to men everywhere to repent (of their sins), because He has appointed (same root word as "determine and boundaries" in vs.26) a Man to judge the world in righteousness, giving proof by raising Him from the dead (vs.31; 2:25-32). For the philosophers, "resurrecting from the dead" was a difficult thing to figure out (or rationalize—vs.32) and just a few became believers (vs.32; note the three different responses to Paul's message—some sneered, others wanted to hear him again and some believed (vss.32,34).

Acts 18:1-17—Paul now came to the seaport of Corinth, east of Athens (vs.1). Here he hooked up with Aquila and Priscilla, natives of Pontus of far northeastern Asia Minor, above Galatia (vs.2). They had recently come from Italy because of a dispersion of the Jews there (vs.2). Aquila was a tent-maker like Paul (vs.3). No matter how often Paul had been rejected and even driven out of town by his fellow Jews, he always had the heart for them to come to know Jesus as Savior, Lord and Messiah (vss.4-6; see Rom.9:1-5). Reasoning with them on the Sabbath days, the Jews resisted him at Corinth (vs.6), yet many Corinthians came to believe in Jesus and were baptized (vs.8). The Lord encouraged Paul in a dream to keep on preaching to them, for a great harvest of souls to be won to Jesus was there, and the people would not attack him. So Paul stayed teaching God's word to them for a year and a half (vss.9-11). Some Jews still reacted negatively to Paul and brought him to the governor of Achaia (Greece) Gallio, with attempts to arrest Paul (vss.12, 13). But things they thought Paul was saying contrary to the Jewish law was all they could come up with against him and the governor was not concerned about those things, so nothing happened to Paul (remember vs.10); and then, Paul, after remaining some time longer, decided to head back home to Syria (vss.12-18).

Acts 18:18-23—Paul left Corinth and travelled across the Aegean Sea to Ephesus and left Aquila and Priscilla there and then landed at Caesarea, and went up to Antioch in Syria, where the brethren had sent him out on his first two missionary journeys.

Acts 18:24-28—Luke now writes about the appearance of Apollos and the great benefit he was to the early church. He was from Alexandria, a central northern seaport of Egypt. It was founded and named after Alexander the Great (331 BC) and soon came to have the largest library in the world, and became a great center for the production of copies of the Scriptures (Unger). He came to Ephesus and was a very learned man, not only about the Scriptures, but also about the things concerning Jesus (vss.24, 25). Though speaking out boldly in the synagogues, he was only acquainted with the baptism of John (see 19:1-7). Aquila and Priscilla helped show him the way of God more accurately (i.e., conversion and the baptism of the Holy Spirit, implied by the following passage, 19:1-7). He went over to Achaia (Greece) and helped greatly the believers there, while also "refuting completely" (BAGD) the Jews in public discourse, showing in the Scriptures that Jesus is the Messiah (vss.26-28).

Acts 19:1-41—Paul now begins his third missionary journey and travels through the Galatian region and arrives in western Asia Minor at Ephesus (18:23; 19:1). Here he meets some disciples, who had only received the baptism of John (vs.3; see also previously, 18:25 about Apollos). Paul gave the Gospel message, baptized them and, when he laid hands on them, they received the Holy Spirit (vss.1-7). After preaching in the synagogue there for three months, the Jews became resistant to Paul and he went to preach from the school of Tyrannus (an open lecture hall) and many Jews and Greeks heard the word of God (vss.8-10). God also did many great miracles there through Paul's ministry (vss.11, 12). For the Jewish high priest's son trying to cast out demons, see Mt.12:23-28. Many also who had previously practiced magic, came to believe in Jesus and stopped those former activities (vss.8, 19). The word of God thus kept growing and prevailing (vs.20). For Paul's desire to go to Rome, see 23:11.

Even the truth Paul and Steven proclaimed that God does not dwell in structures made by man's hand (17:24; 7:48-50) was being heard and having its effect in Ephesus and on some of its economy (vss.23-27). The idol Artemis was one of the Seven Wonders of the World (vs.35; note the claim "falling from heaven" in this verse; note God's claim and "proven fact" to all men—17:31). The one making these temples to this false god began a local riot, along with other similar tradesmen, against Paul (vss.23-29). The Roman Empire was a polytheistic empire, which, as we have seen, is often why cases could not be brought up against someone of different religious belief; but they could try and stage riots (as we have seen this in Acts) against people (often with Paul and the other Apostles), to try and get them arrested and even to leave town (see 17:8-10). Here, with good wisdom and common sense about government procedures regarding crime and uproars from the local town clerk (vs.35), this public disturbance comes to nothing again, as the town clerk steps in and tactfully dismisses the disorderly gathering (vss.35-41).

Acts 20:1-12—In the last nine chapters of the book of Acts, Luke records 7 great proclaimed testimonial speeches given by the Apostle Paul, as the theme of Acts (1:8) continues to be declared and worked out from the start to the very conclusion of the book (to the Ephesian elders; to the public crowd in Jerusalem; to the Sanhedrin; to governors Felix and Festus; to King Agrippa and to the Jewish leaders in Rome (Acts 20-28). To complete his third missionary journey, the Apostle Paul left Ephesus and travelled across the Aegean Sea to Macedonia (vs.1) and then down to Greece (vs.2). He decided to go back to Syria and hopefully reach there in time for the Feast of Pentecost (vss.3, 16). A plot formed against him by the Jews in Greece caused him to carefully choose his route back home. He stayed travelling by sea and returned the same route he took to Greece, heading back up to Macedonia, and from Philippi crossed the Aegean Sea over to Troas (vss.3, 5, 6). He sent his co-ministers over to Troas ahead of him to wait for him there (vs.4).

At Troas, Paul gave a long discourse and message, lasting till daybreak (vs.11). In the upper room there, a young man began to fall asleep and sitting on the window sill fell down to the ground and was picked up dead. Paul immediately went down to him and fell on him and declared that his life was still in him (vs.10). All those there were greatly comforted then (vs.12) and Paul left at daybreak.

Acts 20:13-38—Now on his way back to Syria, Paul leaves Troas and travels by foot to Assos, a seaport town about 30 miles by sea to the south (Unger) but somewhat shorter by land (vs.13; see vss.3,19). Paul stayed on the sea or close to it all the way back till finally going back inland at Jerusalem. Thirty-six miles south of Ephesus (Unger), at a coastal town called Miletus, Paul met with the Ephesian elders (vs.17). Here are some key notes of his exhortation speech to them: Note, the description of his kind of ministry to them in his own words (vss.18-21, 24, 27, 31,33-35); "the whole counsel (purpose) of God" in vs.27 is "all the divine will of God," that he did not hold back declaring to them, even in "counseling" (admonishing) type of circumstances—vs.31, see helpful vss.20 and 13:36); Paul uses the theme word of Acts 1:8 in four of six verses (vss.21-26)—his public and house to house ministry of the Gospel (vss.21,34), the Holy Spirit's witness to him of potential persecutions and imprisonments (vs.23), and his witness of innocence in his ministry to them (vs.26; see 18:6). The ministry of an elder in the church (shepherding overseeing the ones that Jesus purchased with His own blood—vss.28-30); note the goals of the ministry (vs.32); avoiding going against the tenth Commandment (Ex.20:17), Paul worked hard with his own craft

(18:2,3) to provide the needs of him and his associates in ministry, and to be able to give to others also, which is more blessed to do than to receive, as Jesus said (a possible quote from Lk.6:38). For the strong emotions expressed in his departure, see the same verb used in vs.37 of the dad of the prodigal son (Lk.15:20).

Acts 21:1-16—Paul now travelled through the Mediterranean Sea and arrived back in Syria at the city of Tyre (vss.1-3). At first glance, vs.4 can appear to contradict vs.11, but they are actually saying the same thing. The disciples in Tyre knew what Paul was in store for going to Jerusalem, confirmed by the prophet Agabus (vss.10-14). Paul knew, as well (20:22-24). They were all saying to him the same thing as a result (vss.4, 12). Yet Paul, for sometime now, had felt by necessity that he must go to Rome (19:21). If that was to be so, he would have to survive "his trial" coming up in Jerusalem. That "necessity" he felt would soon be confirmed by the Lord (23:11). After visiting the Apostle Philip and his four virgin daughters (vss.8-10), Paul left and arrived with a glad welcome by the brethren at Jerusalem (vs.17).

Acts 21:17-22:30—Having met with James (the brother of Jesus) and the elders in Jerusalem, James encouraged Paul to conform to a Jewish tradition on vow-taking, to follow the law procedure to keep peace with the local Jews (vss.18-26; 18:18; Num.6:1-9). The Jews coming from Asia Minor, though, thought he had done something to defile the temple in Jerusalem and stirred up a riot against Paul (vss.27-30). They sought to kill him (vs.31) and were beating him (vs.32) until the Roman soldiers intervened and stopped them doing this (vss.32, 33). Paul, talking with the commander of the soldiers, asked permission to speak to the Jewish crowd and it was granted to him to do so (vss.37-40).

Paul delivers to his fellow Jews in Jerusalem not so much of a "preaching Gospel" message as more of a "relational Gospel" testimonial here to them. He gave them his "personal witness" of how he found Jesus, or more, realistically, how Jesus found him (brought Paul into the Family of God—22:3-21). Here are some notable points about Paul's proclamation to the Jews: great contacts with the Jews made with them in his background shared in vss.3, 12, 13; he used to persecute Christians, their Lord whom he now devotes his whole life to (vss.4, 5; 26:15); he consented to Stephan's death (Acts 7), whom Paul calls here as the Lord's "witness" (Stephan) before him—vss.19, 20, which now Paul was called to be the same—vs.15); it's God's miracle he was there to "see" and now tell them this (vss.11-13); he did include sharing the Gospel (vs.16); they didn't want to hear of Paul going to the Gentiles (vs.21), now also displaying God's mercy to them through Paul's ministry, but they didn't see that and God's hand upon this (Eph.2:11-22). The Jews reacted to Paul similar to the way they treated Jesus in His trial (Jn.19:6, 15). Finding out that Paul was a Roman citizen (vs.28), the commander could do nothing to him and so, took Paul to the leading Jewish Council, the Sanhedrin, for further investigation (vs.30).

Acts 23:1-35—The Apostles knew for sometime as Jesus said to them, that they would have the opportunity to be a testimony and "witness" to kings and governors of their time (Lk.21:12-15). So now Paul came before the Sanhedrin (vs.1). Seeing there were Pharisees and Sadducees present, Paul elected to let them wrestle out why he was on trial—for the hope and resurrection of the dead (of Jesus). They became divided and so, to avoid another riot, Paul was put in the barracks (soldiers housing) for protection till further notice (vss.1-10). But the Jews sought to kill Paul and formed a plot to ambush him (vss.12-15). The son of Paul's sister heard about the plot and told Paul, who had him tell the commander what he heard (vss.16-22). Protected by a large infantry, Paul was taken to the coastal town of Caesarea and awaited his trial to stand before the governor Felix (vss.16-35).

Acts 24:1-27—Now before the governor of Judea, Felix, Paul has to change courses here as he defends himself against an attorney opposing him (vss.1, 2). The attorney tries to hit hard and fast against Paul, trying to gather hearsay statements against him and using coarse words to try and get Paul riled and upset; but Paul has a great testimonial response (defense) and spoke graciously to the governor.

The attorney called Paul a "pest" (actual word for "pestilence," an infectious malady possible to people – vs.5); said he stirred up riots when it was the Jews doing so continuously against him (vs.5), and he was a leader ("ringleader") of a division called Nazarenes (when he was one of many leaders in the Christian faith, vs.5); not desecrating the temple, he knew the Law's requirement and followed them (21:23-26); note vs.7 is omitted because it was considered by many to be a later addition to explain the end of vs. 6; and while the Jews joined in, they on a regular basis were the ones starting the riots (which was one way to get one arrested in a polytheistic empire—vss.9,12,13). Paul's defense was noble and respectful, and done so (remarkably) cheerfully (vss.10, 11). No proof of charges were (or could be) presented (vss.11-13, 18-20). Paul in good conscience did what the Law of the Jews required, and said what the prophets had written about, the resurrection of the dead (vss.14-16; note how Paul restated vs.16 from 23:1). His real cry (literally) was the proclamation of Jesus' resurrection (vs.21; 23:6). Felix even talked to Paul in private, but to please the Jews, kept Paul in custody for two years (vss.24-27; see Jesus' trial in Mk.15:15).

Acts 25:1-27—Now under new governorship, Paul is brought out to testify to Festus. His message is brief to the governor and knew it was not safe (or necessary) to go back to Jerusalem (23:12-15). So, no one still having any roof of wrong doing (see Mk.14:55-59), Paul appealed to Caesar in Rome, knowing also, some way that God would see him there, to be a testimony to them, also (23:11). Festus explained his dilemma about Paul to King Agrippa, who was in town then (vss.13-22), and before going to Rome, King Agrippa wanted to hear Paul also (the verb here is an ongoing tense in the past, showing prior interest—vs.22). The governor was hoping that this hearing may prove something of substantial evidence in his perplexity about Paul and the Jews (though his favor was previously decided—vss.9, 23-27).

Acts 26:1-32—Paul once again goes to sharing his testimonial conversion here before King Agrippa. While Paul uses the word "defense" in the beginning of his speech (vs.2), we can see by the words he uses that he is actually on the "offense," being a "witness" for Jesus (vss.2, 16, 22). Much of his testimony here is similar to the one given to the Jewish crowd in chapter 22. In verse 8, the word you is plural, so, "you people" (NASB). Paul mentions in vs.14 that the Lord said to him that it is hard for him to kick against the goads (a pointed stick to get animals to move; Paul kept working against God's divine will then). Twice Paul uses the word "witness" (the theme of Acts in 1:8, so people can come into the Family of God—see Rom.10:8-15), first in vs.16 in his calling to serve the Lord; then in vs.22, "witnessing" in his message to the king about Jesus the Messiah. Note the effects of the Gospel to those who believe—have their eyes opened (spiritually), turning from darkness to light from Satan's dominion to God's dominion (Eph.2:1-11), receiving forgiveness of sins and an inheritance with those sanctified by faith in Jesus (vs.18; see Lk.12:32). Paul declares the full scope of territory that he had shared the Gospel, beginning immediately at his conversion (vss.19, 20). He testifies to the king that Jesus is the Messiah, and along with vss.18, 20, gives the full proclamation of the Gospel, presented to both Jew and Gentile (vss.22, 23). Verse 28 has been interpreted as either a statement or a question (NIV). With the decision of the king made, either way it would have gone, Paul is on his way to Rome (vss.30-32).

Acts 27:1-28:31—Finally boarding a ship to Rome, a total of 276 persons would eventually make the trip (27:37). Paul travelled up to Sidon before setting out for Rome (27:3). They sailed north of the island of Cyprus and landed at Myra (far south end of Asia Minor, current day Turkey), changing ships to go to Rome there (vss.5, 6). With difficult winds occurring, they then sailed to the far southwest part of Asia Minor and then travelled south, going south of the island of Crete (south of Greece) and coming to Fair Havens (the far south central part of the island—27:7, 8). The big decision here was to stay on land or risk strong northeastern winds to get to Italy. Paul suggested it was too dangerous, but was outvoted, so they continued on to take the risk (27:9-13). A strong northeastern wind did come up and took the ship off its course (27:14, 15). Going past the shelter of a small island southwest of Crete, they feared being driven all the way to coastal Africa to the south (Syrtis—vs.17, (Unger); 27:16, 17). And so, they were driven along in the Mediterranean Sea, hungry and without hope of getting through the storm (27:17-20). But an angel of God appeared to Paul and brought them comfort that only damage to the ship would occur, as Paul must stand before Caesar (27:21-26). Being tossed about in the Adriatic Sea (lower region of this sea between Italy and Greece—27:27), Paul stated to the head master and his soldiers that all aboard must remain on the ship in order to be saved from the violent storm (27:27-32). Going fourteen days without eating on the ship during the storm, Paul proceeded to have a "communion-like" meal with them, thanking God in their presence and distributing food to them; and all were renourished and encouraged (27:33:37). After having a rocky landing, they arrived safely on the island of Malta (still there today, a little southwest of Italy; 27:38-28:1). They were received kindly on the island, and picking up kindling to start a fire, a viper landed on Paul's arm, but he shook it off to no harm (28:2-6). God used Paul to bring healing of their people on the island—the father of one of the leading men and many others were cured of their diseases (28:7-9). After three months they set out on a new ship that had wintered there at the island, and supplied with all they needed, headed off to Rome (28:10, 11). Travelling between Italy and Sicily (the large island just southwest of Italy), they continued on up the west coast of Italy, and greeted with good encouragement by some brethren along the way, they finally arrived at Rome (28:12-16). Once in Rome, along with a soldier guarding him, Paul called for the local Jewish leaders and briefly explained his dilemma of why he was there at Rome (28:17-22). The Book of Acts closes with this "witness and testimonial" Paul gave to the Jewish leaders, who came to see him in large numbers. He "witnessed" to them about the Kingdom of God (see 1:6 for what this meant to Jews), trying to persuade them from the Law and the Prophets, from morning till evening (28:23). Some were being persuaded and some began to leave after Paul quoted Is.6:9, 10 to them (28:24-28). Some would "hear" and some would not. Jesus used this quote from Isaiah to introduce His parables in Matthew, chapter 13 (see that commentary for the explanation on this quote). For two full years Paul continued to proclaim the Lord Jesus to them, openly and unhindered (some note the word of triumph here in the ending of the book—28:30-31).

Romans

The themes that the Apostle Paul chose when writing his letters to different churches at large are faith, hope and love (1 Cor.13:13). A number of his letters have these clearly laid out as such, while others he integrates them in with his chosen topics of his writing (in the Corinthian letters Paul addresses certain specific problems; one still finds these in his first letter, but more intertwined in his second letter to them).

Paul writes an excellent presentation of the Gospel of God's salvation in His sent Messiah, Jesus Christ. He writes this for both the Jew and the nations. He begins to address his fellow Jews first of these groups in 2:17. As seen in Acts, his custom in taking the Gospel to the world was to first go into a Jewish synagogue and present the Gospel. He had not visited Rome before when he wrote this letter to them (1:11-15). So what we have here in Romans is in high probability of what he presented to the Jews when speaking in their synagogues (or at least in large part what he shared with them). This makes this book even more special and educational for us, having been preserved well over the church age for us to learn so much from the Apostle Paul's writing.

Rom.1:1-7—Paul's rather lengthy introduction gives us good information on several topics: his call by God to be an Apostle for the Gospel to the nations (vss.1,5); specifics about the Gospel promised beforehand by God's prophets in His holy writings of the Bible (vs.2); the Gospel is about His Son (Ps.2; Heb.1:1-6), the prophesied One coming through the seed of David (vs.3; Sam.7; Mt.1:1; Lk.3:23, 31, 38), declared the Son of God (which He has been eternally (Jn.1:1-3,18), according to the Spirit of holiness (note the Trinity here; see Book 1 of <u>The Family Bible Studies Series, The Family of God—Foundation</u> for more understanding of the Trinity, their character and functions), in power by His resurrection from the dead—Jesus Christ our Lord (vs.4); each believer coming into the Family of God is a calling of God (vss.6,7); and, at his ending, Paul's characteristic greeting in his letter to the recipients, to receive God's grace and peace (vs.7; grace—God's outward blessings; and peace—His inward work of tranquility, that works itself outwardly, as well—Eph.2:1-22).

Rom.1:8-17—While longing to see them at Rome, it is a great testimony here how much Paul prayed for them, and still waiting to see and meet with them (vss.9, 10). His mission is to share the Gospel and he made clear that he was not ashamed of that, because it is the power of God for salvation to all who believe (vss.14-16). From "faith to faith" (vs.17) refers back to Paul's introduction in the letter about the basics of the Gospel in vss.1-4. It was promised back then (vss.2, 3, and people should have been eagerly looking for Him), and now fulfilled—by the resurrection from the dead (vs.4); and so, man should live according to this faith in God and His Messiah, back then according to His word, and now with faith in Jesus and His word, the One sent from God to be our Messiah (Acts 3:19-21).

Rom.1:18-2:16—Paul begins his presentation of the Gospel by declaring why the world is now under (though not completed) the judgment of God, because of Jesus' death and resurrection from the dead (vss.1-5), for those who suppress this truth and continue in unrighteous living, which brings the wrath of God (vs.18; see Jesus' words in John 3:16-21). God makes these things known about Him and His work—both inside and outside in His creation (vss.19, 20). Paul says those who do not receive the truth continue to suppress it, and exchange it for a lie (vss.21-25). Without God's presence and power within them, people do not have the strength to "suppress" evil, and all kinds of immoral actions can take place (a list of over 20 is given by the Apostle here—vss.26-31). Though they know the "ordinance" of God (the right thing to do, plus the consequences), suppressing the right thing to do can lead to worse things and even negative influence on others (vs.32). Thus, those practicing such things cannot express judgment to another, as it applies already to them (2:1, 2). God's righteous judgment will give to each person according to their deeds performed (vs.6), both attributively, good and unrighteous actions that were done, again, knowing the good they are to do (1:32; 2:3-16).

Rom.2:17-3:20—Paul now begins to address his fellow Jews (2:17). He wants them to know that what he has said previously in this letter applies to them, to decide for or against Jesus and the Gospel message. He asks them first to be introspective about themselves (2:17-23) and honest about their own life before God. Knowing all they know about God and His laws, are they a good testimony to the nations also (2:24)? It is those who practice God's word that benefit of it (2:24; 10:5; Lev. 18:5; Dt.29:9). Otherwise, those who do not even know God's laws may possibly prove to be a better demonstrator (2:25-27). A Jew is one inwardly, following God from their heart (and so for anyone following after God—2:28, 29), and comes through the Holy Spirit, for God looks at the heart (1 Sam.16:7; Rom.7:6). Paul says that the benefits for the Jew is quite great, and gives quite an added extensive list in 9:1-5 (3:1, 2). But he also gives quite a few quotes from the Old Testament of why both Jews and the nations are all under sin (3:9-18), which brings all accountable to God (3:19, 20; 1:18-21, 32; Jn.3:16-21; 1 Jn.2:1,2), and the need of His deliverance (3:21-30; Acts 2:34-40).

Rom.3:21-31—God's deliverance for mankind is in the Gospel message of His Son, Jesus Christ. In Jesus is the righteousness of God, to deliver mankind from sin and death (vss.21-23; 1:1-4, 16, 17; note that the "righteousness of God" was also demonstrated to Adam and Eve for their sin in Gen.3; now the sacrifice was the human body of Jesus, His shed blood once and for all for mankind, to bring us to God (vs.25; 6:10; 1 Pet.1:17-19; 3:18). Note the "righteousness of God" is mentioned here four times in six verses (vss.21-26). For all those who believe in Jesus and receive Him into their life (Jn.1:12, 13; see the Prayer in the back of the book), they come into the Family of God and are justified by God's gift in Jesus to them (meaning, declared righteous, by believing in Jesus—vss.24-26, 29, 30). That is God's righteousness given as a gift of His grace to us in Jesus Christ His Son (vs.24; redemption here is Jesus' sacrifice by His shed blood for us as the payment to God, dying for our sins). The word "propitiation" in vs.25 refers to His sacrificial offering for us; used only twice in the New Testament, it refers to the "cover" on top of the Ark of the Covenant, from also the Hebrew word which means "a cover" (Vine). And so, He has "covered over" our sins. For the "passing over" sins previously, see Acts 14:16; 17:30, 31. God had to be the "Justifier" also, since mankind cannot pay for his sins and live (vss.20, 23, 24-26, 30; 6:22, 23). The Gospel is offered for and to all mankind (vss.29, 30), created in the image of God (Gen.1:27; 51; see Book One of <u>The Family Bible Studies Series</u>, <u>The Family of God—Foundation</u>, for further insights on mankind created in the image of God and what that means, pg.7). Verse 28 is a good summary by Paul of what he is saying in this section. Thus, the law is established and not nullified (meaning, man's inability to fulfill the Law demonstrates his need for the Savior Jesus, vs.31; see also 10:4; 2 Cor.5:21).

Rom.4:1-25—Paul now demonstrates by the life of Abraham that God's righteousness to mankind comes (as stated in the previous section) by believing God's word through faith for His salvation and not by one's own personal works or actions (vss.5, 23-25). Abraham showed his faith in response to God's vision to him in Gen.15:1-6 (vss.1-3), as well as David's declaration in Ps.32:1, 2 (vss.6-8). Paul makes clear that this took place in Abraham's life before he was circumcised, as circumcision was a demonstration of faith, not a condition of it (or try to achieve it—vss.3-5, 10-12). Abraham believed God at His promise and lived it out in his life, that he would be the Father of many nations (vss.13-23; Gen.17:4-6; 22:17, 18). As this promise is being worked out, Abraham is the Father of both Jew and Gentile, who come to believe, with exemplified faith as Abraham, in Jesus as Savior and Lord (see the previous section), whom God raised from the dead, so we may become right (righteous) with God, and live out His righteousness (vss.23-25; 2 Cor.5:20, 21; Phil.2:12, 13; see Book 4 of <u>The Family Bible Studies Series</u>, <u>The Theology of the Bible—The Family of God</u> for how this is worked out; also, Book 2, <u>The Levels of Relationships</u>, for an encouraging summary of the life of Abraham, pgs. 14-16).

Rom.5:1-21—Paul now begins to amplify the effects of receiving God's righteousness to the believer in Jesus Christ (justification). Peace with God (and carrying over to others—Eph.2) is the first thing he mentions, being free from sin and no longer separated from God (vs.1; 6:1, 18-23). Freed from His wrath, the believer now stands in His grace (vss.2, 9). Compared to any previous boasting (3:27), the believer now boasts in the wonderful hope of His glory (vss.2, 3, 11; 6:4, 5, 8; 1 Jn. 3:1, 2) and even in trials and tribulations in this life, knowing, as we grow and trust in God, it brings about proven character (maturity process—vss.2-5; 6:1-23; Eph.4:13). Note in the first five verses here Paul's mention of faith, hope and love; plus, the work of the Trinity. Verse six says, as we were helpless (mankind's inability to save himself—see previous 3:19-31), Christ came at the right time with His salvation life and Gospel message. "At the right time" may have something to do with transferring the kingdom from Israel (Acts 1:6) to the Kingdom of God (Mk.1:15). With the nations not having hope (see 3:29, 30) and only some harvest Jesus reaped in Israel in His first coming (see commentary on

Mt.21:1-11), He put the enmity between them to death and brought His offer of eternal life to both (Eph. 2), and will see a completed harvest upon His second coming, at the finish of the Great Tribulation (Rev.14:14-20; 19:11-18). Reconciliation goes back to vs.1, where Christ, as our Mediator, brings peace between God and man (vss.10, 11; 2 Cor.5:20, 21; Eph.2). Paul concludes this section of his writing (vss.12-21) by comparing the huge magnitude of difference between the trespass (sin) of Adam and the grace and free gift of God's salvation in His Son Jesus Christ. The magnificence of God's glory has no comparison with the trespasses of man (vss.2, 19-21; 8:17, 18).

Rom.6:1-23—Paul now gives the believer good guidelines in overcoming sin in one's life and living out God's righteous. Baptism signifies this changed life for the believer, who now lives out a "resurrected life" in and for the Lord (vss.1-8). Sin no longer has master over the believer—the Master does (vss.9-11)! The believer now sees that one's physical makeup becomes instruments of righteousness for God (vss.12-14). Being once a slave to sin, the believer is now a slave to God's righteousness in serving Him (vss.15-18; 3:21-31). This process of growth is called "sanctification," which is literally growing in God's holiness, confessing sin and growing in His character (the benefit, literally, the fruit—that is, God's produce—vss.22, 23) of knowing and growing in the Lord—the spiritual birth (Jn.1:12, 13; 3:1-16); and the outcome, eternal life and glory with the Lord—vss.19-23; 3-11; 5:2; 8:18; 2 Cor.4:17; 1 Jn.3:1, 2). See Book 3 of <u>The Family Bible Studies Series, Growing in God's Wisdom,</u> for a very helpful aid in growing in this process of God's wisdom and knowing better how to pray for it.

Rom.7:1-25—Paul now speaks to his fellow Jewish believers (vss.1,4), reminding them that they are free from bondage to the Law and now free to serve the Lord in their new resurrected life of God's righteousness by faith (3:19-31), and so, to bear fruit for God, which comes through the Holy Spirit (vss.1-6; Jn.15:16; Gal.5:22-26). He reminds them of their (including himself) previous life ("in the flesh"—vs.5, and once apart from the Law—vs.9) and the battle and bondage that sin presented (note for the believer that this is not now the case; (see chapter 6), unless one does not execute faith and gives into it—1 Jn.3:4-6; Rom.6). Paul describes the real previous battle in being in bondage to sin and its effects on one's total being –even when one knew the good to do (as the 10 commandments) and wanted to do them, resulting at times, doing the very thing one hated (vs.15). So Paul says he then knew it was "sin within" him that was the root cause, concurring with the Law that it is good to tell him these things (vs.12). The battle in the mind knew and was serving God, but the bondage of the flesh kept serving the law of sin (vss.22-25). Who could ever set us free from this ongoing battle? Only Christ Jesus can (chapter 6), by the "law of faith" (vs.25; 3:19-31), through the "law of the Spirit of Life" (8:1-4; 7:6).

Rom.8:1-17—Paul now marks out for the believer numerous benefits and guidelines for the new life in the Spirit. Note the work and unity of the Trinity in the first four verses (see <u>The Family of God-Foundation</u>, Book 1 of <u>The Family Bible Studies Series</u> for more understanding of the character and functions of the Trinity).

The Holy Spirit enables us to live out God's righteous life by His works within us and through us, and gives life (God's life) to our mortal bodies (vss.1-12). Note believers possess the Spirit of God within them, necessary to be God's child (vss.9, 14, 16; Jn.1:12, 13; 3:1-18—the spiritual birth; see also the Prayer in the back of the book). The Holy Spirit helps us put to death the misdeeds of the flesh (body, mind, soul and spirit—vss.12-14; 3-8) and instead, to display the character of a child of God, which we call God our Father (vss.14-16; Mt.6:9-15; the word "adoption" in the Greek literally means "placing a son" (or daughter, here), into the Family of God through the spiritual birth -vs.15). Believers have the wonderful "kingdom blessings" from God (see Lk.12:31, 32) as being joint-heirs with Jesus in His kingdom (vs.17; Mt.6:9-15; Dan.7:13, 14) and the outstanding miraculous transformation to come (8:18-25; Phil.3:20, 21; though sufferings for His name sake in this life is part of our service to Him, as He said would take place, also (vss.17, 18; Jn. 15:20; 2 Tim.3:12).

Rom. 8:18-30—Paul now builds on all his previous discussions of faith and presents his writing on "hope" for the children of God (see the introduction to Romans for the explanation of his themes). His proclamation of hope here is about the redemption of our bodies and the glory to come (1 Jn.3:1, 2; see also God's present work now in us and through us—2 Cor.3:16-18). The eternal glory to come has no comparison to our temporary sufferings here on earth, though some have had great sufferings in their lifetime, while also, remembering the sufferings Jesus willing went through for us. It is sometimes difficult to see this, though, when we go through them (vs.22; 1 Cor.10:13). The word "groan" in the

Greek means "an inward, unexpressed feeling of sorrow," a type of grief (Vine), used well here by the Apostle Paul (vss.22, 23, 26). Hope has the characteristic of being waited for, and, in this case, eagerly so (vss.24, 25). The Holy Spirit takes hold with us and helps bear our weaknesses (Greek word here). He intercedes (literally) without words for us (vs.26), according to God's will (vs.27); and we know that those called to His purposes, can look forward to His love for us, watching how He works out all things together for good, to those who love Him (vs.28); and looking forward to His glorification for the believer (vss.29, 30), in God's wonderful hope to come for us (vss.19-25, 30; 5:1, 2, 5).

Rom.8:31-39—Here in Romans is where Paul begins and discusses quite elaborately on God's love, carrying along his faith, hope and love themes to the middle of chapter 15. While Paul in other epistles presents in his writings the human attempt to grasp the great measure and depth of God's love (Eph. 3:16-19), he is close here in doing the same, declaring the tremendous magnitude of the unconditional and unfailing love of God. Who can be against us, as a result, knowing this (vs.33) or try to condemn us, with Jesus at the right hand of God interceding for the believer (vs.34; 8: 1, 2)? Could anything ever separate us from God's love for us in Christ Jesus (vss.32, 35)? Paul gives quite a lengthy list of "conditions" one may face in life (vss.35, 36), and then, powers of "created things" we confront in our world, also (vss.38, 39). His answer is nothing shall separate us from God's love in Christ Jesus. And why? He has set us free (the believer in Christ) from sin and death, and by His resurrection from the dead, now intercedes for us at God's right hand; and so, makes us overcomers (literally, conquering over) whatever we face by our trust in Him (the law of faith—3: 27, 28), because of His great love for us, knowing whatever we face, He has (will) overcome it for us (vss.32, 34, 37-39; see Jn.16:33; Lk.12:31, 32).

Rom.9-11—Paul now discusses in these next three chapters his great love and heart's desire (and carried out in his preaching ministry) for the salvation of his fellow Israelites (9:1-3; 10:1). He begins by acknowledging the great heritage that the Israelites have in their relationship to God, which includes God's sending the Messiah into the world through them (9:1-5). The "seed" of this promise of the Messiah, though, comes through Isaac and Jacob, as God declared (9:6-13; also see Jesus' words in Mt.22:32). God's mercy and choosing is not based on "fleshly" descent (9:8), as God looks at the heart, to those who will believe and serve Him (9:4-18; 10:8-13). Paul declares God's longsuffering toward mankind, that He has endured when He could have demonstrated His wrath; instead, now extends His salvation and righteousness to the nations as well as Israel (9:19-26, 30; 3:21-30). The nation Israel as a whole, though, did not receive Jesus, God's Messiah sent to them (and to the world, Acts 3:19-26) and "stumbled" over Him (9:30-33; see Isaiah's prophecy of this occurrence—Is.8:11-15). But throughout time, God has maintained His remnant of Israel (9:27; 11:1-10), so they are not ever destroyed and God's promises (to them and the world) may be fulfilled (see important Old Testament verses leading up to the appearing of Jesus the Messiah about the remnant in Book 4 <u>of The Family Bible Studies Series</u>, <u>The Theology of the Bible</u>—<u>The Family of God</u>, on pgs.

23, 24). All these prophecies and promises are so important, seeing how God builds His Family throughout the ages.

Paul wants his fellow Israelites to be saved and receive Jesus, the Messiah, whom God has sent for them (10:1), so he shares the Gospel of God's salvation with them in this writing. In God's righteousness, Jesus is the fulfillment of the law (10:4; Mt.5:17) and demonstrated living out God's righteousness for us in His life on the earth (10:5). So one cannot say, "Bring Him down to earth for us to see" (10:6), or "raise Him up from the dead so we can see Him" (10:7); no, instead, that has already been fulfilled and now is the powerful message being proclaimed throughout all the earth for all mankind to be saved (10:8-18; Col.1:6, 23). It is the "word of faith" (10:8-13) and comes by hearing the spoken word about Jesus (10:14-17); and by receiving Him into one's life as Lord and Savior, resulting in salvation to the believer (10:9-13; Jn.1:12, 13; see the Prayer of Salvation in the back of the book). By the nations receiving God's salvation in Jesus, that God had prophesied through Moses (Dt.32:15-22), Paul hoped the same for them and to provoke the nation Israel to become jealous, and hopefully receive the Gospel for themselves (10:19-21; 11:11, 14, 30, 31).

In an effort then to try and save some of his fellow Israelites, Paul now speaks to the Gentiles, and explains how the remnant of Israel is already taking place and will one day be fulfilled. In vs.16, the incoming "firstfruit" ("first piece of the dough," since this refers to a bread—like baking, here, referring to the first harvest of Jewish Christians—Pentecost, Acts 2:41; 4:4 and onward) is holy, and so is all of the dough (lump, those of Israel who follow likewise). Their root, being in the Old Testament prophecies and promises of God, is holy; and so will be the branches (the continual ingathering of Jews receiving Jesus the Messiah). Paul, then, addresses someone (or someone who would ever do this of the Gentiles) being arrogant toward the Jews (11:18, 20), reminding them that the Jewish roots support the Gentiles, not the other way around (11:18, 24; arrogant in the Greek means show superiority over, not a fruit of Christian character and one the Apostle Paul would not allow in the church—10:12; 12:16). Beginning in 11:17 to 11:24, the word "you" in the Greek is singular, showing Paul is directing this to any individual where this would apply (the plural "you" picks back up in 11:25 to the Gentiles at large), and, with this kind of character in mind, addresses this as to an unbeliever, since the similar language of being "cut off" (11:22) is used of the unbelieving Israelite "broken off" in their disbelief of Jesus and unlike the remnant in 11:16 (11:17-22; same as a circumstance like 1 Cor.15:2 may also be applying here, one had not become a believer yet, the meaning of "in vain" there). And so, God is able to graft in both Jew and Gentile, in their belief in coming to receive Jesus as Lord and Savior of their lives (11:23, 24; 10:8-13; "kindness" in 11:22 refers to the graciousness of God extending the Gospel to them (the Gentiles) by faith—11:20-22). Verse 11:24 is the general truth to Jews and Gentiles, to whoever it would apply (conditional clause here).

In 11:25, the "mystery" (the "grafting—11:17, 24) brought a "partial hardening" to Israel; partial, because like Paul and other Israelites as the "first fruit" remnants (11:16), some believed (10:13) and others did not (9:31-33). The "fullness of the Gentiles" is the same as the "times of the Gentiles" to be fulfilled in Lk.21:24—this is the time when the Babylonians took away Israel's kingdom (586 BC) till the time the worldly kingdoms are put to a finish and Jesus returns to earth at the end of the Great Tribulation to rule in His millennial reign and temple (Rev.17:9-14; 19:11-18; 20:1-6; Ezk.40-48). The Great Tribulation brings the judgment of God and the final harvest of both Jews and Gentiles (Rev.7:13-17; 14:14-16). So, bringing in all the remnant of Israel (11:16), all Israel will be saved (11:26), when Jesus returns and reigns from Jerusalem (11:26, 27; see the prophecy in Is.59:20, 21 and Heb.8:8-12; Zech.14). With Israel's roots and God's promises to them, with the developing remnant occurring, and the extension of the Gospel through them to the Gentiles—they are loved by God's choice of them and, for the sake of their fathers and promises through Abraham, making their gifts (benefits) and calling something God would not ever regret or take back (11:29; Ps.94:14; Is.54:1-10; Heb.2:17, 7:11-28). So, because of God's great mercy and salvation brought to us in His Son Jesus Christ, He has "closed up together" (the Greek verb in 11:32; 10:8-13) all disobedience, that He may through Jesus display His magnificent mercy, forgiveness and love to all, awaiting the return of Jesus to rule and reign upon the earth. The depth of God's unsearchable judgments and incomprehensible ways are part of the great riches found in His wisdom and knowledge (11:33-35; Prov.21:30; Job 28:28; Is.33:5, 6). For as Creator and Lord of the universe (Gen.1:1), "from Him and through Him and to Him are all things," and He will receive the glory forever and ever (11:36; Rev.4:8-11; 5:13, 14).

Rom.12:1-21—Having expressed his love for his fellow Israelites, Paul continues on with the theme of love and gives us great examples for its expression in the Family of God. Having received God's mercy by accepting the Gospel of Jesus Christ (11:32; Jn.1:12, 13; 3:1-16), Paul now earnestly exhorts the believers by the compassions of God to perform their priestly duty of offering themselves (body, mind, soul and spirit) holy and well-pleasing to God, as sacrifices for His service, which is the reasonable thing to do for all He has done and will do for us (vs.1). He urges them not to be conformed to this transient world, but to be transformed (Greek word means to change into another form, with the emphasis on the inward change finding expression in character—Vine) by the renewing of the mind (the Bible being foundational here), in order to prove God's will in their lives (vs.2). See 1:28, where the word for "prove" is used twice there, two times demonstrating in the negative way of the mind that is not acceptable to God (disapproved and not acceptable in that particular verse). The last part of vs.2 here presents to us some good guidelines for discerning God's will. In the Greek, a single article comes before the words "good" and "well-pleasing" and "perfect," describing the will of God here. The one article here before the word "good" connects the three words together, meaning they all go together as one unit. "Good" refers to being "right" and would conform to God's word in the Bible; "well-pleasing" (same word in vs.1 for the sacrifice of ourselves to God's service and purposes) means doing what is pleasing to God above all else (including when multiple choices exist on an issue, making a decision about something); and "perfect" can also mean "complete;" thus taking no short cuts to its finished work. All these go together as helpful directives knowing and in carrying out God's will for our lives.

Paul then explains that one humble way that God's people express their love to one another is in the gifts given to the church for building each other up in the Lord. Here he lists seven in particular ones. He first says that the gifts are to display a humble character about them in their expression (vss.3, 10; see the commentary on Mt.11:25-30 for a practical definition of humble, seen in Jesus' words and expression about His character). Like the human body, we are members of one another in Christ Jesus, with differing gifts (vss.4-6), as one of the Apostle Paul's gifts was apostleship—vs.3; 1:5; 2 Tim.1:11). The gifts are to be expressed in the complementary way of the faith of the one who possesses the gift (vs.6, that is, not to go beyond what God has given and that which faith receives; see one example in 1 Cor.14:31-33). Prophecy is primarily a forth-telling of the word of God. This is the prime use in the church (see 1 Cor.14:3). It can be a fore-telling, but whatever is said must come true (Dt.18:22; Jn.17:17). In teaching, one must teach the word of God (in its context, a primary guideline), because teachers will be held more accountable to God (James 3:1). In ministry, we are all (in the body of Christ) ministers, in some way and form, yet, some will be designated with positions to carry out church functions (elders, deacons, etc.; see 1 Tim.3:8-13). Exhorting is an encouragement gift, obviously with broad applications, both individually and collectively to the Church; it also contains the use of warnings, admonishment and advisement. Sharing or giving here is listed as a gift with the other gifts. The gift here is qualified by saying to do so in "simplicity" (the primary thought here; see 2

Cor.9:7 for the main gist of the meaning here; "hidden motives" (more on the negative side) would also be included here to avoid to keep things "simplistic." One who leads (literally, takes the lead) is used with a father over his household (1 Tim.3:4, 5, 12) and elders of the church (1 Tim.5:17; 3:4, 5). In the broader use of the word, it could be someone leading a project or function in the church; the word is qualified by doing so "diligently," indicating enthusiasm, and good value included in the function taking place. The gift of mercy is a wonderful expression of God's love to those in need. The word "compassion" in vs.1 is the feeling of distress through the ills of others (Vine). Mercy is the act of God's love brought forward to meet or help meet the one in need. According to Jesus' promise, the merciful can also look forward to receiving God's mercy (Mt.5:7; James 5:11; Rom.11:32). The merciful are to express their acts of kindness cheerfully (vs.8; that joyousness that is prompt to do anything (Vine); our English word "hilarious" comes from this Greek word); for God loves a cheerful giver (2 Cor.9:7).

The Apostle Paul then follows these seven gifts of the Spirit with a listed presentation of "God's love in action" in the body of Christ (note Paul's description of "love's character" in 1 Cor.13:4-8). Love's display is not hypocritical (the Greek word here, pretending to be something else—Mk.7:6). Loves expression is genuine. Love detests what is evil and clings to the good (Greek word is "glue," a manufactures glue for making products; see the same word in God's word for marriage—Mt.19:5, for cleave in that verse). God's love contains two other kinds of love here next—brotherly love and an affectionate family love (parents for children and visa versa, quite appropriate for God's Family love ingredients, vs.10;

KJ's translation brings these out well). Love shows preference for one another in honor (respect, care and regard for someone; see Phil.2:3, 4); the Greek word "preference" means "taking the lead" in doing so. (vs.10). Love also includes "diligence" (see vs.8), and being "fervent in spirit" (earnest, devoted) in serving the Lord (vs.11). Love rejoices in hope (5:5; 8:24, 25; 15:4), endures in God's love and strength when experiencing trials and tribulations (5:3-5; 8:33-39; 1 Cor.10:13; Jn.16:33) and does not stop praying in trusting God (vs.12; see Act 1:14; 2:42; Col.4:2). Love in God's family shares with one another to help meet needs of one another (example, Acts 4:32-37), while also pursuing hospitality, another love of God's love here, (literally, loving strangers, the Greek word here for hospitality; for Paul, love, gifts and hospitality go together, as this worked well in their primarily small settings of the early church—vs.13; 1 Tim.5:10). God's love turns the tide and blesses those persecuting them (vs.14; see vss.17-21; Mt.5:10-16). In the full dimensions of the Family of God's love (see vs.10 and 8:31-39), they weep with one another and rejoice with one another (vs.15). Also, with humble attitudes toward one another, God's Family learns to think the same toward one another (vss.16, 1-6; 15:5), not being wise in their own eyes (vs.16; 11:25; Prov.3:5-8; see Book 3 of <u>The Family Bible Studies Series</u> titled <u>Growing In God's Wisdom</u> for a very helpful word study on the "ingredients" of God's wisdom and praying for them). The last five verses of chapter twelve all go together, emphasizing the importance of consistency in expressing God's love to others, giving back love and good, even when wrong and something bad or evil comes our way. Note the double blessing that comes in doing so. Instead of returning evil for evil, the verse says to (literally) take thought for "good things" before all men (vs.17) and, as much as possible, be at peace (literally, seeking peace) with <u>all</u> men (vss.17, 18). God's <u>double</u> blessing comes through the next two Scripture verses—letting <u>God</u> be the Avenger, He will repay (blessing number one; Dt.32:35); and, when one responds with God's love to someone who would look to harm or do wrong to them, God says that He will reward those who do so (vss.14, 17-20; read the full verses of Prov.25:21, 22; see also Ex.23:4, 5; blessing number two). Since believers are now more that conquerors in Jesus Christ (8:31-39), the believer conquers the evil by doing the good (vs.21).

Rom.13:1-14—Included in Paul's love discourse here is the appropriateness of submitting to God's governing authorities. Why would this be added in his "love" passage? Verses 8-10 gives us our answer—love fulfills the law. Love is a guide with what is good (vs.3), as sure as wrongdoing brings punishment (vss.3, 4; see also 1 Jn.4:16-21). Those in government authority are in their positions as public servants on God's behalf to carry out His righteousness to the people they serve, constantly attending these responsibilities (vss.4-6). In the Greek, the word authority (vss.1-3) means "the right to act." So God raises up positions and people to carry out His regulations and righteousness (the Bible; so, the authority to carry it out). But how are the authorities that exist established by God (vs.1)? Keep in mind what was previously mentioned here and note "God's government" from the beginning of time through history—the regulations and management responsibilities given to Adam and Eve in the Garden of Eden (Gen.1:27,28; 2:8, 9, 15-24; Gen.9:1-7); then, Cain, after committing murder, left God's presence and went out and established his own city (Gen.4:16-24; see Book 1 of <u>The Family Bible Studies Series</u>, <u>The Family of God—Foundation</u>, for further commentary on Genesis, chapters 1-4); then, note the Tower of Babel (Gen.11:1-9), not only the attempt to establish the government of man upon the earth (note the fear and rebellion against God's command—11:4; 1:28; 9:1), but possibly (and probably) "world government" pursuit (at least for that time in which they were living). And what has God done since that time, when men tried to establish their "world government" (empires) apart from God and His righteousness over the earth? God "scattered" them again (Gen.11:9) and brought about His "righteous indignation" and destroyed them and they perished from the earth (for more understanding here see Job 36:1-12). And so will be in the final battle of Armageddon (Rev.16-19), when the Lord Jesus returns to earth to rule and reign, whose government will increase and never end, for the government will be on His shoulders (Is.9:6, 7; Lk.1:26-33; Mt.22:41-44; 1 Cor.15:25).

Thus, one pays their due taxes to the government (vss.6, 7; Mt.22:15-22). Paul says that it is best to not owe anyone anything, but to love one another, which fulfills the law (vss.8-10); and the believer does this by allowing the Righteous King Jesus to rule and reign in their life, and "putting on God's righteousness," by His "law of faith" (vss.11-14; 3:21-28; 10:4) through Jesus Christ.

Rom.14:1-23—Paul continues on his journey of believers expressing God's love to one another in the Family of God here in chapter 14. With Jew and Gentiles now coming together as one in the Church of Jesus Christ and all being members of one another (3:29; 12:4,5), issues of food, honored days, practices and matters of conscience do arise as important concerns to be worked out. Paul concludes that it is up to each one's own convictions to decide on matters of personal practices (vs.22) and one must respect the differences of others and not be a stumbling block (offense) to them (vss.13-20). The "practices" of righteousness, peace and joy in the Holy Spirit are the most important things to observe (vss.16, 17; 12:10, 18). On strong matters of conviction, one must not go against their own convincing until affirmed of a better way, also (vss.22, 23). Collectively, each one must pursue the things that make for peace in looking to build one another up in the Lord (vss.17-19; 12:9, 10, 13).

Rom.15:1-13—Paul now closes his discussion on love with his plea to love one another (vss.1-37) and call to unity (one mind, one accord and glorifying God with one voice –vss.5-13). His encouragement to them is that they would find continual instruction through endurance and comfort in the Scriptures, and through them the God of hope would fill them with joy and peace, and to abound with hope by the power of the Holy Spirit (vss.4, 13).

Rom.15:14-33—Paul reminds them that he has written to them by the grace given to him as an apostle to the Gentiles (vss.15-17; 1:5), though he is convinced that they are filled with goodness and knowledge, enabling them to admonish one another (training by word implied here through the Scriptures—see vs.4, whether by encouragement or by necessary reproof—Vine). He provides being a good example to them, not speaking anything except what God has accomplished through him (not putting himself above or below what God has done in his life and through his life), by the power of miraculous signs of the Holy Spirit (vss.18,19). He preached from Jerusalem to Illyricum (east of Italy across the Adriatic Sea) and always looked proclaim the Gospel where Jesus had not yet been preached (vss.19-21).

He urged them to pray for him, that he would safely come to them. After gathering a collection from the Gentiles, he would deliver the gift to the Jerusalem saints, and pray that he would be delivered from those opposing him in Jerusalem, and then come and find refreshment with the saints in Rome. After his visit, he hoped to move on to new territory as far as Spain and hoped the saints in Rome would help him along his way and with his necessary expenses (vss.22-23; 1:8-15).

Rom.16:1-27—As Paul writes his conclusion of his letter to Rome, he lists 27 names (in my count) in his letter (8 woman appear to be addressed also here) for people to greet. Not having visited Rome yet, how did he know so many people there to greet? In 49 AD, the Roman Emperor Claudius expelled all the Jews from Rome. That is how Paul met Prisca and Aquila (Acts 18:1, 2). Now it appears they must have later returned (vs.3), probably along with others who did the same. Paul travelled throughout Macedonia and Greece, so he met some of them there (vs.3; Acts 18:2). He may have heard of others there and was getting relations recognized there in Rome for his visit. Phoebe (names means "radiant"—Unger) who he met from nearby Cenchrea (close to Corinth), may have been the one (possibly) to deliver Paul's letter to Rome, going by the first two verses (the word for "helper" in vs.2 is a "protectress," in Athens the title of a citizen who had the responsibility of seeing to the welfare of residents—Vine). Paul gives her a great recommendation, having helped him as well (vs.2). The "personableness" of the Apostle Paul here is a great tribute to his ability to meet and develop relationships with others. Prisca and Aquila also risked their lives for him and the church at large (vs.4). The "apostles" in vs.7 is the broader use of the term there. The "first convert" in vs.5 appears to mean Paul's first convert in the western province of Asia Minor (western Turkey today). "Kinsmen" in vs.7 refer to Jewish Christians. A few of the names here (according to some church traditions) may have been some of the "70 disciples" chosen by Jesus in His ministry (Lk.10). Rufus (vs.13) and his mother helped minister to and with the Apostle Paul. Philologus in vs.15 means "fond of talk" and may have been one of the "70 disciples" also (Unger).

Paul exhorts them to be aware and avoid those causing dissensions and stumbling blocks in the church, but stay to the teaching of God's word, the Bible, and be wise of the good and innocent of evil (vss.17-20; 12:9; 14:13). He sends the greeting of his fellow-workers in the ministry and closes his letter with the similar testimony he gave at the very beginning of his letter (vss.25-27; 1:1-5): The Gospel understanding was a mystery kept secret (or silent) for many ages past, but now made known by the written, prophetic Bible passages and manifested to all the nations by the commandment of God sending out His witnesses (vs.26; 1:5; Acts 1:8), to the obedience of faith in offering His free gift of salvation, of coming to personally know His Son, the Messiah, Jesus Christ (vs.27; 3:21-30; 6:23; 10:8-13; Acts 3:19-21; see the Prayer in the back of the book).

1 Corinthians

Paul is writing to the Corinthians from Ephesus (western Asia Minor, western Turkey today—16:8) on his third missionary journey. He is reminding them that he plans to visit them soon and to take the collection of their gift and the other churches who donate to the saints in Jerusalem (16:1-8). In this book of First Corinthians, Paul writes to them and addresses seven particular problems that they were facing in their individual church setting. These topics plus the collection of their gift to the saints in Jerusalem take up the full address of his letter to them. He maintains his faith, hope and love themes, but works hope and love in more toward the end of his letter, with hope coming in his resurrection topic of chapter fifteen.

1 Cor.1:1-9—See the introduction to Romans 1:1-7 as quite a few similarities occur with his beginning here to the Corinthians. Hard to prove in vs.1 who Sosthenes is, as many doubt the same person in Acts 18:17 (unless he was converted and came over from Corinth and was helping Paul in some way. It was a popular name of that time –Unger). Paul acknowledged their testimony of coming to know Christ Jesus by the giftedness given to them—in speech (speaking gifts—see 1 Pet. 4:10, 11) and all knowledge

(2 Cor.8:7). Paul encourages them that God will confirm them blameless, eagerly awaiting the revelation of the day of the Lord Jesus, having been called into fellowship with God's Son, the Lord Jesus Christ (vss.4-9; 1 Jn. 1:1-3; the Greek word "confirm" means to make firm, secure, stable, thus, establish, in their growing in the Lord (Vine); note the emphasis here that this is <u>God's work</u> in the believer, vs.8).

1 Cor.1:10-31—Paul begins by addressing the first problem in his letter (of seven he writes to them about) and continues this discussion to the end of chapter four in 1 Corinthians. It is about "divisions" within their church setting (vs.10). The Greek word means "to split." Some were elevating and following after their "gifted instructors" they had there—Paul, Apollos, Cephas (understood as Peter—John 1:42—or one who had brought his teachings to the fellowship there) and "of Christ" (understood in the next verse, with a past meaning, "has Christ been divided?" or a present meaning (to the Greek perfect tense) "Is Christ divided?"). These were bringing about quarrels (strife, contentions) in their fellowship (vs.11). Paul goes on to declare, as far as he is concerned, his message is not to point to himself, but to Jesus, and the cross He died on for the sins of mankind (vss.17, 18, 23), a hard message to "glamorize" or present with "clever speech," for sure (vss.17-19; 2:1-5). In fact, the Gospel is God's wisdom to the world that <u>He did it</u>—something man could not do—save mankind from their sins and the consequence of them—death. It is the "power of God "and "wisdom of God" displayed, of which both of those come to the one believing in Jesus (vss.18-15, 30, 31; Rom.6:22, 23). This nullifies the "wisdom" of the world's attempt to do this (vss.19-21,

25, 28). Thus, those who do not rely on their "own wisdom" (Prov. 3:5-8) or the "wisdom of the world" (see the "deceits" of the evil one, in the cunning attempt speaking to Jesus in Mt. 4:1-11) are more open to "God's wisdom" and solution to what they cannot do or achieve on their own (the Gospel). Low status (or even high status) in this world and coming into God's family is all worth it, coming to know God's wisdom and righteousness and sanctification and redemption, through and the Gospel message in Christ Jesus the Lord, resulting in the believer's boast in Him (vss.26-31, 18, 24; 3:21-23).

1 Cor.2:1-16—Paul elaborates more here on the verses in 1:17-19. His proclamation of the Gospel message to the Corinthians was not in "superiority of speech" presented to them (vs.1; see the commentary on 1:17-19). In much weakness (of the flesh) and trembling, he presented the Gospel message to them (vs.3) and so, as he proclaimed (had to trust God for) the Gospel in the "power of God" (vs.4), so he wanted their faith to rest in the same (vs.5). Paul declared that the Gospel is a "mystery" of God's wisdom (Rom.16:25, 26; 11:33-36) that had been previously hidden from man (but now is declared throughout the world—Rom.10:16-18; Col.1:6, 23), which the "world" rulers did not or could not understand (vss.6-9; Col.2:15). Only the Spirit of God can make known the thoughts of God, and He does so to "spiritual" people (i.e., those who have the Spirit of God in them). He explains spiritual things (truths) to spiritual people (vss.13-15; note, part of His work is to reveal the things freely given to us by God, vs.12; example, the Gospel, Rom.6:23; gifts of the Spirit, 12:7-11; etc.). The "spiritual" man (or woman) is able to discern

all things then with God's help, while he (or she) is not judged by no man (vs.15; Rom.8:1, 2); for through the Holy Spirit, God now gives the believer the mind of Christ Jesus (vs.16; Jn.14:25, 26; 15:15, 26; 16:13-15).

1 Cor.3:1-23—Paul here in chapter three restates why he is addressing this problem to the Corinthians—jealousy and strife (vs.3; note jealousy wants something somebody else has for oneself, while strife (1:11) is contentiousness, and can involve enmity, which can bring negative feelings that someone is trying to work against oneself or someone else; thus, these are on an opposite spectrum of negative emotions). Everyone involved has their part to play in God's growing process of the believer, but it is God who causes the growth to happen (vss.4-8). Believers are God's cultivating field (see Jn.15:1, 2, 16—see the commentary on John 15 for further explanation of those verses); and believers are God's temple building (vss. 8, 9, 16; 1 Pet.2:4-10; Eph.2:19-22). Paul laid the foundation of Christ Jesus in his ministry (vs.10; Rom.15:20) and others built upon it (vss.10, 11; examples, Apollos (vs.6) and Timothy—4:17; 1 Thess.3:2). Each one's quality of work will be tested and rewarded accordingly by the Lord to the saints (vss.12-15; 4:5; Mt.16:27; Eph.6:8; 2 Thess.1:6-10; Rev.22:12; see a guideline for this in Jesus' words found in Jn.3:16-21). Paul declares that the church is God's temple now (vs.16) and if anyone destroys it, they will be destroyed (vs.17; the Babylonians destroyed God's temple and they were destroyed; the Romans did it to the Jews in 70 AD and their kingdom was destroyed). So God will do the same to those who do it to His people today. With this in mind, the believer is to always trust God for His

protection (Ps.3:3; 1 Pet.1:3-5) and take care of and not defile (the Greek word here) His temple (Rom.12:1, 2; 1 Cor.6:17-20; 1 Thess.4:1-8). Paul's final exhortation in this chapter is to know God's wisdom through the Gospel (1:20, 23, 24, 30) and not to boast in man but in the Lord for what He does, and has done and (in faith) will do (vss.18-23; 1:29-31; 3:8, 21-23).

1 Cor.4:1-21—Here in chapter four Paul finishes his discourse on the address of the first problem in the Corinthian church (see previous commentary on 1 Cor.1:10-31). In the variety of giftedness, believers are to simply see each other as servants of Christ, and their leaders as stewards (managers of a household or estate) of the mysteries of God (vss.1,2; Rom.16:25-27; 11:25; 1 Cor.15:51-58). He reminds them not to pass judgment, as judgment is the work of the Lord (vss.3-5; Mt.7:1; Rom. 2:1-3). Paul says that as he and Apollos work hard to be faithful stewards of God, the Corinthians are to be careful not to go beyond God's word (1:19,31) and divide the group according to their instructors (vss.6-8; 3:8, 21-23). Live by God's word as their instructors teach them (vs.7). If they want to "elevate" him in some way, Paul then says to them to follow his example and imitate his life for the Lord (vss.6,17), though they should consider their own calling first and then the very descriptive list that Paul gives of his own life, in following his life style in serving the Lord (vss.9-13). He became a "father" to them through the Gospel, so he is exhorting his "children" accordingly to help them grow in the Lord by removing obstacles (vss.14, 15), which includes the proper discipline to those causing these divisions in their church, which he strongly

urges them to take care of so he won't have to when he visits them (vss.17-21; Mt.18:15-20).

1 Cor.5:1-13—The second problem that Paul speaks to the Corinthian church about is a particular case of incest in their church setting (vs.9, stated from a previous correspondence by Paul). God had made known in the Old Testament that this was strictly forbidden (Lev.18:6-8). So with God's standard, Paul said that he had already judged the person who did this, even though he was not there present at their church (vss.1-3). Unless the person would have a truly repentant heart, Paul said that he would deliver that person over to Satan which could reach the destruction of the flesh for that person (vss.5, 10), that their spirit may be saved (vs.5). Because of Christ's death and resurrection, believers should now celebrate Jesus dying for ours in sins, in new life of truth and sincerity (vss.6-8; 6:20; Rom.6). Keeping good company with those who do likewise is Paul's principle being taught here (vss.9-12; 15:33). Unless remorseful and repentant for such an act, Paul says to remove such one from their gathering (vs.13).

1 Cor.6:1-20—The third problem that Paul addresses in the church at Corinth is going to the courts in the world to solve cases of complaints of people against each other in the church. Paul declares to them that the church will judge the world and angels and so, should be competent to reconcile their own disagreements within the church. Church settings should be able to do so (see Rm.15:14). But to go to unbelievers shows they were already defeated (vss.6, 7). He admonished them to find a wise individual in the Lord to help solve their case, or simply admit the wrong doing from those who did so. Bad behavior will be obvious of those

who continue to practice such things and not inherit the kingdom of God (vss.9, 10). But believers are washed and sanctified by the Lord from past unrighteous deeds (vs.11; note the Trinity in this verse (vss.1-11; see Book 1 of <u>The Family Bible Studies Series, The Family of God—Foundation</u>, for more understanding of the character and functions of the Trinity).

Believers actually have great freedom in serving the Lord under His laws (vs.12; 7:22, 23; 9:19-23; Rom.3:21-31; 8:1, 2); yet, not all things we may do may be profitable (vs.12; 3:10-15; Rom.14:19). To achieve the Lord's goals in his calling (9:19-23), Paul would not allow himself to be mastered by anyone (or thing; the word "mastered" is from the word "authority" in the Greek, which means "the right to act;" he knew who his Masters is, vs.12). Our bodies have been made to be honorable to God (vss.13-15; we are His "representative figure" here on earth—Strong's Exhaustive Concordance, the Hebrew word for "image" in Gen.1:27 –<u>The Family of God—Foundation</u>, pg.7). Believers are "members of Christ" (vs.15; 12:12-27) and "one in spirit" with Him (vs.17). Body, mind, soul and spirit—we are His (vss.19, 20; 2:16) and His temple (vs.19: 3:16; Eph.2:19-22), and so, to glorify Him with all our being (vs.20).

1 Cor.7:1-40—Paul now discusses the topic of marriage in his letter to the Corinthians, and replies back to them regarding issues that they had previously written to him about and needing his counsel (vs.1). He replies back to them about various statuses regarding marriage (married, unmarried, virgin, widow, etc.) in giving guidance to them. The word "touch" in vs.1 means "to take hold of," referring one trying to "take hold of" (possess or call

one's own) outside of marriage and contains the prohibition of the benefits that go with marriage (vss.2-7; see 1 Thess.4:1-8 for further guidance and explanation written also by the Apostle Paul on this). Paul's recommendation throughout the chapter is for people unmarried to remain as he was (understood as unmarried), to be able to solely focus on serving the Lord (vss.8; 38-40). He realizes that each individual has their own gift in life (to be married or not—vss.7-10). The married should remain married (see Mk.10:2-9), but an unbelieving spouse, married to a believer, should not be prohibited to leave the believing spouse if the unbelieving spouse so chooses to leave. Paul says it is permissible for the sake of peace and the Gospel (vss.10-16; note, not advisable, just permissible, if needed so to be, remembering Jesus' words in Mk.10:2-9). Paul advocates them to remain in the position they are in (depending on their gifts, as previously stated) to be free to serve the Lord (vss.20, 26, 32, 40; 9:1), but whatever decision, not to become slaves of men (vss.17-24), since Christ Jesus has purchased them with His own blood (vss.23, 24; 1 Pet.1:17-19). He mentions this to virgins also, in determining their own gifts (vss.25-28; see Rev.14:4 for the word "virgin" used there for men, also). He bases his statements on the fact that our current world and its outward form is passing away, and so to be working for eternal rewards and undistracted devotion to the Lord (vss.25-35). The father helps determine the gifting of his daughter, also, as Paul advises his previous counsel in their situation, too (vss.36-38). Paul stresses at the end that marriage is a lifetime bond between the man and the woman (Mk.10:2-9), and if death occurs to one in marriage, he still gives them his advice to remain as one is then in life (with their gifting in mind again, as well—vss.7, 39, 40).

1 Cor.8:1-13—Chapters 8-10 are tied together in the Apostle Paul's writing. This fifth problem he addresses in his reply back to the Corinthians deals with things involving sacrifices to idols (vss.1, 4; 10:7, 28). He finishes writing about this as he started out writing about it (8:12, 13; 10:28, 29, 32, 33). We will see how the topics in between are connected with it.

Paul makes clear from the beginning here where he is coming from—his foundation is love, instead of simply pursuit of knowledge, and most important—love for God (vss.1-3). In this subject of discussion it is important to see that idols do not exist in reality (man's making a material image; see the prohibition in Dt. 5:8-10). Only God has existed eternally (vss.4-6; Gen.21:33; Dt.4:35, 39; Ps.90:2; Is.40:28; 43:10; 44:6; 1 Tim.1:17), our Creator and Lord. Paul states that food in and of itself does not bring us closer to God (vs.8; see what does in a similar passage of discussion in Rom.14:17, 18). But some people may still feel uncomfortable eating meat or food sacrificed to an idol (vs.7). So Paul states that if such a person be uncomfortable by eating such food, he says then do not eat it (vs.12) and cause a brother to stumble in one's freedom of it. Paul says he would not eat meat again if it is a stumbling block to another brother (vss.9-13).

1 Cor.9:1-27—To emphasize how the Apostle Paul sought not to be a stumbling block to the brethren 8:12,13) or to others in ministering the Gospel (vss.19-23), he demonstrates this by how he lives his life out in his service as an apostle to God. This connects chapters 8 and 9. He is a free man (vss.1, 19), but makes

himself as slave to all (vs.19), in order to save some (vss.22, 23). As the Corinthians were the "seal" (proof) of his apostleship in God's service (vss.1, 2), he states that with this comes privileges or rights to also carry this out (examples, food granted, taking a believing wife along in the ministry, not having to work, if one has that option—vss.3-4; see Mt.10:7-15; Lk.9:3-5; 10:2-11). But Paul makes clear that he did not make use of these rights and privileges (vss.12, 15), and is not writing his letter to change that (vs.15). He does this "voluntarily," as part of his responsibility to the Lord's calling and work (vs.17). Why? So he may present the Gospel "free of charge" to the people who hear him (vs.18). Why again? So there would be no hindrance in his presenting the Gospel (vss.12, 18; no "stumbling block," like 8:12, 13 to the brethren, as example), preaching the Gospel to mankind. He became a slave to all (vs.19), being all things to all people, so that he may save some (vss.20-23). To emphasize this further, Paul uses the discipline necessary for athletes to compete and win their goal in competition. He applied this to himself in his ministry with his goal to save people (vss.22, 23), and (in keeping with his context here), not being "disqualified" in his preaching and life in achieving his goal (vss.24-27; 10:31-33).

1 Cor.10:1-33—Paul finishes up his topic that he started in chapter eight and writes to his fellow Israelites (addressing them specifically as he did in Rom.9:1-11:10). He uses the "wilderness experience" of the Jews to point out current lessons to be learned (and not repeated) by them (vs.6, 11). Going through the wilderness under Moses' leadership, God provided "spiritual food," the manna, for them from heaven (Ex.16:4, 22-36). The

water that gave "spiritual drink" (provided by God) that came from a "spiritual Rock" which followed them, Paul declares was the preincarnate Christ Jesus (with the article in the Greek, and so, the Messiah (vss.1-4); see Ex.17:6 and Dt.32:4—the Rock and the declared character of God; also Is.26:4). Still, except for Caleb and Joshua, that generation perished in the wilderness until the next generation came about to go into the Promised Land to Israel (vs.5; Num.14:26-35; Neh.9:16-21). Paul admonishes them not to do four mistakes they made in the wilderness journey— do not be idolaters (vss.6, 7; Ex.32); do not commit fornication (vs.8; Num.25:1-9; 31:16); do not try or put the Lord to the test (vs.9; Num.21:4-9; Mt.4:7); and not to "grumble" (complain in a negative way or attitude), against God or man (vs.10; Num.16:41; 17:5, 10; 21:5). Paul's instruction is for them to always be alert not to fall upon these and any negative behaviors (vs.12; 15:33) and if ever tempted of these, to notice it for what it is, and not to fall into it, and pray to God to provide the way of escape (vs.13; 2 Pet.2:9; 3:17,18). Paul reiterates to them to flee idolatry (vs.14; 8:1, 4, 6) and not to share in it in any way (vss.15-22). Ever thing in the created earth is the Lord's (Ex.19:5, 6; Ps.24:1). One can eat meat without bothering one's conscience (from idolatrous sacrifices), since it is all the Lord's (see Gen.9:3; Mk.7:18, 19; Acts 10:15; 11:9). But if someone's conscience is weak and could or would stumble over this, Paul then says for their sake do not eat it (vss.28-30; back to chapter 8, vss.7, 9, 12, 13). So, while it is lawful to do so, this would not be profitable or edifying to the other who could or would stumble over this (vss.23, 24, 32, 33). All that we do should be for the glory of the Lord (vs.31;

Habakkuk 2:14; Mt.5:16) and doing beneficial things for others (vss.24, 32, 33).

1 Cor.11:1-34—The Apostle Paul now begins to write in the next four chapters about proper order in their church services (14:30). The proper order starts with the foundation of proper authority in God's design (vss.1-3; Eph.5:22-25; 1 Cor.3:23). This passage is understood by its conclusion in vs.16— this was a "custom" of those times, though the "principles" still apply for today. Note the equality in these verses, though different roles to be lived out (vss.8-12; see Gen.2:16, 17, 19, 20; 1:27-30; 2:18, 22-24; 1 Pet.3:1-7). Angels in vs.10 were present at God's creation (Job 38:4-7) and help deliver and carryout His word (Acts 7:38; Heb. 1:6, 7 from Ps.104:4) and purposes (see angles and their roles in the Book of Revelation).

Next, Paul addresses to them the proper understanding and respect to be carried out when celebrating the Lord's Supper (vss.17-34). The gathering appears to be much like a "potluck" arrangement, often like we have today (see Acts 2:46; 20:7, 11). One eating ahead of time in the gathering (even if hungry) or in a drunken appearance is disrespectful and could encounter judgment from God (vss. 21, 27-31; 2 Cor.5:10). The Lord's Supper is the "recalling" of His bodily death and shed blood for our sins (vss.23-26). The utmost respect is required because of this in the celebration (vss. 27, 28, 31, 33, 34).

1 Cor.12:1-31—Paul now gives instruction about spiritual gifts and understanding of the body of Christ. He first prefaces the subject by saying that to have or possess spiritual gifts one must have the Holy Spirit living in their life (vss.1-3, 7, 11). Next, he

emphasizes the work of the Trinity in their harmonious activities in the life of believers (vss.4-7, 11; see Book 1 of <u>The Family Bible Studies Series</u>, <u>The Family of God—Foundation</u>, for more understanding about the Trinity and their character, functions and harmonious workings together). There are different gifts given by God, and different ministries and operations (vss. 4-7). Paul here lists nine different gifts that God distributes to the church. The first two are words of wisdom and knowledge (vs.8). Wisdom sees the bigger picture of things while knowledge fills in the specific parts. We see this worked out in God's creation stated in Prov. 8:22-31; 3:19, 20; see these other related passages that help bring this out—Prov.8:10-12; 15:2,7; 22:17-21; 24:3-6; Eccl.7:11,12; 12:9-11; also, see Book 3 of <u>The Family Bible Studies Series, Growing In God's Wisdom</u>, for more in-depth discovery of this and how to pray for God's "ingredients" of wisdom. Faith is being able to "see" beyond the ordinary" (and even just visible things) and trust God to accomplish things to be done (vs.9; see 13:2; 2 Cor.4:13). Gifts of healings are plural here and similar to faith, has many distributions and effectual outcomes. Miracles, plural here also, line up with the two previous but go to other circumstances in life with or beyond the gifts of healing (vs.10; Mt.8:23-27; Acts 5:17-22; 12:4-11; 16:25-34). For prophecy, see the commentary on Rm.12:1-21 and 1 Cor.13:2, 8-10. Discerning of spirits determines the cutting edge between good and evil disguises (spirits; plural here once again; 2 Cor.11:1-15; Heb.5:13, 14; 1 Kg.3:16-28). The gift of tongues (languages—see 13:1) is plural and can be seen in its wide distribution at Pentecost (Acts 2:1-21; a thought that has occurred to me with the passage of Pentecost is wondering if Pentecost was, in part, a restoration of the tower of Babel, where instead of confusion then, now God demonstrates His power and works to reach anyone, individual or groups and the nations, with the Gospel; they also have a personal spiritual edification factor for the one with the gift—1 Cor.14:1-4. Interpretation of tongues is the explanation given after the language of the speech (tongue) is given (vs.10; 14:5). The Holy Spirit is the Distributor of the gifts (vs.11). Paul then compares the members of the Body of Christ to be in similarity to the parts jointed together of the human body, for believers are all baptized with the Holy Spirit (vs.13; Mk.1:8—note, Jesus does the baptizing). The key here is the "oneness" in the body of Christ, with no gifting having an elevation (see 1:10-13; 1 Cor.12:25-27) or a lower dimension or status than another (vss.12-14, 18-20, 25-27); and all have their place, just as God has placed each believer in the Body of Christ (vss.11, 18, 24, 28-31). Those who do not appear "visibly or outwardly noticeable," Paul says that God gives them more abundant honor, than those who do already have it and receive its benefits (vss.22-25), so no division occurs (1:10-13; 11:19), but each member should have the same care for one another (vss.25-27; 10:24).

1 Cor.13:1-13—Here is where Paul enters in his theme of love to the Corinthians (and, of course, for us too; see the commentary on the introduction to Paul's letter to the Romans). Paul touched on this briefly in 8:1-3, but now gives a beautiful description of "love's character" here in vss.4-8. The manifestation by God of the gifts of the Spirit are a powerful demonstration of God's might and wisdom right in the midst of the people hearing and/or seeing

it (Mt.4:23,24; Mk.13:11; Rom.15:18,19; 1 Pet.4:10,11). But without love, Paul says it profits him nothing (vs.3; 10:23, 24). Love is longsuffering (the Greek word here) and kind (fit for kindly use; vs.4). It is not jealous (see commentary on 3:3) and does not brag or "elevate" itself (vs.4; see commentary on the character of Jesus in Mt.11:25-30). Love does not act dishonorably toward others (vs.5; see Rm.12:10; Phil.2:3, 4) or seek things just for its own good (vs.5; 10:24, 31-33). Love is not provoked (i.e., to wrath; see Rm.1:18; 2:1-8; 12:17-21) and does not take account of evil done to it (vs.5; 2 Cor. 5:18, 19; Eph.4: 29-32). Love does not rejoice in unrighteousness, but rejoices with the truth (vs.6; Jn.8:31, 32; 1 Jn.4:6; 3 Jn.3, 4). Love "covers" all things (i.e. preserves by covering, keeps off something that threatens, thus, protects—Vine; vs.7; the verb is used with the meaning of "endurance" in 9:12); it believes all things (of the truth—vs.6); hopes all things (i.e., things related to our Christian hope, vs.7; compare Prov.13:12; Rm.5:3-5; 8:18-25); endures (in) all things (vs.7; see the word in Rm.12:12; Heb.12:2, 7; James 1:12; 5:11; Rev.1:9; 1Cor.10:13); love never fails (or comes to an end, vs.8; Ex.34:5-7; Ps.25:4-10; Ps.136; 1 Jn.4:7-21; Jn.3:16, 17). Paul then goes on to say that one day the gifts will cease (when the Perfect One, the Lord, returns—vs.10), and, thus, we are to go on to maturity, as one day we will fully know as we are fully known (vss.11,12). Paul makes the declaration that in his three great topics that he chooses to write his epistles on—faith, hope and love—the greatest of these is love (vs.13; Mk.12:28-31; Jn.3:16, 17; 1 Jn.4:10, 19).

1 Cor.14:1-40—With the Corinthian church being zealous for spiritual gifts (vs.12), Paul saw the necessity to bring order and guidelines for their practice of them in their church gatherings (vs.40). He emphasizes here the gift of prophecy and gift of tongues (other languages) as his main topic of discussion for their instruction. With the gift of tongues being primarily spoken to God (vs.2), in their church gatherings Paul wants them to desire the gift of prophecy so the church may be edified (built up in the Lord, vss.3-5, 12). Tongues (other language spoken) would need to be interpreted to accomplish the same result (vss.5-19). Paul quotes an interesting passage from Is.28:9-13 (vs.11, specifically, here) to distinguish more clearly how these two gifts are designed to work and serve those who hear them. In vss.10 and 13 of Isaiah, these state (like a child muttering statements in trying to speak) how Israel did not understand (actually, receive) Isaiah's message, and so, it sounded like a "foreign language" to them. Paul says that is how the gift of tongues comes out initially (good comparison) and so reaches out to unbelievers (compare Pentecost), unless understood in the language (like Pentecost) or interpreted (stories have been told on the missionary field how this gift has been used to share the Gospel in people's native language). Prophecy (in the church) is for believers, who hear out the message, distinguish it (vs.29), and can receive the benefits from the gift (vss.3, 5, 12, 26, 31). The additional benefit of prophecy is that unbelievers and those not so acquainted with spiritual gifts can gain the advantage for them also, as "secrets" of their hearts can be declared, acknowledging God's presence in their midst (vss.24, 25). Paul goes on to give a recommended order for both gifts being carried

out in their church services (vss.26-33, basically, a one by one and one at a time order, in the Greek wording, with prophets being careful to control and submit to other prophet's in turn with their own spirit—vs.32). Women speaking in the church (compare 11:5) is clear to understand by the wording used here (wanting to "learn" something or "questioning" something, vs.35), either of which it says to ask their husbands or if single, a church leader about what they seek (vs.35). The reference to "the law" in vs.34, I believe is Paul's reference to being "under authority," stated back in 1:8-10, which draws from Gen. 3:16, of the husband "ruling" over his wife, which the Hebrew word explains having a "governing authority over " (i.e., as a governor carrying out responsibilities, as Adam was to do—Gen.2:8, 9, 15-24; 1:26-30; Strong's Exhaustive Concordance of the Bible).

1 Cor.15:1-58—Paul now addresses the seventh issue of concern with the Corinthian church and that is about the resurrection of Jesus. Paul shares the Gospel with them in these early verses, as what was first and most important when he came to visit them (vs.3). He encourages them to hold fast to the Gospel message, unless they did not believe it when he first presented it to them (to the ones where this applies; vs.2), in which case, now is the time to believe the Gospel of Jesus Christ (vss.3, 4; 2 Cor.6:1, 2). Paul gives us quite a number of people and groups who saw Jesus after His resurrection from the dead, including himself—one untimely born (compared to the original twelve Apostles, unworthy and not fit to be called on a Apostle; yet he received the Gospel, and God's transformation and grace proved very effective in his service and calling to the Lord, vss.8-11). Cephas is Peter (see 1:12; Jn.21) in

vs.5; the twelve refer to Jesus' appearance to them in John 20:19-31 (vs.5). James in vs.7 is taken to be Jesus' brother, who succeeded the Apostle James after his martyrdom (Acts 12:2, 17). Then, to "all the Apostles," is taken to refer to Jesus' visit with them before his ascension (Lk.24:36-53).

Paul now contends with some of those who were saying that there is no resurrection (vs.12). He goes on to declare a number of "false claims" that would have to exist, if Jesus had not risen from the dead—him and others proclaiming this would then be "false witnesses," which would put them in a class to be quite pitied among men," if it was not true (vss.12-19). But the fact is that He has been raised from the dead (vss.3-8; according to the Scriptures in vs.4 refers back to Mt.16:21); and so, all believers will follow likewise (vss.20-24), necessarily so, because He will abolish all rule, authority and power contrary to God, and His Word (Rev.19:11-21), and deliver the kingdom to God the Father (vs.24). He reigns until this is completed (vss.26-28; Ps.2; Ps.110; Mt.22:41-46; Heb.1:1-3) and then will begin His Millennial reign on earth (Rev.20:1-6; Ezk.40-48; Is.9:6, 7).

Paul goes back to his defense of the resurrection in verses 29-34. "The baptism of the dead" is a topic not covered in the Bible. Paul simply brings it up because his readers would be familiar with it, emphasizing his point about the resurrection, that others believed also in a resurrection of the dead (vs.29). His sacrifices and sufferings in his ministry for the Lord also declared validity of Jesus' resurrection, suffering in some ways as Jesus did (vss.30-32, 20-24; 2 Tim.3:12). So he urges them to keep "good company" and be clear minded, according to the truth and God's word (vss.33,

34). When asked about the resurrected body and its formation, Paul delineates some very nice examples in life of different kinds of flesh and physical body make-ups (fish, stars, seeds of grain, mankind –vss.36-41, God giving them just what He wanted them to have—vs.38). Note Paul's description of the believers resurrected body—raised imperishable, in glory, in power and a spiritual body (vss.42-49), based on Jesus' resurrection and His giving of eternal life to the believer (vss.44-49; Jn.1:12,13; 3:16; Phil.3:20, 21; 1 Jn.3:1,2). This will take place for the church at the Rapture of the Church to heaven (vss.50-58; 1 Thess.4:13-18; 2 Cor.4:14; Jn.5:28); this is Paul's hope passage in the Corinthian letter. The last trumpet refers to the last call to the church before the Great Tribulation begins. Similar to Israel, the last trumpet signified their last call to leave where they were staying in the wilderness and move on to their next destination (see Num.10). Jesus has given us this victory over death and promise to be with Him in heaven forever (vs.54-57; Jn.14:1, 2; Phil.3:20, 21; Col.3:1-4; 1 Thess.4:17, 18). Paul exhorts them to be "immovable" with these truths and continue abounding in God's work, which is not in vain serving the Lord (vs.58).

1 Cor.16:1-24—Paul closes his letter to the Corinthians by directing them to take a collection for the needy in the church of Jerusalem, as he had directed the churches of Galatia to do, so he may collect it when he comes to visit them (vss.1-14). He hoped to stay with them awhile when he comes and not just pass through Corinth, as he wrote this from Ephesus (vss.5-9). In a nice, gentle word, Paul encourages them to receive Timothy, his fellow-worker in the Lord, so that he has no fear when he comes

to them (vss.10, 11). Paul wanted Apollos to come to them again (Acts 19:1), but said he would come when he had an opportunity, but not at the time of Paul's writing this letter (vs.12). Paul exhorts them to be watchful (Mt.24:42), stand firm in the faith (16:1), "act like men" (1x in the New Testament) and be strong (in the Lord; Eph.6:10; 3:16), and do all things in love (vss.13, 14). He acknowledges the three men coming to him with needed information from Corinth and says to the Corinthian church to acknowledge such men as these (vss.15-18). Paul sends them the greeting from Prisca and Aquila from their home, as they have been encouragement and helpful to Paul and Apollos in the past, as well (Acts 18:2, 24-26). Most attest that Paul dictated his letters (Rm.16:22), but also wrote at least some "greetings" himself (vs.21; Gal.6:11). The final signoff is thought to have been used in early communion services. Maranatha first meant "The Lord has come; then, "O Lord, come" (Vine). John may have had this in mind finishing The Book of Revelation (22:20), though he did not use this word, but the straight Greek words for this greeting to the Lord, especially possible since the Lord said three times in Rev.22 "I am coming quickly" (22:7, 12, 20). Paul sends them his love and closes his letter as he began it, with God's grace to be with them (vss.22-24; 1:3-9).

2 Corinthians

Like Paul's letter in First Corinthians, he once again continues to address certain problems and previous issues in the Corinthian church. His theme in second Corinthians is God, the Father of mercies and the God of all comfort (1:3). We see this carried out in various ways and specifically throughout the letter (2:7; 7:2-13; 13:11). The book of Second Corinthians comes together in selected topics of concern written by the Apostle Paul—his introduction and escaping perils of death to come to see them (chapter one); forgiveness in the church (2:1-11; 7:2-16); Paul explaining his ministry (2:12-7:1); principles in giving in the church (chapters 8 and 9); Paul's defense of his ministry (chapters 10-12); his closing remarks and exhortations (chapter 13).

2 Cor.1:1-7—For Paul's greeting in vss.1, 2, see Rom.1:1-7. Paul explains how God's comfort spreads to many, in varieties of life's sufferings and afflictions. Compassion is a feeling of distress through the ills of others (Vine) and comfort is the same word for the Holy Spirit (Jn.14:16, 26; 15:26; 16:7-14, the capability or adaptability for giving aid—Vine). Sharing in the sufferings of Christ, we share in God's comfort (vs.5; see 12:10). All this enables one to then share God's comfort with others (vss.4, 7).

2 Cor.1:8-11—Coming from Ephesus (1 Cor.16:8) and in Macedonia writing this letter (1 Cor.16:5; 2 Cor.7:5), Paul writes that he escaped perils of death in coming to the Corinthians (1 Cor.15:32; 2 Cor.1:8-10), even to the point of despairing life itself (vs.9). But Vine catches very well how the Apostle's faith pulled him through this (these) time(s) and the truth that did it in vs.9. Translations say that they had the "sentence of death" within themselves. The word "sentence" occurs in this form only once in the New Testament and means "a judicial sentence," thus an official decision (BAGD). The very similar word form of this word means "answer," and appears four times in the New Testament writings (Jn.1:22; 19:9; Acts 2:47; 20:26). So, it is like one who awaited an official pronouncement on a crime or an offense. Paul, then, was saying they had an official (answer) of death within themselves and begins the verse with a strong adversative conjunction (alla, in the Greek, but, in English), contrasting it with the strong preceding statement in vs.8 he made of despairing even life itself (for Greek studiers, I believe it is a descriptive genitive here). Paul said in the perfect tense here (past completion with current affects) that they already for sometime had this (the—the article is in the Greek before the word "answer" is here) "answer of (about) death" within them (vs.9). The answer is given in the rest of vs.9—God, the one raising the dead, and that was his answer. So, as Vine brings out here, Paul already had the "answer of God" to his appeal, and this gave the Apostle strong confidence, even in the face of death, with the Lord inside him; the one who raises the dead, so they wouldn't rely on themselves, but (same strong adversative conjunction here) on God, who raises the dead, based on the resurrection of Jesus

Christ (see 2 Cor.4:14). And this they set their hope on (vs.10) and gave thanks for the many who pray for them, believing this very same thing as they do (vs.11).

2 Cor.1:1-24—Paul is proud about the testimony of him and his assistants and how they presented themselves to the Corinthians—in holiness and (literally) moral purity, all by the grace of God (vss.12, 13); and because of this, the Corinthians should be proud of Paul, as Paul is of them (vs.14).

Paul wanted to originally come to them twice, but had to change this and flee to protect his own life (vss.15-17; Acts 20:3); he assures them that he was doing the right thing, because God is faithful, and he bases his ministry (and life) on the promises of God (God's word—vss.18-20). Paul affirms them that God anointed him and his team (vs.19) for this ministry, and establishes the believers in Christ (meaning, to make firm and secure, i.e., build them up in God's security). God has initiated this by giving the believer the "seal of the Holy Spirit" (the Divine Pledge of belonging to God and securely His to the "day of our Lord Jesus"—vss.21, 22, 14; 4: 14). Paul wanted them to deal with their problems (First Corinthians) before he came, and reminded them that this life for the believer is a journey of faith (4:18; 5:7), and that is how they stand (vss.23, 24).

2 Cor.2:1-11—In dealing with an incident of forgiveness in the church, once the wrong-doing has been made known to the church (vss.1-6; Mt.18:15-20) and agreement has been made about the offense (Mt.18:15, 19), the church should extend forgiveness and comfort to the one(s) involved, with reaffirming

love (vss.7-11), and not allow the devil to have an advantage in all the circumstance involved (vss.7-11).

2 Cor.2:17-17—Paul now begins to explain to the Corinthians various aspects of his ministry and with his assistants. After leaving Ephasus, Paul stopped in Troas for a ministering of the Gospel to the people there (far northwest section of modern day Turkey). He waited there also for Titus to bring information back to Paul on the First Corinthian letter written from Ephesus. Not finding him, Paul went over to Macedonia (northern Greece today) and was greeted there in sharing the Gospel with conflicts and fears; but Titus came and brought great comfort to Paul and a good report on how the Corinthians had favorably dealt with Paul's letter to them in First Corinthians, with repentance and changed character, resulting in joy to Titus and confidence of Paul in them for such a good response by the Corinthians (2:12, 13; 7:2-16). Thus, Paul was thankful that the "fragrance of Christ" was spreading "in every place" (vs.14), to save unbelievers, and growing in Christ's life for the believers, with his own contribution, by the grace of God, going forth in "moral purity" (same word as in 1:12; vs.17), speaking for Christ in the sight of God (vss.14-17).

2 Cor.3:1-18—Here in chapter three, Paul expands some previous points he wants to make clear to the Corinthians. The "personableness" of his ministry is very clear to them, reaching their "hearts" with the Gospel and their conversions, along with the presence of the Holy Spirit in the lives of the believers (vss.1-3; 4:6). All this testimony gave Paul confidence in them for what had taken place (vs.4; 7:16). Paul affirms to them again that only God could make them adequate for this ministry, evidenced by

the presence of the Holy Spirit working though them (vss.5, 6, 17, 18). Paul then uses the example of the glory of God shining on the face of Moses (Ex. 34:34, 35). The glory that shined on Moses' face after meeting with God in the tabernacle of the wilderness then for Israel, faded from Moses; but for the believer now, it is an ongoing transformation, being changed from "glory to glory" into the image of God, believing and trusting God through the presence of the Holy Spirit within the believer (vss.7-11, 18). Note the Deity of the Holy Spirit here (vss.17, 18; see also Heb.9:14, which includes the Trinity in that verse). Similar in analogy to the unbeliever, a "veil" remains over them until one comes to know Jesus and the Holy Spirit, giving freedom and truth (4:2; Jn.14:17), comes into their life, and the veil is removed (vss.12-18; 4:34). The word "transformed" is used only three other times in the New Testament, twice for the Transfiguration of Jesus (Mt.17:2; Mk.9:2) and once more for the believer (Rom.12:2), denoting one's new life (character) in Christ Jesus.

2 Cor.4:1-18—Because of these great "transformations" (3:18) in the lives of believers, and God's calling of Paul to his ministry (2:14-17; 3:5-11; Acts 13:1-3), Paul and his companions do not lose heart, since receiving God's mercy themselves (vs.1; Rom.11:30-32). Their commendation in their ministry (beginning with themselves) is that they have conducted themselves in truth to God and with a good conscience (vs.2; see previous 1:12-14) toward God and man. Their message is preaching the Gospel of Jesus Christ and His gift of salvation to mankind, and not preaching themselves. This is "shone" to others by God shining His light through them, vss.3-6; (see also Jn.1:4, 5, 9; 8:12; Mt.5:16).

Paul then declares that the "treasure" the believer now has (probably refers to the previous verse, vs.6) was designed by God to show His power accomplished this and not a work of man (vs.7). As a result, even in Paul's lists of afflictions here, the result is so the life of Jesus (vs.6) may continue to shine forth through them, and even bring His life to others—an absolutely remarkable work of God!—vss.7-12; note how in his listing, the difficulties he experiences do not reach a final completion or ending, because of vs.6 (see also vss.17, 18; 5:7-9; Jn.1:4,5—in vs.5, I prefer the word "overcome"; Rom.8:28-39). Paul also quotes Ps.116:10 here (read Ps.116:5-11 in its context) and applies the same assurance of the writer of Ps.116 of overcoming his afflictions and one day "walking before the Lord in the land of the living" (Ps.116:9). Paul addresses this to the Rapture of the church, when, in meeting the Lord in the air, the church is presented to the Father by Jesus in glorious resurrected bodies (vss.13, 14; the New American Standard Bible has 1 Thess.4:14 in the side margin of this verse; see also Eph.5:27, Col.1:22 and Jude 24, 25). All this in God's design, for His glory, and not the work of man, but by the power of God (vss.15, 7). So, Paul and his assistants do not lose heart (vss.16, 1), knowing these promises are eternal matters and not seen by sight till they take place, and the comparatively passing "light afflictions" will one day produce (in the same "spirit of faith"—see vs.13 from Ps.116) an eternal weight (Greek word emphasizes "heavy weight") of glory, everlasting glory, by comparison. These truths and God's presence within the believer renew the strength of the inner man of the believer, day by day (vss.16-18).

2 Cor.5:1-21—Continuing on from chapter four, Paul says, knowing this in advance, we long to be "clothed" with the new heavenly body to come, as we go through the "groanings" of our earthly body (vss.1-4; see also Rom.8:18-25; Phil.3:20, 21). The assurance of this promise is God's Divine pledge of the Holy Spirit (vs.5; 1:22), giving the believer great expectant hope and courage (vs.8; 3:12), walking by faith and trusting God (vs.7; 4:18), and looking to please Him always, as the result (i.e., make it one's aim; the Greek word combines two words—love and honor, and so, the love of honoring God—vs.9). Paul declares that we must appear one day before Christ, to receive recompense for our deeds done, whether good or bad (vs.10; see also 1 Cor.3:10-15). Knowing this day to come, Paul says that he then persuades man (for the Gospel and doing good deeds for God—vss.9,20; 3:12) and hopes this (his) conscience before God is seen to the Corinthians as well, and to take pride in him, for the right reasons demonstrated to them (vss.11,12;1:13,14). God's love compels him and his team to do this, since Christ died for all, so all may live for Him—in this world and the one to come (vss.14, 15). The new birth (spiritual birth—Jn.1:12, 13; 3:1-16) brings about a new creation, as the believer comes into the Family of God (Jn.1:12, 13), and God now demonstrates His life and character and growth through the believer (vs.17; see 3:16-18). This is God's work to "reconcile" mankind to Himself through belief in Jesus Christ ("reconcile" is from two words—again (re) and to conciliate (make friendly); the Greek word took on the meaning "to exchange," such as in money; and so, to change from the previous state of still being in one's sins (enmity), to friendship—Vine; see Eph.2:11-22). Paul

says that this is the ministry that God gave him and his team of associates to do—that God, not counting their trespasses (sins) against them, gave them this ministry of the Gospel to share to mankind, accepting Christ's payment on the cross for our sins, who knew no sin, so that through the spiritual birth we may become the righteousness of God (vss.18-21; see Rom.3:21-30).

2 Cor.6:1-7:1—Paul now concludes his explanation of his ministry and apostleship to the Corinthians in rather dramatic fashion, listing nearly all possible conflicts and hardships that he has experienced up to this time in vss.4-10. He begins with a salvation invitation message in continuation of his exhortation in 5:20, 21 (see also the Prayer found in the back of the book). He quotes from Is.49:8, with the coming of Israel's Redeemer—the Servant of Rulers (the Lord Jesus Christ in Is.49:7)—and God's message of salvation going forth to distant lands and nations (Is.49:5, 6, 12), and God's eventual restoration of the land of Israel (Is.49:5-13). With Jesus' work on earth completed in His first coming to earth to bring God's offer of salvation to all mankind, now is the day and acceptable time to receive His free gift of salvation (vss.1, 2). In the list of Paul's hardships in this passage, note God's character traits found here along with the outward conflicts in vss.6, 7. The Gospel goes forth to make many "rich" (spiritual gains and other blessings), while going forth and offered as a free gift from God (vs.10; see Rom.6:23, Jn.3:16, 17). Paul's plea is for the Corinthians to open their hearts wide to the Apostle Paul and his associates, as they have been to them, seeing all they have done for them and no restrictions prevent the Corinthians from doing so to them (vss.11-13). Paul finishes his discourse on

the topic of his ministry example and explanation with the call to holy living, as he started his letter with this topic by sighting his example for them to follow (1:12-14). The term "Belial" is probable reference to the devil (vs.15). He exhorts them to live in holiness to God (follow His word in the Bible), because now they are His people (family) and walk with Him (vss.14-18; 9:5).

2 Cor.7:2-16—See the previous discourse of this in 2 Cor.2:12-17.

2 Cor.8:1-24—Paul now returns to the subject of the financial collection of the Gentile churches for the saints in Jerusalem (1 Cor.16:1-3; Rom.15:31). Being in Macedonia and writing to the church in Corinth, he declares how the Macedonians gave generously to the endeavor of this gift, even in the midst of their afflictions and poverty circumstances (vs.2). Some great principles, guidelines and considerations are given here by the Apostle Paul, which are beneficial in learning to give to the work of God. I will highlight as many as I can glean throughout these two chapters of eight and nine in Second Corinthians. First, Paul says they gave beyond their means of their own circumstances, even "earnestly requesting" to participate in this contribution to Jerusalem (vss.2-4; see also Lk.21:1-4). Next, they gave their gifts first to the Lord, recognizing His will to do so in this collective effort (vs.5); and so he encourages the Corinthians to follow such a good example (vss.6-8, 10, 11). Paul reminds them of Jesus' example to us—though rich He became poor (in material possessions) in coming to earth, to help us become rich (in spiritual "wealth" and other blessings, as well, vs.9; 6:10; Prov.3:13-18; see Book 3 of <u>The Family Bible Studies Series</u>, <u>Growing In God's Wisdom</u>, for more

discoveries of the ingredients and "riches" of God's wisdom and praying for them). Then, Paul says, if the "earnestness" is there (present), one is to give according to what one has, not what one doesn't have, for the reason to establish equality (vss.12-15; see Prov.1:3 and 2:9 for this (equality) as an "ingredient" of God's wisdom, explained further in Book 3, pg.53). The "earnestness" to do this began with Paul and through Titus to the churches and an appointed brother (unknown) to carry their gift to Jerusalem (vss.16-24). Fellow workers for such honorable service are to be treated with love (vs.24) and respectful servants should be chosen, so no discredit (fault or blame) should come about in carrying out the importance of the gift and its fulfillment and minisrty (vss.20, 21).

2 Cor.9:1-15—Paul continues his discussion about giving to the saints in Jerusalem here in chapter nine and urges them to fulfill their willingness to give, which began the previous year by the Corinthians (vss.1-5). Since there has been some time passing since then, he wants to be sure of the initial willingness to give is still there and for them not to be "covetous" (unwilling to do so now—vs.5). A principle in giving (actually, in sowing and reaping—Gal.6:7) is that one reaps in the proportion of the gift they sow (vs.6; consider also The Sower and The Seed—Mt.13:1-9, 18-23). Another important principle is to be making such a decision from the heart (vs.7; see 1 Sam.16:7; 1 Kg.8:39; Jn.2:24, 25), for this is what God looks at most (Ps.19:13, 14; Lk.8:15; Col.3:15). To help in this decision, Paul gives three helpful guidelines to consider: 1) not giving with a grudge (reluctance or resentment; the Greek word is "grief"; and so, not out of "grief"); 2) or out

of compulsion (i.e., by force; the Greek word is "necessity" here; and so, because you have to do it); and 3) because God loves a "cheerful" giver (vss.7-9; see the similar Greek word in Rom.12:8; see also Lk.6:35-38). Paul concludes this topic of discussion with the amazement of how God causes such gift-giving to spread and abound and bring blessing to so many others as well (I believe this is his indescribable (literally, inexpressible) gift mentioned last in vs.15, how it spreads so bountifully to so many others, also with its positive effects—vss.8,12-14), showing how God causes His grace to abound to so many, that only He would fully comprehend it (or do it!—vss.8-15; Rom.11:33-36; Eph.3:14-21).

2 Cor.10:1-18—Paul now addresses his last topic to the Corinthians in Second Corinthians—the defense of his ministry in serving the Lord. He begins presenting this in a spirit of meekness and gentleness (vs.1; for "meekness," see the commentary on Mt.11:25-30; "gentleness" is the Greek word for being fair and considerate—"a considerateness that looks humbly and reasonably at the facts of a case" (Vine); see how both words are found in James 3:13, 17 in his list of "wisdom" words). Paul's contention and defense here is that some regard him as conducting himself solely by walking in the flesh (vs.2, i.e., strictly on purposes, ambitions and accomplishments for himself and for his own achievements). He also presents his case against those "cutting in" on his ministry and trying to put themselves on the same level of ministry as himself ("false apostles" and "deceitful workers"—11:12-15). He begins by stating that the "weapons" he uses in his service to the Lord are not man's weapons but "Divine weapons," with God working powerfully through him to overthrow strongholds (those

things in which mere human confidence is placed—Vine, used only 1 time here in the New Testament; 6:7). God's word and power take down man's "imaginations" and "devices of the mind" against the knowledge of God, and in Paul's ministry, they take man's thoughts to bring them to obedience to Christ (vss.3-6, 13). Paul reminds them not to look at outward things only (vs.7; 4:18; 5:7); and his authority used is to build them up and not to tear them down, bringing no shame to him or his ministry (vss.7-11; 13:10). In contrast to the "deceivers" trying to put themselves on the Apostle's level and ministry, Paul said that he and his associates do not "compare" themselves by themselves or "with" themselves (simply meaning, they don't compare themselves with anyone). They only declare their ministry to those that they have reached for the Lord and not in another man's work. Their commendation (praise) only looks to the Lord and the ultimate rewards from Him, and their personal boasting is in the Lord and His working through them (vss.12-18; 1Cor.1:31; 4:5.

2 Cor.11:1-33—Paul continues from chapter ten with the aspects of the defense of his ministry for the Lord. He has a "godly" jealousy for the Corinthians (note—not his own), and joining them to one Husband (Jesus Christ), to present them to Christ one day as a "pure" (same root as the word "holy"—7:1) virgin (vss.1, 2, 11; 4:14; Eph.5:25-27). Paul said that they were too complaisant in accepting views that opposed the Gospel (that was presented to them and accepted by them –another gospel, spirit or Jesus—vss.3, 4, 20). Paul was knowledgeable about these things and made the truths about the Gospel and Jesus known to them (vss.5, 6). He was also not a burden to them in his ministry

to them, having aid from the churches in Macedonia and being a tent-maker too in supplying his needs and the one's assisting him (vss.5-11; 1 Cor.9:12, 18; Acts 18:1-3; 20:33-35). He was also not going to allow "false apostles" to come in and mislead them and try to take away the work and ministry he did there in Corinth to begin and build up this church setting in the Lord (vss.12-15, 2, 3). Paul goes on to say that he has reasons to boast as anyone else (if he chose to), but that he will confine his boasting to his "weaknesses," so no one would "elevate" him beyond just himself and what he has said and done (vss.16-33; 10:17; 12:5,6). Paul once again demonstrates his ministry, giving quite an extensive list of personal hardships and sacrifices, as well as physical afflictions and pains done to him, and dangers constantly associated with one on the move taking the Gospel to Jews and the nations; he seems to put the escape from Damascus at the end as an afterthought he wanted to include with his listing here.

2 Cor.12:1-21—Paul continues to make his points of defending his ministry and says he could boast about receiving "heavenly visions" too (if he chose to), but it would not only be nonprofitable (vs.1), yet, also, may "elevate" him beyond himself and what he has said and done (vss.2-6; the vision appears to be his, according to vs.5). He said that God had allowed a physical weakness to remain with him, as a reminder to be humble in the Lord's service, and most of all, to know His power is perfected (present tense passive verb) in (or through) weakness, which is all a part of God's sufficient and available grace (vss.6-9; 1 Cor.10:13). So, as Paul summarizes his hardships in ministry here, he learned contentment with and through them for the Lord's sake, and to

know God's power to work in him and through him during those times as well, and so, to be strong in the Lord (vss.9, 10; 4:7; 13:4; Eph.6:10).

Paul declares in the defense of his ministry that the signs of a "true apostle" were performed and seen by the Corinthians—signs, wonders and miracles (see the commentary on Acts 5:12 for more description about "signs and wonders"). This makes no room for any comparisons (vss.11-13; 11:4, 12-15). Paul says that, as in his previous visits, he will continue not to be a burden to them and will graciously "spend" himself on them for the sake of Christ and the ministry (vss.14-18; this "third" visit is hard to determine since we only have record of his "two" missionary visits there, depending how they occurred and how he numbered his visits himself—see Acts 20:1-3). All the things he has been saying to them are for the purpose to build them up in the Lord. He wants them to take care of their own matters, as he will not spare those sinning or creating hardships in their gathering, if he needs to exercise his apostolic authority to do so, and they have not taken care of their matters or not repented of their sins when he comes (vss.19-21; 13:2, 3, 10; 11:2, 11).

2 Cor.13:1-14—Paul concludes this letter by declaring that Jesus was crucified in the flesh for us (see Phil.2:7-11; i.e., by reason (purpose) of the body for us), but lives because of the power of God (vs.4). So, we are to live by God's power likewise, remembering the believer does and also will live with Him by the power of God (vss.1-4; 4:14; 5:6-9). Paul exhorts them in their gathering to test and examine to see that they are in the faith (see 1 Cor.15:1, 2; Rom.8:9-11). He prays for them that

they will do no wrong (vs.7; the Greek has two negative words in the sentence, and so would read—do no evil at all (BAGD) or "will not do anything wrong" –NIV), but only, as Paul's example, living for the truth (vs.8; 4:1, 2; Jn.14:6). He encourages them to rejoice; let God do His "completing" (growing work in their lives –same word here as at the end of vs.9); be comforted (passive imperative verb here; remember Paul's theme and how it's carried out throughout the letter—see 1:3-7); and to be "like-minded," to live in peace, and God's love and peace will be with them (vss.11-13; his greetings included here). He closes with some of the various manifestations of the Trinity to be with them all—God's grace, love and fellowship (vs.14; see Book 1 of <u>The Family Bible Studies Series</u>, <u>The Family of God—Foundation</u>, for more understanding of the Trinity, Their character and Their functions).

Galatians

In similar purpose, presentation and plea as in 2nd Corinthians, the Apostle Paul writes to the Galatians (central modern day Turkey) to not accept a different Gospel other than the one he preached to them (1:6; 2 Cor.11:4). He defends his exhortation by referring to the life of Abraham (similar to Rom.4, see that particular commentary), that God's righteousness comes by faith, and now faith in Jesus Christ and His Gospel life and message (Gal.3). We also see clearly here in Paul's letter to the Galatians his consistent topics he writes to the churches at large about, faith, hope and love—faith (the explanation of God's truth and doctrine—see how often the word "faith" is used in the first three chapters of Galatians); hope (the eager expectation of the return of Jesus—see how faith is used here with hope and love; Gal.5:5,6); and love (living out the unconditional love of Jesus Christ in the church and world we live in (Gal.5:6, 13, 14, 22).

Gal.1:1-24—One of the principle points that the Apostle Paul declares to the Galatians is that his apostleship is a genuine calling from the Lord and came by His revelation to the Apostle Paul (1:1, 11, 12; Acts 9). For his regular greeting of "grace and peace," see the introduction to Romans 1:1-7 (vs.3). He presents a "snap shot" of the Gospel in vss.4, 5—Jesus giving His life to die for our sins, to deliver us from the evil in the world according to God's will, and to Him receives the glory forever and ever.

Paul strongly exhorts the Galatians not to leave the "Gospel of grace" of Jesus Christ that was preached to them (note the strong wording he uses in vss.8, 9 for those who preach a different Gospel; the word different" in vs.6 means another of a <u>different</u> sort; in vs.7, the word "another " refers to one of the <u>same</u> sort; so neither, both being different (regardless of their wording and preaching), could be correct, since it is a <u>different</u> gospel vss.6-10; there is a strong implication in vs.6 that the "different gospel" would be one based on "works righteousness," instead of the "gift" (grace) of Jesus Christ and faith in Him alone for salvation and God's righteousness; Rom.6:23; Eph.2:4-10; see the commentary for this in Romans 3:21-31; Acts 4:12).

Paul next gives a chronological presentation of his travels after his conversion experience including seeing two other Apostles (Peter and James—vss.18, 19). With his conversion coming by a revelation of the Lord (vss.11, 12), and his apostleship calling coming through teachers and prophets of the church by the Holy Spirit at Antioch Syria (Acts 13:1-3), Paul's wants to establish this with the other Apostles, and be accepted on the same level of calling as them. He was especially concerned of this and hoped that they would do this, being acquainted with his previous actions toward the church (pre-conversion days) and former ways in Judaism (vss.13, 14), and thus, hoping his visit would not be in vain (2:2). But hearing about his ministry and converted changed life, he was not only accepted, but they all gave glory to God for his ministry and the great work God was doing in and through his life (vss.23, 24; 11-24).

Gal.2:1-21—Paul now begins to address the issue of circumcision related to salvation in Jesus, an important topic the early church had to explain at the Jerusalem Council (see Acts 15). As determined at that council, circumcision has no bearing with the salvation experience and Gentiles should not be troubled by it at all (Acts 15:8-11, 19; Gal.5:6), being that salvation is a gift from God and comes by faith in Jesus Christ. So Paul did not give in to those trying to force it upon others, to maintain the truth of the Gospel (vss.4, 5). It was established that Peter's ministry was to the Jews and Paul's was to the Gentiles, and so they gave Paul and Barnabas their acceptance and the right hand of fellowship with them (vss.1-10).

Now that the church of Jesus Christ is one in Him (no divisions of Jews or Gentile—3:28), Paul addressed Peter on this issue not to separate himself from the Gentiles, and not to be intimidated about the issue of circumcision by those trying to force it upon others (vss.11-15). He reminds him that God's salvation and righteousness comes only by faith in Jesus Christ and not by works of the Law (vss. 16, 19, 21). Paul said that he now lives because Christ lives in him (all the believers), and he lives by faith in God's Son Jesus Christ, who gave His life to pay for our sins, so that we may receive His gift of eternal life (life eternal—as He has it; vss.20, 21; Jn.1:12, 13; 3:1-18).

Gal.3:1-29—In chapter three of Paul's letter to the Galatian church, he gives a beautiful discourse about how God's righteousness comes to the believer by faith in Jesus Christ. It is a similar discussion as in Romans, chapters three and four. In Romans chapter four, most of the emphasis there is on <u>Abraham's</u> faith in God's word and promises, transferred over to the believer in Jesus in last two verses of Romans chapter four. Here in Galatians, Paul emphasizes <u>the believer's</u> faith, and that in the Seed of Abraham, Jesus Christ, according to the promise given to Abraham (vss.16-22, 25-29). So his faith transfers over to the believer's faith, based on the promise to Abraham, fulfilled in Jesus Christ (vss.7-9, 18, 22). In vs.19, the Law was given to Moses (the mediator) through angels (i.e., helped in the administration of it). The Law was a "tutor" to lead people to Jesus (vs.24). Once again the Apostle Paul states the "oneness" believers have in Christ (vs.28; Col.3:11; Jn.17:21, 22); and since believer's have received the promise given to Abraham, they become an heir by faith of the promise given to Abraham, as Abraham also believed it and received by faith in God (vss.6-9, 18, 19, 29; Rom.1:17; 4: 3, 20-25; for a more elaborate understanding on God's fulfilling His promise to Abraham, see Book 4 of <u>The Family Bible Studies Series</u>, <u>The Theology of the Bible—The Family of God</u>, on how God works out His promise through the history of mankind and grows the Family of God).

Gal.4:1-31—In this chapter, the Apostle Paul continues on to emphasize that the believers in Christ are heirs according to the promise given to Abraham (vss.1-7; 3:29). As children we were held to "elementary principles" (including the Law—vs.3; 3:23, 24) of this world. So, Christ Jesus came to redeem us (bring us to God through the Gospel) from this bondage and into God's Family through the spiritual birth (Jn.1:12, 13), so as His children, we may then call God, our heavenly Father, who He truly is—"our

Father" (vss.4-6; see Mt.6:9-13; Eph.3:14, 15; see Book 1 of <u>The Family Bible Studies Series, The Family of God—Foundation</u>, for further insights into this marvelous truth and reality for the believer in Jesus). Now as a child of God, the believer in Jesus becomes an heir of God (vs.7; see Rom.4:13; Phil.3:20). As a result, Paul exhorts them not to return to "elementary principles" of this world (bondage of legalizing laws of this world and making them a religious guideline instead of faith in Christ Jesus; vss.8-11, 17-20; see Col.2:8, 20-23; 3:1-4). Paul's "weakness of the flesh" remains under discussion to this day, but appears to be related in some fashion to his eyesight, otherwise vs.15 would have no meaning (vss.13-15). Paul wants them to live in the freedom of the Spirit, as he does, and as all believers have come into the freedom of Christ (vs.12; 2:4, 5; 5:1, 22-25; Rom.8:1-6).

Paul then illustrates an analogy from Sarah and Hagar and Abraham's two sons, Isaac and Ishmael. God's continuation of the promise to Abraham was passed on to (and through) Isaac (vss.23, 28; Gen.17:19-21; 21:12). Paul stresses here the freedom of the believers in Christ (from sin and death, with the gift of the Holy Spirit within them—the Jerusalem above—vss.23, 26, 30, 31; Rom.8:1, 2; Heb.12:22-24; 11:8-20), while unbelievers remain in bondage to this, sin and death (vss.24, 25; Jn.3:16-21). Believers in Christ join in the promise given to Abraham and continued through Isaac and are set free in Christ from what used to hold them in bondage and slavery (vss.28-31; 2:4; 3:22-29; 5:1, 13-25; Rom.8:1-6), also declared here by the larger number of them that will exceed (vss.26, 27; Heb.11:16, 39, 40; 12:1, 22-24; Rev.7:9-17).

Gal.5:1-26—Paul now begins to leave the regular discussion of the topic of circumcision by reminding them that it they receive it (as a means of trying to be justified before God), they have fallen from grace and are under obligation to keep the whole Law. He says to them not to be subject again to a yoke of slavery (vss.1-4).

In vss.5, 6, Paul switches his topics over to hope and love. In vs.5, he declares by the Holy Spirit, believers are (present tense) "eagerly awaiting" (the Greek word here) for our Hope of Righteousness, the return of the Lord Jesus Christ (see also Jer.23; 5, 6; 33:15-17; Ps.89:30-37; Is.9:6, 7; Tit.2:11-14).

Then, he begins his "love discussions" (vs.6 and following to 6:10), saying, this is all that matters—faith operating (Greek word) through love (vs.6; 6:16). Paul assures them of his confidence in them that they will not adopt any other view than God's word and the Gospel preached to them (vs.10), and desires those teaching anything contrary would be cut off from them (vs.12; 1:7-9). Paul declares to them Jesus' reply about the greatest commandment from Lev.19:18—the fulfilling of God's love—vss.13-15; Mk.12:28-31—loving the Lord first and also one's neighbor as oneself; Rom.13:10—the verb here is the same root word as in vs.6.

Walking by the Holy Spirit is certainly a great means of sharing God's love with others, as Paul devotes the rest of chapter five to this subject (vss.16, 25). It prevents one from carrying out the desires of the flesh (vss.16, 17). Walking by the Spirit discovers the freedom of the Holy Spirit (2 Cor.3:17, 18), not being under law (see the purpose of the Law in 1 Tim.1:9; Rom.7:4-6), but under grace (Rm.3:27, 28; 6:14; 7:4), to bear fruit for God (vss.22,23;

Rm.7:4; Jn.15:16, 17—consider here "fruit that will last" and the workings of the Eternal Spirit of God—Jn.15:16; Heb.9:14; 2 Cor.3:17, 18). Paul gives here quite a lengthy list of works of the flesh being evident (vss.19-21; the word "sorcery" is the word" pharmakia" in Greek, the use of drugs, also found in the Book of Revelation—9:21; 18:23, and similar derivatives in 21:8 and 22:15). Note how these are opposites of the fruit of the Spirit (vss.22, 23). Paul gives stern warning that those who practice (present participle) such things will not inherit the kingdom of God (vs.21). Each "fruit of the Spirit" is a unique expression of God Himself (vss.22,23), beginning with love; for joy, see Jn.16:22; 17:13; for peace, see Jn.14:27; 16:33; Rom.5:1,2; for patience (the Greek word here is "long suffering"), see 1 Cor.13:4; Eph.4:2; 2 Pet.3:9; kindness is that which is fitting and beneficial, springing forth as a disposition of the heart—see Mt.11:30; Eph.2:7; 4:32; goodness can carry a "rightness" and correct moral judgment or character with its expression—6:10; Phil.1:6; 2 Tim.3:16, 17; Mt.7:11, 17; Heb.9:11; 13:20, 21; for faithfulness, see Jn.14:1-3; 1 Cor.1:21; 2:4, 5; Rm.1:17; 3: 21-30; Gal.2:20; Heb.11; the word gentleness is the Greek word "meekness", for which see the commentary of this with explanation about the character of Jesus in Mt.11:25-30 in vs.29, and in James 3:13; and self-control is literally, "in strength," finding our strength and control in the Lord (Acts 24:24; Titus 1:8; 2 Pet.1:5-8 in vs.6; 2 Cor.12:9, 10; Phil.4:11-13; Eph.1:18-20). No law governs these things—they are sought for and found only in God, and His definitions, and from His work in the believer's life (vss.23-26).

Gal.6:1-18—Here in chapter six of Galatians, Paul gives some instruction on continued "love actions" for the church to take. Paul says if one is caught in a trespass (could be a sin, a false step or blunder of some sort; "caught" can also involve being taken off guard—Vine), one who is spiritual and could handle the situation should help restore such a person in a "spirit of meekness" (vss.1, 2; see back at 5:23 for the word and definition at James 3:13). One also must be careful to not get caught up in the problem at hand itself (vss.1-5; consider Gal.3:20). For examining one's own work in vs.4, see 2 Cor.10:12, 13. The word "load or burden" in vs.2 refers to something heavy or burdensome; the word "burden" in vs.5 means something to bear, without reference to weight (Vine); see the word used in Mt.11:30 and its verb form (second in order there) used in Mt.11:28. Sharing an "act of love" is thanking teachers who teach them the word of God (vs.6). Then, Paul says for them to do good to all men (vs.10), for what we sow, we reap (a basic principle of life—vs.7-9; see Ps.126:4-6; Job 4:8; 15:31; Prov.22:8, 9). Paul concludes his letter with his last thoughts on circumcision, saying what really matters is the "new birth" in Christ, coming into the Family of God (vs.15; 2 Cor.5:17; see the Prayer in the back of the book); and his "boasting" is in Jesus and His death and resurrection for us, not in the works of man (vss.11-15; 2:20; 1 Cor.1:31; Jer.9:23, 24). For the "Israel of God" in vs.16, see Rom.9:6-8. The "brand-marks" of Jesus refer to Paul's physical scars (here in the Greek, a genitive of association and found only here in the New Testament).

Ephesians

Paul wrote this letter to the Ephesians during his first imprisonment in Rome (Acts 28:16, 30, 31). He continues to follow and adapt his favorite topics of faith, hope and love to the Ephesians, also (1:12, 15-18; 3:17-19; 4:2-5; 4:15-6:9 on the interaction and applications of God's love). He finishes with seven dimensions of the "armor of God," praying to God for and applying the various kinds of His strength in His victory of salvation for the believer in everyday life (6:10-20).

Eph.1:1-14—For Paul's initial greeting of grace and peace, see Rom.1:1-7. Paul explains that the believer in Christ has "every spiritual blessing in the heavenly places" in Christ Jesus, who upon His resurrection and ascension, sat down at the right hand of God (1:20; Ps.110:1; Heb.1:1-3); and now, having believed in Christ as Savior and Lord, the believer with the indwelling Christ is seated in the heavenly places (spiritually) with Christ Jesus (2:6; Col.3:1-4; Phil.3:20). This came through God's choosing the "adoption of sons" to come into His Family, redeeming (buying back with the paid price—the blood of Jesus Christ—for the payment of the sins of mankind) mankind and his receiving this payment and offer of salvation to him by believing and receiving Jesus Christ into their life—the "gospel of your salvation" (vss.7-13; Jn.1:12, 13). God had "predestined" this plan, and knew those who would receive it—receiving God's gift of grace of His Son Jesus Christ (vss.4-6). The believer is "sealed" with the Holy Spirit, having been redeemed by God and now being "God's own possession" (vss.13, 14; Jn.10:27-30; 2 Cor.5:4, 5; 1 Pet.2:9, 10). The believer also shares now in the "inheritance of the saints" (vss.11-14, 18)—the blessings and promises of God the Father, including the one day "hope of glory" in Christ Jesus (vss.12-14; Col.1:27; 3:1-4; Phil.3:20, 21; 1 Jn.3:1, 2). While God's administration and working out His plan of salvation for mankind was a mystery to man, it was all according to the council and purposes (fulfilling the Scriptures) of His will and plan, and all being summed up (involving completion and fulfillment) in His Son Jesus Christ, revealed to mankind (vss.7-10). The "fullness of times" (vs.10) is partly explained in this; see also Mk.1:15—"the time is fulfilled" is Jesus' first coming to fulfill the Scriptures, and "the kingdom of God is at hand" is the King now growing the Kingdom through the Family of God, and will one day rule and reign (His second coming) on the earth (Jn.1:5; 16:33; Rev.17:14; 19:11-20:6).

Eph.1:15-23—Paul finishes this chapter with a prayer for the Ephesians. He prays that they will continue to know God better (NIV, vs.17), as God makes Himself known more to them and through His wisdom for them (vs.17; see Book 3 of <u>The Family Bible Studies Series—Growing In God's Wisdom</u>—for learning more "ingredients" of God's wisdom, along with definitions from the Hebrew, and how to pray for them). Paul refers to God as the "Father of Glory" in his prayer. Vine describes "glory" as "the character and ways of God exhibited through Christ and to and through believers," a fitting explanation for the context of this prayer of the Apostle Paul. He wants them to know the "riches" of God's glory as part of their inheritance in the saints, and to understand better the hope of their calling in Christ (vs.18; 4:1, 4). Part of knowing this calling is understanding the strength of God available ("surpassing greatness"—vs.19) to those who believe. Three kinds of "strengths of God" are mentioned here—1) His power (referring to His inherent power within Himself); 2)"the strength" (His ever all-powerful ability to perfect and complete; His manifested power and strength (example, the creation of heaven and earth, Gen.1, 2; see Book 4 of <u>The Family Bible Studies Series—The Theology of the Bible: The</u> <u>Family of God</u>, chapter eight, The Creation Passage, for expanded insights on this "strength of God" in creating heaven and earth in Genesis chapters 1 and 2); and 3) "of His might" (His strength, especially physical strength given as a gift (example, Samson, the Book of Judges, chapters 13-16; Eph.1:19). All these "strengths" combined were exemplified in the raising of Jesus from the dead and He was seated at the right hand of God (vs.20; Ps.110:1); and He was given the name above all names, and authority, power and dominion forever (vss.21, 22; Phil.2:9-11; Mt.28: 18; Col.2:10), and was appointed as the Head of the Church, His body (vss.22, 23; Col.1:18). As the One in whom all things in heaven and earth were created (Col.1:18; Jn.1:3), and in whom "all the fullness of the Deity dwells in bodily form" (Col.1:19; 2:9; Jn.1:14-18), the One Who went from heaven to earth and back to heaven (Eph.4:8-10; Jn.3:13), from the creation of heaven and earth to the new heavens and new earth (Rev.21,22), He will be the One to fill all things in everything (vs.23; 3:19; 4:10, 13; 5:18 and following; Jn.3:1,2; Phil.3:20, 21; Col.3:1-4).

Eph.2:1-22—Paul on several occasions in Ephesians reminds them of how God has delivered them from their former way of living (2:1; 11-13; 3:14, 17, 22). The Gentiles had no hope in the world and, before those becoming a believer, were without God and separated from the covenants of promise given to Israel (vs.11-13). But there was hope for the Gentiles prophesied in the Old Testament (see Is.9:1-7; 19:22-25; 42:1-13; 49:5-7, 22, 23; 56:6-8; Jer.1:5; 4:2; 33:9; Mic.4:2; Mal.1:11; Gen.22:18). All these prophecies are brought about and fulfilled in the Messiah, Jesus Christ (Lk.24:44-48), who brought this beginning hope and the start of its fulfillment to the Gentiles in His first coming, and ministry on earth (Mt.12:15-21; Mk.1:15).

Paul reminds them how they used to conduct their life under the deceptions of the devil and doing things for selfish gain alone, and by that nature were "children of wrath," being under God's judgment (vss.1-3). Yet, for those who receive the Gospel and God's gift of salvation in Jesus through the spiritual birth (Jn.1:12, 13; 3:1-17; see the Prayer in back of the book), they are "made alive" (due to His resurrection) together with Christ (vs.4-9), showing the believer the "riches of His grace," by which we are saved (vss.5, 8, 9); so then, as a result, the believer may do good works for God, through His work in and through the believer in Christ (vs.10).

Paul then gives one of the most beautiful declarations and explanations of God's miracle in the heart of the believer, even destroying the strongest, most negative emotional state that man could have—enmity and hatred toward another—and bring peace to both Jew and Gentile, including also—peace with God (14-17; Rom. 5:1, 2). The relationship of Jew and Gentile, without hope and God in the world for the Gentile (vs.12), and ordinances of Jews excluding the Gentiles from Jewish worship and ways (they had to stay in the outer court in the Jewish temple area) often brought much animosity and enmity between them (vss.14-16); but the Gospel "destroyed this" and created "one new man" in Christ, bringing God's peace to one another (vss.15, 16). Though Gentiles were far away, the Gospel began to quickly spread throughout the world (Col.1:6, 23; Rom.10:18; 1Tim.3:16) to reach even the distant places (vs.17; Mt.24:14); and now, the believers in Christ are "fellow-citizens" in God's Family (vs.19; Phil.3:20) and are being "fitted together" as the temple God dwells in (vss.21, 22; 1Cor.3:16; 6:19), allowing them now direct access to God through the Holy Spirit indwelling them (vss.18; 3:12; Heb.4:14-16; Mt.27:51). The foundation of the temple was built upon the apostles and prophets, with Jesus the "corner stone" (the main One Who upholds it—vs.20; 3:5; Acts 4:11, 12; Eph.1:22, 23; Col.1:18, 19).

Eph.3:1-13—Paul next wants to comfort the Ephesians to know that his hardships, sufferings and tribulations have been willingly done for their benefit, since they have received the Gospel and come into The Family of God (vs.13). He reminds them of his calling to ministry by the revelation of Jesus (vs.3; Gal.1:11-13; Acts 9) to preach the Gospel of Jesus Christ (vss.8, 9), also made known to and through the apostles and prophets by the Holy

Spirit (vs.5). The mystery of the Gospel (vs.4; Rom.16:25-27), hidden in previous ages (vs.9, i.e., though prophecies for both Jew and Gentile for salvation and better days ahead, were in the Old Testament; see previous chapter). I don't think very many saw this coming, especially the way it did through God's Messiah (Acts 3:19-26), that would affect both Jew and Gentile in such a profound, personal way by God's miraculous work and power, both inside them and outside, to bring peace and stability to them both. It makes them both "fellow-heirs" (inheritors; see chapter one, vss.1-14 for the previous discussion of the "inheritance"), members of the same body (the church of Jesus Christ (1:22, 23; 2:14-22; 4:4; 5:30-32); and "fellow-sharers" of the promise in Christ through the Gospel (2:19-22; 3:6). This "manifold wisdom of God" (vs.10) was made known through the victory of the church of Jesus Christ to the "rulers and authorities" in the heavenly places (signifying their defeat—2:2; Col.2:13-15; 1 Jn.3:8; Jn.1:5; 16:33; the word "manifold" means "many sided"— they cannot stop God's work; see Prov.21:30). So, God's work and promises <u>always</u> prevail (vss.11, 12; see Is.40:13, 14, 18; 42:13; 43:10-13; 45:11-13; 46:8-11; 49:6, 7; Rm.11:33-36).

Eph.3:14-21—For this reason (vs.13), Paul kneels before the Father to pray for the Ephesians (and all the saints—vss.13-19). Verse 15 can appear somewhat complicated at first, but a closer look at the word order of Paul gives this an exciting insight and understanding of why Paul prays for "all the saints" in this prayer. The adjective "every," modifying "family," is singular, as is the word family. The noun in the singular here without a definite article emphasizes the individual members of the class denoted by the noun (BAGD). Thus, children or members of the family are the emphasis here, meaning "every member" of the family, that is, all the children and members of God's family, in heaven and on earth, derive their name (being in His family) from Him. So, we have here, The Family of God, in heaven and on earth, all derive their name (Christian, God's Family) from being a member of His family (vs.15; 2:19; Phil.3:20), all those who have had the spiritual birth (Jn.1:12, 13; 3:1-17) and have come into (and those who will) The Family of God (note how God is growing (building) His Family—in heaven and on earth). Thus, Paul prays for all the family. A very good prayer example indeed! Paul brings up once again the importance of God's "strength" to be active in the "inner man" of the believer (vs.16; 4:24; see previous definitions of God's strength in 1:19) through the Holy Spirit. Their faith is rooted and grounded in God's love and he desires that <u>all</u> the saints grow in it to the fullest (vss.18, 19). His love has no boundaries to its width, length, height and depth; and so, cannot be fully comprehended, but certainly known and experienced (vss.17-19; 1:4-6; 2:4-7; 5:2). Paul concludes his prayer with the proclamation that God is able to do "exceeding abundantly" beyond all we ask or think, through His power working within and through the believer in Jesus Christ (vss.20, 21).

Eph.4:1-32—Paul now, as he writes toward the end of his letters and as he often finishes with the topic of God's love, encourages here also the "interactions" and "demonstrations" of God's love among The Family of God, which is what they have been called to do (vss.1-3; 1:18); and to maintain the unity of the Spirit in the bond of peace that He has brought them (vs.3;

2:14-16; 4:32). Paul lists seven important "unity factors" of the body of Christ—one body, one Spirit, one hope, one Lord, one faith, one baptism and One God and Father and in and over His Family (vss.4-6); for "one baptism," see the commentary on John 3:1-21). As in Romans and First Corinthians, Paul writes about the gifts given to the church in his "love passage," for the building up the body of Christ, as each does its part in God's expression of love (vss.15, 16; 5:2). Paul quotes Ps.68:18 as a declaration that as Jesus went back to heaven in His ascension, He gave gifts to men (the church, for its building itself up in His love—vss.8-11, 16). The discussion about how "far" Jesus went when He descended into the lower parts (regions) of the earth still continues today. It is important to first recognize that the context of the passage is God giving His gifts for the building up of the church (vss.7-16). In the original Greek, no word follows "lower" in vs.9, so "parts" were added to complete the meaning. BAGD states that the passage refers to "regions" of the earth, which by definition would refer to the earth's surface. This seems to be a good answer to fit the context since all the Apostle Paul is trying to bring out here is Christ's "descension" and "ascension," having covered that expanded territory, "that He might fill all things" (in heaven and earth; see the commentary at the end of chapter one on this discussion). Leading a "host of captives" in vs.8 I believe refers to the "first-fruits" that Jesus won in His ministry on earth (see Is.61:1-3; Lk.4:16-22). Note the reasons the Apostle Paul states why God gives gifts to the church—equipping for the works of His service; to build up His Family in Christ; maintaining unity of the faith (based on the truth of God, 1:13; 4:15, 21; 6:14); and for personal and collective growth, maturing into the fullness of Christ (vss.11-13; 1:23). This last point made is elaborated more in vs.15, which helps the "body of Christ" mature and grow as each part of the body, does its work in love (vss.14-16).

With this practice, Paul reminds them again not to walk in their former way of life before knowing Christ Jesus—the ways of the "old (former) man" (vss.17-22), but to renew the spirit of their minds (reading the Bible—vs.21; Rm.12:1-3) and live-out their new life (man) in Christ, (literally) according to God, who has created the believer new (2 Cor.5:17), to live in righteousness and holiness of the truth, (vss.23,24).

Paul completes chapter four by giving a list of practical "love actions" for the church to follow. Being members of each other, Paul says to speak truth with one's neighbor (see Zech.8:16; 4:15, 25; 2 Cor.13:8). Paul says not to harbor anger inside or to sin regarding it, but clear oneself immediately for sure or before the day ends (vss.26, 27; Ps.4; Mt.5:21-24). Paul set a good example by working to meet his needs and companions with him and in order to be able to give to others, as well, and exhorts them to do likewise (vs.28; Acts 20:33-35). Our words in serving the Lord should be "graceful" (a gift), to build others up and to meet needs and not to speak out bad things (vs.29; Prov.10:19; 15:23; 17:28; 18:20; 22:11). Paul then states not to grieve the Holy Spirit (knowing the right thing to do in whatever we face—present tense verb; vs.30; see Ps.15); and putting away all anger and bitterness (vss.25-27; Heb.12:14, 15), living in God's forgiveness to us and extending it also to others, as God forgave us in Christ, with kindness and compassion (vss.31, 32; Mt.6:11-13).

Eph.5:1-14—Paul once again reminds the church at Ephesis not to live according to their days before becoming a believer in Jesus Christ (vs.8). He simply lays out before them previous "unfruitful deeds of darkness" compared to living now as "children of light" (vss.1, 8, 11). "Deeds of darkness" to avoid include bad (filthy) speech of any kind (vss.4, 6, 7), along with those who do such thing; plus, immorality of any sort (which include greed, impurities and idolatry—vss.3, 5-7, 12). Instead, to walk with the fruits of the children of light—love (vss.1, 2), thanksgiving (vs.4), goodness, righteousness and truth (vs.9), and deeds that are pleasing to the Lord (vss. 1,10), even "exposing" evil deeds (vss.11-14), that is, bring them to the light, which can also involve reproof (in the meaning of this Greek word). Paul's quote from Is.26:19 uses words for evangelistic purposes here, it appears most likely, as a Christian would already be raised up with Christ (2:5, 6). When people hear or read his letters he would certainly want unbelievers to receive God's gift of salvation in Jesus ("sleeper" in this verse is a present participle, also, showing continuous action involved; if a Christian has committed such an act, 1 John1: 9,10 would apply to them, with similar effects from vs.14 occurring).

Eph.5:15-15—6:9—Paul finishes his subject on love to the Ephesians by addressing six groups of people—wives, husbands, children, fathers, slaves and masters. All of them include a submissive and/or accountability factor with them in relation to the others involved in relationship to them. Coming out of lifestyles previous to their Christian conversion, Paul exhorts them to be careful to walk as wise people now before the Lord (the Greek word for "careful" is where the English word "acrobat" comes from), and to make the most of the time they have now in serving the Lord and doing His will (vss.15-17). "Drunkenness" leads to wastefulness, but "filled with the Spirit" brings much joy in the Lord, beneficial individually and collectively, bringing so many beautiful songs also during the church age (vss.18-21, being a part of the Lord's "filling up" progressive works—1:23; 3:19; 4:10, 13). "Psalms" in verse 19 is a sacred song sung to music; "hymns" are songs of praise addressed to God; and "spiritual songs" is the general word for "song," here with spiritual content (vs.19; Vine). Note these are done from the heart with thanksgiving to God (vss.19, 20).

The verb "being subject" to one another (respectfully humble and accountable) is a participle that comes out of the main verb (that is, the ones following out of the main verb) "be filled with the Spirit" (vs.18 and following). Paul first applies this to the church at large (vs.21). Next, to wives in relationship with their husbands (vss.22-24), acknowledging God's design of the relationship (see Genesis, chapters 1 and 2; plus the chapter, The First Family on Earth, of Book 1 in The Family Bible Studies Series for further insights on this topic), as the church is subject to Christ (vs.24, Col.1:18; 1 Cor.11:3).

Then, Paul addresses husbands to love their wives as Christ does the church (vss.25, 33). Three primary reasons are expressed here in doing this: 1) spiritual holiness, not only in the present, daily life (vss.25, 26), but, as a "bride in the Lord," without spot or wrinkle, when one day Jesus presents (the church) to the Father (i.e., without bame—vs.27; 2 Cor.4:14; 11:2; Jude 24,25); 2) physical nourishment and care of health and strength (vss.28-30;

"nourish" used only twice in the New Testament— in 6:4 for the other use ("bring up"); "cherish" means to keep warm, as a mother bird hovering over her young ones with her feathers—Dt.22:6,7; Vine; and 3) to help "fill the earth" (Gen.1:28; 2:24; Eph.4:10), with the two previous reasons above also, to fulfill God's first commandment given for both Adam and Eve—"to fill the earth" and subdue (govern over) it (Gen.1:28, the "one flesh" expressed in the offspring—vs.31; see Ps.127). Note carefully here "the filling up" of the earth with the fulfillment prophecies in Ephesians (1:23; 3:19; 4:10, 5:18 and following), until God's Family is "full" in the eternal dwelling with Him in the New Heavens, New Earth and New Jerusalem (Rev.21, 22). This explains also how Paul says that this "mystery" that God works out refers to Christ and the church (vs.32; see Book 1 of The Family Bible Studies Series for more understanding of God's plan in creating Adam and Eve, to begin to fill up the earth and family development; and Book 4 The Theology of the Bible—The Family of God about how God develops and fulfills His Family throughout the time of the Bible and history).

The Apostle Paul continues his submission/accountability theme with four more groups of people. After addressing husband and wife, children are next discussed (vss.1-4). In vs.1 someone may ask, "what if my parents do not know the Lord?" The answer is in vs.2—honor (show respect) for your father and mother, which comes with a promise (vs.3) and is beneficial for all involved. Verse four is a key and primary responsibility for the father (and one would have to include parents here also) to carry out—bringing them up (remember the word "nourish" here used also in 5:29) in the <u>discipline</u> (active training) and <u>instruction</u> (training by word, literally, to place in the mind) of the Lord (God's word, the Bible, and appropriate applications). Note that this is the responsibility of the father (parents) in God's design (see Dt.6:4-9; 4:9; Prov.1:8; 22:6; 23:15-21; also, Book 1 of <u>The Family Bible Studies Series</u> for a more complete understanding of this and helpful aids to carry out this responsibility to God).

Slaves (servants) are to be obedient unto the Lord with fear and trembling (vs.5; <u>fear</u> is respect due to officials and masters in their positions; <u>trembling</u> is respect under responsibility; Vine). Their "eye service" is first unto the Lord, knowing the good they do the Lord will repay them (vss.6-8; sowing and reaping—Gal.6:6, 7). Masters likewise are to respect their servants, knowing that both have an impartial Master in heaven (vs.9).

Eph.6:10-24—Paul actually now returns to his prayer for "God's strength" for the Ephesians and practical application to victoriously carry it out (see 1:19, as Paul uses the same three words of "God's strength" and how they are defined). Paul illustrates the believer applying "God's strength" here by listing a "warriors coat of armor" and compares seven spiritual dimensions of a believers walk with God to them—the truth, righteousness, the Gospel, faith, salvation, the Holy Spirit and prayer. Several important principles are to be noted here: first, the "coat of armor" all goes together for the believer—the complete armor of God (vss.11, 13; I believe a subjective genitive here in the Greek as God actually works them out through the believer); always remember they work together, so wear the "full armor of God"; second, stand (one of the major goals here) from start to finish throughout whatever battle one faces (vss.11-14; see and pray the ultimate goal of "standing" also that Jesus said for us to pray in Lk.21:36); third, the battles are "spiritual battles" that we face (vs.12; 2:2; note the proclaimed victory with this in 3:10-12); and so, "salvation is a present experience of the Lord's deliverance of believers as those who are engaged in spiritual conflict"—Vine, under helmet. Our job is to pray and resist the evil (and their forces vs.12; James 4:7; 1 Pet.5:6-9) and stand with the Lord (vs.13; Jn.16:33). Fourthly, apply the appropriate armor as needed (truth, righteousness, the Gospel, faith (one does not want to put out a larger fire, but the dart that had fire on it—vs.16), salvation (the victory placed over (in) the head—the helmet—vs.17), the Holy Spirit and God's word—the sword, referring back to the Holy Spirit—see Lk.12:11, 12; Mt.10:19, 20; Acts 13:1-4; and prayer in the Holy Spirit (vs.17 and Rom.8:26-28), with alertness and all perseverance and requests for all the saints—vss.18-20; 3:14-19).

Paul would often send his fellow workers to comfort the churches about his circumstances (vss.21, 22; Timothy in 1 Cor.4:17, etc). He closes with a proclamation (undoubtedly his prayer for them) of peace, love and faith to be with them from the God the Father and the Lord Jesus (vs.23); and grace to be with all who love the Lord (literally) in incorruptibility (i.e., that which cannot be corrupted, tarnished or ever changed; thus, unfailing and never stopping or dying).

Philippians

The Apostle Paul visited Philippi in northeastern Macedonia for the first time in his ministry on his second missionary journey. He wrote to them this letter during his first imprisonment in Rome (Acts 28:16, 30, 31). He maintains writing on his important topics of faith, hope and love, but doing so more sporadically in this letter to the Philippians. He continues on in strong and confident faith (1:25-27; 2:17, 18; 3:8-11); persistent and always persevering in hope (1:20; 2:15, 16; 3:20, 21); and constantly focusing on growing in the love of Christ (1:8-11) and exhorting the churches in living out its powerful, interactive displays toward and for one another (2:1-13; 4:1-9).

Phil. 1:1-30—Paul writes to the Philippian church and their leaders and mentions in chapter two that he soon plans to send Timothy to them for ministry and current updates (1:1; 2:19-23). He thanks them and prays joyfully for them for their participation in the Gospel right from the beginning and is confident that God will continue this good work in their lives and perfect it till the day of Christ Jesus (vss.3-7). In his love for them, he prays their love will grow and abound so they may prove the things that are excellent (i.e., the things that really matter – BAGD) and producing the fruit (singular) of righteousness through Jesus Christ, to the praise and glory of God (vss.8-11).

He makes known to them that his imprisonment has worked out for the greater progress of the Gospel (vss.12, 13), and has even encouraged other brothers to be more bold in sharing their faith. However, not all of them were doing it from love, goodwill and pure motives (vss.12-17, possibly in jealousy of Paul's success in his ministry which had now entered into their territory of Rome through his imprisonment—see 2 Cor.10:12-18). Either way, Paul was not interested in being contentious, but only that the Gospel was going forth (vs.18) and that through his life, whether in life or death, Christ Jesus would be exalted through him, and by this, he would continue on in ministry for their progress and joy in the faith (vss.19-26).

So Paul exhorts the Philippians to live their lives as citizens now of heaven (Greek word for "conduct," vs.27; 3:20, 21), standing together in the "oneness" of spirit, mind and faith of the Gospel (vs.27) and not alarmed by opponents to them, since it warns them of their destruction (unless, they receive the Gospel message), but salvation for the believer (vs.28), recognizing also that entering in Christ's sufferings are part of the believer's experience to help set other's free and receive Christ as their Savior and Lord (vss.29, 30; Jn.3:16-21).

Phil.2:1-30—Paul continues his "oneness" (unity) emphasis he began in 1:27 (see Jn.17:11, 21, 22) by first encouraging them to share Christ's comfort, consolation (literally, speaking chose to someone, here in this passage in love), fellowship (literally, sharing) of the Spirit (i.e., the work and character of the Holy Spirit, example Gal.5:22-25; Phil.3:3), and affections and compassions with one another (vs.1). He asks them to make his joy complete by "thinking the same" (i.e., in Christ, His concerns and affairs—see vs.21), having the "same love" (of Christ), being "one in soul" together, and (literally translated) focusing on "one thinking" (vs.2; see this picked up in vs.5 and following). Regarding one another as more important than themselves is an important part of sharing Christ's love and humility with one another (vs.3; see commentary on Mt.11:25-30 for a practical definition of "humility"), being concerned for other's interest along with one's own personal interests (vs.4).

Paul goes on to share that the humility of Christ is the example of humility for the believer (vs.5). Though existing in the form of God (the nature or essence existing in the person Himself, specific form and character (Vine); Jn.1:1; 10:30; Col.1:19; 2:9), He did not consider equality with God something to be grasped (vs.6; "something to be grasped" is the noun from of the verb for "rapture" in 1 Thess.4:17, to seize or take away by force; as a noun it means "prize or treasure;" and so, here in its context with Jesus, means He did not regard His being on an equality of glory and majesty with God as a prize or a treasure to be held fast (Vine; see Jn.17:4, 5), but instead, laid them aside (the majesty and glory in heaven with the Father –Jn.17:5), taking on the form (same word as in vs.6) of a bond-servant, being made in the likeness of men (vs.7; Jn.1:14); and found in appearance (figure; see 2 Cor.4:4, Col.1:15), as a man (see Book 1 of The Family Bible Studies Series, pgs. 7 and 8, for more insights into the correlation between the physical body of Jesus and mankind), He humbled Himself and became obedient (to God as His Bond—Servant, for the salvation given to mankind on earth) to the point of His death on the cross (vs.8). Having accomplished this (suffered, died, resurrected and ascended to heaven—Col.3:1,2; Heb.1:3; 12:1-3), God gave Him the Name above every name, that mankind will bow their knee to and confess His Lordship, to the glory and honor of God the Father (vss.9-11; Mt.28:18; Ps.2; Ps.110; Acts 4:12).

Based on this wonderful demonstration of humility and obedience to God by Jesus, Paul speaks earnestly to the Philippians to work out their salvation, given and accepted by them from God, with fear and trembling (see Eph.6:5 commentary for helpful meaning of "fear and trembling"); for it is God working all this out for the believer, in them and through them, according to His purpose and goodwill (vss.12, 13; Eph.1:5; Jn.3:19-21). He wants them to be blameless, innocent and without moral disgrace children of God, shining as "God's light" in the world (vss.14, 15; Mt.5:16; Dan.12:3), holding true to God's word, remembering their Hope in the return of Jesus (vs.16; 3:20, 21). In his service to the Lord for their faith in Christ, Paul encourages them to rejoice with him and share their joy with him also (vss.17, 18).

Paul writes that he plans to send Timothy to them soon, a trustworthy and proven servant in his help in advancing the Gospel and hopes to see them soon himself as well (vss.19-23). Epaphroditus, another faithful fellow worker and fellow soldier ministering to and for Paul in the Lord's work, risked his life and was sick to the point of death in Christ's work for them (mentioned twice about this by the Apostle Paul here—vss.27, 30); but, God had mercy on him, spearing much sorrow to many, and so Paul sent him back to them that they all may see and receive him joyfully in the Lord (vss.25-30).

Phil.3:1-21—Paul now begins to move toward the close of his letter to the Philippians. He warns them to beware of those who would insist that a person must be circumcised to be saved (see the issue dealt with in Acts 15). He declares that believers are the true circumcision (Rm.2:29), who have the Spirit of God, and glory in Christ Jesus, and bringing His salvation by faith through the Gospel message to all mankind. If anyone similar to his background should put confidence in their religious accomplishments for their benefit, he has quite a list himself in his background (vss.4-6, outside of persecuting the church—vs.6). But all <u>that</u> he gladly counts as lost to gain Christ Jesus in his life (vs.7). He gladly counts all things lost to gain Christ, which is <u>God's righteousness</u> coming to the believer by faith in Jesus Christ (vss.8, 9; see also Rom.3:21-30). Paul wants to live out the resurrected life of Jesus living in him (the meaning of the word "resurrection" in vs.11, which in the Greek has a prefix before it and means "the out-resurrection," i.e., to live it out in his life; vss.10-12). Paul's goal in his life now is like one running or competing in an athletic event—stretching out and moving forward (probably a correlation to the foot races of that time—vs.13), as one concentrates on the goal of the competition (the finish line or completion of the event) to win the prize—God's reward(s)—that come from His calling and ministry for us in His plan of serving Him in our lives (vss.14-16; 2:12, 13). He warns them to beware of people who are "enemies of the cross of Christ," that set their minds on selfish gains and earthly things (vss.17-19).

But believers are "citizens of heaven," eagerly awaiting" our Savior from there, who will "transform" our current physical bodies to be "conformed" (literally, having the same form) as His glorious body, by His mighty power to even subject all things to Himself (vss.20, 21; 1 Jn.3:1, 2; 1 Cor.15:27, 28).

Phil. 4:1-33—As Paul finishes his letter to the Philippians, he encourages them to "keep standing" (present tense) in the Lord (see also Eph.6:10-20). He urges two people in their church setting to "think alike" in the Lord (same words here as the first exhortation in 2:2), and appears to be addressing another individual there in vs.3 but the wording or context does not clarify who that may be. He encourages them again to rejoice in the Lord (vs.4; 3:1) and to be considerate, fair and forbearing (the Greek word here) with one another (see also in James 3:17). Most think his statement of "the Lord is near" refers to the Lord's return (1:20; 3:20, 21). He continues to encourage them, as our Lord Jesus did, to not be "anxious" (worry, be over eager in desiring something) about anything (see Mt.6:25-34), but by different kinds of prayers (general prayers, wantings or needs, and askings—three Greek words here) with thanksgiving, to make them known (pray) to God (vs.6); and to know God's peace that surpasses all understanding (vs.7) that guards our hearts in Christ Jesus (vss.5-7; see Jn.14:1, 27; 16:33; Mk.9:34, 50; Rom.12:14-21; 14:17-19). Part of being peaceful is thinking peaceful (wholesome) thoughts. Paul gives a list of some of these in vs.8—God's truth (see Jn.16:13-15; Rom.14:17-19; 2 Cor.13:8); things honorable (Greek word means seriousness in purpose and self-respectful in conduct (Vine); also used as a characteristic of church leadership and exemplary conduct—see 1 Tim.3:8, 11; Tit.2:2); things that are just (right thing to do—see Rm.1:17; 4:3; 14:17; Eph.4:24; Phil.1:11); things that are pure (same root word as "holy" here; see Eph.4:24; Col.1:22; 3:12; 1 Pet.1:13-21); things that lovely (pleasing, agreeable and lovely—to the Lord (Rm.12:1,2; 14:17, 18; Eph.5:8-10); things that are spoken well of (2 Cor.8:18-21; Phil.2:19-22; Eph.4:29; Ps.19; Ps.23; Ps.27:1-6; Ps.119:1-8; Prov.3:1-8); things that are of virtue (pre-eminent estimation for a person or thing; moral goodness (Vine); see the only other uses of this word in Peter's letters—2 Pet.1:3 (the last word in the verse) and vs.5 (the first word in his listing here—moral excellence), and used of "God's virtues" in 1 Pet.2:9 to be proclaimed); and things that are worthy of praise (commendable of good character and well-doing). Paul says to take account of the character of these things and think upon them (the meaning of the Greek word here for "thinking upon this things). These meditations along with "good practices" keep one in the peace of God" (vss.6-9).

Paul concludes his letter by thanking the Philippians for supporting him in his ministry and going out of their way to do so. He knew how to work for his own needs (vs.11; Acts 20:31-35) and trust God for what else he may need (probably this being the foundation of his "secret" of contentment—vss.11-18). They will reap well also in giving to him and his ministry (vss.18-20; 2 Cor.9:6-15). The concluding verses show how Paul's imprisonment was helping to spread the Gospel, even to those in government circles (vss.21-22; 1:12-14); and he blesses them that the grace of the Lord Jesus Christ be with their spirit (vs.23).

Colossians

The Apostle Paul writes this letter to the church in Colossae (southwestern current day Turkey), even though he had not previously visited them (2:1; someone there may have seen him before, but not the church at large). His bond-servant Epaphras, though, is from there (1:7; 4:12). Martyrdom recordings have listed Epaphras as their first bishop and suffered martyrdom there (Unger). Paul writes his letter to them during his first imprisonment in Rome (Acts 28:16, 30, 31).

Paul's continuous encouraging main topics of faith, hope and love are easily recognized at the beginning of his letter (vss.4, 5). He brings his message of faith in grand style presenting the deity and supremacy of Jesus Christ (1:15-20; 2:9) and exhorting them to stay clear of philosophies and teachings contrary to Christ Jesus (Chapter 2). He delivers his proclamation of hope in vivid presentation of the life of the believer being with Jesus, seated at the right hand of God, who is our hope of glory (1:27; 3:1-4; see 1 Jn.3:1, 2). He concludes by giving his "love in action" teachings, similar to the end of Ephesians, yet refreshing to see new expressions (chapters 3 and 4).

Col.1:1-29—For Paul's introduction, see Rom.1:1-7. Paul lays out his topics of faith, hope, and love, and encourages them for belief and practices of them (vss.2-5). They heard them and received them by God's word of truth—the Gospel, which amazingly, even then was spreading throughout the world and constantly bearing and increasing "fruit production" for God from its proclamation (vss.5, 6, 23). They learned it from Epaphras, a faithful servant of Christ on Paul's behalf in his ministry, who informed Paul of their (the Colossians) love in the Spirit (vss.7-8).

Paul prays for them that they be filled with the knowledge of God's will, in all spiritual wisdom and understanding (vs.9), so they may walk in a manner pleasing to God and to bear good fruit for Him and grow in the knowledge of Him (vs.10); being strengthened by His power and glorious might (see Eph.1:19 and 6:10), for all endurance and longsuffering (Greek word here—vs.11); and giving thanks to the Father who has qualified the believers to share in His inheritance of the saints in light (vs.12; see Eph.1:18), because of Jesus, who delivered the believer from the domain of darkness (see Eph.2:1-7) and transferred us to His beloved Son's kingdom, redeeming the believer in Christ (purchasing us—see Rev.5:9, 10) through the price He paid on the cross for us to receive forgiveness of our sins (vss.13, 14).

With His completed and victorious accomplishment in redemption (vs.14; 2:9, 14, 15), God has bestowed to Jesus the "Name above all names" (Phil.2:9-11) and He has "first place" in everything (vss.15-18). The "image of the invisible God" (vs.15) involves "representation and manifestation;" Jesus is the visible representation and manifestation of the invisible God to created beings"—Vine; Col.1:19; 2:9; Jn.1:14-18; Heb.1:1-3; "firstborn of all creation" is the literal translation in Greek without an article, and so, first place of (over) all creation (vss.15, 18), since He created all things (vs.16), and existed (eternal nature of His Deity) when He created all things (vs.17; Jn.1:1, 2); and in Him all things hold together (vs.17; Heb.1:3). He is the Head of His body, the church, and calls all the believers in Him "brethren" (Heb.2:11, 12), with many more "children of God" to come and be completed for God's Family (Heb.2:13; Rev.21, 22), with Jesus being the <u>first</u> to rise from the dead and all God's Family in His body, the Church, to follow (vs.22; 1 Thess.4:16-18; 2 Cor.4:14; Rev.20:4), making all, because of Jesus' redemptive work, from one Father (Heb.2:11; see also the commentary on Eph.3:15). All this and Christ's manifested Deity was the good pleasure of the Father (vs.19; 2:9; John 1:14-18; 3:16; Eph.1:5-9-14), to reconcile (see commentary on 2 Cor.5 for the definition) all things together in Christ (Eph.1:9-12), making peace through His shed blood on the cross, whether things in heaven or on earth (vs.16, 20), to present the church holy, blameless (without fault or blame) and beyond reproach (not anything called to one's account against them—the Greek word here; vs.22; 1 Jn.1:3, 7, 9); and so, Paul exhorts them to stand firm in their faith (literally, established and settled) and the hope of the Gospel, that is being proclaimed in all creation under heaven (vs.23).

Paul acknowledges to them the willingness of his sacrificial sufferings in Christ for them to carry out his ministry of the Gospel, because of the resulting benefits for them to understand the ministry of the Gospel, so they can be saved (vss.24-26; see

Eph.3:1-13)—the mystery being Christ within the believer, the Hope of glory (vss.27; 3:1-4). The goal in his instructions through God's wisdom (vss.9, 10) is for their maturity growth in the Lord (see also Eph.4:10-16; 1 Tim.1:5), all in God's power and mighty strength working through him (to them and to us—vss.10, 11, 28, 29).

Col.2:1-23—Paul's concern for the Colossians is that they do not allow themselves to be deceived by false reasoning (Greek meaning of "delude" here (Vine; see the only other use of this word in the New Testament in James 1:22) or simply by "persuasive argument" (that is, plausible argument in contrast to demonstration), instead of following Christ Jesus, who demonstrates both (words and actions of truth—1:13, 14; 2:3, 9, 12-15). Philosophy alone, empty deception (literally, without content), traditions only according to men and the simple "elements (elementary ones) of the world" (word means any first things from which others in a series or, a composite whole, take their rise (example, letters of the alphabet as elements of speech—Vine); see vss.2:20; Gal.4:3, 9; also, Rom.1:19, 20, 25), are other examples that Paul warns them about, instead of following the teachings of Christ (vss.1-3 8-10) and pursuit of the knowledge of God (1:9, 10; 2:2, 3; 3:1-4; Rom.11:33-36). Jesus is the One who has set the believer free from sin and death (vss.10-13) and made us alive (spiritually) with Him (vss.12, 13; Jn.5:24; Rom.6:21-23; this includes the "handwritten ordinances" (vs.14), for which see vss.20-23 and Eph.2:14-16 and its commentary). Therefore, let no one judge another about this (vss.16, 18). He adds certain "religious practices" of their time to the list, too (vss.16, 18, 20-22)—the body casts a shadow, but the body is the issue (vss. 17, 19). Such things "appear" to "cast" a glimpse of wisdom, but are only "self" attempts to try and demonstrate it (already accomplished in Jesus—vss.2, 3, 13-15, who "disarmed" (literally, stripped them of their armor and power) the evil heavenly spiritual rulers and authorities—vss.12-15; Eph.2:2, 14-16; 3:9, 10), according to God's purpose and plan (Eph.1:9, 10; 3:11, 12) in Christ Jesus. Some of those "religious practices" only harmed the body and brought no care or benefit to it all (vs.23, KJ; compare Eph.5:29).

Col.3:1-4:6—Paul now presents in the beginning of this chapter a beautiful presentation of the believer's life hidden with Christ in God and the wonderful "hope of glory" in Christ to come (vss.1-4; 1:23, 27; 1 Jn.3:1,2). He now leaves his "faith proclamations" and teachings and speaks more elaborately on the believer's "hope of glory" in Christ to come (see also Phil.3:20, 21; Jn.14:1-3). He notes "Christ seated at the right hand of God, in fulfillment of Ps.110:1 (Mk.16:19; Heb.1:1-3), and so, exhorting believers to seek Christ there (vss.1, 2; Eph.2:17-22; 3:12; Heb.4:14-16; 1 Jn.2:1). Having died with Christ to our old nature (vs.3; 2:12, 13; Rm.6: 5-11; Eph.4:22-24), our "new life" is now with (in) Christ (vss. 3, 10) in God (Rm.6:17-23; Eph.4:24-5:10). In fact, He is our Life (vs.4) and the believer eagerly looks forward to being in glorified body with their Lord Jesus (vs.4; Phil.3:20, 21; 1 Jn.3:1, 2; 1 Thess.4:13-18).

Paul now writes on his "love topics," their recognition and active displays, especially in contrast to the "old ways" of life (vss.5-9). The "new life" is now to take over, done in the image of the One who created us to display them (1 Pet.2:9, 10; consider the restoration of this from the beginning and the fall of man—Gen. 1-4; see Book 1 of The Family Bible Studies Series for a commentary on Gen.1-4, pgs. 7-11), which includes no distinction (literally, no place for) partiality in backgrounds (vss.10, 11). The "new life," based on (and in) God's holiness and love (vs.12; Eph.1:4-6; 2:4-7), is presented in compassion, kindness, humility (see commentary on Mt.11:25-30 for a practical definition found in the character of Christ), meekness (see commentary on Mt.5:5 and James 3:13 for a definition), long-suffering, forbearance, forgiveness and thankfulness (literally), the bond of the completeness of love (a genitive of a degree here), showing the clear end result and the display of God's love throughout, which encapsulates all the rest (vss.12-14). With this, they are to let Christ's peace rule in them (see Phil.3:4-9) and God's word dwell richly in them (vss.16, 17; Dt.11:1; Ps.19:7-11; 119:15,16, 41, 42, 89, 105; Prov.3:1-8; the word of God's peace "ruling" in one's heart is the word for "umpire," as deciding all matters in the heart—to arbitrate; Vine); and to do all we do in word or need for the Lord, giving thanks to the Father in Jesus' name (vs.17).

For the exhortations to the six groups that Paul speaks to here, see Eph.5:22-Eph.6:9, 18-20 (vss.3:18-4:6; for "sincerity of heart" in vs.22, see the same words in Acts 2:46). For vs.4:5, see Eph.5:15-17; and for vs.4:6, see Eph.4:29 and Mk.9:50.

Col.4:7-18—Paul closes his letter by addressing 10 individuals specifically, either in compliments or with instructions (note the two helpers of Paul with Jewish heritage, Mark and Justus, who proved a comfort to Paul; see Acts 15:36-41). Epaphras was undoubtedly a key resource for Paul on how to address and pray for the church at Colossae (1:7; 4:12, 13; Philemon 23) Demas (vs.14; Philemon 24), eventually deserted Paul (2 Tim.4:10). It appears as understood here that Paul wrote a letter to the Laodiceans, but no copy or remains of this exists to the date of this writing (vss.15, 16). It is often thought, in closing his epistles, that Paul "signed" the greeting, but often had it dictated (the main content of the letter) to someone else to write for him when possible (vs.18; 1 Cor.16:21; Rom.16:22). He closes by asking them to remember his imprisonment, and the blessing of God's grace to be with them (as he began his letter with the same; vs.18; 1:2).

1 Thessalonians

Paul established the church at Thessalonica on his second missionary journey. There was a harvest there for the Gospel, but opposition as well, and Paul was driven out of the city to Berea (west of Thessalonica) and then went to Athens and eventually to Corinth, where this letter was written (Acts 17:1-18:1). The city still exists today (spelled Thessaloniki) in northern Greece on the Aegean Sea.

1 Thess.1:1-10—Paul's favorite subjects to write on to the churches at large—faith, hope and love—are noticeably seen at the beginning and toward the close of his letter, also (1:3;5:8). Paul covers his faith discussion through the first 3 chapters and through the first eight verses of chapter four. He begins his "love interactions" for the church in 4:9-12, then, on the subject of comfort for a deceased loved one in their church, he presents great understanding on the Rapture of the Church and Christ's second coming, both from 4:13 through 5:11; and finishes with "church love interactions" (within the church and outside—5:14, 15) to the close of his epistle.

Paul acknowledges his close fellow-workers in the Lord's work of sharing the Gospel and church affairs to follow, Silvanus (probably Silas) and Timothy (vs.1). He greets the church with his common greeting of grace and peace (vs.2; see Rom.1:1-7 for more elaboration on this). He commends them for their "work of faith, labor of love and endurance (Greek word) of hope" in the Lord Jesus in the presence of God the Father (vs.3), declaring God's choosing of them (reception of the Gospel), as the Gospel came to them in word, power of the Holy Spirit and full conviction (assurance—vss.4, 5). They became imitators of him and the Lord Jesus and examples to others in receiving the Gospel in the midst of tribulation, and with the joy of the Holy Spirit (vss.6-8). They turned from "idols" to serve the living and true God (vs.9), as God gives the believer the hope of Christ's return, and also, delivers the believer from the wrath to come (vs.10; 5:9; Rev.6:17).

1 Thess.2:1-20—Paul recounts and reminds the Thessalonian church about his visit to them. Even though suffering and shameful treating occurred leaving Philippi, Paul and his fellow-servants were still bold in presenting the Gospel of the Lord Jesus, even while encountering similar opposition in Thessalonica (vss.1, 2). Their exhortation to them was not in error, impurity or deceit (vs.3). God had entrusted them to go forth and preach the Gospel, so their motive was to please God and not as "man-pleasers," with an approval to God (the Greek word), who examines our hearts (vss.4, 5). They did not declare the Gospel to them with flattering speech (Greek word with motives of self-interest here, Vine), nor in a "disguise of greed" or seeking glory from men (vss.5, 6). They could have been "burdensome" to them with their authority (vs.6), but instead, were gentle (mild) with them, as a mother tenderly handles and cherishes her children (even in trying

moments—the Greek word used here by Paul, Vine; vs.7). Having a fond affection for them, they were glad to impart to them, not only the Gospel, but their own lives as well, in their personal hard work and labors to and for them (vss.8,9), in proclaiming the Gospel. Their conduct was holy, righteous and without blame, as a father encourages, consoles (speaks closely to, the Greek word here; see also 5:14) and testifies (literally, witnessing) to them to walk in a manner pleasing to God, who has called us into His kingdom and glory (vss.10-12).

Paul elaborates more on chapter one, verse 6. As the Thessalonians received God's word as truly from Him—which actively works in and through believers (see Heb.4:12)—they became imitators of the Christian churches of Judea, enduring suffering at the hands of their own countrymen, being hostile to them and trying to hinder them from furthering the Gospel of Christ Jesus to others, and so, encountering God's wrath, unless they repent and receive Jesus in the Gospel message (vss.13-16; compare vss.7-11). Paul was eager to see them again, but had been detained more than once, for the new believers were his crown and joy in his ministry, and also in the day of Christ's coming (vss.17-20).

1 Thess.3:1-13—With Paul in Athens alone and then going over to Corinth (west of Athens), when Timothy and Silas came to Paul (Acts 17:15), Paul then sent Timothy back to Thessalonica to see how the church there was doing, and not to be disturbed over Paul and his fellow-workers trials and hardships for the Gospel (vss.1-5). Timothy returned and brought them good news on how their faith and love was growing among them, even in distresses

and afflictions of their own (vss.6-8). So, Paul encouraged them to "keep standing firm" in the Lord (1:3) and in thankfulness and joy he prays earnestly to see them soon, and help their progress (moving to completion, the Greek word here) and growth in their faith (vss.9, 10). His prayer in written form here reflects all this for them, plus their developing and increasing in God's love, for all men, as God continues their growth in their hearts (establishes them), to be "blameless in holiness" at the coming of the Lord Jesus with His (literally) holy ones (vss.11-13; two line of thoughts can come from the Greek wording of Paul here in vs.13: if it refers to the Rapture of the church (meeting Jesus in the air and then presenting the church to the Father—1 Thess.4:13-18; Col.1:22;2 Cor.4:14), then all stands as the NASB and KJ translate; if this refers to the second coming of Christ, then the Greek word "holy ones" (NIV) would refer to "angels" (BAGD), as Jesus (Mt.16:27;25:31; Mk.8:38) and the rest of the New Testament writers on the subject made known (2 Thess.1:7; Jude 14); note Jesus does come back with a selected, chosen and described army in coming back to earth in His second coming—Rev.17:14).

1 Thess.4:1-18—As the Apostle Paul now moves toward his final address in his letter to the Thessalonian church, he, as he customarily does, gives exhorting "love interactions" for the church. Here the topic is "sanctification" (continued growth in the holiness of the Lord), which is God's will for them (vss.3, 7). Love of God expressed is acquiring one's mate for life in the holiness and honorable process of God (vss.3-6; see Book 2 of <u>The Family Bible Studies Series—The Levels of Relationships</u> for the importance of friendship before companionship). Rejecting

(literally, setting it aside instead of following it) this would be to reject God, who gives us His Holy Spirit (the verb here is a present tense verb referring to the continual process and work of the Holy Spirit in the life of the believer, vss.7,8).

Paul then brings out two kinds of love for the Thessalonians to follow—brotherly love (the word "Philadelphia," more of an affectionate, caring-for-one-another love) and God's "agape love," which is God's unconditional love for one another (and even all mankind—vss.9,12; 2:6-12). Paul encourages them to continue to do these "love actions" with one another; and live a quiet and peaceful life; and do practical work to provide for their needs; and to be a good example toward outsiders (vss.11, 12; see Mk.4:11).

In an effort to encourage one who may grieve over someone who has died in the Lord (another Christian), Paul here gives the teaching on the Rapture of the Church (4:13-18), for comfort to one another and to give them the hope in the Lord (vss.13, 18, by the Lord's word, vs.15). It is important here to see how he explains this important event and key words that help us understand it. The summary of this is given to us in vs.14. Based on the resurrection of Jesus, the Church will experience the same bodily resurrection for them (vss.14-17; Phil.3:20, 21; Col.3:1-4; 1 Jn.3:1, 2). A key word to note here in vs.14 in this understanding for us is the word "bring." What is all happening and going on with this event? Who is "bringing" something to somebody else? Notice God will "bring" with Jesus those who have fallen asleep (died) in Him (vs.14). So, God gives the command and a shout is given (possibly something like, "come up here" or "arise") and Jesus descends from heaven (vs.16—note the Lord Himself, it says) with a shout (literally, a shout of command, NASB in the margin of this verse); and a voice of the archangel (note how they (here "he," the archangel) gets to participate in this grand event for the church, being warriors for God's people throughout time; Dan.10; Jude 9); and a "trumpet of God" occurs (trumpets alert the people about the timing of an event—Num.10—and the "last trumpet" in 1 Cor.15: 52, 53 (in the same context) indicates (as was in Israel's time) that it is time to move out to the next destination; see Ex.40:34-38). Then, those deceased in the Lord rise to meet the Lord in air, followed by the church alive on earth at that time, rising up likewise to meet the Lord in the clouds (vss.15-17; the word "rapture" is the Latin word for the Greek word here meaning "seize by force suddenly" (Vine), caught up, i.e., going against gravity, in vs.17). Then, from the clouds and sky, the church is brought by Jesus (the word "bring" back in vs.14) and presented to God the Father as His beautiful, glorified Bride (5:23, 24; 1 Jn.3:1,2; see about the presentation in Col.1:22; Eph.1:4-6; 5:26,27; 2 Cor.4:14; John 3:29; and Jesus' prayer and intention in love for the church in Jn.17:24 and His prayer for us to pray in meeting Him in Lk.21:34-36). Thus (the comfort), the believer will always be with the Lord (their place is in heaven—Jn.14:1-3, similar language, in the "dwelling places" provided by God in heaven). Comforting words indeed by Jesus that the believers are to share with one another (vs.18; 5:11), their "hope of glory" (Col.1:27; 1 Thess.1:3; 5:8; 1 Jn.3:1, 2).

1 Thess.5:1-28—With the Rapture of the Church now declared (4:13-18), many would now ask—"when does this occur?" (a similar question the Apostles had regarding Israel's kingdom in Acts 1:6-8, using the same words as in vs.1 here; see that commentary and

answer on the definition of those words, "times and epochs"). Paul now addresses "the second coming of the Lord" (vs.4, the Day of the Lord), so they would know (comfort) that they were not in the time of God's wrath (as reason for writing this; vs.9; 1:10; 2 Thess.2:1-4; see the previous commentary on 1:10, the Great Tribulation—Mt.24:21, 29; Rev.6-19). One indication of that time to come is the proclamation that there is "peace and safety," when instead, destruction comes and, like birth pangs (see the same language used by Jesus there in Mt.24:8; Mk.13:8), people under God's wrath will not escape (vss.3, 9; 2 Thess.1:6-9). So believers are to be alert to meet the Lord (vss.4-8; Mt.24:37-44; see this commentary in the believer's taken to be with the Lord in the Rapture there and being alert for it). We are called by God to live in holiness and honor to God, and before our fellowman (vss.8, 9; 4:3, 4, 12; 3:13; 2:10-12). Thus, to be alert for the meeting of the Lord (4:17; 5:4-6) and living together with Him (vs.10; 4:17), whether asleep or awake (the latter follows His command (Mt.24:42, 44; vss.10, 11), and encouraging one another for that day and building each other up in the Lord (vs.11).

Paul finishes up his "love in actions" with encouraging words to the Thessalonians. He says "in love" to express their appreciation to the ones who give them instruction in the Lord; and to live peacefully with one another (vss.12, 13; 4:11, 12). Help train (by word of encouragement or reproof, if necessary) with any who need help with personal disciplines (idle, lazy, to help them put things in proper order); speak with tenderness to those who are disheartened over something, and help support any who are weak (of course in any area, but especially in faith—see Rom.14:1: 1

Cor.9:22, 23; BAGD); and to be "longsuffering" (Greek word, including in one's temperament) with all men (vs.14). Don't return evil to someone, but only what is good for one another and to all men (vs.15). Always rejoice (see Neh.8:10, 12; John 16:22; Phil.4:4), pray unceasingly (Eph.6:18) and give thanks in all things (always something to be thankful to the Lord for), for this is God's will to do (vss.16-18). Not "quenching" the Spirit means not to "put out" the "fire" of His workings (see Mt.3:11; Acts 2 at Pentecost, etc., that is, determine His working at the time); and "test out" prophecies that are given (with God's word and Biblically with discerning spiritual people—vss.19, 20); and keep away from all forms (and appearances) of evil (vss.14-22). Continue in the Lord's sanctification (4:3; Heb.10:14) to one's entirety and whole being (spirit, soul and body; two Greek words here—complete and entire), setting the goal to be blameless (2:10-12; 3:11-13) at the coming of the Lord, which is the work of God in the life of the believer (vss.23, 24; 4:7, 8; Phil.1:6). Paul charged them to read this letter to all of them and finishes his letter with the pronouncement of God's grace to be with them, just as he began his letter in 1:1.

2 Thessalonians

Paul's second letter to the church of the Thessalonians presents a clearer picture of the coming of the antichrist, the judgment of God upon the wickedness of the world and the second coming of Jesus Christ to earth to rule in His millennial reign. It appears to be a takeoff from chapter five of first Thessalonians, giving detail about the long time prophecy of the Day of the Lord (Is.2:21; Joel 1:15; 2:1, 2, 11, 31; 3:14, 15, 18-21; Amos 5:18-20; 9:11, 12; Mic.4:6, 7; Zeph.1:7,14-18; Zech.14:1-15; Mal.4:5, 6). See the connection at 1 Thess.5:2 and 2 Thess.2:2. In the midst of their persecution at Thessalonica, they were wondering if the Day of the Lord had come. Paul had made known to them in 1 Thess.5 that the Day of the Lord is a time of God's wrath upon the unbelief and wickedness of the world and the church is not destined for that (1 Thess.1:10; 4:13-18; 5:9-11; see that previous commentary). And so he goes on to explain to them that this time does not take place till the events of 2 Thess.2 occur.

2 Thess. 1:1-12—See 1 Thess.1:1 for the greeting to them. Paul gladly commends the Thessalonians for their growing faith and love toward one another in the midst of their persecutions, and afflictions, and their growing endurance (standing firm under

their trials) through their sufferings for the Lord (vss.3-5). Their suffering for the Gospel of Jesus demonstrates God's righteous judgment, and that they are considered worth of the Kingdom of God (see Phil.1:28; 2:9-11; Acts 5:41), and that same righteous judgment will bring the penalty of eternal destruction and just retribution to those who do not know God or obey the Gospel of the Jesus Christ (vss.6-10). This will occur when the Lord returns to earth with His mighty angels in flaming fire (vs.7; 1 Thess.3:13—see that commentary) and to be glorified and marveled at in His saints (the church at large—"all who have believed"—vs.10; see the King's return and entering into His temple—Ezk.43:1-9). Paul prays for them that the Lord Jesus be continued to be glorified in their lives by God's grace, and thus being counted worthy of their calling (1 Thess.2:12), and that God would fulfill their every desire for goodness, through their faith and God's power working in them (vss.11,12).

2 Thess.2:1-17—Paul now addresses specifically to the Thessalonians why they are not in the Day of the Lord in the time of their own persecutions (vss.1-3). He begins by making reference to the Lord's return in His second coming to earth (note the language of "gathering" here and Mk.13:26, 27; also Dt.30:3-5; plus, the reference again to the Day of the Lord—vs.2, for which see the previous commentary of the introduction to Second Thessalonians; (our gathering in vs.1 is Paul's reference to the believers at the second coming.) Paul did not want anyone to tell them anything different (vss.2, 3), because the Day of the Lord will not occur until two events first take place—1) the apostasy—the word here means "rebellion," that takes place in concurrence with

the antichrist or conceivably, events leading up to his appearance (BAGD; a defection or revolt—Vine; the only other occurrence in the New Testament of this word is found in Acts 21:21, and, in a religious sense, a falling away apostasy—BAGD). This kind of terminology and understanding fits the context well here, leading up to the next event; 2) the appearance of the antichrist (the man of lawlessness, the son of destruction—vs.3). Paul references the antichrist with the "abomination of desolation" (vs.4: Dan.9:27; Mt.24:15; see also Is.14:14; Gen.3:4, 5). Until he appears, though, One is retraining the "mystery of lawlessness" at work (vss.6, 7; what <u>activity</u> restrains him now (and lawlessness at work) is, in the Greek, a neuter present participle action (vs.6), and the Holy Spirit is in the neuter gender, when referred to directly; the One now restraining (vs.7, referring to a specific person) him (the antichrist and lawlessness at work), is, in the Greek, a masculine present participle active; five times in the Gospel of John, the Holy Spirit is referred to directly in those passages with the Greek masculine personal pronoun (He or Him, "ekeinos"—see in Jn.14:26; 15:26; 16:8, 13, 14), until He is taken out of the way, at the Rapture of the church—1 Thess. 4:17). It is also not that surprising that the Holy Spirit would be referred to in the masculine gender (spirit, in general, is in the neuter gender). So, this seems to best fit the context of the events here and currently taking place.

Paul then goes on to reveal what takes place (remember the Thessalonians concern—vs.2) when the antichrist appears—the Lord will slay him at His coming to earth (vs.8; Rev.19:15,16); the antichrist comes in the activity of Satan's power, and false signs and wonders (vs.9; see Rev.13) and in deceit of wickedness, with followers who perish, because they did not receive the love of the truth to be saved (vs.10-12; 1:7-9).

In contrast to vs.12, Paul gives thanks to the believers, who are loved by the Lord and have responded and received the Gospel of Jesus Christ, by faith in the truth (compare vss.11,12), by the sanctifying (holiness development) work of the Holy Spirit; and growing in God's glory (2 Cor.3:17,18), to one day receive the glory of the Lord Jesus, that He will share with the believers (vs. 14; Jn.17:22-24; Phil.3:20,21; Col.3:1-4; 1 Jn.3:1,2). Paul reminds them to hold on to what he and his fellow-servants had taught them, by mouth or by an epistle (compare vs.2; and so for us to follow the Bible). He prays that the Lord Jesus Himself and God our Father, who loves us and has given us eternal comfort (1:5, 10, 11; 2:13-15; Rom.15:4) and good hope by grace (1:10; 2:8, 13-15; Rom.5:1-5; Col.1:26, 27), will comfort their hearts (with His eternal comfort) and strengthen them (growing in the faith) for every good work and deed (vss.16, 17; 1:11, 12).

2 Thess.3:1-18—Paul requests them to pray for him and his team ministers for the continued spreading of the Gospel through them and for God to deliver them from (literally) unreasonable and evil men, as God will strengthen and protect him and them from the evil one (vss.1-3; see 1 Pet.1:3-5). Paul had confidence in them that they would follow what they were charging them to do (vs.4) and prayed that God would direct (make straight) their hearts into God's love and the endurance of Christ Jesus (vs.5; 2:14, 16, 17).

Paul gives one final instruction to some in their church setting who were not willing to work (idle or disorderly in some way or manner) in their church group (vss.6, 11; see the initial direction given by Paul back in 1 Thess.5:14). Paul is firm on the principle that if one is not willing to work, then neither let him eat (vs.10). Paul lived that way to be an example to them, by working night and day to provide for his own needs and those in ministry with him (vss.7-9; he was not "idle" (same word) among them (vs.7); see also Acts 20:33-35). So he commands them to work to provide their own needs, as well (vss.10-12; "busybodies" in vs.11 literally means "working around" work—doing none at all—as said previously in this verse). Paul says not to associate with ones of that lifestyle, and not to treat them as an enemy, but admonish (to train by word, whether by encouragement or corrective urgency—Vine) such a person as a brother (vss.14, 15). But the church is not to grow weary of doing what is good (vs.13; Eph.6:8) and accept and follow what Paul said (vss.12-14; 2:15). As a final blessing, Paul prays that God's peace be with them in all they do (vs.16). See the commentary at the end of Colossians for Paul's closing of his letters to the churches.

1 Timothy

The Apostle Paul is writing to young Timothy (4:12) in his responsibilities to pastor the church at Ephasus (1:3). The theme and encouragement of this book is for Timothy to "fight the good fight of faith" in carrying out his duties (1:18; 6:12; 2 Tim.4:7). It is generally agreed that Paul wrote this letter after the release of his first imprisonment to Timothy. Paul here gives good guidelines and instructions on proper conduct in the household of God (3:15). Paul knows the battle well, from the outside and inside the church, living in godliness, and taking hold of the God's promises in the present life and also those in the life to come, and fixing his (our) hope on the living God, the Savior of all men (4:9, 10; 1:1). In his pastoral duties, Timothy was now in the battle with those responsibilities, also.

1 Tim.1:1-20—Paul begins his letter to Timothy by reminding him of Paul's authority by the command of God to his calling to be apostle for the Lord, God our Savior and Christ Jesus our hope (vs.1; Acts 3:1-4). Timothy was a true child in the faith, as Paul was like a "father" in the Lord to Timothy (Phil.2:22; 1 Cor.4:17). Paul extends God's grace, mercy and peace to Timothy and from Christ Jesus our Lord (vs.2).

With all the worship of false gods in the Ephasus area (a center for Artemis (Greek) or Diana (Latin), one of the seven wonders of the world), Paul instructs Timothy to direct certain men not to teach "strange doctrines" instead of God's word (vs.3). Myths or fables (fictional stories or accounts where there is a falsification of facts—Vine) and "endless genealogies," rising to mere speculations, were just a couple of the problems Timothy faced there at Ephasus (vss.3, 4). Paul lays out the "goal" for Timothy in presenting the teaching of God's word—the demonstration of God's love, from a good conscience and (literally) unhypocritical faith (not pretending to be something else). "Fruitless discussion" can otherwise be the result, with others asserting things they do not understand or over presenting themselves (as about the Jewish Law back in those times, not surprising about all this in light of vs.4—vss.5-7). Paul affirms on the topic of the Law that the Law is good, if used properly (lawfully), remembering that it was given for those who are lawless, and rebellious and immoral, etc., things contrary to sound teaching and the glorious Gospel of God in Jesus Christ (vss.8-11, 1).

Paul recounts to Timothy how blessed they are to be in the ministry (vs.12; 4:14) and recalls to Timothy God's calling of him (Paul) to the ministry (2:6, 7). He affirms this high honor, especially since Paul had previously persecuted the church and acted ignorantly in unbelief (vss.12, 13), but now declares how God's mercy, grace, faith and love were far greater in abundance than the sins he committed (vss.12-15). Now as a believer, he is a demonstrator, having found God's mercy, of "all the longsuffering" (Greek word) in Christ Jesus in his service to Him, as an example for believers to see and find encouragement by his life and faith in ministry for Christ Jesus (vss.15-16). Paul declares and gives glory and honor to God—to the King of the ages (literally) and to the unchanging (incorruptible—not liable to corruption or decay—so, immortal) and invisible and only God, forever and ever (vs.17; 2:5; Dt.4:39).

Paul exhorts Timothy to "fight the good of fight" (vs.18, see the introduction of first Timothy), keeping faith and a good conscience (vs.19, 5) according to his calling (vss.18, 19; 4:14). Two people who fit in the category of 1:3, Paul points out to Timothy to beware of in his ministry (vs.20). See also 2 Tim.2:16-18 (the meaning of the "resurrection already taken place" is uncertain and difficult to precisely sort out; could mean that the resurrection already taken place may not follow with any others to take place, undermining 1 Thess.4:17 and other resurrection verses in the Bible to come, example, Rev.20); but God's foundation and promises stand sure and firm—2 Tim.2:19. For the statement "hand over to Satan," see 1 Cor.5:5; and not to blaspheme (dishonor or speak against God or other people), see 6:1 and Titus 2:5; 3:1, 2).

1 Tim.2:1-15—The first thing in basic responsibilities that Paul asks earnestly for Timothy to do is to pray, and lists four kinds of prayers—prayer for needs; general prayers; intercessions (which can include petitions to superiors); and thanksgivings (vs.1)—praying for kings and authorities in high positions, in order that we may live quiet and peaceful manners of life (the Greek words here prefer to both inner and outer tranquility), in godliness and dignity (Greek word refers to integrity; seriousness in purpose and self-respect in conduct; see the word also in 3:4; Phil. 4:8—the

second word in the list; Tit.2:7—the last word); and prayers for salvation, as God desires that all men be saved and come to the knowledge of the truth of the Gospel of Jesus Christ, the One Mediator between God and man, for man to be saved (vss.1-6); Acts 4:12; Gal.3:20-22; Heb.9:13-15; 12:24). "Ransom" in vs.6 is a payment made for another that is due them to set them free of it (especially a slave or criminal), similar in meaning to the word "redemption" (see Rom.3:23, 24; Col.1:13, 14; Heb.9:11-15). Christ paid the "ransom" for all (vs.6), effective by faith, in the spiritual birth (Jn.1:12, 13; 3:1-17; Rom.3:21-28). Paul declares to Timothy that this is his proclamation, appointed as a preacher, teacher and apostle to the Gentiles in faith and truth (vs.7). With this calling, he wants all men to pray to God with holy hands and without wrath and disputing (vs.8).

For women in the church, Paul directs them in writing to Timothy to be modest in dress and appearance, to be of a sound mind and to live a life of good works, and have demonstration of godly character (vss.9, 10). They are to be willing to learn and be submissive to the church authorities (vs.11; see also 1 Cor.14:34, 35, 3-5, 10—see the commentary on 1 Cor.11 for details on that chapter). By God's design, women are not to have teaching positions in the church exercising positions of or over men (either self appointed or have authority, the Greek word in vs.12 for "exercise authority"), or appointed by another to do so (literally "to have authority of a man, a subjective genitive here); see God's design in Gen.2:7, 15-24; 1 Tim.3 for the designs of both and serving in the church; see also Book 1 of <u>The Family Bible Studies Series, The Family of God—Foundation</u>, the chapter, The First

Family on Earth, a commentary on Genesis 1-4 for further details and insights about God's design of man and woman, as Paul refers to this as his basis for his statement in vss.13-1). Paul refers to God's design from his statement in vs.12 in the last three verses of chapter two here, with the blessings of God to women, continuing in faith, love, holiness (growth in sanctification) and (literally) a sound mind (same word as in vs.9; vss.13-15).

1 Tim.3:1-16—Paul now gives Timothy directions for leadership in the church. As mentioned previously about God's design in 1 Tim.2:11-15 (see the commentary on those verses), it is a good thing if a man desires and reaches (seeks, Greek word here) after being in church leadership (literally here, an overseer in the church—vs.1). Characteristics are then given by Paul for this position (as one who oversees and becomes an example for God's people to serve (see also 1 Pet.5:1-4 and Tit.1:5-9); the Greek has the word "necessary" as a prelude to the overseer's characteristics listed here in Timothy chapter three; KJ says "then must be..."). First, there is to be no discredit or blame to the one desiring to minister; then, the husband of one wife (that is within God's guidelines for marriage—Eph.5:21-33; 1 Cor.7; 2 Cor.6:14-18, etc); free from the influence of intoxicants (alcohol, illegal drugs, etc., so moderate in use of alcohol—vs.2); sound judgment (sensible); orderly conduct and appearance (the word cosmetic here in Greek); hospitable (to strangers and guests); able to teach (God's word and guidelines in life—see 2 Tim.2:24); not given over to the effects of wine (literally here; alcohol in general—vs.5:3); not a physical fighter or violent person; but instead (contrast here), a fair, equitable person, not always

insisting on the letter of the law, but considerate and reasonable in decision making (the Greek word here); and not contentious or a quarrelsome person (that is, argumentative or fault finding—remember the preceding verse); not a "lover of money" or greedy (see 6:6-10); managing one's household well (family with self respect and to each other, with children honoring their parents and well devoted to and with them; dignity—see the last word in 2:2 and in 3:8 and Tit.2:7; vss.4, 5); not a recent convert to the faith (overseer and elder are sometimes used interchangeably—see 4:14; so then, to exemplify the humility of Jesus (see a definition in the commentary of Mt.11:25-30; vs.6); and the last listing by Paul here is to have a good witness in the community (to outsiders of the church; vs.7)—vss.1-7.

Paul next addresses the character and responsibilities of a deacon (general meaning—a servant; here looked at as an appointed position under a higher authority in the church, normally, the elders). First for deacons is being serious in purpose and self-respect in conduct (vss.8, 4); not contradictory (saying one thing to one person and different to another, i.e., double-talk); not given over to the effects of wine or addiction to alcohol or illegal drugs (vss.8, 2, 3); not fond of or pursuing dishonest gain (vs.8); holding (present tense) the mystery of the faith with a clear (literally, clean) conscience (vss.9,16; 1:5; Eph.3:1-11); and have a time of proving for the opportunity of service (with the view to approval); and then, allowed to serve (minister), without any charge or accusation against one devoted to serving (vs.10).

Under the context here, it seems fitting that women appointed to service (deaconess—see commentary on vs.12) in the church presents the best understanding in vs.11. Their characteristics are—serious in purpose, and self-respect in conduct (see vss.4, 8); not fault-finders, accusing of others or malicious in speech; free from the influence of intoxicants (alcohol, illegal drugs, etc., so moderate in alcohol use); and faithful in all things (vs.11).

Deacons are also to be husbands of one wife (see vs.2 commentary) and manage their households well (vs.12; see commentary on vs.4). Those who minister well acquire a good standing and great confidence in faith in Christ Jesus (vs.13). Paul says that these things are necessary (Greek word as in vs. 2—see the commentary there) for good conduct in the church of the living God (whom we live for), the pillar (upholding the church) and foundation (NIV) of the truth (vs.15). Paul concludes with the testimony of the common confession of the faith (see vs.9), a mystery now made more clear (see Eph.3:1-11; Rom.16:25-27) about the coming to earth of God's Son, our Savior and Lord (1:17) Jesus Christ, covering His full ministry from birth to His ascension in vs.16. Called "the mystery of godliness," of God bringing His Son to earth to save mankind from his sins, and rose from the grave and was taken back to His glory to be with God once again (Jn.1:1, 2; 17:5, 24; Heb. 1:1-3). All these verbs in vs.16 are passive verbs, showing how God fulfills His plan to build His family through the faithfulness of His Son Jesus Christ (Mk.1:15; Acts 3:19-21; Eph.1:9-14; 3:14, 15—see the commentary on these two verses for God building His family, in heaven and on earth).

I Tim.4:1-16—In light of 3:16 just covered, Paul declares how opposite behaviors will take place in the days before the return of

Jesus coming back to earth and to reign (see 2 Tim.1-9; 2 Pet.3:3-7), regarding the faith (3:16): The presence of deceiving spirits and teachings of demons (vs.1; again, compare 3:16); hypocritical liars (see the same root word in 1:5 with Paul's goal there), being as "branded" in their conscience (like a permanent mark, as used on animals—vs.2); people forbidding marriages and abstinences of certain foods (vs.3; see Dan.7:24-27; sounds possibly tied in with cultic religious teaching; see vs.1). All this instead of giving thanks to God (quite simplistic in comparison), who created everything in His creation good (vss.3, 4; Gen.1:31; Heb.11:3), all set apart and created by God for our enjoyment and service to Him, affirmed by the word of God (Gen.1:31; 9:1-3, 7) and prayer (the word intercession here, remembering our daily prayer in Mt.6:11, as well as the prayers that go up to God in need of His blessing and provision for others; vs. 5; 2:1,8). Timothy is instructed by Paul to continue being "nourished" (see the same root word in Eph.5:29 and 6:4) on the words the faith and the good teaching of God's word and to share these with the brethren in his ministry (vs.6; Rm.1:17; 15:4; Heb.11). He is to avoid "tales and fables" (see about these in 1:4) and concentrate on living a godly life (vs.7), which is profitable for all things—this life and the life to come (vss.8, 9). Paul says for this we strive and labor, fixing our hope on the living God, the Savior of all men, especially believers (vss.10, 11; Heb.12:1, 2; Dt.10:17-20). Paul finishes this chapter with several exhortations to Timothy: show your progress and maturity, growing both in speech and conduct, in love, faith and purity (root word of holiness here; 1 Pet.1:16), and being an example for the believers (vss.12, 15; 1:16; Tit.2:7);

continue in the public proclamation, teaching and exhortation of the Scriptures, connected with using his spiritual gift prophesied over him by the presbytery (probably the elders at that time; vs.13, 14); and Paul stresses to Timothy to carefully watch himself and his teaching to the brethren, which will enable them both to work out their salvation in service to the Lord (vs.16; Phil.2:12, 13), experiencing His blessings, direction and deliverances along the way.

1 Tim.5:1-25—In regards to relationships in carrying out his ministry, Paul gives Timothy directions for respectful conduct in his interaction with others in the church. Paul says not to be disrespectful to older men (literally, to strike at), but to encourage them with proper or required advice. Relate to younger men as brothers, younger women as sisters and older women as mothers—all in purity (vss.1, 2; 4:12). Paul gives lengthy advice here in the proper handling of widows in the church (vss.3-16). He exhorts those widows who have children and/or grandchildren to help care for them, which also helps provide opportunity for mutual exchange between them (vss.4, along with having any with dependent widows, also—vs.16; see also Dt.4:9). The single widows can help in God's work more freely, including prayer (needs and general prayer here—vss.5-7; see Lk.2:36-38). It is one's responsibility to care for their own first (vs.8; Dt.4:9). Paul gives a character trait listing here for widows too, a testimony of a good witness to others and devotion to every good work (vss.9, 10), but for younger widows to marry and to serve in carrying out household responsibilities, and to help manage things well, and not give the enemy an occasion for (literally) verbal abuse

(not that some problems won't occur, as is well known in family development). Taking care of one's own then, will not burden the church (vs.16).

Paul concludes chapter five by instructing Timothy to honor those who both teach and preach God's word in the church, even if fitting with a financial blessing in return (vss.17, 18); and not to bring an accusation against an elder without two or more witnesses (see Jesus' words in Mt.18:15-20), where also, if a sin is acknowledged (Mt.18:15-20) and continues on, the church may bring the rebuke to the attention and presence of the church for them to learn from it (vss.19, 20). Paul says to carry this out without partiality (vs.21). Appointments to church positions and service should be tested and approved with a reasonable time frame, to keep free from sins of others unchecked (vss.22-25; 4:14; 3:8-13), with the concentration of doing good deeds for God's servants, whether seen or unseen (vs.25).

1 Tim.6:1-21— Paul exhorts Timothy to speak to servants and workers to honor respectfully their masters, whether an unbeliever or believer, to keep consistent with Christian belief and respect to authorities, realizing also the benefit believers bring to their masters (vss.1,2; Rom.13:1; Eph.6:5-9; note this respect can be maintained even with disagreements). Avoid arguments with those advocating different doctrine of the faith (in Jesus and godliness—vs.3), as pride and lack of understandings, when continued, can only lead to strife and envy and "evil suspicions" (vss.3-5), instead of "the doctrine conforming to godliness in Christ" (vs.3; 4:12;1:4,5) Some in opposition may only be looking for financial or personal gain (vs.5), without knowing the great personal, and collective

gain (in the church) of godliness (growing in the Lord; see 4:8; "contentment" is satisfaction with what one has—vss.6-8; see the other occurrence in the New Testament in 2 Cor.9:8; also, Book 3 of <u>The Family Bible Studies Series, Growing In God's Wisdom</u>, for more "ingredients" of wisdom and how to pray for them). Pursuit of money primarily or simply just for personal financial gain, can lead one down many erroneous pathways and traps and snares, even eventually into ruin and destruction (vss.7, 9; see Lk.12:13-34); for "loving money" in and of itself finds itself at the root of many evils, and such pursuits would be contrary to the faith, and bring many pains in life (vss.9, 10; instead, see Mt.6:19-21; Lk.6:35-38). Paul, then, instructs Timothy, on the other hand, to pursue godly and everlasting things—seven to be sure: righteousness, godliness (4:8, 9), faith, love, endurance (the Greek word; so, perseverance), meekness (see the commentary on Mt.5:5 and James 3:13 for a helpful definition) and eternal life (vss.11, 12), which Paul calls this (the theme of this letter)—"fighting the good fight of faith" (vs.12; 1:18; 4:10-12). He reminds Timothy to recall his good testimony given, leading him to his ministry, remembering also the "faithful witnessing" of Jesus before Pontus Pilate (John 18, 19), and to keep "fighting the good fight" until the Lord's return (vss.13-15)—The Sovereign Lord and King of kings, to Him be the honor and dominion forever—Amen (vss.15, 16; Mt.28:18; John 1:14-18).

Paul gives to Timothy the guidance to share with those who are rich to set their hope on the certainty of God and not riches of the earth (see Prov.3:9,10, 13-26); for God is the One who supplies us with all good things (4:4,5), and instructs us to be "rich" in good works and ready to share from one's own belongings with others, and so, to store up a good foundation for the future, taking hold of "real life" (eternal life) indeed (vss.17-19, 12; Eph.6:7, 8; Col.3:17, 23, 24; 1 Tim.4:8-11).

Timothy is instructed by Paul to "guard his deposit" (for which see 2 Tim.1:12-14; 1 Tim.4:12-16; 6:12-14) and avoid "empty discussions" and arguments and such things that are falsely called "knowledge," which some profess and "missed the mark" regarding the faith (vss.20, 21; see Col.2:2, 3; 1 Cor.1:30-2:16; Prov.21:30). Paul blesses Timothy with God's grace to be with him in closing (vss.20, 21; 1:1, 2).

2 Timothy

Paul sends this letter to Timothy while in his second imprisonment in Rome (1:8, 16, 17). He knows that his time of departing from the earth is now soon (4:6-8). He instructs Timothy on some last guidelines and directions for his ministry.

2 Tim.1:1-18—Paul begins his letter by reminding Timothy of Paul's calling to begin an apostle for the Lord Jesus Christ, by God's will according to the promise of life in Christ Jesus (vs.1; 2:10; 1 Tim.4:8; 6:12). He passes on to Timothy God's mercy, grace and peace from God the Father and Christ Jesus our Lord (vs.2). Paul maintains a clear conscience, as his faithful previous forefathers (Rom.1:7), and constantly prays for Timothy day and night, longing to see him again (vss.3, 4). Paul acknowledges Timothy's sincere faith (Greek word un-hypocritical faith) and his great instruction and training he received from his grandmother and his mother (Dt.4:9, 6:1, 2), gaining wonderful education of the Scriptures from childhood (vs.5; 3:14-17). With this background and calling now to the ministry, Paul reminds him to use his gifting that came to him through Paul's laying his hands upon him (vs.6; 1 Tim.4:14). Part of being in ministry for Christ's is overcoming sufferings for Him in His service and purposes with

His power, strength, love and grace and sound judgment (literally, a sound mind—vs.7) through the Holy Spirit (vss.7-9; Jn.16:33; 2 Cor.12:9). Through the gospel, Christ's appearing has put "death to death" and brought "life eternal" to light for mankind to be saved from sin and death (vs.10; Jn.1:1-18), which Paul was appointed for a preacher, apostle and teacher (vs.11; 1 Tim.2:7); and so he accepts those sufferings that go with the ministry (2:10), knowing God is able to protect and guard the "proceeds" that come from his ministry in the Lord's work, all entrusted to Him, with His promises and rewards in mind (vss.12, 8-10; 4:8; 1 Tim.4:8-11; Tit.1:1-3; 2 Pet.2:3,4). Paul then instructs Timothy to be likewise in his ministry—guarding his ministry and gifting in the Lord and entrusting the same to the Lord, as Paul said he did in vs.12 (vss.13,14; 1 Tim.6:20). Paul knows the commitment to ministry (4:7, 8), as some left him (vs.15), while the house of Onesiphorus was faithful to Paul, seeking him out and finding Paul, regardless of him being in prison (vss.8, 16, 17). Onesiphorus also had a testimony of good service to the Lord in Ephesus (vs.18; 4:19).

2 Tim.2:1-26—Paul now exhorts Timothy to be strong in God's grace (vs.1; 2 Cor.12:9; Phil.4:13) and to impart Paul's teachings and instructions on to other faithful men, also, so they can pass them on as well (vs.2). Paul instructs Timothy to be a faithful soldier to His Master, the Lord Jesus Christ—not "entangled" in civilian affairs or pursuits (vs.4; see the word in 2 Pet.2:20 also; Prov.3:1-8), competing by the rules to win the prize in the "good fight of faith" (vs.5; Phil.3:13, 14; 1 Cor.9:24-27; 1 Tim.4:8-10; 6:12), and receiving of his needs from the generosity from others (Prov.3:9, 10), as part of "sharing of the

crops" (fruit, produce) from his ministry (vss.6, 7; 1 Cor.9:10, 11; Lk.10:7). Paul endures the hardships of his Gospel ministry (vss.8-10)—even imprisoned like a criminal for the Gospel, yet, God's word is not "imprisoned" (that is, bound up—see Phil.1:12-14; Col.1:6,23)—for the sake God's chosen ones (His Family), so they may obtain God's salvation with its eternal glory (vs.10; Phil.3:20,21; Col.1:25-27; 3:1-4; 1 Jn.3:1,2; Jn.17:10,22-24).

The next three verses 11-13, though appearing a bit difficult at first, are more helpfully understood by the tenses of the verb—vs.11 is a past understood tense ("died with Him"—aorist in Greek), followed by a future promise (see Rm.6 for a fuller understanding of this for the believer); "endure" (vs.12) is a present tense (1:8; 2:3, 4, 10; 4:5,7, 8) with another future promise; "deny" is a future tense verb, probably with more of a present tense understanding (as is possible with the Greek future tense), unless this refers to the unbeliever (in a future occurrence) at the final judgment, as lived out in their life –Heb.9:27; Rev.20); otherwise, the present tense meaning would apply to the unbeliever as well, and not be a <u>sure applied</u> thing to a believer, in light of Peter's testimony in Jn.21; "disbelieving" (faithless) in vs.13 is also a present tense verb, and so, not applying to the believer, but simply states that one disbelieving does not change the truth of the Lord, about who He is, or what He has said and done (1 Tim.1:15-17; 3:16; 2 Tim.1:8-10; 2:8, 9; 4:1; Is.55:6-13; Mt.24:35).

With the Gospel and truth presented, Paul directs Timothy to not get caught up in (literally, the Greek word) "fights over words" in the ministry, which is not useful (as a fight) and can be to the ruin of the ones hearing (vss.14, 24-26; 1 Tim.6:4; instead—1

Tim.4:6). Timothy is to present himself as an approved workman for the Lord unashamedly, (literally) "cutting straight" the word of truth (genitive of content here, presenting straight the word of God, the truth, vs.15; Jn.14:6; 16:13-15; 17:17), and to avoid profane and empty talk, leading to further ungodliness, which can spread like a sickness can, and possibly upset the faith of some (vss.16-18; for "the resurrection already taken place," see the commentary on 1 Tim.1:20). Paul assures Timothy of God's sure foundation (1 Tim.3:15, 16) and that God knows those who are His, and that those who name the Lord's name are to (literally) "stand away" from wickedness (Lk.13:27; 1 Pet.1:15, 16); and so, to be a "vessel of honor" for the Lord, sanctified, useful and prepared for every good work (vss.19-21; for the word "seal" in vs.19, see Jn.3:33). Timothy is also to flee youthful ways and lusts and pursue God's righteousness, faith, love and peace, calling on the Lord with a clean heart (vs.22), and shun away from uninstructed disputes and quarrels (vss.22,23; Prov.17:14). The Lord's servant is to be gentle to all (see the other use of this word in 1 Thess.2:7), able to teach, patient of wrong doing or saying, and able to instruct (same root word as "uninstructed" in vs.23) those who oppose him in meekness (see the commentary on Mt.5:5 and James 3:13 for helpful understanding of meekness), if God should grant repentance to those opposing the truth and give them knowledge to understand and accept it and escape the devil's snare (or trap), which they were caught to do the devil's will ("his" agrees in the Greek case (the end of the word) with the word, "devil," said previously—vss.24-26).

2 Tim.3:1-17—In chapter three, Paul exhorts Timothy on numerous appearances of negative behavior and character exemplified in the last days before the return of Jesus to rule and reign on the earth, and says those days will be hard to bear (vs.1). The list here is quite extensive and carries throughout the chapter, emphasizing some specific, brief descriptions of that time in vss.2-4. I will highlight a few notable words from those verses, beginning with "lovers of self" and "lovers of money (vs.2). The breakdown of some home and family settings are obvious here, showing the basic and vital importance for the family to set their foundation and get their daily strength from God's word (Ps.119:41, 42, 89, 105, 114, 130, 140; Ps.122; Jn.17:17). "Disobedient to parents" means unwilling to be persuaded, Vine; vs.2). "Unloving" at the start of vs.3 has the Greek root word for "the love of the family" and natural affections, especially parents to children and children to their parents. It has a negative prefix in front of the word to show its lacking in these times (see also the word used in Rm.1:31; refer to Mt.24:12, 13 for another notable verse about these times). Right after this word, "irreconcilable" means who cannot be persuaded to enter into a covenant" (Vine)…"haters of good things" (literally, not loving the good—vs.3)…"lovers of pleasure" rather than "lovers of God" (vs.4). Some have even a resemblance of godliness, but deny its (true) power in God (vs.5). Paul's command to Timothy is (literally, the Greek word) to "turn away" from them (vs.5). Some will try to take advantage of idle women, who have negative personal behavior habits, and with this taking place, though still learning, yet never able to come to the knowledge of the truth (vss.6, 7; see 2:25, 26). There will be those

opposing the truth, but will not make progress because of their folly being obvious to all, like James and Jambres opposing Moses (vss.8, 9, known in Jewish tradition to be in the group of magicians opposing Moses—Ex.7:12; 8:18; 9:11). Paul gives Timothy a nice list of positive counter character traits of faithful servants of God, which Timothy has been following in his service to the Lord (1 Tim.4:6)—Paul's teachings, conduct (way of life examples), purpose, faith, longsuffering (Greek word), love, endurance, persecutions and sufferings—the last two Paul says that godly people will experience living righteously for the Lord (vss.10-12); and Paul rejoiced that God had brought him out (rescued him) from them all (vs.11). But evil men and swindlers (cheaters) will proceed from bad to worse, deceiving others and being deceived themselves (vs.13; see Gal.6:6-10). So, Paul encourages Timothy to keep walking in the ways he was taught and has come to know, knowing the Scriptures that give him (us) wisdom that leads us to salvation through faith in Jesus Christ (vss.14, 15; 1 Cor.1:30, 31; Rom.3:21-30; Eph.2:8-10). All scripture is "God-breathed" (God is the Originator, Source and Author of them) and profitable (gainful) for teaching (to be passed on—2:2) of the truth of God's purpose, direction and guidelines in life; reproof (bringing proper persuasions and direction to take—Ps.119:67-72; Prov.1:23, 25, 33; 3:11, 12); correction—restoration to an upright or right state; improvement of life and character (Vine, only time used here in the New Testament); and instruction (and training) in righteousness (the right way to live; see also Eph.6:4; 1 Tim.4:6-11). The purpose of these "proper persuasions," and "trainings" is so God's servant may be "complete" (here capable, in that process—the word in Greek is "limb," as God puts the parts of the body together to make a "complete" person), and so, (literally) "completely furnished" for every good work (a point often not stressed enough as one of the highlights, purposes and benefits of God's word, the Bible, for us; vss.16, 17).

2 Tim.4:1-22—Paul now finalizes his last encouragements to Timothy. He charged him in the presence of God and of Christ Jesus, the coming Judge of all mankind, by His coming appearance and kingdom reign, to preach the word, being ready in season and out of season (planned and unplanned, that is, God's event and timing), and to reprove (see the word in 3:16), rebuke (charge strictly when necessary), exhort (advise or urge earnestly) with all long-suffering and teaching (vss.1-3). "The time will come" appears to refer to the prophetic words shared by Paul concerning the last days in 3:1 and following. Some will not be pursuing sound doctrine, but only want to listen to teaching according to their own desires, turning their ears from the truth and turning to myths (vss.3, 4; see the commentary on this word in 1 Tim.1:4 for better understanding). Timothy is to be serious and reasonable in his ministry, being willing to endure hardship in His work for the Lord to accomplish His goals, doing evangelistic service to help bring in the harvest for (of) God, and to fulfill his ministry and duties in God's calling for his life (vs.5). Paul knows the time of his departing the earth is coming, as noted in his wording of his life to be sacrificed for the Lord in upcoming days (vs.6). He has "fought the good fight" and about to finish his race (1 Cor.9:24-27; Phil.3:13, 14), looking forward to the reward of the "crown of righteousness," from the righteous Judge, not only for himself,

but also to all who long for His appearing (vss.6-8, 1; Phil.1:6; Col.3:1-4; 1 Jn.3:1,2; 1 Cor.9:25; Tit.2:11-14).

The remainder of Paul's letter to Timothy concerns greetings, acknowledgements and directions to those in the Lord's service and one warning about one in opposition to them (vss.14, 15; may be the same one in 1 Tim.1:20, but difficult to be totally certain). It is a good positive statement to see Mark's benefit with the Apostle Paul in the Lord's work (vs.11; Acts 15:36-41; Philemon 24). Paul realizes whoever is there or not there at his trials, God will bring him safely to His heavenly kingdom (vss.8-21; 1 Pet.1:3-9; 2 Pet.2:9). In signing off, Paul blesses Timothy with God's grace to be with him (vs.22; Phil.4:23).

Titus

Paul and Titus originally met and hooked up together in ministry in Antioch Syria (Gal.2:1-3). In between Paul's two imprisonments in Rome, he and Titus went and evangelized throughout the island of Crete (in the Mediterranean Sea, south of Greece; Tit.1:5; Unger). Paul left Titus there to help make arrangements in the church settings and appoint elders for their leadership (Tit.1:5). His letter directs for the character of elders in the church, plus for the development of good, Christian character traits for the believers in the church gatherings for various ages.

Tit.1:1-16—Paul reminds Titus at the beginning of his letter that he is a bond servant and an apostle of the Lord Jesus Christ, for the chosen ones of God (His Family), and for the knowledge of the truth (God's truth) and godliness (living in God's ways and character; vss.1,2). The promise from God who does not lie, is the hope of eternal life in Jesus Christ, (literally) "before times eternal," that is, before the world began (KJ; vs.2), which God brought in His known proper time in the Gospel of Jesus His Son, which is the proclamation Paul was entrusted with, by the command of God our Savior (vs.3). Paul greets Titus as a genuine child in the grace and peace from God the Father and Jesus Christ our Savior (vs.4).

As Paul states the "character traits" for Titus to look for in choosing the leaders for the young church settings in Crete, the word for "elder" in vs.5 (used also in 2:2) is almost interchangeable with the word "bishop" (overseer) in vs.7. If there is any distinction, the former would emphasize the "character" of the term, while the latter would stress the position and work carried out (Vine, under bishop). They are to be with "no charges against them" as God's steward (manager of His people and affairs—vss. 6, 7); husband of one wife (see 1 Tim.3 for the commentary on this and similar traits listed there for elders); have believing children (not always easy for parents to determine this, but here indicates the importance of sharing the Gospel with children early in their lives), not rebellious, in bad habits or disobedient (vs.6); not self-seeking or self-pleasing, not quick tempered (Pr.16:32; Eccl.10:4); not given over to the effects of alcohol (and drugs); not a "fighter" (physical; 1 Tim.6:12); not greedy or pursuer of dishonest gain (vs.7); hospitable, lover of good things, of sound mind and judgment, just and fair, holy and self-controlled (vs.8); and holding fast and true to God's word, the Bible, in order to urge people to accept and live by its sound teaching and to effectively refute those who contradict it (vs.9).

Paul gives Titus examples of those who do not present or hold to the sound teaching of God's word (vss.10-16)—rebellious people (literally, not under submission); empty, fruitless discussions (see the word in 1 Tim.1:6, also); "deceivers" (literally, mind deceivers; fantasies); and some from the Jewish circumcision persuasion, emphasizing "commandments of men" (see Mk.7:1-13; Col.2:20-23) and turning people's attention certain to Jewish tales (myths; vs.14; see this meaning of this word at the commentary in 1 Tim.1:4), which were overturning some whole households, and for dishonest gain (vss.11, 12; the quote of one of their prophets was simply to prove Paul's point—not what they said was true, but it was true they said it—vss.12,13). Paul commanded Titus to "silence" them and "reprove" them (remembering previously stated in vs.9; vss.11-13), so the church may be sound in faith and truth (vss.13, 14; see also 2 Tim.2:24-26 and 2 Tim.4:3, 4). Paul directly points out differences between pure and impure—to the pure, all things are pure (that is, they find it); to the impure, their minds and conscience become defiled (impure) and their deeds (detestable and disobedient) do not back up what they profess to know, about God, or anything good (vss.15, 16).

Titus 2:1-15—In light of the last two verses of chapter one, Paul instructs Titus to speak the things that are fitting and proper and the sound teaching of God's word in the Bible (vs.1). Part of proper and fitting teaching is to encourage people in the various age groups to grow in godly character. Older men are to be serious in purposes and good examples of self-respect in conduct; plus of good judgment, and sound in thinking, faith, love and endurance (perseverance—vs.2). Older women are to be likewise in conduct, reverent and respectful; not speaking bad things about or to others; not given over to the affects of alcohol (or drugs); teachers of good things and of good judgment, and a sound mind, to be able to train young women to love their family and help them grow in the Lord; and so, to work with their husbands in all things for the family's personal and collective benefits, pure and good workers in their homes they care for with their family (vss.3-5). Young men are to develop in sound thinking (vs.1) in all things and demonstrate patterns (consistency) of good works and sound doctrine; serious in purpose, and self-respect in conduct, including honorable speech, not speaking things self-condemning (see 3:11), so that anyone opposing may sense their own shame and not have negative statements about the ministry in what was said (vss.6-8). Servants and workers are to be subject to their own masters, well-pleasing, not argumentative or speaking against them (vs.9), or stealing (Dt.5:19), but showing all good faith, doing credit to God's word (BAGD) and making the Scriptures and all its teachings attractive (the word "cosmetic" used here) to others in all things (vss.9,10). Paul's urging to live in these ways is because God's grace of salvation in Jesus Christ has appeared, instructing us to deny (say no to) all ungodliness and worldly lusts and desires, and to live with sound thinking, in righteousness and godliness (His character) in our days here on earth (and, of course, forever more—vs.12); as we favorably wait for and expect the appearing of the Blessed Hope and Glory of our great God and Savior Jesus Christ (vs.13; 2 Tim.1:10; 4:1, 8). Paul states four things that come as blessings to the believer because of Jesus dying for our sins and rising from the dead to bring us God's gift of eternal life through the spiritual birth (Jn.1:12, 13; 3:1-17)—redeems us (purchases us to and for God—Rev.5:8-10) from every lawless deed (see Ps.130:8;1 Pet.1:17-21); purifies us (Ezk.37:23; Heb.1:3; 9:14; 1 Jn.1:7, 9; 3:3); brings us into God's Family as a child of God (Jn.1:12, 13; Rom.8:16; 1 Jn.3:1), making us through the spiritual birth God's people, His very own possession (Ex.19:5,6; Rev.1:6; 5:9,10; Dt.14:2; 1 Pet.2:9, 10); and making us zealous (fervent) for good deeds (it has been said—that "jealous" and "zealous" may not be far apart in this context (Vine, under zealous; vss.13,14). Titus is to speak these things, earnestly urging and reproving where necessary, with all his duties in charge, setting things in order (1:5) for the churches in Crete. Paul said in carrying this out to not let people disregard him (be disrespectful in fulfilling his responsibilities; word means "to turn over in one's mind, having thoughts beyond; thus, despise; Vine; vs.15).

Titus 3:1-15—In conjunction with the spiritual birth discussed by Paul previously in 2:11-14, Paul continues to emphasize the importance in living a life of good works (vss.1, 8, 14; Eph.2:8-10; Phil.2:12, 13), displaying them in subjection to rulers and authorities (vs.1), not being contentious, but forbearing (fair, equitable, not always insisting on the letters of the law, but considerate and reasonable in decision making—see the word in 1 Tim.3:3, the word "gentle" there), and showing "meekness" to all men (see James 3:13 for understanding the word "meekness;" vs.2). Paul then explains the salvation experience, reminding Titus (us) that we were once foolish, disobedient, (being) deceived, following pleasures and lusts of the world (1 Jn.2:16,17), harboring even evil intents, envy and hate (if so experienced—vs.3); but then God, with His kindness and love for us, reached out and came to save us, not by our works of righteousness, but by His mercy He saved us, by the cleansing, and regeneration (taking away our sins; 1 Pet.1:18-21; 3:21, 22) and renewal of the believer by the Holy Spirit coming into one's life, being poured out richly to us through

Jesus Christ our Savior in the spiritual birth (Jn.1:12, 13; 3:16, 17, 33-36; see the Prayer in back of the book); and now then, the believer is justified (made right before God) through faith in Jesus Christ (see Rm.5:1-11), and made an heir with His gift and hope of eternal life to the believer in Jesus (vss.4-7; Jn.3:16; Rom.6:23; for "inheritance" see the commentaries on Rom.8:12-25 and Eph.1:15-23). So, then, Paul exhorts Titus to speak these things confidently, to help the church engage in good deeds in their life, which is profitable for them to do (vs.8; Eph.6:8).

In contrast to the instruction to live a life of good deeds in daily service to the Lord, Paul closes his directions for Titus by emphasizing four activities that are <u>not</u> profitable to do: "Foolish disputes" (see the word in instructions to Timothy in 2 Tim.2:23); "genealogies" (see commentary on 1 Tim.1:4, where this word occurs, and the root word for "disputes" also); "strife" (especially with the words in this context in mind; Gal.5:19,20; 2 Cor.12:20); and "useless battles" and speculations (even controversies) concerning the Law (Rom.10:4). Paul says to Titus to avoid such things, for they are, unprofitable, and are "fruitless discussions" (void of results—Vine; vs.9; see the word in 1 Tim.1:6). A "factious" person is to be admonished (reproved by training by word, God's word primary here—1:9; 2 Tim.2:24-26) and declined after two warnings (vs.10, "factious" is stressing an opinion, especially a self-willed opinion, which is substituted for submission to the power of truth and can lead to a division—Vine). Such a person has (literally) "turned aside" and if so from the truth, is self-condemned (on account of doing himself what he condemns in others; vss.10, 11; 1:9; Rm.2:1, 2; 14:22).

Paul gives final instructions to Titus regarding some of their fellow workers and emphasizes the importance of doing good deeds and to help meet pressing needs of one another (vss.12-14; Nicopolis in vs.12 is a port in northwestern Greece). Paul signs off by sending his greetings with others who are with him and asks Titus to greet those with him who love Paul, and his fellow workers in the faith. He blesses Titus with God's grace, to him and to all in Crete (vs.15; 1:4).

Philemon

Paul is writing this letter to Philemon during his first imprisonment. The letter has connections with the church at Colossae, by the names mentioned in the letter (vs.2; Col.4:17; vs.24; Col.4:10). There was a house church gathering that met in Philemon's house (vs.2; the name "Philemon" means "affectionate"—Unger). For the introductive greeting of "grace and peace," see the commentary on Rom.1:1-7.

Paul commends Philemon for his love and faith expressed to the saints (vss.5, 7). He prays this fellowship of the faith will grow into the knowledge of every good thing in us for the sake of Christ Jesus (vs.6; see similar prayer in Eph.1:18-20). Paul appeals to him in love (vs.9) about his slave Onesimus, whom Paul had the opportunity to lead him into the Family of God (vs.10). His name means, "useful" and now as a Christian Paul wants to do the right thing and send him back to Philemon (vss.11-14), now, more "useful" than ever (vss.15, 16). Paul asks Philemon to accept Onesimus back and if any wrong was done or anything needs to be paid back, Paul would do it for him (vss.17-20). He had confidence in Philemon doing the right thing and even more for Onesimus (vs.21) and hoped to see him again soon (vs.22). For Epaphras, see Col.1:7, 8. Paul closes with the same word of grace as to the Philippians (4:23).

Hebrews

The Book of Hebrews is a beautiful well written book about Jesus becoming the Merciful and Faithful High Priest pertaining to the things of God (part of His faithful Messianic Majesty—2:17; Jude 25; see Book 4 of <u>The Family Bible Studies Series, The Theology of the Bible—The Family of God</u>, to see the development through the Bible of Jesus' role and fulfillment as The Prophet, Priest and King). This is the theme of the Book of Hebrews (the writer's main "sermon" theme), describing Jesus' prophetic coming, demonstration and fulfillment of His High Priestly role and character (2:17; 5:10; 7:3; 7:26). The writer of Hebrews also emphasizes Jesus' "once for all time" sacrifice for the sins of mankind (1:3; 9:12, 15, 26-28). He did this through suffering (2:10; 5:7-9; 9:11-14; 12:2; Lk.22:39-45; 23:34-43; Jn.20:25; Is.52:13-53:12), beyond what man himself can imagine, and yet without sin (4:15). And now having been made perfect (completed His mission—Jn.17:4), He became the Source of eternal salvation to all who believe in Him (5:9; Jn.1:12,13; 3:16,17); "perfect" (in His eternal character) He already was (see Book 1 of <u>The Family Bible Studies Series, The</u> <u>Family of God—Foundation</u> for a helpful understanding of the character and functions of the Trinity—the Father, the Son and The Holy Spirit), and so, this means His fulfilling mission of God's work, during His first coming to earth (with His second coming due to come—9:28; John 17:2-4), including the Old Testament Scriptures written about Him (Is.7:14; 52:13—53:12; Mic.5:2-5; Lk.24:44); and through suffering and temptations, did so without sin (4:14), flawless in all He said and did, and thus, the "unblemished" and "perfect" sacrifice to God on mankind's behalf for our sins (9:11-15; 1 Pet.1:18-21), and the Source of eternal salvation for all who believe in Him (5:8, 9; 9:26-28; 10:10,14; see also 2:10; Jn.3:16,17).

Hebrews to this day still does not have an agreeable author by Bible researchers and scholars. Some have suggested Paul, Barnabas or Apollos to name a few of the notable ones of possibility. However, the book has been well attested by early church fathers and continues to be a great source of teaching, encouragement and blessing to us and throughout the church age (Rom.15:4-6; 2 Tim.3:16,17).

Heb.1:1-14—The writer of Hebrews begins the epistle by declaring that the "ways and various means" that God spoke to the forefathers by the prophets to form the Old Testament Scriptures had now closed with the coming of His Son to earth. He now spoke to us in His Son, because they (the prophets) spoke about Him (vss.1, 2; Lk.24:27, 44; Rm.1:1-4; Eph.1:9-12). "The last days" in vs.2 means the end of these days, that is, the Old Testament prophets and their role then (and so, realistically, fulfilled). God has appointed His Son Jesus as the heir of all things, in fulfillment of Ps.2:8 (also, Mt.28:18; Jn.17:1, 2; Eph.1:9, 10;

Col.1:16, 17), and through whom He made the world (vs.2; literally, the "ages"—a period(s) marked by spiritual or moral characteristics—Vine; Jn.1:1-3; Eph.1:18-23; Col.1:16, 17). The Son is the "radiance" (light) of God's glory (vs.3; Jn.1:5, 9; 8:12) and the author declares the Deity of Jesus Christ, testifying He is the "exact representation" (the Greek word where we get the English word "character") of God's nature (see also, Jn.1:1-18; Col.1:19, 2;9; the second Person of the Trinity—the Trinity having the same nature (characteristics) and different functions; see Book 1 of <u>The Family Bible Studies Series</u> for Their characteristics and functions). The Son upholds all things by His powerful word (His spoken word here, in the Greek; vs.3; Eph.1:22; Col.1:17). Having completed His mission upon His first coming to earth to die for the sins of mankind (vs.3; 9:11-15; 10:12), He returned to heaven by His resurrection and ascension (see the commentary on Mt.28 for the Gospel harmonies of the resurrection, and Acts 1:9-11 for the ascension), and sat down at the right hand of God (vs.3; 8:1; 10:12; 12:2). These first three verses are a great summary of the work and nature of God's Son, Jesus Christ, the Messiah (6:1; Acts 3:19-26; 26:22, 23).

With much of the world, including the Roman Empire of that time, being polytheistic (many gods), worship of angels (see 2:6-8; Col.2:18) the "elevating" of angels (by some) about their status as God's servants (vs.14) and created beings, at times needed to be addressed in the church, and so, the writer of Hebrews does so in the first two chapters. Here in chapter one, the writer of Hebrews points out distinctive differences between the victorious Son of God and God's created angels: first, the Son has inherited a more excellent name than them (by His name—Jesus (Savior—see vs.14, and Christ—the "Anointed One," the Messiah; see Eph.1:20-23; Phil.2:9-11) by His nature and fulfilling work (and yet to come) on earth (vs.3); second, He is God's Son, and by this the angels <u>worship Him</u> (vss.5-7); third, the angels have their <u>own mission</u> assisting God and His work of salvation to the world (vss.7,14); fourth, the Son is eternal (vss.9-12—note in vs.9—"God, thy God, hath anointed thee"); and fifth, His victorious rule, seated at the right hand of God (vss.8, 9,13; 2:6-8).

Heb.2:1-18—Throughout the Book of Hebrews the writer is looking to achieve three goals speaking to his audience—encourage Christians in the church, especially of Jewish heritage; reaching primarily a Jewish crowd for the Gospel; and also trying to prevent Jews from retreating back into Judaism. All three of these desires to his listeners become quite noticeable in their particular contexts of the Scripture writings. Beginning in chapter two, the writer of Hebrews gives a specific warning about neglecting the salvation message and remaining in unbelief (vss.1-3). He exhorts them to pay close attention to the salvation message and not drift away (vs.1), since what one sows is what one reaps (vs.2; Gal.6:7, 8; see also Acts 7:53). The salvation message was delivered, and heard from Jesus, then confirmed and witnessed by signs and wonders (see the helpful definition in Acts 5:12 for these words) by the Apostles and followers of Jesus (vss.3.4; Acts 2:42; 5:12). In another statement about the angels, the writer reminds his listeners and readers that God has subjected His world to come to be handled and governed by His Son (vss.5-8, quoting from Ps.8; see Ps.2; Eph.1:22; Jn.17:2; 1 Cor.15:23-28; Is.9:6, 7; Rev.19,

20), who now rules by God's side, till coming back to reign on earth (1:13; 2:6-8; 10:13). By the suffering of His death that He gave for everyone for the sins of mankind, He was crowned with glory and honor, (vs.9; see Jn.5:23, 24). Jesus' accomplished work of salvation for mankind will bring many sons to glory into the Family of God—(vs.10), and the author says that it was fitting that the leader of their salvation was perfected through sufferings (vss.10; 5:7-9; for "perfected" see the introduction to Hebrews). As we the people here on earth who do not like to undergo suffering, it is natural for us to ask "why" this had to be so? Yet, throughout the remaining discussion of chapter two, the writer gives us many reasons why this was necessary, and beneficial for all—1) This was the <u>only</u> way for mankind to be saved—Jesus dying for our sins and raising from the dead to bring us the free gift through His love for us of eternal life, and thus, bring many people into the Family of God (many brethren, children of God into His Family—vss.10-13; Jn.3:16; Rm.6:23); 2) It brings His Family into the sanctification process till God's Family is "perfected" (completed) in heaven (vs.11; 10:10-14; 11:40; Mt.5:48; 1 Jn.3:1,2); 3) Through His death and resurrection, it rendered the devil powerless (defeating sin and death—vs.14; Jn.1:5; 12:31-33; 16:33; 1 Jn.3:7-9; Eph.3:8-12); 4) This takes the believer out of "death's slavery" and turns the fear into hope and confident expectation of the inheritance of eternal life (vs.15; Phil.3:20,21; Rom.8:15-25; Heb.9:15); 5) To become our Faithful and Merciful High Priest, making first the successful payment for the sins of mankind through the cross (the word "propitiation" here; see the word in 1 Jn.2:2, also), and He continues to be our

Advocate (the Victorious Mediator between God and man) for the sins of mankind—1 Jn.2:1,2; Heb.2:16,17; and 6) through His sufferings and temptations, coming through all of them without sin (4:15), He is certainly able to come to the aid of those who come to Him (remember where He sits—1:3; 8:1) for help in their time of need (vs.18; 4:14-16; 1 Cor.10:13; 2 Thess.3:3; 1 Pet.1:3-8; 2 Pet.2:9). Though not stated by the author here, Jesus' fulfillment of Is.52:13—53:12 fits here in His High Priestly role and is explained by Peter (Acts 3:18-21) and Paul (Acts 26:22, 23) about the Messiah's necessary suffering for mankind.

Heb.3:1-19—In the next two chapters, three and four of Hebrews, the author reaches out to Jewish unbelievers (3:12, 19; 4:5) and encourages them to enter into God's Sabbath rest by receiving in faith the Good News of the Gospel of Jesus Christ, the Messiah (4:4-6, 11; 6:1). "Holding fast our confidence" in vs.6 is a statement of faith and encouragement for the believer (4:3, 14; 6:11;10:23), who is to walk faithfully with Jesus, their Apostle and High Priest, who was faithful to God, who appointed Him as the Faithful and Merciful High Priest in God's service (vss.1,2; 2:17; 4:14-16). Moses was faithful in all God's house (see Num.12:3), but Jesus receives more glory as the Son, faithful <u>over</u> God's house, who is the Builder of all things (vss.3-6; 4:3; Jn.1:17, 18; Eph.1:20-23; Col.1:16-19; 1 Cor.3:7-9; Gen.1). However, the context of vs.7 and following, points to a warning and a lesson from Israel's wilderness experience and so, not hardening their hearts in unbelief to the Gospel message (vss.12, 19; 4:5-7; not to "harden their hearts" is quoted from Ps.95:6,7 three times in these two chapters (3:8, 15; 4:7) and "not enter His rest" is mentioned four times (3:11, 18; 4:3, 5; vss.7-11). So, in vs.12, the "brothers" would refer to the author's Jewish audience, which have not yet come to believe in the Messiah (since "unbelieving" would not refer to the believers in Christ; 4:3; see also Paul's use of this word in Rom.9:3). They have been "partakers" of Christ only (that is, by contact with Jewish Christians and the gathering together of the believers, similar as explained by the author in 6:4-12). Consequently, they are urged by the author (and speaker to them), while the time is still "Today" (vs.13; 2 Cor.6:1, 2), not to get caught with a "hardened and evil heart" (vs.12) in disobedience and unbelief (vss.14-19), and receive the Gospel message, and Jesus their Messiah (4:1, 2, 6, 11; 6:1; Acts 3:19-21).

Heb.4:1-16—This chapter continues the message of chapter three, with the urgency while it is still called "Today" (3:15; 4:7), to enter God's rest (vss.1, 9, 11). The author acknowledges that the listeners have had the "Good News" preached to them (vss.2-6), but failed in disobedience to believe and receive the Gospel of Jesus by faith (vss.2, 6). God rested from His works (vs.4) and now they are exhorted to rest from theirs, and believe in Jesus the Messiah, the Faithful and Merciful High Priest for their salvation, learning from and not repeating the disobedience in the wilderness experience (vss.9-11). The writer brings all his message home to them by reminding them how active and alive and sharp and penetrating the word of God is, even to the "inward reasonings" and "intents" (the Greek words here) of the heart (vs.12), because nothing is hid from God, to whom everyone one day must give an account (vs.13; 9:27, 28).

The author now goes back to where this part of the message began and the theme of Hebrews—Jesus, the Merciful and Faithful High Priest (vs.14; 2:17). The presentation started with this in 2:17-3:1 and now picks up from there and continues through 10:18, where the content of the message then switches over to the exhortations given to the listeners (and now us the readers). He gives another stern warning, though, to unbelievers in chapter six. The author's message in vs.14 to "hold fast our confession" of the faith comes as encouragement (as we see now) to the believers and warning (in the message that followed) to the unbelievers of the Gospel (3:6, 7; 6:11, 10:22, 23). Our High Priest is sympathetic (literally, suffers with us) and understands our weaknesses (great comfort here), because He was tempted in all things as us (Mt.4:1-11; 26:41; Lk.23:34), yet without sin (vs.15; 2 Cor.5:20, 21). And now, with the veil removed from the Holy of Holies (6:19, 20; 9:1-3; 10:19-22), the believer may go directly to the throne of God through Jesus our Great High Priest, and find His grace and mercy to help us in our time of need (vs.16; the Greek word is "timely help," and so, "well-timed"—BAGD; Eccl. 8:5-9; Prov.15:23).

Heb.5:1-14—As we begin chapter five of the Book of Hebrews, we are close to the midway point of the book. Here is a brief summary of the remaining message of the author and how the book continues and finishes from here.

Starting three verses back in 4:14, the writer returns to his main theme of Jesus, the Faithful and Merciful High Priest, which he began in 2:17. He discusses this more now up to vs.10 in chapter five. In 5:11 he then turns to the necessity of going on to "maturity" for the believer through 6:3. The word "maturity" is the same word for "perfect" used a number of times in the book (see this helpful and encouraging word study of this topic at the end of this commentary on Hebrews). The author then presents a very hard and stern warning again to the unbelievers, who heard the great presentations of the Gospel and God's word (6:5-note again, "partakers" only, as some gathered with the believers in their assemblies, along with the previous warning, in 3:12-14; see Paul's terminology of such in Gal.2:4, 5) and still remained in unbelief (6:6; 3:12-19). He returns to building up the believers in faith, emphasizing God's strong promises in 6:9-20. In 6:20 he picks up the High Priest theme again from 5:10 and continues this through the main course of his message to 10:18. He then addresses the rest of the book to his "exhortations and encouragements" to the believers. Two brief discourses to the unbelievers given in 10:26-31 and 12:14-17, with similar language and principle pointed out again, likened to that in 6:6. He closes with personal notices at the end (13:22-25).

Returning to his High Priest theme of Jesus, the writer teaches and reminds his audience of the responsibilities of the earthly high priests—offering gifts and various sacrifices, including sins for the people and themselves, along with a "gentle and understanding" disposition in "counseling" others in the ways of God (moderate his feelings, is the Greek word here; vss.1-3). His calling and placement of high priest must be from God, as Aaron's was (vs.4; Ex.28). And so was Jesus' calling (2:17), based on the prophecy of Melchizedek and His Sonship (vss.5, 6, 8; 1:5, 6; 7:3). His sufferings were difficult and deeply felt, but His serving and dependence on God came always first, demonstrating this by

His reverent life for God. As a result, He was obedient to God in the midst of His sufferings (vss.7,8) and having "perfected" His mission (see the introduction of Hebrews; Jn.17:4,5; Phil.2:5-11), He became to all who believe in Him the Source (the cause brought about) of eternal salvation, designated (literally, to be called to) by God according to the order of Melchizedek (vss.9, 10; 7:1-3; see the end of chapter two about the sufferings of Jesus).

The author now emphasizes the need to go on to "maturity" for the believers (see the "perfection" theme at the end of this Hebrew's commentary; see also Eph.4:10-16). He points out that some had become "dull in hearing" (sluggish) and needed to have the basics of the faith taught to them again (6:1, 2). Maturity (going on to perfection—Mt.5:48) is building on the basics, not always having to repeat those basics (foundational beliefs), as one learns to discern (to sort out) the difference between good and evil (vss.11-14; see Book 3 of <u>The Family Bible Studies Series, Growing in God's Wisdom</u>, for learning how to pray for this, in learning the six words of understanding from Proverbs on pgs.19-40, with the helpful summary chart on pg.102).

Heb.6:1-20—Desiring to go on past the elementary teachings of the faith and moving on to maturity, the author firstly gives his most stern and pointed words yet to the unbelievers who have heard the Gospel preaching and God's word and still choose to remain in their unbelief. Being "partakers" only (vs.4; 2:14-19) of the good things of God in the believers gatherings (vss.4,5), if they refuse to repent and believe in Jesus, the Messiah and "fall away" (to fall in one's way—Vine; only time used in The New Testament), there remains no way out for them, since Jesus the

Messiah is the "once for all" sacrifice for man's sins, who alone offers mankind the free gift of eternal life. The writer brings out harsh words of what they do to Jesus, with all previously stated, remaining in their unbelief of Him, God's Messiah (vss.4-8; 7:26-28; 9:11-15; 10:10-14; Acts 3:19-24).

But for the believers, the author is convinced of better things for them—things that accompany salvation (vs.9; 4:3); for God will reward those who diligently seek Him (KJ; literally, seek after Him) and their good works in ministering His love and goodness to others (vs.10; Heb.11:6; Eph.6:8). The writer wants to assure them of this in their faithful works, remembering the inheritance of His promises, and being diligent to do the good works all their life, and imitate those, who through their faith and patience in the Lord, inherit the promises (vss.11, 12; Heb.11). He continues to encourage them in the assurance of God's promise, pointing out God's promise to Abraham by His own authority (vss.13, 14); and Abraham, waiting patiently (for God to fulfill His word), received the promise (vss.14, 15; Israel was greatly multiplied (Ex.1:7); and see Abraham's blessing –Jn.8:56)! And God confirmed this with an oath (vs.14, declaration to keep a statement or promise), to give "strong encouragement" for the believers, as this hope (promises and oath of God's word) serves as an "anchor" of the soul (a heavy metal object with pointed ends to dig in the ground to keep a ship from drifting, usually when docked), safe and firm (vss.16-19). The "hope" and fulfillment of God's word is Jesus (Eph.1:9-11), who has now opened the door to come directly to God's throne (2:17,18; 4:14-16), as our forerunner where He now sits (1:3; 8:1; 10:12, 13; 12:1,2), serving as our Advocate—our Supporter and Intercessor for the forgiveness of our sins (vss.19, 20; 7:25; 9:24; 1 Jn.2:1,2; Mt.5:9-15; Rm.8:34; Heb.5:1, 4-6) and High Priest forever, according to the order of Melchizedek (vss.19, 20; 7:3, 17).

Heb.7:1-28—Chapter seven discusses the validity and longevity of Jesus' High Priestly reign in fulfillment of God's promises (see Book 4 of <u>The Family Bible Studies Series, The Theology of the Bible—The Family of God</u>, for helpful insights into Jesus' role and fulfillment of God's Messiah—The Prophet, Priest and King). The author teaches us about the connection between Jesus and Melchizedek (Gen.14:18-20). Melchizedek means king of righteousness, and he was the king of Salem (King of peace—vss.1, 2). Without a genealogy, he has an endless lineage, like the Son of God and, so abides (remains) a priest continually (vs.3). After Abraham defeated the kings (Gen.14), Melchizedek blessed him and Abraham gave him a tenth of the victory spoils (vss.1, 4-7). The summary here is that Abraham and Levi, his heritage, paid tithes (a tenth) to Melchizedek, the one who lives on (vs.8). And so, the "real blessing" here is that "the one who lives on" blessed Abraham (who was given the promises) and Levi, for the lesser is blessed by the greater, Melchizedek, the priest of God, vss.7, 1. And Jesus was the prophesied type of Melchizedek (Ps.110:4), designated by God as His (and our) High Priest forever (vs.3; 5:10), who is the "blessing" and "fulfillment" of God's promises for all mankind (vss.7-10; 9:11-15; Eph.1:9-12), so those who believe in Jesus may receive His free gift of eternal life (Jn.3:16, 17; 17:3; Rom.6:23; Heb.9:15).

Remembering that the author wants to help bring growth and maturity to the believers (5:14-6:2), the writer presents this using the "perfection theme" word in vss.11 and 28, showing how this takes place by the "endless" reign of Jesus the High Priest. Stating that the Levitical priesthood and law could not bring about perfection (vss.11, 19, 28; see also Rom.7:7; 1 Tim.1: 9, 10), Jesus came in the "likeness of Melchizedek," and demonstrated this by His indestructible (endless) life (vss.15-17, 28), by His resurrection from the dead and ascension to heaven (1:3; 8:1; 10:12; 12:2). Changing the Law which brought weakness (vss.12-14, 18, 19, 28), this High Priest (Jesus), because of His endless life and fulfilling the prophetic "priest" coming in the order of Melchizedek (vs.1; Ps.110:4), brings a better hope that draws the believer in Him near to God (vss.19, 25; 4:4-16). With His priesthood forever (vss.17, 21, 23, 24, 28; 6:20) and stated with an oath (vss.20, 21, 28; 6:16-20), He has become the "guarantee" of a better covenant (vs.22; 8:6-13; the word "guarantee" is the word "bail," and so, Jesus is the personal "guarantee" of the terms of the new and better covenant, secured on the grounds of His perfect sacrifice—Vine; vs.28; 9:11-15). The result then is that He can save forever (Greek word—for all time) those who draw near to God trusting in Him, because He lives to make intercession for them (vss.25; 9:24; Rm.8:34). By His character and life demonstration, it is fitting for Him to be the High Priest—holy, innocent, undefiled (free from contamination), separated from sinners (4:15) and exalted above the heavens (vs.26; 1:3; 4:14-16), offering Himself once for all for the sins of mankind (vs.27; 9:11-15, 26; 10:10), appointed by God (5:10), made perfect forever (vs.28; see the introduction to this commentary of Hebrews for "made perfect" and the helpful and encouraging listing of the "perfection" verses in Hebrews at the end of this Hebrew commentary).

Heb. 8:1-13—The writer of the Book of Hebrews continues on with the theme of Jesus, the Merciful and Faithful High Priest (vs.1). He now also includes discourse on Jesus' more excellent ministry (vs.6 and following)—the New Covenant (7:22). He starts out by declaring that Jesus, seated at the right hand of the throne of the Majesty in heaven, (vs.1), is a "Minister" in the true tabernacle of God in heaven (vs.2-5;7:25), that is, He works right at the throne of God in continuing His ministry (see Jn.5:17). The New Covenant is the covenant of His blood, shed for the sins of the world, declared in the Gospel message, going out to all the world (Lk.22:20; 9:11-15; 10:10-12; Col.1:6, 23; Mt.24:14). The New Covenant transcends the Old Covenant (Ex.20-24), with a "Mediator" who died for the sins of all mankind (vs.6; 9:15; 12:24; 1 Jn.2:1, 2) and brings peace between God and man (Eph.2:14-17), bringing the believer into the Family of God (Jn.1:12, 13; 3:16, 17; 17:2, 3). The New Covenant also brings better promises, long lasting ones (vss.6, 10-12; 9:15; 7:25; 4:14-16; 11:16, 40; 13:5, 6). These long lasting promises will also include God's fulfillment of the promises to Israel (Ezk.36-48) and salvation and hope to the nations as well (see Mt.12:17-21; Is.9:1,2). God's laws will be on their minds and hearts, and God will be their God (to both—Eph.2:14-17) and they will be His people, because they will all know the Lord (vss.10, 11; Ezk.36:26, 27; 37:24-28; Jer.32:40, 41; 33:7-9; Eph.2:11-22); and He will be merciful to their (our) iniquities (sins) and remember them no more (vss.12, 13; 2:17; 2 Cor.5:20, 21; Eph.2:14-17; Jer.31:31-34; Micah 7:18-20).

Heb.9:1-28—In chapter eight of the Book of Hebrews the writer reveals the New Covenant in Jesus; and in chapter nine through chapter 10:18, he tells us how that was accomplished. He starts this out in chapter nine by comparing two tabernacles—one on earth and one in heaven. The first 10 verses relate to the earthly sanctuary—their articles (vs.2), the location of the Holy of Holies (vs.3), the ark of the covenant, with its design and objects contained inside it (vss.4, 5) and its overall limitations and shortcomings, two of which are brought out here: no one but the high priest was allowed in the Holy of Holies (and that only once a year—vss.7, 8), and this form of divine service and worship (vss.1, 6, 9) could not "perfect" (growth and development in God's holiness and character) the worshiper in conscience (vss.9, 10). The "physical" aspect through the cleansing of blood (vss.20-23) is the main focus here (vs.10), till the time of "reformation" (an "amendment;" a right ordering, where the imperfect is supersede by the better order of things—Vine). One also might think of this as a moving from the outward to the inner matter of things pertaining to God—beginning with His mercy for us (2:17, 18; 4:14-16; 6:10).

The first tabernacle on earth was given to Moses as a copy of the one in heaven (8:5). On Jesus' ascension, He went into the tabernacle in heaven—the greater and more "perfect" one (vs.11). He entered by His perfect sacrifice given for the sins of mankind (5:9; 7:26-28; 10:12)—by His own blood—and obtained eternal redemption, through His sacrificial death and resurrection for mankind (redemption—release by paying a ransom price, here His blood for the sins of mankind—vss.12, 15, 26; Eph.1:7-14). The result to the believer is the cleansing of the conscience from sin and dead works (vs.14; contrast the outward work only of the first covenant in vss. 9, 10, 13; see also 1 Pet.3:21). Note the character and the ministry declared of the Trinity in vs.14—the blood of Christ…offered without blemish to God…the eternal Spirit…to serve the living God. Also, it is without blemish…that can cleanse (one's conscience; 1 Pet.1:18-21; 3:21, 22). And so, Christ Jesus is the Mediator of a new and better covenant (vs.15; 8:6-13), with His death and sacrifice taking place for the redemption of sins committed under the first covenant (all those leading up to His sacrificial death), as well as those of the whole world onward (1 Jn.2:1, 2), so that believers may receive eternal life (life as God has it, Jn.3:16) and the promise of the eternal inheritance (vs.15; 6:17-20).

The author goes on to say that a covenant is much like a will (a disposition (agreement) of property by will or otherwise—the Greek word for "covenant" here; Vine), that comes to enforcement (like a will) at the time of death (vss.16-18). In Lev.17:11, it states that it is the blood by reason of the life that makes atonement for sin (see also Lev.17:14). And so, when the 10 commandments and ordinances were given to Moses (Ex.21-24), he cleansed the book they were written in and the people, (and later on the tabernacle and vessels—Lev.16:14-16) with the sacrificial blood of calves and goats (water, scarlet wool and hyssop representing sin sacrifice and atonement with it—Lev.14:4; Is.1:18), showing the "blood of the covenant" which God commanded (Ex.21:24;

24:1-8); for without the shedding of blood there is no forgiveness (vss.19-22; Gen.3:21). So the earthly copies of the heavenly things needed to be cleansed as such, but the heavenly has better sacrifices than these (vs.23; for the heavenly articles and sacrifices, consider Rev.8:3; Heb.8:5).

The writer then returns to the topic of Christ Jesus entering the greater and more perfect sanctuary in heaven, where He sits at the right hand of the throne of God as our Intercessor and Advocate (vs.24; 1:3; 7:25; 8;1, 6; 9:15; 10:12; 12:2; Rm.8:34; 1 Jn.2:1, 2; Heb.6:19, 20). Unlike the high priests making their sacrifices often on a regular basis, Jesus the Great High Priest offered Himself and His own blood (9:11-15; 10:10, 12), once for all time, for the sins of mankind (vs.28), to put away sin, by the sacrifice of Himself (vss.25,26; "consummation" means "bringing a completion together;" the heading up of all the various epochs (periods of time, including here fulfilling the Old Testament prophesies about Him), in His first coming to earth, awaiting His second to come, vs.28), appointed by Divine counsels (God's will; Vine, with my addition of the fulfillment of the prophecies about Him; see expanded understanding in Eph.1:9-11). As it is appointed for men to die once (Gen.3:19) and then the judgment (2 Cor.5:10; 1 Jn.4:17), so Christ, having died once for the sins of many (people, that is), will appear the second time, not to bear sin (NIV), but coming for those eagerly awaiting Him for salvation (vss.27, 28; see the word "eagerly awaiting" in Phil.3:20 and similar word in Titus 2:13).

Heb.10:1-39—The author continues on with his theme and intention in 6:1 to help the saints press on to maturity (the "perfection" theme; see the introduction and ending of Hebrews for this development). He reminds them that the Law could not do this, being only a shadow (not the real images) of the good things to come and unable to fully clear (or perfect) the conscience of sins (vss.1-4; see the commentary on this previous discussion in 7:11-19; also, 9:9; 1 Pet.3:21). "Therefore," the writer says, this condition of mankind paves the way for the coming of Christ and His sacrificial life, death and resurrection (quoting Ps.40:6,7 from the Septuagint—the translation of the Hebrew Bible into Greek), all according to the "councils" (will) of God (vss.5-10; 9:26). This establishes God's new order—with all its benefits (vs.9; 7:12; 8:8-13; 9:11-15, 26, 28; 10:10-14; 11:16; Rom.3:21-28), bringing sanctification (growth in holiness) and "perfection" (growing in Christ to its perfect completion—1 Jn.3:1, 2) to the believer in Jesus Christ (vss.10-14). The greatest of these being the cleansing of one's sins before God and the gift given to the believer of eternal life, coming into the Family of God (vss.15-17; Jn.1:12, 13; 3:16, 17; 5:24; 10:27-30; 11:25, 26; Heb.6:17-20; 9:15; 10:14; see the Prayer in back of the book). And so, now there being forgiveness of this things, with Jesus' death and resurrection once and for all for the sins of mankind (9:28; 10:12), there is no longer any sacrificial offering for sin (vss.18, 11, 1; 9:8-15). For vs.6, "But a body Thou has prepared for Me," see Book 1 of The Family Bible Studies Series, The Family of God—Foundation, for more insights on this verse from Gen.1 and man being created in the "image of God," and the relationship between the body of Jesus and ours in God's creation (pgs.7, 8 in that book).

The writer of Hebrews now switches the content of his message to his exhortations (applications) and encouragement to the church. Two more stern warnings in his remaining discourse are also delivered to unbelievers. "Therefore," the author writes, since Jesus has opened the door to the throne of God for the believer to now come directly to God, by His sacrificial blood offering for their sins (10:10-18), he exhorts them to "draw near to God" with (literally) a "true heart" (in the Greek; KJ also) and in full assurance of faith, having been "cleansed and washed clean" from our sins by God (perfect tense verb, meaning past action completed with present on-going effects), since we have a Great High Priest, Jesus Christ, over the house of God (vss.19-22; 2:17; 4:16; 6:17-20). God is faithful to His promises (2:17; 9:15; 11:11; 1 Cor.1:9; Rev.19:11) and so, the author encourages the believer, as he has been doing, to "hold fast" to the confession of our hope, without wavering (Greek word is "unbending;"vs.23; 4:14; 6:11, 17, 18-20). Also, to stimulate (encourage—BAGD) one another to love and good works (possibly the two highest demonstrated characteristics that portray the Christian life, along with faith and our hope in Jesus, vs.24; 6:17-20; 7:19; 1 Cor.13:13; Heb.13:15,16); and not to forsake the assembling together, and all the more so as we see the Lord's return (the Rapture and the Second Coming) drawing near (vs.25; one possible problem may have been converted Jews switching their gathering from the Jewish Sabbath (Friday night to Saturday night) to the Christian gathering on Sunday, since the writer uses the word "custom" in this verse; Acts 20:7).

The author of Hebrews one again addresses a strong and stern warning to the unbelievers hearing his message (vss.26-31). If they willfully continue to sin (present participle) after hearing the knowledge of the truth about the Gospel of Jesus (9:24-28; 10:12), no sacrifice remains for sins (vs.26; recall 6:4-6), with only judgment one day to come (vs.27, from Is.26:11; Heb.6:6-8; 9:27; 10:18; see Jn.3:16-21). The writer uses again his regular indirect pronoun "anyone" to point to the individualistic concern of his hearers (see 3:12; 13; 4:1), that if they who know the Law of Moses set it aside instead of responding to its fulfillment in the Gospel of Jesus (Lk.24:44; Jn.5:45-47; Rom.3:19-30; 10:4), no mercy or sacrifice remains for their sins, even testified by others, when they die (vs.28; see the example in Dt.17:2-6; Heb.2:2). This would be especially true to those who (literally) "tread underfoot" God's Son (see similar in 6:6) and regard His sacrifice as something unclean (see 4:14; 9:11-15, 26), which those who have heard and received it in principle only, having been in contact with the Christians gathering ("sanctified"—see the similar circumstance in 1 Cor.7:14 (BAGD), and Heb.6:4-6) and yet did not receive and follow Christ (vs.26), instead, also insult the spirit of grace (vs.29; Jn.16:7-11; Heb.9:11-15, 10:15-18). For God will avenge and repay, and judge His people and all the earth (vss.30, 31; Is.2; Is.24; Ps.96:13; Rev.19:11-21; Dt.32:35, 36; for Christians, see 1 Cor.3:10-15; Eph.6:5-8; Heb.10:34, 35; 11:16).

Much suffering and persecution occurred during the time of the early church, even up to the time of Constantine (emperor of Rome from 306-37 A.D.). The author reminds and lists some of those sufferings that some in his congregation experienced and endured previously (vss.32, 33). Even the taking of their property occurred, yet, they knew they have better and long-lasting ones to come (vs.34; 11:13-16), while they also showed sympathy to those who were put in prison (vs.34). He encourages them to not lose their confidence for there is great reward ahead, and they simply need to seek God for His strength and endurance, focusing on and doing His will, looking to the promises ahead (vss.35,36; see the commentary of the Armor of God in Eph.6:10-20 and about God's strength in Eph.1:19; Rom.15:4,5; Col.1:10-12; Rev.3:10—His "word of endurance;" 4:14-16; 6:17-20; 9:15; 11:13-16). And by faith, live by God's righteousness (Hab.2:4), persevering in their faith to the "possession" of the soul (vss.37-39, for which, see this word "possession" in 1 Pet.2:9).

Heb.11:1-40—The chapter here in Hebrews eleven is called the Great Faith Chapter. It gives us examples of men and women who have lived out their life with faith in God, and gained His approval (literally, obtained a witness, in the Greek—vs.2). The author details some key "ingredients" of faith in vs.1 and then explains in vs.3 what it does for us and gives us better understanding about God and how He created the world.

First, faith is the "assurance" (or reality—see this word in Heb.1:3, where Jesus is the "reality" of the character of God, that is, His Deity in bodily form—Col.1:19; 2:9) of things "being hoped for" (a present participle passive verb—and so, ongoing (see Rm.8:24, 25) and passive, brought about by God), and the "proof" (or evidence) of things not seen. How is faith the "reality" of "things hoped for" and "proof" of what we don't see? All found in the revelation (reality) of His Son Jesus coming to earth to fulfill God's mission (Jn.1:14-18; 3:16, 5:24; 17:3, 4; Lk.24:44). He is our "proof" (2:8, 9). In the Old Testament it was by God's revelation, and also His creation of the world and mankind in His image (see Book 1 of The Family Bible Studies Series, The Family of God—Foundation, pg.7, for the important understanding of the word "image"), Noah and the Flood, the Tower of Babel, promises to Abraham, Moses and the Israelites crossing the Red Sea, Joshua conquering Jericho and the Promise Land for Israel (see the promises in Gen.22:17; 26:4; Dt.4:40), etc. God also spoke (revealed His will) through the prophets (1:1-3; Amos 3:7). By these 'proofs" (God's revelations) we gain understanding by our faith that God created the world (ages; see the commentary on Heb.1:1-3 for understanding the word "ages") by His spoken word (vs.3; Gen.1; 5:1, 2); so that (with the result in mind here) the "things which appear" (BAGD) did not come about (or were made) out of the "thing" being seen (same verb form as discussed in vs.1—ongoing and brought about by God, the passive verb again). So, what the writer is telling us is that since God created the world by His spoken word, no material thing existed to bring this about. Plus, by seeing and studying what God created, we can clearly see that the thing which we see created by God did not have the power or makeup to create themselves, meaning, whatever God created did not have the power or ability to create itself (vs.3).

As the author exhorts the listeners (and readers) to be strong and confident (maturing) in their hope and faith in the Lord (4:14-16; 6:1, 11, 12, 17-20; 10:23), he wants them to be imitators of those who through faith and patience inherit the promises (6:11, 12; 13:7, 8). He now testifies to a good number of them who did this in chapter eleven, as good examples of their faith and lives they lived before Almighty God.

Abel offered a better sacrifice than Cain. Genesis chapter four tells us that Cain brought an offering of the fruit of the ground, while Abel gave of the firstlings (firstborn) of his flock and of their fat portions. This was declared again about Abel in vs.4 as God testified about receiving his gifts. Later on, Abel's type of sacrifice became the standard God required from Israel in their sacrifices to God (Ex.13:2; Lev.3:16, 17); and so, his faith (faithfulness) still speaks out today (vss. 3, 4; 12:24).

Enoch (meaning "dedicated," "initiated"—Unger) was pleasing to God (note—obtained the witness) and God took him up to heaven without dying on earth (vs.5; similar to the occurrence for the church in the rapture—1 Thess.4:17, 18). The author affirms that faith must be present and active to please God (see Rom.14:23; 1:17; 3:21-30; 4:13, 21, 22), for the one coming to God, must believe that He is (a slight pause here to ask "that He is" what? The answer is found in six words looking back—that He is God! Look how this statement boosts ones faith); and God rewards those seeking (literally, "seeking after") Him, (a present participle verb here—vs.6).

Noah's building the ark (Gen.6:13-22) was done so with "reverence to God," as God warned him about the things not yet seen (the coming judgment—Heb.11:1—and for the salvation of his household). His righteousness to God condemned the world of its coming judgment (2 Thess.1:5) and he became an heir of the righteousness that comes by faith (vs.7; Gen.6:9; Rom.4:13, 22).

Abraham was called by God to leave his home (Mesopotamia, modern northern Syria and Iraq) and go to the land He promised him to receive as an inheritance (Israel, called Canaan at his time), though he knew not where he was going (i.e., unfamiliar territory; vs.8). He lived there as a foreigner, as did Isaac and Jacob, the fellow-heirs of the promise to Abraham (vs.9). Living in tents, Abraham was looking for the city with foundations, who's architect (Greek word is our English word "technician" (Designer) and builder is God (Maker; actual framer; used only here in the New Testament literally means "one who works for the people," like a constructor, and so, Builder—Vine, vs.10—God, the Designer and Builder of the New Jerusalem to come—vs.16; Rev.21, 22). Sarah trusted God for His promise He gave to them, and conceived even beyond her normal time of having children, considering God faithful who gave them the promise (vs.11; Gen.17, 21; see also Rm.4:18-22). From one man comes many descendants as God promised (vs.12; Gen.15:5; 22:17; 32:12; Ex.1:7), and yet to come into the Family of God, to fill up the New Jerusalem forever (see Book 4 of The Family Bible Studies Series, The Theology of the Bible, The Family of God, for this development and fulfillment by God throughout the whole course of time).

The next four verses are interjected summary verses by the writer of Hebrews. He states that the people previously mentioned lived out their lives of faith without receiving the promises, yet looked forward to them ahead, because they were citizens of heaven and, thus, strangers on the earth (vs.13; Phil.3:20,21). They were seeking their own country, not desiring previous cities and countries where they had been, but the heavenly city, that

God has prepared to be together with His family (vss.10, 14-16, 39, 40; 13:14).

Abraham's faith was tested when God asked him to offer his only son, who would carry on the promises, in a sacrifice to Him (vss.17, 18). In faith Abraham reasoned that God can raise the dead, and so, received his son back without sacrificing him, as God provided the sacrifice for Abraham, so it is being similar (in a parable (analogy), the Greek word here), as God did, giving (sacrificing) His only Son Jesus, for us, and then received Him back to heaven (vs.19; 1:1-3; Jn.3:16, 17; Gen.21:12; Gen.22).

By faith, Isaac blessed Jacob and Esau (Gen.27), as Jacob and Joseph continued the sharing of blessings and promises to their sons, regarding things yet to come (vss.20-22).

Moses was raised in a life of faith and continued to live a life of faith, leading the Israelites up to their Promised Land. Not fearing the king's edict (order; Ex.1:16), his parents hid him for three months (vs.23) Ex.2:2), and growing up he refused to be called the son of Pharaoh's daughter, choosing ill-treatment with God's people rather than enjoyment of the pleasures of sin (vss.24, 25). He considered the reproach of Christ (see Heb.13:13; 12:1-3; the "disgrace" that was similar to Christ Jesus at times in fulfilling God's mission, a genitive of association; see Moses' plea in Num.11:10-15; also Heb.5:7-9; 12:2, 3) of greater riches than the treasures of Egypt, because of the focused reward (vss.26, 6, 13-16). Moses endured the trials with the Pharaoh, not fearing his wrath toward him (Ex.10:28, 29), seeing the One who is unseen in the burning bush (vs.27; Ex.3). He kept the Passover and the sprinkling of the blood on the doorposts to save the first-born of the Israelites, while the judgment fell upon Egypt (vs.28; Ex.12); and they passed through the Red Sea as on dry land, while Egypt's army was drowned (vs.29).

Great faith and patience was exercised by Joshua in conquering Jericho (vs.30; Josh. 6); and Rahab, being faithful and teaming with the spies of God's people, to save herself and family from God's judgment on Jericho (vs.31; Josh. 2:1-21; 6:22-25). The author also includes seven other names or groups (the prophets) who could easily be listed in this faith chapter, but did not speak about them in detail (vs.32). Note here in the specific listing is Jephthah (Jud.11, 12). Standing out and named specifically by the writer with the others in this faith chapter, as the New American Standard Bible translates Jud. 11:31, Jephthah may have had an "option" stated there when he returned home from battle. It has been said, according to Jewish tradition, that if no one claims a faithful virgin Jewish daughter as their wife, she may be dedicated to the service of helping in the Jewish temple. This would make good sense, also, for a man of faith (Jud.11:38-40); plus, stated in the context, she should not have to "suffer" because of her virginity. The writer goes on to elaborate on numerous courageous "acts of faith" in righteousness by those who performed them, as well as heart-gripping "acts of martyrdom," by those who truly lived and died for the Lord (vss.33-38). The writer concludes that chapter saying that these _all_ "obtained a witness" through their faith (vs.39), but not yet the promise at that time (vss.39, 1, 2, 13-16). God foresaw (planned) something better—the "perfection" of His whole family, in the perfect, everlasting city, with Him for eternity (vss.40, 10, 16; 12:22-24; 13:14; Rev.21, 22).

Heb.12:1-29—With such great witnesses surrounding us in the heavens (Heb.11), the author now returns in his exhortations to a theme and encouragement he brought up earlier in 10:36, especially in light of sufferings experienced for the Lord (see 1 Pet.3:13-17)—the need of endurance (10:32-36). "Endurance" is mentioned in vss.1-3, 7. "Endurance" means to hold up under circumstances that one faces in life, that is, hold up under the circumstances with the Lord in His strength (see 2 Cor.12:9, 10), and run the race set before us (vs.1; see 1 Cor.9:24-27; Phil.3:13, 14). Part of running a race is overcoming the obstacles. The writer mentions two here—dealing with and putting aside "heavy burdens" (the Greek word here; see Mt.11:25-30) and any sins that "easily entangles" one (one that can take advantage or prevail over one—Vine; vs.1; 1 Jn.1:9). Many athletic contests come down to the successful strength of endurance. So the writer exhorts the believers to "fix our eyes on Jesus" (who has victoriously run the race—see Jn.1:5, 16:33; 17:4); He is the Author and Perfecter of the faith (vs.2; 2:10; see the "perfection" theme at the end of this Hebrew commentary; in the Greek, the article is before the word "faith," which I think is significant here, focusing on Jesus, the Author and the Finisher (ultimate Fulfiller) of <u>the</u> faith; and so, an objective genitive here, seeing our Victorious Champion where He now sits (vs.2) and our life there, hidden with Him in God—Col.3:1-4). "The joy set before Him" (see again where He victoriously sits) enabled Him to "endure" the cross, despising the shame (of the cross and treatment done to Him; yet, <u>He had no shame</u>, instead being sinless, died for our sins in His love for us, so that we may live with Him and live a righteous life to serve Him—4:15;, 9:15; 2 Cor.5:2; Jn.3:16, 17); and so, He could "despise" the shame that took place, and now, victoriously rejoices—vs.2; Eph.3:8-12; Col.2:13-15; Heb.1:1-3). Knowing the Author and Perfecter of the (our) faith, the writer encourages us to consider what He endured—and was victorious—so then not to grow weary or lose courage or heart in the trials we face in serving our Lord (vss.3, 4; 2:17, 18—our Merciful and Faithful High Priest; 2:17; 4:14-16; 10:10-14).

"Endurance" is God's inner strength with perseverance for the believer that enables us to grow in discipline and obedience to serve the Lord (vss.5-9; 5:7-9). The word "disciple" comes from the word "discipline" and this is a factor of the Father's love for us, so that we may share in His character, including His holiness (vss.5, 6, 9, 10; 10:14; Col.1:9-14). The "discipline" can appear as "grief" (the Greek word here) at first (vs.11), but later on produces the "fruit (product) of God" in our lives that He desires us to have—the peaceful fruit of righteous (vs.11; Jn.15:16; Gal.5:22-25; see this as a part of James' description of wisdom in James 3:16, 17). And so, the believer is encouraged to go to God and pray for His strength to accomplish the tasks God has daily for us (vs.12; see the verb "making straight" in Luke 13:13) and for the lame to be healed (vs.13; see of this in Acts 3:1-10).

The author gives another warning to the unbelievers in his listening (and reading) audience (vss.14-17). He exhorts them to "pursue peace" with all men (Rom.12:17, 18; 14:19) and the Lord (Rom.4:24-Rm.5:9), for without <u>the</u> sanctification (the article is in the Greek, and so the translation in the New American Standard version; refers to the spiritual birth, beginning the growth in

God's holiness for the believer—Jn.1:12, 13; 10:10, 14), no one will see the Lord (vs.14; Rm.8:9-11), and gives the example from the life of Esau (vss.15-17; note the emphasis on "anyone" (here, "no one") again in delivering his message—vs.15; see 3:12, 13; 3:1). "Comes short of God's grace" means be lacking, come short (BAGD), not falling away, but not having arrived (3:12; see the explanation in the Old Testament in Dt.29:17-20 and so, vs.14; 6:4-8).

The writer now explains to the believers that they have come to the "heavenly Jerusalem," "the city of the living God" (vs.18-22, quite unlike the gathering at Mt. Sinai of the past—Ex.19). Zion is the city that David captured (2 Sam.5:7). See the ongoing gathering now before the throne of God (Rev.4). "The general assembly" is one word in the Greek and used only here in The New Testament and means "a festival gathering" (BAGD), literally, "all gathering," "The spirits of righteous men made perfect" is reference to the believer reaching their "perfect" state, yet, awaiting the Rapture for completion together of the church age (vs.23; 1 Thess.4:18-18; 2 Cor.4:14; Heb.11:39, 40). For Jesus, the Mediator of the New Covenant, see chapter eight. For the "sprinkled blood," see 9:11-15, 22-26.

The author now gives one final warning of God's coming judgment upon unbelievers (vss.25-27, 29; Dt.4:24). Note the repetition of the consequences of refusing to "hear His voice" (vs.25; 3:7, 15; 4:7), with the judgment upcoming before the Lord's return to earth (vss.26, 27; Hag.2:6-9; see Rev.16:17-21). The writer then refers back to the believers, encouraging them to offer acceptable service with gratitude to God, having reverence and awe, in His unshakeable kingdom (vs.28; 6:7-12; Dan.2:44).

Heb.13:1-25—Back in Hebrews 10:19 the author began to give his listeners exhortations to follow. Here in chapter thirteen he finishes his message (which he felt was brief to them—vs.22) with his final encouragements. Continuing in brotherly love is an important Christian theme and expression (vs.1; a kindred love for all those in the body of Christ; see this important "love expression" in these passages, also—Rm.12:10; 1 Thess.4:9; 2 Pet.1:7). Showing hospitality is another important Christian practice and some have even entertained angels "without knowing it" (New American Standard Bible translation; vs.2; Gen. 18, 19; Judges 13; the word hospitality and entertain have the same root word—foreigner or guest). With the sufferings of some taking place in the early church (and some today; see 10:32-34), they are to remember and pray for those in prison and ill-treated, as if being with them (vs.3; Eph.6:18-20; Philemon 22). Christians are to model God's design for marriage, free from fornication and adultery, and honorable to each other and the family, before God and man (vs.4; Ex. 20:14-17; Mk.10:6-9; Eph.5:22-33). Christians are not to be "in love with money" (see 1 Tim.3:3; 6:6-10), but always love God first in everything (Mk.12:28-31; Rom.12:9-21; 1 Cor.13:1-8); and look at His love for us!—vss.5, 6; Jn.3:16, 17; 13:1; 17:1-26). Follow the outcome (way of life) of faithful leaders and teachers of God's word. Correlations should be recognized with vs.8 (vss.7, 8). Everyone should study God's word in the Bible (regularly, even daily) to determine the difference between truth and error (vs.9, God's strengthening grace to the heart and mind; 5:14; 2 Tim.3:16, 17; Titus 1:7-9). The believer celebrates the sacrificial blood of Jesus shed for our sins once for all time (vs.10; 9:11-15, 26; 10:10, 14; 12:2). Going outside the camp has to do with the sin offerings required in the Old Testament for the Jews (Ex.29:14; Lev.4:12, 21; 9:11; 16:27; Num.19:3, 7—all these have to do with "sin offerings."). And so, Jesus went outside the camp and offered His blood, as the Messiah, once for all time, so believers could receive His gift of eternal life and the promise of the eternal inheritance (vss.10-14; 9:11-15, 26; 10:10, 14; Jn.1:12, 13; Rom.6:22, 23; Acts 3:19-25). By this great gift, the believer offers the continual sacrifice of praise to God, giving thanks to His Name, and the doing of good works and sharing God's blessings to others (vss.15, 16; Phil.2:12, 13; 1 Pet. 2:12). Faithful leaders in the church deserve honor and submission, keeping in mind what their responsibilities are to the Lord, so it will be joyful and profitable for one and all (vs.17).

The writer now closes his writing, requesting prayer and encouraging his listeners to have the right motives and desires in all they do, and also hopes to see them soon (vss.18, 19). He expresses a beautiful prayer for them, that the God peace (see Phil.4:6-9; Jn.14:27), who brought up from the dead our Great Shepherd of the sheep (Jn.10:1-18; 1 Pet.2:25), through the eternal covenant (Heb.8; 9:15), Jesus Christ our Lord, equip them (us) in every good thing to do His will (for "equip," see the word in 10:5; 11:3; and Eph.4:10-13 in vs.12), to do what is pleasing in His sight (see the word pleasing in vs.16; 11:6; 12:28 and Rm.12:1,2), through Jesus Christ, to whom be the glory forever and ever. Amen (vss.20, 21; Rev.4, 5). No more is known (at this writing) of the imprisonment of Timothy (vs.23). The author either writes from Italy or is sending his greetings from a group that is from there in his writing to his destination (vs.24, also remembering Acts 18:2 as possible influence here). He closes extending God's grace to them (vs.25).

The Perfection Theme in Hebrews

2:10—Jesus, the Author of our salvation, perfected through suffering (in fulfilling His mission on earth; see the introduction on this).

5:8, 9—Learned obedience through suffering, being made perfect (fulfilling His earthly mission), became the Source of eternal salvation.

5:14; 6:1—Let us press on to maturity.

7:11, 19—The Law made nothing perfect.

7:28—The Son, made perfect forever (see the introduction to Hebrews for this).

9:9—Sacrifices from the Law cannot make the worshiper perfect in conscience.

9:11—Jesus entered the perfect tabernacle in heaven (8:5).

10:1—The same repeated sacrifices of the Law cannot make perfect those who draw near.

10:14—By Jesus' once and for all time sacrifice for the sins of mankind, He has perfected for all time those who are being sanctified (beginning at one's spiritual birth—Jn.1:12, 13; Heb.9:14, 26; 10:10; 1 Jn.3:1, 2).

11:40—Perfection experienced when all the church is gathered in God's promised eternal inheritance

(1 Thess.4:16-18; 2 Cor.4:14; Phil.3:20, 21; Col.3:4; Heb.9:15; 1 Jn.3:1, 2).

12:23—In the heavenly Jerusalem, the spirits of righteous men made perfect.

Mt.5:48—See Jesus' statement and the process here.

James

James is one the four writers of the "general epistles" in the New Testament (others being the Apostles Peter and John and the other is Jude). James was one of the earthly family brothers of Jesus, as was Jude (Judas; see Mt.13:55; Mk.6:3). The "general" epistles were sent out to the church at large and not just one specific church. With all the specific topics that James covers, it is difficult to arrive at just one title theme for his epistle. "Endurance" seems to be a major focus, though, from the start to finish (1:3, 4; 5:11), but the goal of this is to become "perfect," (mature) and "complete" (sound in every part; 1:4), similar to the "perfection" theme in Hebrews (see the commentary at the end of the Hebrews).

James 1:1-27—James begins by acknowledging himself as a bond-servant of God and of the Lord Jesus Christ (vs.1). He is writing primarily to the dispersed Jews, who went to live in other areas of the Roman Empire (vs.1; see Acts 8:1). He wants them to see the "development process" in their personal growth when they encounter various kinds trails in life and he gives good guidelines to help overcome them. First, he says to consider it all joy in those encounters, because of God's development work and "character growth" in the end result (vss.2, 4). Great attitude and perspective here. Next, to make them a growth step in faith (vs.3; see Dt.8:1-6; and the great encouragement shared by Peter in 1 Pet.4:12-14 and by Jesus in Mt.5:10-16). Then, James says that this "process of development" builds the strength of "endurance" (literally, holding up under trials, with the Lord and His strength to overcome them), which develops perseverance and character development through the process of problem solving (vss.3, 12; see 5:11; Prov.3:5-8). Then, following it through, one reaps the benefit of a good end result (the "produce" involved)—becoming more mature in the Lord (see Heb.5:14 and Rm.5:1-5) and more complete (toward "soundness" in every part of our being; vs.4; 3:17, 18).

James goes on to say that if anyone lacks something (in the problem solving process to become more mature and complete—important goals in God's eyes for our personal development in the Lord), all one needs to do is "ask" God for His wisdom, who gives to all men generously, without fault-finding or blame, and it will be given to him (see Prov.2:1-11; see Book 3 of The Family Bible Studies Series, Growing In God's Wisdom, a word study on the Hebrew words of Prov.1:1-7, to know more "ingredients" of God's wisdom and how to pray for them more specifically, knowing what they mean). When any one asks God for His wisdom, it must be in faith (present imperative verb) and not doubt, that is, keep trusting God and don't separate oneself from the "faith in God" prayer (Greek meaning of not "doubting;" see Prov.3:5,6, "understanding" here means" knowledge and meaning" of our own in 3:5). One cannot be "unsettled" and/or "double-minded" (literally, "two-souled") in light of the clear certainty presented in vs.5 (vss.5-8; see also the commentary on Heb.11:6).

James continues this discussion by encouraging the brother in humble circumstances (with the various trials—vss.2-4) to pride oneself in their "high position" (following vss.2-5, 12), while those looking to their riches (that is, counting on them alone and their pursuits just for that—see Eccl.10:19, 20 and Lk.12:15-21), will watch them fade away, as a flower does in its passing season (vss.9-11). And so, the one who endures through their trials they encounter (vss.2-5), having proven faith and love for the Lord (the word "approved" in vs.12 is the same word as "testing" in vs.3; see this in Rom.5:4—"proven character," the result), will receive the "crown of life" (1 Cor.9:25; 2 Tim.4:7, 8; note here the demonstration of their love and faith in the Lord, and, given to them—the "crown of life"), as the Lord promised to those who love Him (vs.12; Jn.3:16; Heb.9:15).

When being tempted, one should not ever say that God is tempting them, as God cannot be tempted by evil nor does He tempt anyone (vs.13; see Dt.32:3,4; Lev.11:44; 1Pet.1:15-17). Man is tempted when he is "lured" (as in fishing) and "drawn away" by his own lusts (passions, desires; vs.14). If it conceives (to take together with; catches), gives birth to sin, and if becomes full growing, it brings forth death (vs.15). When trials (vss.2, 12) and temptations come (vs.13, 14; Mt.4:1-11), James says do not deceive yourselves (vs.16; contrast vs.12 with vss-13, 14). The good and perfect gifts come from the Father of lights above, with whom there is no change or shifting shadow (vs.17; Num.23:19; Mal.3:6; Heb.13:8). By His goodwill for us, He (literally) "birthed us" by the word of truth ("birth" here is the same word for "brings forth" in vs.15; here, referring to the spiritual birth of the believer coming into the Family of God—Jn.1:12, 13; Jn.3:1-16), as the early believers became the "first fruits" (as in the early produce of the harvest) among His creatures to believe in Him (vs.18; Acts 2; 1 Cor.15:5-8, 20-23; see also Rev.14:4).

James addresses two important aspects of human behavior in his letter—our works and our speech—both to be pleasing to God. He wants believers to be quick to hear, slow to speak and slow to anger (vss.19, 20, probably with vss.2, 13 in mind, handling their various trials they face; see also Prov.16:32; Eccl.7:9). Therefore, they are exhorted to put away all filthiness (moral defilement) and "surplus" of evil, and in meekness (Greek word, see 3:13) receive God's word, being able to save them (that is, saving (delivering) them from those things, not the basic salvation message, which they already received—the word planted in them, vs.21; "meekness" (see 3:13) is a grace of the soul, exercised first toward God, then man; close to humility; opposite of self-assertive and self-interest; a calm and undisturbed spirit, not elated or cast down, because it is not occupied with self at all—Vine; Mt.11:28; see this also in Gal.5:23; James 3:13; Eph.4:2. Then, on the other side of behavior, James desires for the believers to become (present imperative verb) "doers of the word" (see 2:22) and not just "listeners" of it, otherwise, they (us) may forget it (vss.22-24). But looking intently (see this word in Lk.24:12; 1 Pet.1:12) into the "perfect law," the "law of liberty" (Rom.8:1, 2; 2 Cor.3:12-18), the believer is to be an "effectual doer" of God's word, and so blessed of God in doing so (vs.25). James retreats back to his topic of speech initially (vs.19) and declares that true (pure) religion involves self-control and carefulness in one's speech, otherwise one's religion could be "void of results" (the Greek word here; vs. 26; see also 3:1-12; Prov.10:19-21; 11:12; 12:17-20; 15:4; 17:27, 28; 31:26; Jn.12:49,50). True religion is looking after (NIV) orphans and widows in their distress (sufferings due to the pressure of circumstances—Vine; see Dt.24:17-22) and to keep oneself "unstained" (moral blemishes) from (by) the world (vs.27; see this is 1 Pet.1:17-21 in vs.19).

James 2:1-26—James addresses two topics in chapter two—the downfall of being partial and faith without works. The Bible says that being partial is a sin (vs.9; see also Dt.1:17; Prov.24:23; Rm.2:11; Gal.2:6). It makes distinctions (even discriminations) toward others; makes one out to be a judge (see 4:12; 5:9) and involves "evil reasonings" (vs.4). Believers are to be "rich in their faith," with love for God and their neighbor (the "royal law"—vs.8; Mk.12:28-31; Lk.12:16-21) and live by the "law of liberty" (Rm.8:1, 2; 2Cor.3:17, 18; Gal.5:22-25). God's mercy triumphs (predominates) over judgment (vss.1-10; see Rm.11:30-32; James 5:11; 2Pet.3:9).

James then testifies to the importance of demonstrating one's faith with good works (vss.14-26). He states that the believer is to exemplify their faith with good works, showing (working out) their salvation in the Lord by their demonstration of their faith (vss.14-16; see Paul's similar proclamation in Phil.2:12, 13). Faith by itself with no works would be dead (vs.17-20). The reference in vs.19 that "God is one" comes from Dt.6:4. The Hebrew word "one" means "unified or united." Thus, the Trinity is united and the believer enters into that union with them. The example of Abraham offering up Isaac as a sacrifice to God is a great demonstration of one's faith being lived out in good works, in which he was called the "friend of God" (vss.21-23; see also 2 Chr.20:7; Jn.15:12-17; see Book 2 of <u>The Family Bible Studies Series, The Levels of Relationships</u>, for a foundational Bible study on the basic words of relationships (stranger, acquaintance, friend, companion, etc.), and an encouraging study on the life of Abraham—the friend of God). Thus, Abraham was justified by his good works, because his faith was working with his works (vss.21-24; "justified" here means "treated as righteous" (BAGD); his righteousness came by faith—vs.23), and so, it is made known by what one does. His works demonstrated his faith, and faith was "perfected" (remember this word from James 1:4) as a result of the works (vs.22), his faith working with his works, as was Rahab (vss.22-25). So faith, joining in with the union of the Trinity, will show itself, demonstrating itself in the good works of the Lord, working in and through the believer (vss.22-26; Mt.5:16).

James 3:1-18—In Chapter three of his general epistle, James returns (or maybe never left it!—1:19, 20, 26; 2:12) to the topic of controlling ones speech. In this context, though, it is in regards to those who desire to be teachers (vs.1; see Rm.2:17-23). God's word is His truth to us (Jn.17:17) and so teachers encounter stricter accountability, needing to be able to not only handle it accurately (2 Tim2:15), but also to present and use it correctly, as well (2 Tim.3:16, 17). James wants teachers to be aware of their potential—positively and negatively (vss.2-6). Though a small part of the body, it is a difficult instrument to tame (vss.7, 8). If one does not stumble in what he says, he is a perfect man (remember this subject and discussion in 1:4), able to bridle the whole body, also (vs.3). Unfortunately, negative and positive things come out and James says as this comes from one good intended instrument, this should not be so (vss.9-12; a great goal in life for all of us for sure; see the verses back in 1:26 for this).

More important for teachers (and all believers on this), it is more important than what we know and understand, in how we conduct ourselves daily (apply what one knows) before God and man; vs.13). In these great verses given to us on what to pray for regarding this conduct and personal behavior of ourselves, James presents a list of important "character presentations" of wisdom, not just definitions (though important) of what consists of wisdom (see Book 3 of The Family Bible Studies Series, Growing In God's Wisdom, for helpful "ingredients" in praying for God's wisdom). He wants believers to know the truth (vs.14) and to live it out in what we say and do, by knowing God's wisdom from above, as "wisdom" strictly from the earth can lead to evil results (vss.15,16; Prov.21:28-31).

James presents here God's wisdom from above, "character demonstrations," in vss.17, 18: first, it is pure (from every fault; connected in its root word to "holy;" see this verb in 4:8); back in vs.13, God's wisdom is presented in a spirit of "meekness" (a genitive of content, meaning one of wisdom's expressions is the character of meekness; see the helpful definition in 1:21 of James); then, it is "peaceful" (that is, with the characteristics of peace); gentle (the word here is more favorable to "forbearing"—what is fitting and fair; not insisting on the letter of the law; it expresses that considerateness that looks humanely and reasonably at the facts of a case; see this word in Phil.4:5); compliant (well to obey; obedient); full of mercy (see 2:13; 5:11; Heb.2:17; Lk.6:36) and good fruits (plural; Gal.5:22, 23; Jn.15:16); unwavering (means not to be parted; not prejudiced; without uncertainty; contrast 1:6); and, without hypocrisy or pretense (definitions from Vine). He concludes this great description of some of wisdoms expressions by saying that the fruit (singular) of righteousness is sown in peace by those making (present tense) peace (vs.18).

James 4:1-17—Chapter four of the epistle of James is centered around one main truth in vs.6—God opposes the proud, but gives grace to the humble (see Mt.11:25-30 for a helpful definition of the word humble). He addresses those who have been caught up in "quarrels and conflicts and wars of the flesh"—personal desires and pleasures sought for, with wrong motives involved (vss.1-3; see 1 Pet.2:11, 12). He warns about establishing "friendship" with the world (not here having friends in the world, but establishing the world's ways; likewise in see 1 Jn.2:15-17). God's grace has tremendously been given to the believer in Jesus with the gift of the Holy Spirit, who longs and battles for us with God's jealousy (vss.4, 5; Ex.20:5; 34:14; Jn.16:8-11; Rm.8:26-28; 1 Pet.2:9,10); yet, God continues to give us more grace—to the humble—expressed here as not being proud, but instead submitting to God, resisting (standing against) the devil and evil, drawing near to God, confessing sins (1 Jn.9), and humbly coming into the presence of God (seeking Him in prayer) that He may lift us up (vss.6-10; Lk.1:49-52; Jn.1:14-18; Rm.5:17; Is.66:1, 2; 1 Pet.5:6-11).

Jesus had warned us about judging others (Mt.7:1, 2; Jn.7:24; also Rm.2:1). James says that those who judge others become a judge, and there is only One Righteous Judge, to whom we must all give an account of our lives (vs.12; Mt.28:18; 2 Tim.4:8; Rom.14:9-13; Jn.5:21-29). And so, our humility before God is to be demonstrated also before our fellow man (vss.6-12), and so fulfill God's royal law (2:5, 8; 1:12).

James often shares reflections of the Sermon on the Mount that Jesus proclaimed in the Gospels in Mt.5-7. He warned about being anxious about tomorrow (Mt.6:24-34) and not being desirous about achieving material gain (Mt.6:27, 28, 34; see also the previous verses in Mt.6:19-23, and Lk.12:15-21, also leading up to this same passage found in Luke 12:22-34). How can one know what tomorrow will be like (vss.13, 14; see Prov.27:1, 2)? Instead, one is to humble himself and come before the presence of God in prayer (vss.6-10) and seek Him and His kingdom first (Mt.6:32-34)—not being anxious, but to discover His will to be done (vs.15; Mt.6:9-13; Lk.22:42). Thus, knowing this is the right thing to do, not doing it but even yet, boasting of uncertain days ahead, one sins (vss.16,17; see the similar in Rm.14:23) and needs to apply vss.7, 8 in the humble process of the heart (vss.6, 7, 10; 2:22; Prov.3:1-12; Jer.29:7, 11-13).

James 5:1-20—James continues his exhortations from the Sermon on the Mount as he warns those who have become wealthy with material gain of storing up their treasures for themselves (vss.1-3; Mt.6:19-21; Lk.12:22-34), when these "material" things can decrease in value and even disappear, instead of being "rich toward God" (Lk.12:16-21) and establishing treasures in heaven

(Mt.6:19-21; Lk.12:32-34). Some even withheld paying their workers (vs.4; see Dt.24:14, 15) and lived a life of pleasure, in "a day of slaughter" (referring what they did to others in vs.4 and possibly vs.6), which reached the Lord's ears and sinned before Him (Dt.24:15; see also Jer.25:34).

The connection between vs.6 and vss.7-11 is that, even in the midst of sufferings and hardships, the Lord will reward His faithful saints, with much better and long-lasting rewards (the prophets (vs.10), Job (vs.11) and believers with the crown of life, according to the Lord's faithful promise; 1:12; Heb.9:15; 2 Tim.4:8). And so, patience is the prayer and the need for the brethren (the word here 3 times is "long-suffering" (vss.7, 8), similar to "endurance" in vs.11 and at the beginning in 1:2-4), remembering that the Lord is full of mercy and compassion (vss.11, 12; 2:12, 13; 1:12, 17, 18).

Verse 12 refers to Mt.5:33-37. Suffering (worked in here with cheerfulness and praises) come into the picture as one of their "various trials" (vs.13, 14; 1:2-5) that they (and we) can experience. They are to come before the elders to be anointed with oil and receive prayer in the name of the Lord (vs.14; see Mk.6:12, 13 for the background here). James says the "prayer of faith" (genitive of Source here—the name of the Lord in vs.14 and the Lord doing the healing in vs.15; Heb.12:2) will restore the one who is sick. If sin is involved, based on confession of it (individually to God (1 Jn.1:9) or to the brethren), they will be forgiven, which can be a factor in their healing (vss.15, 16). The prayer (petition, supplication) literally of the "inward working" of a righteous man is strong (able to do much; the word "strong" here is the word for "strength," especially physical strength, given as a gift from God—Vine, under the word dominion; vs.16). The key here is found back in vs.15—the "prayer of faith;" see that commentary. To Him belongs the glory and dominion forever and ever, Amen—1 Pet.4:11; 5:6-11. James notes Elijah's faith in the midst of his adversities (vss.17, 18; notice the "earnest prayer" in vs.17). He closes his epistle with similar instruction that Jesus gave for reproving a Christian in a sin (Mt.18:15-20; also see Gal.6:1) and helping them recover and prevent future reoccurrences and any other related problems, which could even be from physical death (vss.19, 20; 1:14-18).

1 Peter

Peter is one of the four writers of the "general epistles" in the New Testament (see the introduction to James on this, also). His theme in this epistle is a "priestly" theme, as seen 1:2 and nicely summarized in 2:5, followed through to 2:10. His concentration is focused on how believers in Jesus are to live out their lives, with spiritual sacrifices offered to God in our daily lives, acceptable and pleasing to Him (2:5).

1 Pet.1:1-25—Peter's general target area that he looks to reach with his epistle is the northern, north central and eastern part of current day Turkey (vs.1). He acknowledges the believer's calling and choosing of God by the foreknowledge of God the Father and by the Holy Spirit's sanctifying work (see Jn.16:8-11), to obedience to Jesus Christ and "sprinkling" of His blood (vs.2; "sprinkling" is the allusion to the use of the blood of sacrifices appointed for Israel (see Ex.24:1-8; 29:15-21) and typical of the sacrifice of Christ (Vine; see this in Heb.12:24, the only other use of this word in the New Testament as a noun and in reference to the blood of Jesus; see also the verb in Heb.9:13 and the understanding in vs.14 about the blood of Christ Jesus). The "sprinkling" here refers to the believer's continual commitment to the Lord's sanctifying work

in their life (vs.2; 2:24; 3:15; Heb.10:10, 14) and their "priestly role" and sacrifices of their life service to Him (2:5-10, 24, 25; Rev.1:6; 5:9, 10). For the greeting of "grace and peace," see the introduction to Romans 1:1-7.

Peter's emphasis in the beginning of his epistle is on God's gift to the believer of "a living hope"—God's bringing the believer in Jesus through the spiritual birth (born again vss.3, 23; Jn.1:12, 13; 3:1-17) into the Family of God, by the resurrection of Jesus Christ from the dead (vs.3). The new (spiritual) birth brings an inheritance with it that cannot be corrupted or destroyed and free from all contaminations (vs.4), reserved in heaven for the believer in Jesus (vs.4; Jn.14:1-3; Heb.11:10, 16; Rev.21, 22; see the Prayer in back of the book). Through their faith the believer is protected by the power of God (vs.5; Eph.2:8, 9), for their salvation ready to be revealed in (at) the last time (at the Rapture and then the Second Coming of Christ to rule and reign on the earth—1 Thess.4:13-18; Rev.19, 20).

The believer in Christ, Peter says, greatly rejoices (Greek word here and in vs.8 means "exuberant joy" (Vine) in God's salvation through the spiritual birth (see Jn.16:22), and joyfully too, looking forward to the Lord's return (vs.5; see 2 Tim.4:8; Phil.3:20, 21), though experiencing some grief in various trials (vs.6; 4:12). Those "testings of one's faith" are to prove to each one more valuable than gold—which is tested, tried, proven and purified through fire refinements and processes—so one's faith may result in praise, glory and honor at the revelation of Jesus Christ (vs.7; James 1:1-5); whom we believe in and love, though have not seen Him yet, and greatly rejoice with joy (literally) unable to be told out, and glorified (vs.8; see Rm.8:28-30; 9:23; Jn.16:22; 2 Cor.3:17,18), looking forward to the end (outcome) of our faith—the salvation of our souls (vs.9; Tit.2:10-14; 2 Tim.4:8; 1 Jn.3:1,2).

The coming of the Messiah and salvation, with the prophets predicted sufferings and glories to follow of Him (vss.20, 21), remained a mystery in the past (Rm.16:24-27; Eph.3:1-12; Is.52:13-53:12). The prophets made careful search and inquiries to what (and even whom—see Jn.1:19-27) and what kind of time He would appear (vss.10, 11). But now, with the coming of God's Son to earth, bringing salvation to mankind and fulfilling the Old Testament prophecies about Him in His first coming to earth, and revealed to His holy prophets and apostles by the Holy Spirit, God's salvation through the Gospel message of Jesus is now made known (vss.20, 21; Jn.1:1-18; Acts 2:37, 38; 3:19-21; Eph.1:7-14; 3:4-11). This was announced through those who preached the Gospel of Jesus by the Holy Spirit working in them and through them (Acts 2:14-39; Eph.3:4-11; Col.1:24-27), and now carried over to us in the inspired writings of the New Testament (2 Tim.3:16, 17). Notice that angels long to look into the things announced by those who preach the Gospel message (vs.12). They are God's ministers too, sent out to serve those who will inherit salvation (Heb.1:7, 14). Their intrigue seems to be their marvel how God works through fallen, regenerated mankind to go out and eternally save others through the Gospel message of Jesus; yes, a true mystery of godliness and God's great and powerful work indeed (vss.10-12; Eph.2:11-22; 1 Tim.3:16; Col.1:19-27)! So, Peter exhorts them (us) to be alert in their minds and fix their hope (vss.3, 20, 21) completely on God's grace to come at the revelation of Jesus (vs.13).

The theme of priestly living in holiness and the role of the priesthood of believers are now brought forth by Peter. God's holiness is the model for the believer (vss.14-16; Lev.11:44, 45; 19:2). Our conduct is to be in reverence to God (vs.17), knowing we were redeemed (bought by God) with the price of the precious, unspotted and unstained blood-sacrifice of His Son for our sins and eternal redemption (vss.18, 19; 2:21-25; Heb.9:11-15). He was chosen by God from the foundation of the world (see vss.1, 2; Jn.1:1-3; Acts 2:22-24) on the one hand (in the Greek), while on the other hand, has appeared (note the contrast and some of the "mystery" here) in these last times, for the sake of those who believe (and will believe) in Him—whom God raised from the dead and gave Him glory—so that our faith and hope are in God (vss.20, 21, 3, 13).

With the perfect, unblemished sacrifice (vs.19) of Christ received by the believer (in obedience to the truth of the Gospel message—vss.22, 25) for a sincere (unhypocritical) love to fellow believers, Peter declares for believers to love one another earnestly from the heart (vs.22); reminding them that they experienced the spiritual birth into God's Family by the work of God (vss.3, 23; Jn.1:12, 13; 3:1-17, His "birthing" the believer spiritually into His Family), through the imperishable, living and forever abiding word of God (vss.23,24, from Is.40:6-8; see Mt.24:35)—the prophet's prophesied messages and the fulfillments in Jesus the Messiah (vss.10-12) and His Gospel proclamation (vs.25).

1 Pet.2:1-25—As Peter now presents in his epistle the understanding of the "priesthood of believers" and what that role is to demonstrate, he exhorts the new believers to leave their former way of living (vs.1) and desire the "pure" (true) word of the God, so they may grow and mature in their salvation with the Lord (vss.2, 3). Peter then uses the analogy of each believer being "a living stone" of the Lord, being built into a "spiritual" house of the Lord (temple analogy here; see 1 Cor.3:16; Eph.2:19-22), which is "precious" (literally, held in honor) in the sight of the Lord (vss.4, 5). This "spiritual" house is to make believers a "holy priesthood," to offer up (as priests) "spiritual sacrifices" acceptable to God through Jesus Christ (the theme of first Peter's epistle—1:2; see also Rm.12:1, 2). This is God's intention for His people (see Ex.19:4-6; Rev.1:6; 5:10; 7:15; 20:6; 22:3-5) and to give them this honor (see vss.4-8). And so, the "priesthood" consists of the following: chosen by God (the believers, in response and acceptance of the Gospel message—vs.6; 1:1 2; 2:22-25); a nation (family, akin to the Greek word "begat," and so, beginning with the "spiritual birth," to grow God's Family into a "priestly nation"—vs.9); a royal priesthood (in His kingdom to serve the King as His priests—vss.5, 9; Dan.7:13, 14; Is.61:6; Rev.1:6; 7:15; 22:3-5); a holy nation (1:15-21; Dt.7:6); a people of God's own possession (Ex.19:4-6; Dt.14:2; 1 Pet.1:14-25; 2 Cor.6:16-18; Rev.21:3-7; 22:3-5); that believers may "tell out" His "virtues" (manifestations of His power and moral excellences—Vine; see the other four uses of this word in the New Testament—Phil.4:8; 2 Pet.1:3, 5), having called us out of darkness into His marvelous light (vs.9; Is.9:1-3; 42:5-9; Eph.5:8; Col.1:12-14; Rev.21:22-27);

for once we were not a people, but believers are now God's own possession in His Family (vs.10; Hos.1:10; 2:23; Rom.9:24-26; Rev.21:3); and not having received mercy, now the believer has received God's mercy (vs.10; Lk.1:49-51; Rm.11:30-32; Eph.2:4-7; Heb.2:17; 4:14-16; James 2:13; 5:11; 1 Pet.1:3). So, Peter encourages the believers as aliens and strangers on earth (similar to the wilderness experience like that of the Israelites), to abstain from "fleshly lusts" and have a good conduct before others, so no matter what is said toward us, our good conduct and behavior may be a factor (testimony) to win them over to the Lord in the day of His coming (vss.11, 12, 15; 1:5-7; 4:16).

Peter now gives several "submission" encouragements to his selected groups of people (to institutions, servants to masters, wives to husbands and husbands (in understanding) to wives—up to 3:7). Notice in submission to authorities, it is the will of God doing what is right (and so silencing the ignorance of foolish men—vss.13-15). Our freedom of believers (Gal.5:1) is to be demonstrated by doing what is right in God's eyes, honoring all men, the king, love for all brothers and sisters in Christ, and reverence for God (vss.16, 17).

Servants are to be submissive to their masters (Eph.6:5-9), whether treated kind or rough (vs.18). This finds "favorability," for the sake of "conscience of God" (see vss.23, 24), when one bears some "grief" to experience (that is, sometimes there is not much one can do to bring change or just best to do under those circumstances—not wanting to make things worse—vss.19, 20, 23). Christ has set this example for us, and did so without sin or deceit (vss.21, 22; Is.53:9). The keys to do so are brought out in the next three verses—entrusting (Greek imperfect verb here, so ongoing action in the past—"kept entrusting"—New American Standard Bible) Himself to Him who judges righteously—vs.23); the goal of dying to sin (already done on the cross) and living righteously for God (vs.24; "wounds" here is actually singular, a wound, as from a stripe or stroke to someone; only time used in the New Testament, here meaning (being singular) the stroke of Divine judgment administered to Jesus for our sins on our behalf on the cross (Vine), that we may die to sin as He died for ours, once for all (Heb.9:12-14, 26; 10:12). This is where healing begins (see also James 5:14-18). While we used to stray (as sheep), now the believer has returned (spiritual birth in conversion) to the Shepherd (Jn.10:11-18) and "Overseer" of our souls (same word as "elder"—overseer) in 1 Tim.3:1, 2; vs.25).

1 Pet.3:1-22—Peter continues on with his submission topic, specifically here in the relationship with husband and wife. Wives are to be submissive to their own husbands, even so if some are disobedient to the word they may be won over by their good behavior, in fear (respect) and purity of their wives (vss.1, 2). Their beauty is to be of the primary nature of imperishable qualities—a meek (see definition at James 1:21) and quiet inner spirit, the emphasis on the hidden nature of the heart and not the outward adornment as the priority, as holy women of the past, as Sarah with Abraham, conducted themselves, and not give in to fear of any kind (vss.3-6). Husbands are to be understanding with their wives as their dependent helping spouse (Gen.2:20-24), as a fellow-heir of God's grace of life, so their prayers are not hindered (without obstacles—vss.7, 12).

In summary, Peter gives some harmonious characteristics for believers to strive for and carry out—being of one mind (reading the Bible for this—1:22-25; Phil.2:1, 2), sympathetic, brotherly loving, compassionate, humble-minded (see Mt.11:25-30 commentary for a practical definition of humble), not returning insults but giving blessings to others, which believers are called to do and inherit their blessing (vs.8, 9; 1:4; 2:23-25). Peter goes on to quote more encouragement from Ps.34:12-16: to love life and see good days, not speaking deceitfully; turning away from evil (Prov.4:20-27); and doing good and seeking peace (Mt.5:9; James 3:18); for the eyes of the Lord are on the righteous and to hear their prayers, but against those who do evil (vss.10-12).

Peter now addresses how to handle suffering in a godly way and perspective. Who could harm one if they are zealous (set on) doing what is good (vs.13; see also Rm.8:31; Ps.118:6)? Yet, blessings come by doing the right thing regardless (vs.14). So Peter refers to Is. 8:12-14—not to fear what others fear, or be intimidated or troubled by them (vs.14; see Is.8:12); instead, sanctify (set apart as holy—a priestly duty; now see Is.8:13-15) Christ as Lord (no one else) in your heart, being prepared to give an answer to those who ask of our hope within us (1:3,13; one's conversion testimony is a good example here, too), and doing so in meekness (Greek word here; see commentary on James 1:21 for definition) and reverence (vs.15). Keeping a good conscience is important, so others may feel their wrong doing if speaking against us (or others), demonstrated by one's good behavior (vss.13-16). Suffering for doing right always is better than suffering for doing what is wrong (vs.17). As our example (2:21), Christ died for sins once for all—the Just One for the unjust—in order to bring us to God, having been put to death in the flesh, but made alive by the Spirit (KJ, NIV; vs.18; Rm.8:11); by which (the Holy Spirit) He went and proclaimed to the spirits now in prison, who were disobedient during Noah's time, as God (literally) "kept waiting" during the ark's construction, which eight persons (Noah's family) came through the water safely (vss.19,20). The more recent view of this difficult to sort out passage and that fits the context best that we have today (at this writing), presents commentators saying that Jesus went down to the people of Noah's time and, by the Holy Spirit through Noah, made proclamation of the Gospel at that time to the people, of God's salvation being available, and also announcing the coming judgment on the earth (and so, building the ark); those in prison are those who did not accept God's message of salvation through Noah and are now (see the New American Standard Bible translation of vs.19) in prison as a result, though this was preached to them then while on the earth before the judgment came (see similar thinking of the Tower of Babel—Gen.11:7-9). And God "kept waiting" during the building of the ark (the word "patience" of God in vs.20 is the word "long suffering;" and so, the whole world was reached at that time, though God's "long-suffering" message through Noah; see 2 Pet.3:9). Only a few—Noah and his family of eight total—were brought safely through the water (vs.20; see upcoming 4:5, 6 also).

Peter goes on to say that as Noah and his family were saved through the water of the flood, this representation and analogy of Christian baptism now saves the believer, not the water removing dirt from the flesh, but the "pledge" (NIV), "answer of a good conscience toward God", that is, the believers new life through the spiritual birth, being cleansed from sin with the presence of the Holy Spirit now with them (2:24; Heb.9:11-14; 10:10; Eph.4:4-6; Rom.6:4; see the commentary on John 3:1-21 for more discussion of baptism), through the resurrection of Jesus Christ (vs.21); who now sits at God's right hand, with all authorities, angels and powers subjected to Him (vss.22; Mt.28:18; Col.2:9, 10).

1 Pet.4:1-19—Peter encourages the believers to cease from sin, as Christ Jesus has suffered once for all (3:17) that we may die to sin also and live for righteousness (vs.1; 2:24, 25; 2 Cor.5:21; the word for "arm yourselves" is the verb for the noun "weapons of warfare," for which see in 2 Cor.6:7; 10:3-5). He reminds them once again not to live in former habits of lusts of the flesh (vss.2-4; 1:14), for those who live in those habits will have to give account to Him who is ready to judge the living and the dead (vs.5; Jn.5:21-29; Acts 10:42; 2 Tim.4:1; Rm.14:9). Peter says that is why the Gospel was preached to the dead (see back at 3:18-20), that those who rejected the salvation gift and message from God will be judged, while those who received it "may live" (present tense verb) in the spirit according to God (vs.6).

Peter exhorts the believers about the urgency of the time we live in, to live our lives pleasing to God (vbs.7; Heb.1:1, 2; 9:26; Eph.1:7-12). He gives some more general instructions for believers to carry out in their priestly service to the Lord (2:5)—be of a sound mind and sober spirit for the purposes of one's prayers (vs.7; 3:7); keep a fervent love for one another, which covers over a multitude of sins (vss.8; Prov.10:12; 19:11); hospitality is a basic practice of the church, for fellowship and outreach (vs.9;

Rom.12:13; 1 Tim.5:10; the early church practiced their love, hospitality and gifts together (Rm.12), and so here, too—vss.8-11); Peter divides the gifts to the church in two categories here—speaking gifts and serving gifts, a helpful distinction to remember; note every believer has a least one spiritual gift, to serve and build one another up in the Lord (vs.10; Rm.12:6; 1 Cor.12:7; 14:3): speaking, as God's representative (His words for the moment at hand), and serving, with the strength (physical strength as God's gift to the server) that God gives, so God may be glorified through our Lord Jesus Christ, to whom belongs the glory and dominion forever. Amen (vs.10, 11).

Peter then gives one more teaching and comfort about handling suffering according to the will of God (vss.12-19, summarized in vs.19). The spiritual battle is ongoing, so one must not be surprised but always alert (vs.12; 5:8-10; Mt.24:42; Lk.21:34-36—a prayer to pray). When sufferings for Christ occur, Peter encouragingly says "keep on rejoicing" (see Mt.5:10-16), with the end goal always in mind, seeing the Lord one day, rejoicing then with great jubilation (see 1:6-9), and in His name, glorifying God (vss.13-16; see Acts 5:41, 42; 16:22-34). All the ones not believing in the Lord and doing wrong will receive the just punishment from the Lord (vss.17, 18; Jn.3:16-18; Heb.9:27), while believers receive their just rewards from the Lord (Mt.5:3-16; 6:1-15; 10:41, 42; 1 Cor. 3:10-15; 9:16, 17; Eph.6:6-9; Col.3:23, 24; Heb.11:10, 16, 24-26; Rev.22:12). The key is to "continually entrust" (present tense) their souls (themselves) to our Faithful Creator in doing what is right (vs.19; see 2:21-25; 3:15-17).

1 Pet.5:1-14—Peter speaks now to the elders in the church, as a fellow-elder himself, who has witnessed, not only the life of Christ on earth, but His sufferings, as well; he reminds them of the glory to come (vs.1; 4:13, 14; 1:6-9; see Phil.3:20, 21; 1 Jn.3:1,2). He gives them instructions to shepherd the sheep voluntarily, and not from compulsion (or strict necessity, the Greek word here), which is God's will for a serving elder (vs.1; see 2:25 also); and not for any kind of dishonest gain, but, instead, to serve eagerly (in readiness—vs.2). Also, they are to be examples to the flock, and not abusing their rights and authority in serving the Lord (vs.3; see Paul's examples in 2 Cor.5:5-9; 10:8; 13:10, 11; Philemon 14), but looking forward to the reward (vs.4). Younger men are to be submissive to the older men, as all are to "clothe" themselves with humility toward each other, as God gives grace to such as these (vs.5). And so, believers are to humble themselves under God's mighty hand (see 4:11; 5:11), that He may exalts us at the proper time (vs.6; 1:8, 9; 4:13; see Mt.11:25-30 for a helpful, working definition of humility), and casting all our cares upon Him, because He cares for us (vs.7; Mt.6:25, 32-34). Resist evil and the evil one, and so "accomplish" (finish, don't give in) to the attempted evil (vss.8, 9; see 4:7, 12, 13; also, Mt.4:1-11; 1 Cor.10:13). Note the growth development which can include sufferings for the Lord and doing what is right in vs.10—He will complete, establish (fix firmly), make us stronger, and "lay the foundation and build" us up (lay a foundation, firm and unwavering; see the analogy back in 2:4,5).

Peter closes his epistle with close associations to Silvanus (taken as probably the Silas of Acts) and Mark, the writer of the second

Gospel, working in close relations with Peter (see Acts 12:11-17). Peter acknowledges his epistle as "God's true grace," confirming the validity of his words and exhortations that were written, in which believers are called to stand firm in (God's word; vs.12; 1 Cor.15:1). "Babylon" often in the early church was a reference to Rome. The "kiss of love" is God's unconditional love and Peter extends peace to all those who are in Christ (vs.14).

2 Peter

The theme of second Peter's epistle is his encouragement to the believers to "grow in the grace and knowledge of our Lord and Savior Jesus Christ" (3:18). We see this emphasized at the beginning of his epistle (1:2, 3, 5, 8), stated at the very end (3:18), and with all the in between fitting right in with this, including the emphasis of avoiding "false prophets" and "false teachers" in quite some detail and specific descriptions in chapter two.

2 Pet.1:1-21—Peter declares once again (1 Pet.1:1) his bond-servant role and apostleship to Jesus Christ and writes to those who have the same faith in the Lord as him, having obtained <u>God's</u> righteousness, through the believers coming to know our God and Savior, Jesus Christ (vs.1). He extends and prays God's peace to be multiplied to them in the knowledge of God and of Jesus our Lord (vs.2). Peter testifies that through now knowing the Savior (and growing in their relationship with Him), the believer in Christ, who has been called to His own glory and virtue (moral excellence), through His Devine power has been granted everything pertaining to "life and godliness" (personal growth and life's sufficiencies in Him—vs.3; 3:18). Through these (His gifts of life and growing in godliness), He has granted to us His "of great value" (Greek word)

and "very great" (Greek word is the superlative of "great" here, only time used in the New Testament) promises, so that (with this great blessing) we may become "sharers" (the word for fellowship in the Greek) of the (His) divine nature (godliness)—truly great promises indeed, one must consider, from start to finish; having escaped (from) the corruption in the world by its lust (singular, meaning evil desire(s), vs.5.

So, to now grow in godliness and continue to stay away from worldly lusts (vs.5), Peter teaches seven excellent virtues (moral excellences) for the believer to pray for, to "exercise in," and to develop them for personal growth and attainment (vss.6-9). The first goal of attainment is "moral goodness" (qualities; vs.5; see the other New Testament uses in 1 Pet.2:9; 2 Pet.1:3 and Phil.4:8). Peter says to "diligently bring these in and supply" them to your faith (the Greek words of vs.5). Next is "knowledge" (knowing <u>what</u> to grow in regarding "moral goodness" (vss.5, 6; see Book 3 of <u>The Family Bible Studies Series</u>, <u>Growing In God's Wisdom</u>, for a word study on more "ingredients" of God's wisdom and character building and how to pray for them). Peter then points out "self-control" (a key ingredient in properly handling and developing "moral goodness; see Gal.5:22-25; Acts 24:25; Tit.1:8; Eccl.8:5, 6). Then, the quality of "endurance" (the Greek word, "to hold up" under circumstances, with the Lord help and His strength, vs.6; see the commentary on James 1:1-5). God's will and purposes are extended over time, from start to finish, and the believer needs to pray for this "character strength" from God to fulfill one's short term and long term goals (Heb.10:36; Rev.3:10—"keeping God's word of endurance"). "Godliness" then begins to settle in (be a part of one's being) as these things are prayed for and practiced (vs.6). One then begins to see and experience the wonderful things God can do in and through the "believing" mind and heart in Him (1 Cor.2:9-16; Is.64:4; 26:3, 4; 33:2, 5, 6). Next, "brotherly love" is an expression or outflow of developing "moral goodness," also (loving the brethren as brothers in a family, which they are; see the other four uses in the New Testament—Rom.12:10; 1 Thess.4:9; Heb.13:1; 1 Pet.1:22); and finishing with the eternal quality and godly character trait and best of all—God's unfailing and unconditional love (vs.7; Jn.3:16, 17; Rom.5:1-11; 8:32; 2 Cor.5:21; 1 Cor.13:4-8, 13; Heb.4:14-16; 5;7-9; Titus 2:14). The believer growing in these qualities of "moral goodness" will not prove barren (yielding no return) or fruitless (see Jn.15:16), developing and maturing in the knowledge of the Lord (vss.8, 3; 3:18; see the commentary at the end of Hebrews for the "perfection" theme developed in Hebrews). Not growing in these virtues, Peter says, leaves one blind (to spiritual things and personal growth development) and short-sighted, forgetful of one's past cleansing of sins (vs.9). Therefore, rather (the Greek word here, than vs.9), Peter says to be diligent and certain about their calling and choosing of them by God (vss.10, 3; 1 Pet.1:2), for in doing these things one will not ever stumble (or fall, vs.11; a strong emphatic negative in the Greek here, also showing the sowing and reaping principle in vs.8). Adding these "rich" treasures on earth also brings a "rich supply" (same verb as in vs.5) to those doing them, when entering the kingdom of our Lord and Savior Jesus Christ in heaven (vs.11).

Peter makes known in his epistle here that the time of his departure is not far away (vs.14), and so, he wants to remind them of these things, for the present time and after he leaves for heaven (possibly reflecting on this in vs.11), so they may recall them (and now, part of the New Testament for all to read, also—vss.12-15). Peter testifies to them that the power and coming of the Lord Jesus (second coming) was not a tale or myth made up to them (see the commentary on 1 Tim.1:4 for the definition of "myth" here), but he (along with James and John) were eyewitnesses of His Majesty, on earth (with the rest of the apostles) and on the Mount of Transfiguration, witnessing then His Majestic heavenly glory, and hearing from heaven the testimony that "this is my beloved Son with whom I am well pleased" (vss.16-18; Mt. 17:1-8; see Is.42:1). Peter declares to them that the personal witness of this event, plus being followers of the Lord throughout His whole time of ministry on earth (see Acts 1:21, 22), makes the prophetic word more certain (prophecies of the Messiah's first coming to earth being fulfilled—Acts 3:19-21), and thus, one should pay close attention to this (and prophecies involving His second coming to earth), so one is not left in the "dark" about these things, eagerly looking forward to His return (vs.19; Phil.3:20, 21; 2 Tim.4:8; for "Morning Star, see Rev.2:28 and the commentary on 22:16; Lk.1:77-79). He affirms to them that no prophecy of Scripture is of one's "private interpretation" (KJ, vs.20). The word "interpretation" means literally "a release" (Vine). The meaning then? Next verse—vs.21. No prophecy of Scripture came about by an act (release) of human will, but men moved (impelled) by the

Holy Spirit spoke from God (vs.21; see 1 Pet.1:10-12; Ex.17:14; 34:27; 2 Pet.3:14-16).

2 Pet.2:1-22—Peter remains on the subject of prophecy from 1:19-21, only now he devotes a whole chapter about recognitions and warnings against "false prophets" and "false teachers." He warns against "secret and destructive heresies (divisions developed and brought to an issue; partialities or prejudices—Vine) and blaspheming (to slander or speak against) the truth, bringing swift destruction on themselves (vss.1, 2). In greed they exploit (take advantage of) people with false words (vs.3). But if God did not spare angels when they sinned (vs.4; Tartarus—a place where angels are confined for judgment—Vine), nor the ancient world in Noah's time, or Sodom and Gomorrah during Lot's time and yet, delivered Noah and Lot, righteous men of their time, seeing the wickedness going on all around them (vss.4-8), then the Lord knows how to rescue the godly from temptation (see 1 Cor.10:13) and keep the unrighteous under punishment for the day of judgment (vs.9).

Peter goes on to say that with corrupt desires, they despise authority and revile (speak against) angelic majesties (vs.10); but the angels being greater in might (strength) and power (inherent power), do not revile them back in judgment against them before the Lord (vs.11; see Michael the archangel's response in Jude 9). They revile where they have no knowledge, like unreasoning animals (vs.12). Peter's listings of their character and actions show ones without conviction of right or wrong, and appearing out of control, not ceasing from sin (vss.13-16). Speaking arrogant words of vanity (emptiness) and living in complete sensuality,

Peter says "blackest darkness" is reserved for those who continue to do so nonstop, and do not repent of their deeds (vss.17, 18, 21), while they are promising "freedom," yet being themselves slaves to corruption (vs.19). Whatever a person is overcome by (present tense), to this they are enslaved (vs.9). Some attempted to flee away from their lifestyle of sin (vs.20) by hearing and even knowing the Gospel (the knowledge of the Lord and Savior Jesus Christ, trying to even join in with you—vss.13, 20, 21), but get entangled (word means "to weave") once again in that lifestyle and are overcome again (same word and verb tense as vs.19), and now, turn away (punctiliar, one time action) from the holy commandment (the gospel, the only thing that can save them) delivered to them (vss.20, 21; similar to Heb.6:4-6). The proverb for them then becomes true (vs.22).

2 Pet.3:1-18—As a result of chapter two, Peter "arouses" his audience, reminding them not to forget the Gospel (2:21) spoken by the holy prophets and apostles (vss.1, 2; 1:13-15; 1 Pet.1:10-12). Peter says in the last days mockers will come mocking about where is the Lord's promise about His coming back to earth, as nothing has changed from the beginning of creation (vss.3, 4). Yet, why would they ask such a question, knowing what the Lord's coming is about (see Amos 5:18-20; 4:11-13; 2 Pet.3:9, 10)? Peter says, it willingly (in the Greek) escapes their notice that the heavens existed long ago (Amos 4:13) and the earth was formed (the Greek word probably means "held together" too; see this verb in Col.1:17; also see Heb.1:3) out of water and by water (see Gen.1:9, 10). A similar occurrence took place at the flood (water covering the earth), but with people living contrary to God on

the earth, this was brought by God as His divine judgment on the earth (vss.5, 6; 2:5). The present heavens and earth are reserved for fire, kept for the day of judgment of ungodly men (vss.7, 10-12). Peter declares to them that God is patient (longsuffering in Greek) over His creation (1 Pet.3:20), not wanting (willing) that anyone perish, but all to come to repentance (vss.8, 9, 15; Ps.90:4; Rm.2:4; Rev.2:21, 22). Knowing these things believers are to conduct themselves in holiness and godliness (vss.11, 14; 2:5, 7-9; 1 Pet.1:16-21), knowing the Lord is bringing new heavens and a new earth, in which righteousness dwells (vs.13). Peter affirms that the writings of the apostle Paul would become Scripture, which some unknowledgeable and unstable would "distort" (twist or turn) as other Scriptures also, to their own destruction (vss.15, 16). So, Peter warns them to be on guard and not be carried away by the error of lawless men, but grow in God's grace and knowledge of our Lord and Savior Jesus Christ (vss.17, 18; 1:1-4, 8), to Him be the glory, now and forever. Amen (vs.18).

1 John

The main theme of 1st John is fellowship with God (1:3) and fellow believers (1:7). He teaches on the subject of sin throughout (1:5—2:2; 5:16-21), which is foundational to maintain "fellowship" with both God, fellow believers and a testimony to others. John also addresses different groups of people he desires to reach with his variety of messages (which some are often repeated for emphasis). "Little children" (mentioned seven times—2:1, 12, 28; 3:7, 18; 4:4; 5:21) refers to very young new believers. Another group is "young children," (not brand new, but still young—2:14, 18). Young men and fathers are addressed, also, more mature and responsible in the faith (2:13, 14); and general directions to the "brethren," (3:13-17) and "beloved" (Christians overall) are also spoken to in John's first epistle.

1 Jn.1:1-10—John begins his epistle with a great specific recognition of the incarnation of Jesus Christ (vss.1-3; Jn.1:14-18; Col.2:9). John says in repeated fashion what he and the eyewitnesses discovered—they saw Him with their eyes, heard Him with their ears, touched Him with their hands, as He actually appeared before them, emphasizing the reality, physical appearance and confirmation that the "Word of Life," Jesus Christ, had become

visible (in the flesh) to mankind on earth (see Jn.1:1-5, 9-18, 29, 49; 3:29-36; 8:12; 11:25-27; Acts 3:19-26). John's message that he proclaims (vss.2, 3) is for others to also receive Jesus Christ (the eternal life, vs.2; 5:20; Jn.1:12, 13, 5:20; 17:3; see the Prayer in back of the book) and have fellowship (the "sharing" within the fellowship of Christians together) with them, knowing God personally (vs.3), that their joy (in the Lord) may be "shared" and made complete together (building God's Family, vs.4; see Jn.16:22).

John declares the message that he and the eyewitnesses heard from Him—that God is light and no darkness is in Him at all (vs.5; 1 Tim.6:16; Jn.8:12; 1:4, 5, 9). To walk with God is to follow the truth and not walk in "darkness" (spiritual darkness, vss.6, 7; Jn.1:4, 5, 17; 3:16-21; 8:12; 12:46). God knows, though, that we may sin and simply need to confess that (vs.9), for the blood of Jesus cleanses us from all sin (vss.7, 9; Heb.9:11-15, 26; 10:10, 14; note when we confess our sins to Him, we don't need to ask Him for forgiveness (repent means to turn away from it); we simply (and very thankfully) <u>thank</u> Him for it, which also involves forgiving ourselves, since He did it already upon our confession and repentance to Him, and cleansing one of it—vs.9). One deceives themselves if they say that they have not sinned (present tense) and lie about God's testimony He sent in His Son Jesus to die for our sins and bring His offer of eternal life to mankind (vss.8-10; Jn.3:16-21; Rm.3:23; 6:23; 1 Jn.5:10).

1 Jn.2:1-29—John emphasizes that he writes these things (especially here to those very new and recent to the Christian faith—"little children") so that they will not sin (vs.1). When we

do sin and confess our sins, Jesus is our Advocate before the Father (same word, here the Holy Spirit is called in Jn.14:16, 26—one who appears on another's behalf; helper—BAGD; Heb.1:1-3). He is the "payment" for our sins (propitiation, vs.2; 4:10; Rm.3:24-26), and also for those of the whole world (vs.2; 4:14). John says that keeping His commandments is one demonstration (with their spiritual birth) that one has come to know Him (vss.3, 4; 1:6, 7); also one who keeps His word (present tense) and is being perfected in His love (vss.3-5; 4:16-18; 5:2-5). As the believer lives and grows in the Lord, his/her life should be an example of our Savior and Lord (vs.6).

The Lord Jesus gave the commandment to the church to love one another, as He loves us (Jn.13:34, 35). This was not a "new commandment" because they heard of it early in their Christian experience and was proclaimed by Jesus and the early church (vs.7). Yet, it is "new" because the church had just recently started up, and the commandment follows <u>His</u> example of love for us (vs.7, 8; Jn.13:34; 17:23, 24; Eph.4:32), as the True Light is already shining (Jn.1:4, 5, 9; 8:12; 12:46) and the darkness is passing away (vs.8; 3:8; Jn.1:5; 16:33). Loving the brethren demonstrates one walking in His light (vs.9-11; Jn.1:4, 5, 9; 8:12; Mt.5:14-16) and keeps one from being a "stumbling block," to himself and to others (vs.10; see also 2 Pet.1:1-11; Mk.12:29-31).

John now speaks to four different Christian "age level" groups—little children (new conversions); young children (vss.14, 18), those still young in the Lord; young men and Fathers (vss.12-14). John repeats some of their encouragements to them, stressing the points he brings out to them, to emphasize and affirm them of what took place at their Christian conversion (spiritual birth—Jn.1:12, 13; 3:16) experience. These truths become "cemented" (founded) in their faith in the Lord (Jn.8:31, 32; 17:17). As a result of these great works of the Lord in the lives of believers in Jesus, they are not to love the things in the world, now that their love is from and for the Lord (vss.15, 16—pursuits of the world); for the world is passing away (also with it vs.8), but those doing (present tense) God's will, last forever (vs.17; Prov.21:30, 31; 1 Cor.7:31; Is.46:8-11; Jn.3:16-21).

John then finishes chapter two speaking to the "little children" (vs.28) and "young children" (vs.18). He writes to them because some people were trying to deceive them (vs.26; 3:7) and he points this to the work of "antichrists," speaking against Christ and the truths of the Bible (vs.18). For the last hour in vs.18, see Eph.1:9-11; Heb.1:1-3; 1 Pet.4:7. The appearances of antichrists show that we are in the last times, awaiting Christ's return. The fact they don't stick around Christian settings shows that they are not of them (vs.19; see also Acts 20:28-30). But the believer has the "anointing" from God (vss.20, 27; see 3:24; 4:13) and He guides us into all truth (Jn.16:13) and teaches us all things (Jn.14:17, 26). That is the reference to "you all know" (that is the truth) in and vs.20 and vs.21. The "antichrist" denies the truth of the Father and Jesus His Son (vss.22, 23). And so, they are to let God's truths abide in them and grow in them (vs.24; Jn.14:6, 16, 17; 17:17; Phil.1:6, 9-11). One of those great truths is His promise of eternal life (vs.25; Jn.3:16, 17; 10:27-30; 1 Jn.5:11-13, 20). They are exhorted to "abide" (rest and trust in the Lord continually), having that confidence and looking forward to His coming (3:2) and continuing to do what is right in the eyes of the Lord (vss.28, 29—another way to recognize believers compared to deceptions from antichrists—vs.29, plus vss.21-23; 3:7).

1 Jn.3:1-24—John now begins in chapter three to address the church as a whole, referred to as "beloved" and "brethren." The two very brief exceptions and are in 3:7 and 5:21, speaking to the "little children" once again. John starts by pointing out the wonderful, amazing work of God, that God takes us and delivers us from Satan and evil ways and places the believer into the Family of God, calling us "children of God" (the general word used for children here, from the Greek word to "beget" or to "bear"—Vine). The New International Version catches this excitement with an exclamation point at the end—"and that is what we are!" This is one reason why those who have not become believers do not recognize us (vs.1; 4:5, 6; see the Prayer in back of the book). The great joy for the believer gets even more exciting with the promise in vs.2—absolutely miraculous—to be like Him when we see Him (1 Cor.15:51-53; Phil.3:20, 21;Col.3:1-4). And so, the believer is to walk in the ways pleasing to the Lord, through a pure life living in His promises (vs.3; 1:7-9; 2:25, 29; 3:21, 22; 5:11-13). In light of His promises, John makes known that the believer cannot continue to sin (present tense), as Jesus came to take it away, the One who knew no sin, because of now the Holy Spirit indwelling the believer (vss.4-10, 24; 4:13; 5:18; Heb.9:11-14, 26, 28; 10:10, 14; Jn.16: 8-11; 1 Pet.4:1, 2). The devil has sinned from the beginning (see Jn.8:44) and Jesus came to destroy his works (deliverance from the past to live with and for Him in the present and future—the righteous living, a sign (demonstration)

of the believer in Christ—vss.7-9; Prov.4:18; 2:29, 30; "seed" in vs.9 I believe is the Holy Spirit—placed in us for growth (seed) in the Lord and the work He does in the believer's life and to the world—Jn.16:8-15).

From vs.10 to the beginning of chapter five John focuses on love for one another in the body of Christ, another demonstration of the believer in Christ (vs.18, 19; 4:7, 9, 21; Jn.13:34, 35). The love for Christ is exemplified by showing His love to one another, passing from death and into life, and demonstrating that in practical ways with their life to one another (vss.11-18; 2:10; Jn.5:24). Actions done in love also gives our hearts confidence before God (vs.19). Nothing slips by God because He knows all things (vs.20). So if we are convicted of a wrong doing, we go back to His promise in 1:7, 9 (see that commentary), then proceed on in prayer (vss.21, 3). The faithfulness of God and His love for us is brought out here by John when we pray and keep His commands and our lives are always pleasing to Him—(vss.21, 22; see Jn.8:28, 29; in our faith we are to trust Him for it; Mk.11:24, 25; see also 1 Jn.5:14, 15). His commandment is to believe in His Son Jesus and love one another (vs.23); and to abide with Him is to work with the Holy Spirit (who is with Him, Rev.4, 5) He gave to us (vs.24; 4:11-13; Gal.5:22-25; Rm.8:26-28).

1 Jn.4:1-21—Chapter four of John's epistle addresses three times to the "beloved," the church of Jesus Christ (vss.1, 7, 11). An important factor of fellowship with God and man is to test the spirits to see if they are from God, because of false prophets and false teachers (vs.1; 3:8; 2 Pet.2; Jude 4). John teaches us some specific guidelines for testing spirits: 1) If from God, they

will acknowledge Jesus' incarnation and coming from God (vs.2; 1:1-3; Jn.1:14-18). Those who do not confess (present tense) this truth are of the antichrist that exists in the world (vs.3). 2) John reminds the church that they have overcome them (vs.4; 2:12-14; Jn.1:5; 16:33). 3) God is greater than any creature He has made (vs.4; Jn.12:31; Eph.3:8-11; Col.2:13-15) and gives the believer the Holy Spirit to live within him/her (3:24; 4:13; Jn.14:16, 17; 2 Cor.3:17, 18). 4) And Jesus said that those who are of God hear the words of God (so John says, those that know God, vs.6; Jn.8:47; 10:3-5; 18:37). Good teaching for discerning the spirit of truth and the spirit of error (see also 1 Tim.4:1; Heb.5:14).

Loving the brethren continues fulfilling Jesus' command for the church (vss.7, 8, 11, 12; Jn.13:34, 35; 16:27; 17:23). God loved us first and sent His Son for the "payment" (propitiation) of our sins, so the believer may live and love through Him (vss.9-11, 14-16, 19; 2:2). God's love is a "perfected" (maturing) work in the believer's life (vss.12, 17, 18). The believer knows that he/she abides in Him because of the presence of the Holy Spirit in their life (vs.13-15; 3:24; Rm.8:16). The demonstration of the church in knowing the Lord is their love for one another, as the Lord loves us (vss.19-21; Jn.13:34, 35; Eph.4:32-5:2).

1 Jn.5:1-21—John affirms the spiritual birth for the believer in Jesus, the Messiah in vs.1 (Jn.1:12, 13) and loving the Father results in loving His children (the church—vs.1). Loving God and obeying His commandments also follows right through to loving His children (the Family of God—vss.2, 3; 3:23; 4:21). The believers, His children, have overcome the world by their faith (vss.4, 5), affirmed to them back in 2:12-14 (see that

commentary). The "water and blood" would seem best to refer to His baptism to His death on the cross (vs.6). The Spirit is truth (Jn. 14:17; 15:26; 16:13) and so, along with vs.6, continues to "bear witness" (present participle) to the truth of the testimony of Jesus Christ, the Messiah (vss.7-10; Acts 3:19-25), making the believer through the Holy Spirit a "witness" (affirmed in God's word, the Bible) of the life and testimony of Jesus Christ, which is the testimony (witness) of God to the world (vss.9, 10). Since Jesus rose from the dead and always lives forever (Rm.6:3-11), God gives His gift of eternal life through the spiritual birth to the believer (vss.11-13; 2:25; Jn.1:12, 13; 3:1-21; 10:27-30). These verses along with John 3:16, 10:27-30 and Rm.6:23 are some of the strongest affirmations of God's gift of eternal life given to the believer we have. He wants us to be assured of this, born out by John's gospel and epistles and other Bible passages, along with the sure understanding and meaning of "eternal" itself.

Having confidence in prayer is praying according to His will (the Bible). God always works out what is best and according to His will (rest assured, even if you are not sure what to pray, but trusting God for His answer—see Rm.8:26-28, 34-39; Is.46:8-11; Prov.16:3, 9; 21:30, 31). It is always good to know when we pray according to His will and He hears us and we have His answer to look forward to, worked out in His faithful way (vss.14, 15; see also 3:18-24).

The two "kinds" of sin John teaches us about are those that do not lead to death and those that are capital crimes and lead to capital punishment and death (see Eccl.8:8, 12, 13). Some sins of crime in the Old Testament carried a capital punishment with it (murder, Ex.21:12; adultery, Lev.20:11; kidnapping, Ex. 21:16; causing a miscarriage, Ex.21:22-25; children cursing parents (Dt.5:16; Ex.21:17; etc. see also Gen.9:5-7). The Greek does not have an indefinite article in the language as English does so "sin" not leading to death and "sin" leading to death is an appropriate interpretation here. John, referring back to prayer in vss.14, 15, says to pray for those whose sin is not one leading to death for God's restoration to them (note the power of intercessory prayer here, also—vs.16). Then he says that he is not saying that he should make request for those sins that lead to death (vs.16, as God has made known certain capital punishments for capital crimes in the Bible; see also Rm.13:4). He didn't say that they couldn't; only saying that he wasn't declaring that, as God's desire is that no one should perish, but all come to repentance (2 Pet.3:9) and we live in the time of His mercy to all (Rm.11:30-32). Yet, if one refuses and continues so to not repent, God has declared and made His will known about certain capital crimes, and one would risk the fate of that punishment, if not receiving God's witness about His Son and the Bible and their wrong-doing (vss.9, 10, 16, 17; Num.23:19; Rm.6:23; 13:2-5).

Yet, God protects His family (vs.18; 1 Pet.1:5), while the world lies in the power of the evil one (vs.19; Eph.2:2; Jn.8:44). The believer knows Him who is true (vss.5-11; Jn.14:6; 17:2, 3), the Lord Jesus Christ, who is the true God and eternal life (note the declaration of His deity, vs.20; Jn.1:1, 18—New American Standard Bible). The "little children," in John's closing (and for all, this being God's principle) are exhorted to guard themselves against idols (vs.21; Ex.20:2-6; 1 Cor.10:7-14).

2 John

John writes this epistle to "the chosen lady and her children" (vs.1). I think this would be a more favorable conclusion that this refers to a particular Christian setting (gathering) and to the leader(s) there to carry out the admonitions he addresses to them and, of course, to the church at large (see vss.5, 13 also; might be more protective (discreet) in sending his letter, also). In vs.1 John speaks to all who know the truth—the reception of the Gospel of Jesus Christ and follow God's word, the Bible (1 Jn.4:10, 14, 15; Jn.14:6; 17:17), which abides in the believer and will be with us forever (vs.2; Mt.24:35). John greets them with grace, mercy and peace from God the Father and His Son Jesus Christ (vs.3; Jn.10:30).

John's main subject (the bigger picture here) is that the believer walk in truth, the truth of the Gospel, which the Apostles and Prophets of the early church to proclaimed (vs.4; Eph.1:13; 3:19-22). Walking in truth is to follow the Lord's commands (1 Jn.2:3-6), one of the primary ones given to the church which is to love one another (vss.5, 6; Jn.13:34, 35; 1 Jn.4:21).

John warns them as he wrote in 1 Jn.2:18-27, to beware of antichrists in the world, not confessing the incarnation of Jesus;

for many "deceivers" have gone out into the world (vs.7). He warns them so they won't lose rewards in serving the Lord in truth (vss.8, 4; 3 Jn.3, 4).

John goes on to say that anyone who goes too far (BAGD) or beyond the Gospel message (as denying the incarnation of Jesus) does not have God, as the believer has both the Father and the Son (vs.9; Jn.10:27-30; 14:23). John instructs them not to participate with antichrist teachings, or actions they do, including not to receive them into one's home (vss.10, 11) or give them a greeting.

He keeps his letter brief because he wants to discuss more in meeting with them face to face (vs.12). He sends a greeting from those with him, who are also children chosen of the Lord (fellow believers), to the ones receiving his epistle.

3 John

John addresses this epistle to a fellow believer named Gaius, to him and the fellowship with him, of whom John has some influence with them, including spiritual oversight (vss.1, 10, 12, 14). He prays an encouraging prayer for him, that his health "prosper" (literally, to help on one's way—Vine), as his soul prospers (vs.2). Brethren had come to John and reported how he is "walking in truth," giving great joy to John to hear this (vss.3, 4; 2 Jn.4). Gaius is commended by John in his faithfulness in serving the brethren, and especially of his handling strangers who are believers in the Lord (vss.5-8). Since they take nothing from the Gentiles (vs.7), John directs him to send them out with his (and their) fellowship support in service to the Lord, and be co-workers with them (vs.8).

One in their fellowship, though, was working against the church, putting himself first and not accepting John and other believers, even unjustly accusing them, putting them out of the fellowship and preventing others to come into the fellowship (vs.10; see the warnings in 2 Jn.6-11). John said he would call attention to what he was doing when he comes and encourages the believers to only imitate good examples and what is from God (vs.11; 1 Jn.2:5-10). One example for them was Demetrius in their fellowship, who John acknowledged having a good testimony, as well as others in their fellowship, also (vs.12). John closes his epistle as in 2 John (see that epistle), here calling those with him "friends", and those in their fellowship "friends" also, both having the definite article before the word "friends," and to greet each of them by name (vs.13-15).

Jude

The writer of the epistle of Jude is most commonly agreed to be the brother of Jesus' earthly family (Mt.13:55; Mk.6:3). He is a bond-servant of Jesus Christ and brother of James, the brother of the earthly family of Jesus, also, and the author of the epistle of James (vs.1; Mt.13:55). Jude writes his general epistle to the called and beloved in God the father, and kept for Jesus Christ (vs.1; His church; Jn.17:11; Col.1:16-18). He prays God's mercy, peace and love be multiplied to them (a good collective prayer, to pray for them—and us today, too—vs.2).

Jude says initially he wanted to write to them about "our common salvation," but felt necessary to write about "contending earnestly for the faith," once for all delivered to the saints (vs.3). Some persons "secretly crept in" on some (see also Gal.2:4) and deny our Mater and Lord Jesus Christ, and were turning His grace into "shameless conduct" and living. Jude says that this is what God's judgment is reserved for (an important topic in his epistle), if they refused to repent and receive Jesus into their life, the spiritual birth (Jn.1:12, 13; 3:1-21; see the Prayer in back of the book; vss.4, 6, 7, 15).

Jude reminds them of certain judgments that have taken place in the past, all leading up to the "great day of judgment" of

Almighty God (vs.6). He recalls to them the wilderness experience of Israel (vs.5), fallen angels (vs.6; see also 2 Pet.2:4), and Sodom and Gomorrah (vs.7). He says they (referring back to vs.4) commit acts of immorality ("dreamers"), stated also in the previous verse, while rejecting authorities and speaking against "angelic powers" (Vine; vs.8). He mentions a good example of handling those situations by Michael the archangel, when contending and disputing with the devil about the body of Moses (see Dt.34:6), who simply rebuked him in the Lord's name (vs.9; see Zech.3:1, 2; 1Pet.5:9). Those doing these things slander things they don't understand, and things they do know (and do)—purely natural instincts alone—like unreasoning animals, are destroyed by those very things (vss.10, 8).

Those doing these kind of things follow after the ways of Cain (Gen.4:1-8), and Balaam (compromise for money; Num.22-24; 31:16; see also 2 Pet.2:14-16), and Korah (rebellion against authorities; Num.16; vs.11). They are like "hidden reefs" in their love feats (which most gatherings had their communion services with these also; see 1 Cor.11), caring only for themselves without fear (vs.12; a "reef" can be a set of stones going out into a body of water, which is dangerous to walk on and even more dangerous if covered up by high water or tide). Jude addresses them as "wild waves," casting up on shore their shame, like foam; and wandering stars (no set place), reserved for the blackness of darkness (vs.13). The prophesy of Enoch actually refers to Dt.33:2, the judgment of God coming down at Mt. Sinai (Ex.19-24), as making reference to the judgment also yet to come (vss.14, 15, 6). Their actions and words are repeated and further described by Jude in vs.16.

Jude reminds the believers of the "mockers" to come in the last time before the Lord's return to earth, spoken about by the apostles, and repeats again their actions that go along with their words, (vss.17,18; see 2 Pet.3:1-9). Those practicing these things cause divisions, emphasizing merely natural and worldly things, and do not have the Spirit of God (vs.19).

Jude exhorts the believers, in contrast to ways of the world just pointed out, to build each other up in the holy faith, praying with the help (in) the Holy Spirit (vs.20; Rm.8:26-28; Eph.6:18). Believers are to keep themselves in the love of God, eagerly awaiting His mercy to be revealed and take the believer to eternal life (vs.21; Phil.3:20, 21). In the awaiting time, believers are to be active and alert, sharing the Gospel with others who need to be saved (vss.4-19). Jude presents a contrast in the next two verses—having mercy on those wavering and have not yet made the commitment, and snatching (saving) those they can from the coming judgment (see Zech.3:2), and having mercy (or possibly pity here) on those refusing, hating the sins that they are in bondage to in their lives (note the "garment" or "tunic" here is the "inner garment," thus, even the ones that are not visible; vss.22, 23).

Jude closes his epistle with great words of encouragement: God is the only God (Dt.4:35, 39) and Jesus Christ is our only Savior, (Acts 4:12), who can keep us from stumbling and make us stand in the presence of His glory—blameless (literally, without blame) and with great joy!—be the glory, majesty, dominion and authority, before all time, now and forever—Amen (vss.24, 25; Lk.21:34-36—a prayer Jesus gave believers to pray; Ps.84:1-4).

Revelation

The book of Revelation is appropriately titled—The Revelation of Jesus Christ, as the first few words of the book bring out. The bigger picture of this means the fulfilling and completing all things of God's plan and prophecies in His Son, Jesus Christ (Eph.1:9-12; Rev.19:10; 1 Cor.15:23-28). More specifically also, a number of "revelations of Jesus" comes forth in this book: 1) His Triumphal Character (1:12-16); 2) The Lamb who was slain (5:6-10); 3) The Harvester of the final harvest (14:14-20); and 4) The Triumphant Victorious Warrior and King (19:11-18; see also Zeph.3:14-20). Remarkably and miraculously, add these to Jesus' incarnation, transfiguration and resurrection body, John saw Jesus in seven different appearances in his lifetime—quite the revelations indeed shown to the disciple whom Jesus loved (Jn.21:7, 20)!

Revelation is tied together in four specific visions John received in the Spirit (1:10; 4:2; 17:3; 21:10). All give a specific revelation in God's plan to show His activity and lead to the completion of His everlasting purpose—to fulfill His Family and live with them forever in the New Jerusalem and New Heaven and New Earth (Rev.21, 22; see Book 4 of <u>The Family Bible Studies Series, The Theology of the Bible—The Family of God</u> for a more complete

Bible review on this great work of God throughout time, 41 pages).

Time frame is also a factor in the Book of Revelation—past, present and future (1:19). In 1:10, John says that he was in the Spirit—the general Greek past tense (aorist tense) used here. So, John is writing down his vision in the near recent past for others to read and wonderfully preserved by Almighty God throughout that time since. Presently, John was writing to seven churches in western Asia Minor (western Turkey today). The messages were directed to those seven churches, but the Lord's truths are applicable from that time on, as well (Heb.13:8; Mt.24:35; Jn.17:17. Chapters 4 and 5 present the current worship in heaven (4:8) and the future coming-to-earth-to-reign of God's Lamb and King Jesus (19:11-18), seen in heaven, with all that being played out from chapter six and onward. A sequence of events is more clearly revealed beginning in chapter six with the appearance of the Antichrist (or possibly here his military leader—6:1-4; 13:1-10). Paul gives us a guideline in First Thessalonians, chapters four and five, and Second Thessalonians, chapters one and two (see the commentaries there) that the Antichrist appears after The Rapture of the Church and his "abomination of desolation" occurs during the Great Tribulation (many believe around the middle of those seven years—Dan.9:27; Mt.24:15; 2 Thess.2:3-5). Visions two and three include his brief reign and swift defeat (17:8, 11; 19:19-21).

Rev.1—The word "revelation" means an unveiling or uncovering ("In the ordinary sense, a mystery implies knowledge withheld; its Scriptural significance is truth revealed"—Vine, for the word mystery, used 4 times in Revelation—1:20; 10:7; 17:5, 7). Note God's transmission of this vision—God, to Jesus, through His angel, to John, to His bond-servants (to His many bond-servants, all believers—all those who would hear these words (vss.1-3; 2:29; 22:17-20). The blessing comes to one who reads it (probably the messengers of the churches—2:1, etc.; Mt.11:10) and those who hear this prophecy and keep it (take to heart, guard, heed—apply oneself to it—vs.3; 22:7,9), for the time is near (vs.3; Ps.90:1-4, 2 Pet.3:8,9; Mt.24:44; 1 Cor.7:29-31; Rev.22:6, 7, 10, 18-20; the word "time" means a fixed or definite period, a season—Vine).

John sends this prophecy to the seven churches in Asia Minor (see introduction) and greets them with God's grace and peace vs.4; see the introduction of Romans 1:1-7 for understanding of the greeting of "grace and peace." Note the Trinity referred to here and the description given to each (vss.4, 5; for "first-born of the dead" see the commentary on Col.1:16-19). Great acclamation here given to Jesus—who has freed the believer from their sins (Rom.6:1-11; 8:31-39; Heb.9:26; 10:10-14) and made us to be a kingdom of priests to serve Him forever; and He will receive the glory and dominion forever and ever, (vss.5, 6; 5:9, 10, 12-14; 7:14, 15; 22:3; 1 Pet.2:5, 9, 10). John confirms the Lord's coming and dominion by quoting Dan.7:13 (Mt.24:30) and Zech.12:10—see the full context of Zech.12:10-14 and also, John 19:37; note— every eye will see Him (vs.7; Mt.24:29-31). John reveals that God is the "Alpha and Omega" (vs.8; the first and last letters of the Greek alphabet; we get the word "alphabet" from the first two letters of the Greek alphabet, alpha and beta); see also 1:17; 21:6;

22:13; Is.41:4; 44:6, 7; 46:8-11. The proclamation "Lord God Almighty" is a great declaration repeated in key passages of the Revelation; see their listings here—1:8; 4:8-11; 11:17; 15:3; 16:7, 14; 19:6, 15, 16; 21:22).

John now introduces his circumstances and his intent of the prophecy (John is mentioned by name four times in the Revelation—1:1, 4, 9; 22:8). The receiver of the Revelation is believed to be the Apostle John and confirmed as so by numerous early church fathers (Unger). He begins by stating himself as a brother in the Lord who is a fellow-sharer of the sufferings and endurance (Greek word; for definition, see the commentary on Heb.12:7) that are in Jesus (vs.9). Patmos is a small island a little ways off the coast of Asia Minor (Turkey today), a little south of Ephesus, between Turkey and Greece in the Aegean Sea. It's rocky and barren terrain was used as a place to banish criminals. John was sent there by the Roman Emperor Domitian in 95 AD (Unger; vs.9).

John records the first of his four visions (see introduction about them) in the Revelation (vss.11-20). He was commanded to write it in a book (vs.11). "The Lord's day" is taken by most to refer to Sunday (vs.10). John heard a loud voice like a trumpet and was told to write out his vision (prophecy) and send it to the seven churches (vss.10, 11). John saw seven golden lampstands (referring to the seven churches) and seven stars (probably the messengers delivering the prophecy to their churches; vss.12, 16, 20, 3; angel can also mean messenger, Mt.11:10). The vision refers to the Son of Man (Jesus, in light of Dan.7:13, 14; also see Rev.14:14), standing in the middle of the churches (vs.13; see

Col.1:16-19). The description here of Jesus in the Revelation of this passage is one of Majestic Victorious character (vss.13-16): the garment from head to feet refers to His royal kingship (vss.13, 5, 6; 17:14; 19:11-16); His golden girdle is His priestly authority (vs.13; Lev.8:7, 13; compare also Rev.15:6); His hair of white wool and eyes as a flame of fire demonstrate His purity and removing impurities and injustices carrying out His righteous judgments (vs.14; 2:18; 15:4; 16: 5, 6; 19:11; Is.9:6,7; 11:4,5); burnished bronze refers to His strength and power (Unger; vs.15); voice like many waters is His strength of command and the large sphere in which it is heard (vs.15; 14:2; 19:6; see also Ps.19:1-11; Ezk.43:2); He judges righteously with His sharp two-edged sword (vs.16; 19:15; Is.11:3-5; 49:1-3; Heb.4:12); and His face shining as the sun shows the glory of God, as coming directly from His throne (vs.16; see the angel in 14:1; see Moses in Ex.34:29-35; 2 Cor.3:7; 4:4-6; Ezk.43:1-5). At the vision John fell at His feet as a dead man (see similar in Dan.10:7-9, 18) and Jesus encourages him that He died and lives forever more (Rm.6:9, 10), and has the keys of death (and overcoming death—Rm.6:1-11) and Hades (where the unbelieving dead await judgment; see Lk.16:23; Rev.20:13). John was then instructed to write the vision and record it, along with the messages to the churches and the things to take place in the future (vss.19, 20).

Rev.2—The Roman Empire was a polytheistic empire, though it allowed in some places persecution to Christians and even death sentences (2:13). Some had allegiance to a main god of worship and others had many ("The city was greatly addicted to idolatry" (Unger, on Pergamum). Most if not all of the seven churches had thriving economies in their cities and some manufactured special products they were noted for (ex., medical salve for the eye in Laodicea, 3:18). Five of the churches needed some kind, of repentance, one was a suffering church (Smyrna) and one was remaining faithful, with promises given to them to come (Philadelphia).

Ephesus (vss.1-7)-The main message that comes with the letter to Ephesus is to not lose your first love (vs.4; Mk.12:29-31). With a good list of positive accomplishments (vss.2, 3), there is one very important "work" they needed to remember as top priority—doing the works in love in serving the Lord—like they did a first (vs.5). Pretty simple task of utmost importance in the midst of busy schedules and activities we face, including oppositions that can occur (vss.2, 3, 6). It needed repentance, as well, showing other things became the main focus (vs.5). Not much is known about the Nicolaitans, but appears to be tied in with idolatry and their sacrifices (vss.6, 14, 15). As the Spirit says these messages to the churches, Jesus wants His church to overcome their trials and focus on love for Him, and the "tree of life" in God's Paradise for His Family to come (vs.7; 22:1-5; Rm.8:31-39).

Smyrna (vss.8-11)—The main central message that comes to the church from the letter to those in Smyrna is "to be faithful unto death" (vs.10). Jesus is our example as given in vs.8—the first and the last, dying for our sins and rose from the dead, and alive forevermore (1:13-18); Heb.9:24-28). They experienced sufferings and poverty (even in a thriving economy) and were spoken out against by the Jews (vs.9). A short trial of suffering was coming to them (vs.10), but their focus was to be on Jesus and His overcomings (Jn.1:5; 16:33), and the "crown of life" in His coming world and reign (2 Tim.4:5, 7, 8; Heb.11:10, 14, 16; Rev.11:15; 21:1-7), along with all those overcoming and having life in His name (vs.11; 21:5-8; Jn.3:16-21).

Pergamum (vs.12-17)—The teaching to the church of Pergamum is more implied due to strong warning against false teaching there in the area stated to them—cling, hold fast and teach the Word of God (2 Tim.3:16,17); Heb.4:12; Jn.17:17). False teachers, who do not change and teach the word of God will have to face Him who will judge with His sharp two-edged sword (vss.12, 16; 19:13, 15). Killing a faithful Christian witness is also recorded at Pergamum (Antipas, known to be a bishop there—Unger), declared as the place where Satan dwells (vs.13; see the commentary on the introduction to the churches at Revelation 2). Acts of immorality, associated with food sacrificed to idols, similar to the Old Testament teaching of Balaam (vs.14; Num.25:1; 31:15, 16), which seemed to be similar also to the Nicolaitan teaching (vs.15), was often associated with idol worship. This drew the stern reprimand from the Lord with this entering into the church, or He would come and make war against those doing this, if they did not repent and teach God's word (vs.16). Those overcoming this and come to know Jesus, God will give them the "hidden manna" (the manna that comes "inside," not the literal bread as before—see Jn.6:49-51, eternal life through Jesus—The Bread of Life), and a white stone with a new name on it, that only the one receiving it knows (vs.17; see 19:12; name changes are not unusual, examples are Abraham, Sarah, Jacob, to name a few, representing their true character and purpose God has for them);

a white stone was used to vote and acquit people in court; plus used as admissions to important feasts (Vine; see 19:7).

Thyatira (vss.18-29)—The Lord gives strong advice to the church to and through those at Thyatira to hold fast to what they have and continue to do God's works until the Lord comes (vss.25, 26). They too had a problem of immorality and things, including foods, sacrificed to idols, while allowing someone similar to Jezebel (see 1 Kg.16:31; 21:25; 2 Kg.9:7) in the Old Testament to teach and deceive with this teaching (vs.20). God commends the church's good deeds (vs.19), but they were permitting this to take place, and would not repent of it (vs.21). So, God's Son, with eyes of a flame of fire and feet like burnished bronze (see 1:14, 15), would bring condemnation upon those committing adultery, with sickness and death to her children, unless they repent of this (vss.22,23). They were trying to make their teaching appear to have a divine connection, but instead (as the Lord said), were teaching (and deceiving with) the "deep things of Satan" (vss.24, 20). Only God knows the depths of the mind and heart (vs.23; Rm.8:27; 1 Cor.2:10; Heb.4:12) and His works will be done and displayed through those in faith, love, endurance and service to Him (vss.19, 26; Jn.3:19-21), as He will give to all according to their deeds (vss.23, 26-29). To those overcoming and keeping His deeds, they will be with Him and reign with Him in His everlasting kingdom, overcoming the darkness, with the Bright and Morning Star (vss.26-29; 22:5, 16; Dan.7:13, 14; Lk.1:31:33 Jn.1:1-5; 16:33).

Rev.3—Sardis (vss.1-6)—Sardis was a church with incomplete deeds (vs.2). They knew what their deeds were (vs.3) and needed to return to them (similar to 2:5, 26), and continue to do God's works (vss.1, 3 6; 2:5, 26). Cults and immorality were also known in their city and affected the "garments" of some (vss.3, 4; see also James 1:27), and so, needed to repent (vs.3). Those not "soiling" their garments will walk with the Lord in white garments, being worthy of that gift (see 6:11; 19:7, 8); along with those who overcome, confessing Jesus as Savior and Lord, Jesus will also confess them before the father and His angels (vss.4-6, a Family tribute).

Philadelphia (vss.7-13)—The church of Philadelphia was a faithful church, given a specific ministry by the Lord to be His testimony to the world. The "key of David" refers to Is.22:15-25 and Eliakim in charge of the royal household, as David's representative (Is.22:15, 20, 22-24). So God gives open doors to represent Him and in His service, too (vss.7-9). For "synagogue of Satan," see 2:9. However God fulfills this verse, see Jn.17:23 (vs.9). God's promise to them (and the church) is to keep them out of (Greek preposition "ek") the hour of testing coming upon the earth (vs.10). This is consistent with the Rapture of the Church and the Great Tribulation to follow (see commentary on 1 Thess.4, 5 and 2 Thess. 1, 2). "Coming quickly" has the meaning that when the events before His coming and including His coming occur, they will take place quickly (see 22:7, 12, 20). For the "crown of life," referring to rewards to the believer, see 2:10; 2 Tim.4:7, 8; 1 Cor.3:10-15; 1 Thess.5:1-11. The reward for overcomers is to be made a "pillar in the temple of God" (vs.12; 7:15; 21:22; 1 Sam.2:8; Ps.75:1-3; Prov.9:1-6; Eph.2:19-22; 1 Tim.3:15, 16). His family will be seen, known and identified as His possession, living in the eternal New Jerusalem together forever with Him (vs.12; 1 Pet.2:9). The message here by the Spirit goes out to all the churches (as with all the messages to the seven churches—vs.13).

Laodicea (vss.14-22)—The Laodicean church here is one that lacked zeal for the Lord, being neither hot or cold spiritually (vss.15, 16, 19). Jesus declares Himself to them to be the "Amen" (by man, meaning "so be it;" by God, "it is so"—Vine), the "Faithful and True Witness" (1:5; 19:11), and the Beginning of the Creation of God (Source or Cause here; vs.14; Jn.1:1-3, 10; Col.1:16, 17). The Lord says because they are not hot or cold, evidenced by their deeds, He is about to spit (literally, vomit them out of His mouth (similar as could happen with some foods – vss15, 16). They were declaring "to be rich" (present tense) and "had become rich" (perfect tense, past completion with present ongoing effects; see Hos.12:8), and had need of nothing (vs.17). The Lord declared to them because of saying these things that they are wretched (Greek word is undergoing a hardening, callus effect), miserable (Greek word is mercy only here without mercy, pitiful), poor (and continuing on so; see 2:9), blind (Greek word for "smoke," here spiritually blind; see Mt.13:13, 16), and naked (needing God's garments—vs.17; 19:7, 8; Is.61:10; Rm.13:14). The Lord is quite gentle in His reproof (Prov.3:11, 12) and offers them some sound advice (the word for "advice" is a collective advice in invitation, a "uniting" in counsel, similar to Is.1:18). His gold is refined by fire (and so, similar process) to become rich (see Prov.3:13-21; Heb.12:5-13); His garments are white ones (3:4, 5; 6:11; 19:7, 8, given for righteous works); and <u>His</u> eyesalve will help one truly see (vs.18; Mt.6:19-23; 13:16; see Lk.16:11-15 for "true riches"). The Lord calls for repentance here and says for them to be zealous for Him (note, no alternative here, as the conflicts above; vss.19; 15-17). The Lord reproves (Jn.16:8) and disciplines and counsels (together with them—vs.18) in love (vs.19; Prov.3:11, 12; Heb.12:5-13). The invitation in vs.20 is primarily evangelistic (and at least a part of all the "overcoming" promises here the Lord gives in the letters to the churches and at large in the Revelation, 1:3), because believers have already invited him to come in and with the descriptions given here (vss.15-17), there must be a great enough need for the Lord to do this (2 Pet.3:8, 9; Eph.1:7-11). In personal invitation given by the Lord also, overcomers may sit down with Him at His throne (an invitation not always granted by rulers on earth in world history), for He grants them to serve and reign with Him (vss.21, 22; 5:9, 10; 7:15; 20:4; 22:5; Dan.7:18).

Rev.4—With the invitation given to the believer to come to the throne of God where Jesus is at the right hand of God (3:21; Heb.1:1-3), the Holy Spirit now takes John there in a heavenly vision to see the continual worship going on around the throne of God. This begins the second vision of the four given to John to write down and pass on to God's servants in the body of Christ (1:1, 2, 11, 19; 4:1, 2). As John sees God on His throne (see also Dan.7:9-14), His appearance is like two different kinds of quartz colors—jasper (blue, green, or rosy tints) and sardius (a deep orange red), with a rainbow, like an emerald, around the throne (remember where we see the rainbow and what it means over the earth, and here, where it comes from (vs.3; Gen.9:12-17; also see Ezk.1:28). Twenty-four unidentified elders and thrones are around the throne, wearing golden crowns (overcoming victory crowns, similar in meaning to the ones given out in the Olympics of that time; vs.4; 2:10; 3:11; 2 Tim.4:7, 8; see also 1 Cor.9:25—same word as in vs.4 for "crown" in the Greek). The peals of thunder and lightning flashes refer to impending judgment to occur (vs.5; 8:5; 11:19; 16:18). The seven Spirits of God refer to the complete composition of the Holy Spirit (vs.5; 1:4; 5:6; see also Is.11:2; Jn.16:8-11). For the "sea of glass" in vs.6, see 15:2; 21:18, 21; Ezk.1:22; Ex.24:9-11). The "living creatures" are identified as "cherubim" in Ezekiel's vision (vs.6; Ezk.10:15, 20; an angelic order (Unger), having to do with protection (Gen.3:24; Ex.25:18-20) and here directing the never ending worship before the throne of God (vs.8). Their appearances represent the dominion of four divisions of God's creation (lion—animal kingdom; calf (young bull)—domestic kingdom; man—God's creation of mankind in His image; and eagle—bird kingdom of God's creation—vs.7). The description given of the "living creatures" fit their purposes well (vs.8), with unending "heavenly" energy and motion giving continual praise and acknowledgement to the Lord God Almighty for His holiness (worth repeating), His eternal nature, and forever continual thanksgiving to Him, who lives forever and ever (worth repeating also—vss. 8,9), sitting upon His throne (Ps.145:13; 90:2). In such declaration, the twenty-four elders fall down before the throne and cast their victory crowns before the One who bought them and brought them their victory, putting them before His throne (vs.10; 5:9, 10). They praise our Lord and our God because He is "worthy" (the greatest worth and value and deserves the acclamation), to receive "glory" (His character and accomplished works) and "honor" (highest esteem and respect) and power (Greek word is His "inherent power"—Vine; vss.8, 11); for He created all things (Gen.1:1; Jn.1:1-3; Rev.3:14), and because of His will (purpose), they continually exist (Greek verb here) and were created (vs.11; Ps.33; Ps.104; Is.46:8-11).

Rev.5—Chapter five of the Revelation continues on with the second vision of the four that John receives, with further developments of the heavenly vision. This continuation focuses on the "Lamb who was slain" (Jesus, vss.6, 9). John sees a book held in God's right hand, written front and back, and sealed up with seven seals (vs.1; compare Dan.8:26; 9:24; 12:4, 9). The seals open up the impending judgments of God, followed by the trumpets and plagues. No one was found in the vision who could open up the book and break the seals (vss.2-4; see Jn. 5:22-29). An elder comes up to John with "good news," "that" the Lamb who was slain" is worthy to open the book and break the seals (vs.5). He is described as the "Lion from the tribe of Judah" (vs.5; see Lk.3:33; Hos.11:10; Is.31:4; Joel 3:16; Amos 1:2) and the "Root of David" (22:16; 2 Sam.7:11-14; Is.9:6, 7; 11:1-5, 10; Jer.23:5, 6; 33:17). He has seven horn (seven the number of completion; horns signifies rulership and kingship—see Is.9:6, 7; Ps.89:17, 18, 24-29) and "seven eyes," showing the Person and work of the Holy Spirit, sent out to the whole earth; vs.7; see 4:5 and the related verses there. The "Lamb" is worthy to take the book, because He has overcome the world (vs.5; Jn.16:33) in the mission of His first coming to earth (Jn.16:22; 17:4; Heb.9:28), to bring salvation to the world and purchase for God (bring into the Family of God) by His shed blood, mankind from every tribe, tongue, people and nation (vs.9), and making them a kingdom of priests to reign with Him upon (or over) the earth (vs.10, 22:5; Dan.7:1-14, 18; 1 Pet.1:17-21; 2:9, 10).

As the Lamb takes the book, the four living creatures and the twenty-four elders bow before the Lamb in worship, each with a harp (playing victory songs in praise and worship to God—vs.8; see 14:2; 15:2) and yet, in solemn reverence, holding golden bowls of incense, representing the prayers of the saints coming up to God's throne (vs.8)—and they will continue to keep coming during the judgments of God unfolding (8:3,4). The song they sing is a new song to the Lamb, declaring His victory and His great accomplishments for God, purchasing believers in Christ from the earth, to serve before God forever, as His Kingdom of priests (vss.9, 10; 1:6; 7:14, 15; 22:3-5). And the myriads (a large vast number) of angels joined in saying loudly their praises to the Lamb (in individual declared praises to Him—vss.11, 12; see also 4:9; Jn.5:21-24; "power" in vs.12 refers to physical strength in total makeup (inner and outer), given and provided by God (Vine), here referring to His strength in His ministry and enduring the cross, paying for the sins of mankind; see also Lk.22:39-44; Heb.5:7; 12:1-3). And then, all created things join in, giving also their individual proclamation of praises to God, including His dominion over them, forever and ever (vs.13; "dominion" here is the Greek word for God's created and manifested power—Vine; 1:8; 4:11); as God, because of the Lamb's overcoming (vss.5-10), is building His Family to be with Him forever and will completely restore the whole world (Rev.21, 22).

Rev.6—As the second vision given to John continues to unfold (4:2), the scene returns back to earth, displaying a "white horse rider" who goes out conquering on the earth. John sees the Lamb open one of the seals on the book and the "living creatures" declare the order to begin God's judgments (vss.1, 16, 17). This is quite widely thought by many to be the Antichrist or his military leader during the Great Tribulation (vss.1, 2; 2 Thess.2:1-12; Mt.24:21; Rev.7:14; see also Dan.11:40-45). The next seal broken shows his "plight to fight" (make war), taking peace from the earth, with the occurrence of war taking place (vss.3, 4). The third seal broken and order given by the third living creature is famine on the earth, represented by a black horse (vs.5). With the Antchrist present and war taking place, prices for some common items to eat reach a ridiculously high and practically unaffordable price (vs.6). "Oil" is olive oil, needed for lamps of that day (Mt.24:1-13) and medicinal healing (Lk.10:34). "Wine" was also medicinal in those times (Lk.10:34) and wartime history shows some military leaders and others under stress consuming more of this on a personal level (but see Eph.5:17, 18). Seal number four reveals and ashen (pale-looking) horse, indicating death occurring on a very large scale in various ways (Hades—the place where the unbelieving dead await final judgment—increases its number during these judgments; vss.7, 8; see Jer.24:10; 29:17-19; Rev.22:17-19; 1:3). The fifth seal opened shows those who were killed for their faithfulness to God's word and their testimony for Him (vs.9; see the "overcomers" in Rev.12:10-12). Blood underneath the altar is where the Old Testament sacrifices were poured (Ex.29:12). They cry out to God for mercy, judgment and revenge for this atrocity (vs.10). God comforts them for the moment by giving them (the Greek here, "each one") a white robe (see 19:7 8; Mt.22:1-14), until to the others, this likewise, takes place and the judgments are completed (vs.11; 7:14-17). The sixth seal of judgment gives us a glimpse at the end of the Great Tribulation (the sixth trumpet and plaque do also—9:13-21; 16:12-16). The words are reminiscent of Jesus' words concerning this time, quoting from Joel 2:10; 3:15 in Mt.24:29 (vs.12) and Is.13:10 and 34:4 (vss.13, 14; see also Jer.4:24; Ezk.38:20; Nahum 1:5-7). Men hiding in the caves recall Is.2:12-22, for they realize it is the time of the wrath of God upon the earth (pretty knowledgeable acclamation made by them here—vss.15-17).

Rev.7—Before the judgments resume and the last seal occurs and the trumpets begin to sound, John observes an interlude here—the sealing of the 144,000 from the tribes of Israel and another scene of worship at the throne of God. Appointed angels have already been stationed by God to hold back the winds from blowing on the earth (vs.1; why? Note the first trumpet coming up in 8:7 upon the earth, so no one could blame this on the wind—or something else; it is the time of God's appointed judgments—vss.2, 3, as the angels wait for their signal to begin their duty, until the 144,000 are sealed by God on their foreheads; see Ex.12:7, 13; Ezk.9:4-6). Note the various tribes that are sealed of Israel, bond-servants of God, (vss.4-8) and their honorable acclamations acknowledged by God, and their duty and dedication to the lamb—see 14:1, 4, 5).

John then sees a great uncountable (to us) multitude before the throne from every tribe, nation, people and tongue (5:9), standing before the throne and the Lamb, wearing white robes, with palm branches in their hand (used only one other time in the New Testament at Jesus' Triumphal Entry into Jerusalem—Jn.12:12, 13; see also Lev. 23:39-43), crying out loudly, declaring, "Salvation to our God, who sits on the throne and to the Lamb" (vss.9,10, remembering 6:9-11). The elders and living creatures join in worship, declaring similar in 5:12, and then add—"be to our God forever and ever;" note, "Amen" begins and ends the acclamation here, meaning "so be it" (forever; vss.11,12). After a moment of "question and answer" who these are before the throne, the elder explains to John they have come out of the Great Tribulation (vs.14; Mt.24:21), and "washed" their robes in the blood of the Lamb, coming to believe and receive Jesus, the Savior and Lord (22:14; 1:5; 3:4; 1 Pet.1:17-21); and they will serve before the throne forever in God's presence and care in heaven, and with their Shepherd, the Lord Jesus, wiping away their tears and leading His people to springs of living waters, with no more hunger or thirst to ever experience again (vss.13-17; 3:12; 21:4; 22:1-3; Is.25:8,9; Jn.7:37, 38).

Rev.8—After seeing what the first six seals revealed, the seventh and last seal comes as a rather surprise at first with its content—silence (vs.1). It is important for us to remember the "rainbow" around the throne and what it means from the heart of God (4:3). God's desire is always salvation for His creation of mankind, made in His image (meaning, a representative figure, (Strongs); see this elaborated more upon in Book 1 of <u>The Family Bible Studies Series, The Family of God—Foundation</u> on page 7; see also James 2:13 and 2 Pet.3:9). God then releases the assignments to the angels with their trumpets given to them (vs.2). The first four trumpets have similarity with the first four plagues in their "target" of God's judgment (1st trumpet—land of the earth, 1st plague—people of the earth; 2nd of both on the sea; 3rd of both on springs and rivers; 4th trumpet—sun, moon and starts, 4th plague—on the sun).

Remembering the cry and prayer of the martyrs at the altar in 6:9, 10, God now begins to answer it through His assigned angel in vss.3-5. After many prayers coming up to the throne of God at the "golden altar" (the altar of incense before the throne of God—see Ex.30:1-3), the angel takes fire from it and casts it to the earth, with impending judgment to follow it (vss.4;5; see the commentary on 4:5). The first trumpet burns up a third of the earth, through fire and hail, including grass and trees (remember the "silence" of the wind back at 7:1). The second trumpet, with the fire cast to the earth, turns a third of the sea into blood, also taking out a third of the sea creatures and ships at sea (vss.8, 9). The third trumpet is like a burning torch that strikes a third of rivers and spring waters, making the waters (bitter, called wormwood—a bitter and injurious plant), causing many of mankind to die (vss.10, 11; see Jer.9:15). The fourth trumpet is upon the atmosphere and sky, and darkens a third of the sun, moon and starts, also making dark a third of the day and night (vs.12), as a flying eagle in the atmosphere then gives the warning of three more trumpet blasts to come (vs.13).

Rev.9—Chapter nine contains the fifth and sixth trumpets sounding off. The "star" from heaven falling to the earth is similar to the third trumpet in 8:10. Remember that God is in control of the judgments, with His main goal to bring in the final harvest (7:14-17; 14:14-16; 2 Pet.3:9). Note the star is also a "him" (vs.1), who was given the key to "the shaft of the abyss;" (abyss occurs seven times in the Revelation—9:1, 2, 11; 11:7; 17:8; 20:1,3; "a deep or bottomless pit, referring to the lower regions as the abode of demons, out of which they can be let loose—Vine; see also Lk.8:31). The effect of the opening appears much like a volcanic eruption (vs.2). The appearance of locusts is similar to Joel 1:4-7; but here demonic powers are with them, not just behind it, including painful scorpion stings on mankind without the seal of God on their foreheads (vss.3, 4). Note no harm is done to the earth, as brought about by the previous trumpets (vs.4). Mankind is not allowed to die with this sting (James 2:13), though they even seek it (vss.5, 6). The locust, looking like horses prepared for battle, is reminiscent of the Day of the Lord that Joel describes in Joel 2:1-11. Their gruesome appearance combines features of man and animal (vss.7, 8). Verse nine describes an army off to war (also see Joel 2:4-9). The sting is allowed for five months (the normal life of a locust in spring-summer life; vs.10), with a demonic power (their hierarchy), as their leader (vs.11; unlike real locust—Prov.30:27).

Warfare continues on with the sixth trumpet and a massive huge army leading the way (vs.16), in the time known as the Day of the Lord (Amos 5:18-20; Zeph.1:7-18; 3:8-20; Is.13:1-16; 24:1-23; Zech.14:1-15). The voice from the golden altar goes back to God going forth to answer the prayers of the ones slain on earth for the Lord who are under the altar there crying out to the Lord for justice on their part (vs.13; 6:9-11; 8:3). This trumpet release of judgment puts to death a third of mankind on the earth (vss.15, 18), by plagues, fire, smoke and brimstone (vs.18). This is done by the destructive force of four angels (demons; see the word "angel" of the abyss used in vs.11), who have been bound at the "great Euphrates River" (vss.14, 15). God's angels in heaven are free and ready to serve Him (7:1; 8:2). Some angels have been bound by God (like in the locked-up abyss, vss.1, 2; see also 1 Pet. 3:19; 2 Pet.2:4; Jude 6) and reserved for judgment, and only released (as this time of judgment) at God's command (vss.1, 2, 14, 15), and all for His purposes only (vs.15; see also 16:12, the sixth plague, working in conjunction with this and the huge massive army in 9:16). This army has much destructive power with it weapons, out of the faces and tails of their "horses" (vss.17-19). Even after this judgment, those remaining still did not repent of the terrible sins they were committing (vss.20, 21). Question remains—is this the end or Armageddon? One can see that this is not the end quite yet, with the "Kings of the east" and the dried up Euphrates River making their way westward (vast majority of commentators I have read agree on this time frame). For fast conquering of the Antichrist (6:1, 2) that leads up to Armageddon, see Dan.11:40-45, as this appears, according to history, yet to come and applies to the Antichrist.

Rev.10—John now sees another strong angel (5:2), this one coming down out heaven ("strong" here as in 5:2 is God's strength given to the recipient as a gift). Who is this angel?—is the natural question that comes up, with this glorious description that John presents to us in vs.1? The answer is just as he is stated—a strong angel from God (the reason this is not Jesus is because Jesus does not need to swear by God, being God Himself, the Second Person of the Trinity; see book 1 of The Family Bible Study Series,

<u>The Family of God-Foundation</u>, for further helpful study and insights about the character and functions of the Trinity); also, He created the things of heaven and earth referred to here by the angel (Col.1:16-19), and <u>He</u> lives forever and ever (vs.6). The angel's appearance is just like coming from the throne of God to deliver his message (vs.1). He carried with him an opened little book and stood on the land and seal (vs.2, 5, 8; God's dominion; compare 13: 1, 2, 11; see also Dan.9:24 and 12:7 with vss.5-7 here for God's completion of time and events). Seven peals of thunder then spoke, but John was told not to record what was said (vss.3, 4; see Ps.29:3-9). The angel has a very specific and urgent message (note the element of surprise here)—at the <u>seventh</u> trumpet, the mystery of God is finished, having preached this through His servants the prophets (vs.7). What about the "plagues" yet to come (chapter 16)? One can see in 9:20,21, no one else repented; after "plagues" 4 and 5, they did not repent either (16:9,11); at the last, "plague," they blasphemed God because of it (16:21); and when the Harvester comes in 14:14-16, He sweeps His sickle over the earth (and this before the plagues occur)—because the harvest of the earth (literal Greek word)—was dried up (14:15; followed by vs.16). John then takes the little book from the angel's hand and eats it (see also Ezk.2:8-10) and as it was said, it tasted good, but made his stomach bitter (vss.8-10). Yet, John was instructed to continue prophesying about many peoples and nations and tongues and kings (see 16:14; 17:9-15).

Rev.11—Now awaiting the seventh trumpet coming up in vs.15, John receives some instructions on measuring the temple on earth. Seeing that there will be a physical temple for Israel

during this time, the question arises about why this comes up here in the Revelation. The next two chapters focus on Israel and Jerusalem (11:8). There is another chapter and verse that tell us about a temple during this time and that is in 2 Thess.2, where the Antichrist's "abomination of desolation" takes place in the temple and desecrates it (2 Thess.2:3, 4; see the commentary there and also in Mt.24:15, 16). This gives us the background for the beginning of chapter eleven here in the Revelation.

John is instructed to measure the temple and the people in it (vs.1). He is told that the holy city (Jerusalem) will be trampled down by the nations for 3 1/2 years (the last part of the Great Tribulation—vs.2). Two witnesses then appear and will prophesy for the 3 1/2 years (vs.3, 4, in fulfillment of Zech.4:11-14). Many speculations have been made about the identity of these two witnesses, since the Scripture is silent about this. Their activities are like the past about Moses and Elijah mentioned in vs.6, yet, some have also offered the suggestion that these may be two prophets of their own time, raised up by God for the prophetic work of that day. God gives them a special protective power they may use if anyone should try to harm them (vs.5, a sowing and reaping principle here—Gal.6:7; Rev.22:12). The spiritual condition of Jerusalem of that time is stated in vs.8, necessitating the prophets ministry there (vss.1, 2, referred to above, and vs.8). When their ministry is finished (God's time), the Antichrist (the beast—see Rev.13:1-10) will war against them (6:1, 2) and kill them (vs.7). If the people have not believed in Jesus' resurrection for them yet, they are about to witness a sensational demonstration of God's power to do so right before their own eyes, followed by a rapture (transportation to heaven) to complete a marvelous miracle and testimony of God's power and hope before them (undoubtedly broadcasted to the rest of the world, as well—a great video to see over and over and over again!). An extended "celebration" about their death occurs there; yet, God performs the "true" and long lasting "celebration" to the people right there, before their very own eyes (and to the world to hear and possibly see then), and especially powerful since they would not bury them, causing great fear in their enemies (vss.11, 12). But, glory is given to the God of heaven, by those (the rest—vs.13) who know God (vss.13, 18). There resurrection was followed by an earthquake and death to 7,000 people in the city (vs.13).

As the seventh angel blows his trumpet, celebration resounds in heaven by loud voices there (vs.15), praising God for bringing His kingdom to the world through Jesus the Messiah, who will reign forever and ever (vs.15; Dan.2:44; 7:13, 14; Lk.1:31-33). How can they begin to celebrate yet? See the angel's message back in 10:7. So, the elders fall on their faces and worship before the Lord God Almighty, the One who continues existing and always did exist (the Greek verbs here mean this), and by His great power (inherent power, the Greek word) has begun to reign (vs.17). They acknowledge to the Lord that this is His time of judgment (wrath; 6:15-17), which will bring the time for all the dead to be judged (Rev.20:11-15) and for the rewards to the prophets and all His people (22:12), and destruction to those destroying the earth (vss.18, 19; Jer.51:25, 26). The "ark of the covenant" represents God's presence, as John see it in God's temple opened up in heaven, with impending judgment (4:5; 8:5) and the last plagues are about to come (vs.19; 16:1-21; the last seal and trumpet point to impending judgment, while the last plague brings the final judgment occurring at the end (16:17-21 and chapters 17-19).

Rev.12—Chapter twelve continues with the emphasis on Israel and the birth of the Messiah through them. Verse 1 refers back to Joseph's dream in Gen.37:9. This leads up to the birth of the Messiah in vs.2 (for the pains experienced, see Mt.2:16-18). The devil's opposition to them is given in quite dramatic detail in vs.3—seven heads refers to the seven mountains (worldly kingdoms) in Rev.17:7,9,10; then, authority of the devil given to the Antichrist (the beast; see that commentary in chapter 13); the ten horns refer to the last kingdom of the world given to the beast (see 17:12); and the seven diadems refers to a "form" of kingship (Lk.4:6) that the devil displays over the seven world kingdoms and their kings (17: 9,10). The tail sweeping away a third of the stars is difficult to see without further information, but if it has to do with angelic warfare (vss.7-10), whatever was casted down would soon be able to return (of the good angels), since what the devil did very soon is done to him (vss.9, 12)—and not allowing him to return to heaven ever again (vss.7-12; 20:1-3; 20:10; see also Dan.8:10). As the devil tried to prevent the birth of the Messiah, God was well ahead of the scheme to prevent that from taking place (vss.4, 5; Mt.2), and the Messiah was successful in His ministry and ascended into the heaven (vs.5; Jn.17:4; Acts 1:9-11; Rev.19:15). Verse 6 shows God's preparation and protection of Israel during the Great Tribulation after the "abomination of desolation" (vss.6, 14; Mt.24:5-21; 2 Thess.2:3, 4). The main battle taking place is in the heavens (vss.7-10; Eph.2:2; 3:8-12; 6:12, 13; Dan.10:13, 20,

21; 12:1), but the devil operates his misuse of authority through many worldly kingdoms (13:2; 17:9-14). And now is casted down to earth during the Great Tribulation with his fallen angels and does some persecution to Israel and the church (vss.13-17), before being bound in the Millennial reign of Christ (20:1,2), let loose then for a brief time before casted into the Lake of Fire forever (20:7-10).

With this the ones in heaven rejoice of the devil finally leaving their domain (vss.10-12). His accusations and persecutions did not stop God's people exercising their faith overcoming him through the blood of Jesus and the words of their testimony in knowing the Lord, even to their final death, however that takes place (12:11). Many will know then that the devils time (including him) is now short (vs.12; Jn.12:31; 16:8-11).

God has always maintained a remnant for Israel (see Book 4 of The Family Bible Studies Series, The Theology of the Bible— The Family of God, for important remnant verses in the Old Testament (pg.23) and the commentary on the New Testament remnant in Romans, chapter 11, about how God has carried this out throughout time). The devil tries again to get rid of Israel, by a flood, but God miraculously opens up the earth to catch the water and circumvent his murderous attack once again (vss.14-16; 4, 5). The devil was enraged and went off to persecute those keeping God's commandments and having the testimony of Jesus (vss.17, 11; 19:11; "enraged" is an abiding condition of the mind, often with a view to take revenge—Vine; 12:11).

Rev.13—John now is given some of the activities and description of the Antichrist and false prophet of The Great

Tribulation. For standing on the seashore, see Dan.7:2-8. The description of the beast is similar to 12:3 (see that commentary for similar explanation as here), as the devil transfers his authority to him (vss.1, 2, 4; see Dan.7:4-6 for the description—the kingdom that took away Israel's kingdom (Babylon) and the two worldly kingdoms that followed them (Persia and Greece; Dan.4, 8). The "head as if slain" in vs.3, called his "fatal wound" (of the sword in vs.14), from our perspective before the event, could be real (since he is a man of war himself—6:1-4; 13:7), could be an assassination attempt, or possibly a conspiracy plot (set up) to get the people to follow the Antichrist (vss.3, 4, 7, 8, noting the lack of harvest on the earth then, vs.8; 10;7; 11:15-18, though the saints are on the earth, vs.7; 12:11, 12). For his blasphemous statements and rebellion for 3 1/2 years (vss.5, 6), see the "little horn" in Dan.7:8, 21-27. For "captivity" and the "sword," see likewise in Jer.15:2; Rev.22:10-15. Endurance is what the saints need to pray for (see the definition in James chapter one and Heb.10:36, 37) and read the Bible a lot (vs.10; 1:3; 22:7).

The false prophet exercises the satanic given authority of the Anti-Christ, and looks lamb-like, but speaks as a dragon (vss.11, 12, 2, 5). His job is to "make" the people worship the beast (vs.2; see Dan.2, 3; Rev. 12:11, 12). He even performs great signs, in all deception of wickedness, power and false wonders (vss.13, 14; 16:13, 14; 19:20; 2 Thess.2:8-12; see also Lk.10:17-20). Through a "false resurrection" of the Antichrist, the false prophet tells those dwelling on the earth to make an "image" to the beast (vss.14, 15). They make it look "alive" (false creation to "look" man-like and "speak" like mankind), so that those who do not worship the beast would be killed (vss.14, 15). The false prophet "makes" (the Greek word here, possibly in conjunction with the image of the beast) the people take a mark on their right hand or forehead in order to buy or sell—needing either the mark, name of the beast or number of his name to do so (vss.16, 17; many alphabets have numerical equivalents to them, example, A=1, B=2 and so on). The word "calculate" means "to count," taken from the Greek word "a stone," which was how counting then was often done (by stones or pebbles, voting and court decisions made, for example—Vine; see Acts 26:10). Greek and Hebrew that the Bible was written in have numerical equivalents. Time will tell when the Antichrist appears how his name and numerical equivalents will work out (vs.18).

Rev.14—The fourteenth chapter of the Revelation of Jesus Christ begins with a scene on the earth, followed by a song from heaven (vss. 1, 2). The scene in vs.1 is on Mt. Zion (the western ridge of Jerusalem, then referred to the whole city (Unger); see this in Is.2:1-4; Is.1:27; Ps.48). The picture presented to us here appears to be the start of Christ's millennial reign (vs.1; 11:15; 12:10) in Jerusalem. The 144,000 have come through the Great Tribulation, having the Father's name and the name of His Son Jesus on their foreheads, as God's possession and protection, chosen as "first fruits" to Him as His witness and service during the Great Tribulation (vss.1, 4, 5; 7:4-8; see some of that celebration during this time frame also in Is.25:6-12). Note too they follow the Lamb wherever He goes, indicating the Lord back on the earth, during His second coming and reign on the earth (vs.4; Rev.20:1-6, in light of the declaration in 11:15). They are declared to have excellent character traits to serve the Lord, including no defilement with women (chaste behavior and conduct; the Greek word is "parthenos," the word for a virgin for females, primarily, in Greek); they are "blameless" (without fault—vss.4, 5). In a very honorable tribute, it appears, at least with them in mind, a new song is sung in heaven by the huge multitude there, singing in celebration on their harps, in joyful choral festivity (vs.2, 3; 5:8; 15:2; see similar multitude description in 19:6), which only the 144,000, purchased from the earth (5:9, 10), could learn the song on the earth (vs.3).

Three angels now appear each proclaiming their own individual message to those on the earth. The first declares the "eternal Gospel" to all mankind, giving charge to fear (reverence) God and give Him the glory, who made heaven and earth, including the sea and springs of waters, and to worship Him, for the time of His judgment has come (vss.7, 8; for the eternal Gospel, see 1 Pet.1:25, finishing up God's plan of the Gospel through the prophets and carried on into and through the Millennium and its truth forever and ever; Mt.24:35). The next angel announces the fall of Babylon forever—from the time it became the first kingdom on earth through Nimrod (Gen.10:8-14; 11:4) and took away Israel's kingdom and nation in 586 BC, to its final attempt to have a world kingdom revived in the Great Tribulation (Rev.16-18; see Zech.5; Jer.51:24-26)—they and all the worldly kingdoms will fall, not ever to be found again, with the Lord reigning on the earth, because of all the immorality and fornication they brought on the earth (vs.8; 18:1-24; Dan.2:44, 45). The third angel proclaims God's wrath on anyone who takes the mark of the beast during this time he is on earth (vss.9-11; 13:12, 15-17). The result is eternal torment forever with fire and brimstone, having no rest day or night, who worship the beast (vss.9-11, 7). As John endured and persevered for the Lord (1:9), the saints are called to seek God for His strength and endurance and do likewise (vs.12).

Then, John records another vision of the "son of man" (Jesus; vs.14; 1:13; Dan.7:13, 14; see the introduction to Revelation for the "visions" of Jesus in the Revelation). Here Jesus is seen as the Great Harvester, swinging a sickle over the earth to reap it (harvest it); but as vs.15 states, the harvest is (literally) dried up (New American Standard Bible has the words in the margin outside this verse, "has become dry;" see previous commentary on 10:7). Verse 16 declares the earth was reaped, and the time of God's judgment has come (vss.15, 7; Joel 3:13). And so, the last angel here swings his sickle to bring God's judgment on the unbelief and wickedness of the earth and gather those under God's judgment for the final war (Armageddon) of His wrath before the Lord returns for His Millennial reign, vss.17-20; (9:20,21; 15:1; 21:8; 22:14,15; Jn.3:16-21). With the end soon coming before the Lord's return, the believers who die from that time on are encouraged that they will enter God's rest in heaven, resting from their labors, and rewarded for their good deeds (vs.13; 1 Cor.3:10-15; Eph.6:7, 8).

Rev.15—As John now sees the seven angels ready with the last seven plagues of judgment about to come upon the earth, he declares another (12:1) great and marvelous sign in heaven (vs.1). He also sees those who were victorious over the beast, his image and his name (7:14-17), playing their victory songs, standing on a "sea of glass" (see the commentary on 4:6 for the sea of glass;

for their harps, see previously at 5:8 and 14:2). As John sees this, they (in his vision) "are singing" (present tense) the song of Moses (Ex.15:1-18), the bond-servant of God, and the song of the Lamb (5:9, 10; note also vss.11-14 there), giving great praise and attribution to the Lord in vss.3, 4. They draw from several Old Testament sources (see Dt.32:3, 4; Jer.10:6, 7; Lev.19:2; Ps.86:9, 10; Rev.16:5, 6; 6:9-11; 19:8; for the wonderful proclamation and tribute to "The Lord God Almighty" in the Revelation, see their listings in 1:8).

John next sees the temple of the tabernacle of testimony opened in heaven (vs.5; see Num.1:50-53; Heb.8:5) and the angels who had the seven plagues. They wear linen, bright and clean (compare 19:8) and golden girdles around their breasts (vs.6; see commentary on 1:13, 14). The angels received the golden bowls of the wrath of God, who lives forever and ever, as the temple filled with smoke from the glory of God (Ex.19:18; Is.6:4); and no one could enter the temple till the plagues were finished (vss.7,8).

Rev.16—All the seven plagues cast upon the earth are contained in chapter sixteen. A voice from the temple commands them to go and proceed with them (vs.1). The first one is a malignant sore cast upon those who took the mark of the beast and worshipped his image instead of God (vs.2; see 14:7-11; only other place found for the word "sore" outside this chapter is in Lk.16:21 about Lazarus, visiting the rich man). The second plague is judgment poured on the sea (probably universal here since all the major seas and oceans around the world are interconnected), and they became blood like that of a dead man, killing every living thing in the sea (vs.3; see 8:8, 9). The third angel poured out his bowl on the rivers and springs of water (major drinking sources for most—see Ex.7:17-21) and they became blood, also (vs.4; see 8:10, 11). The angel of the waters declares God's righteous judgment here (15:3), giving back blood to drink to those who killed (took the blood) of saints and prophets of God—that they deserve it (vss.5, 6; 6:9-11). Then finally, the ones who were killed for their faithfulness to the Lord and His word, and have been waiting for the Lord's righteous judgment and retribution to come on their behalf, chime in convincingly with the angel's declaration to the Lord God Almighty, that there is not ever a doubt that His judgments are true and righteous (vss.7, 5; 6:9-11). The fourth angel poured his bowl on the sun, allowing it to scorch men with fire and intense heat. They reacted by blaspheming God and not repenting of their sins, and so, to give Him glory (note the negative responses to the last three plagues—vss.8, 9, 11, 21; 14:7). The fifth angel poured forth his bowl on the throne and kingdom of the beast and it became darkness (see 8:12; Ex.10:21-23). The people gnawed their tongues and felt the pains from their sores (vs.2; note, from their own caused pain, refusing to repent of their deeds and worship God, and instead, entering in these judgments of God; vss.10, 11; 9:20, 21; 14:7-11). The sixth angel pours out his bowl on the great river Euphrates (current central Iraq; see Is.11:15,16—the river was right in the middle of the Assyrian empire and note this is primarily for the remnant of Israel, the positive end here). The kings of the east and the kings of the world are being gathered together by demons (vss.13, 14) for the war of the great day of God the Almighty (see Zeph.1:14-18; Joel 3:9-17; Rev.17:14) at Armageddon (meaning "mound of Megiddo," a little south of Nazareth and west of Nain (Lk.7:11), southwest of the Sea of Galilee; the valley above it, the plain of Jezreel (or the Greek modification name—plain of Esdraelon), is 20 miles long and 14 miles wide—Unger; vss.12-14, 16). The Lord comes as a thief, and man, not knowing the day or hour (see Mt.24:36-44), yet is to know the "season" (signs) of the Lord's second coming (Mt.24:32-35, 4-14; 1 Thess.5:1-11). For the garments, see 3:3-6, 18-22; vs.15. The last plague poured out by the seventh angel is upon the air, where Satan and his demons were once allowed to roam, will finally be casted into the lake of fire, forever (vs.17; 20:2, 7, 10; Eph.2:2; Jn.16:8-11). A voice from heaven said, "It is done," referring to God's completion of the judgments before the Lord Jesus returns to earth (seals, trumpets and plagues; vs.17; see 15:8). The flashes of lighting and thunder roars occur at the end of each judgment (seals—8:5; trumpets—11:19; and here, the last plague and final judgment completion), all showing impending judgment coming; also, see the beginning of all these warnings in 4:5. Here in the last plague, a great earthquake as never seen before ("so great and mighty"—vs.18) occurs and splits the great city of Babylon, called Babylon, into three parts (vs.19; 14:8; 17:18; 18:10, 16, 19), as God remembers it's abominations, sins and impending judgment (vss.19, 18; 17:5; 18:2-8). The islands and mountains disappearing recalls the sixth seal pointing to the end of the judgments (vs.20; 6:12-17; see also Heb.12:26, 27), along with huge hail taking place (a talent was somewhere between 75-100 pounds). Those not believing in God or worshipping Him (14:6, 7) blasphemed (spoke evil about or toward—see 13:5, 6)

God, because of the hail and the plague was so exceedingly great (vs.21).

Rev.17—As people read this chapter of the Revelation, they often wonder—how does Babylon come back into the picture now in the end times before the Lord's return? The answer is in its history trends and Biblical prophecy to be yet completed.

Note its history—First kingdom ever on earth through Nimrod (Gen.10:8-10); its city and the "Tower of Babel," rebelling against God's command (Gen.1:28; 9:7) to establish their own kingdom (Gen.11:1-9); declining, then building up again around 1700 BC with Hammurabi; declined quite quickly through defeat from other countries, including Assyria till they rose again through Nebuchadnezzar the first (1126-1105 BC). The Assyrians routed Babylon again and defeated them in 1027 BC; "tugs of war" continued between the two till 625 BC and Nabopolassar became king of the "new Babylonian era," followed by his son, Nebuchadnessar the second of the Book of Daniel; he destroyed Israel's Jerusalem in 586 BC (see the Book of Habakkuk in the Old Testament); the Persians then destroyed Babylon in 539-538 BC, before Alexander the Great took over them and controlled Babylon in 323 BC, which led to Babylon's diminishing and decline—for the time being in history, anyway (contributive dates and history from Unger's Bible Dictionary). So what then remains of this vast and wide-spread impact that this kingdom and people have had on history?

Note their legacy—they "pop up" and decline…and "pop up" again and decline again. Will they "pop up" again? The Bible says "yes" and God is not through with them yet (see also Zech.5 and

Jer.50, 51), because of what "abominations" they brought on the earth (Rev.17:5—"the mother of harlots"), and still do and will be finally judged by God (Rev.16-18).

Zechariah and Haggai were contemporary prophets for their time, <u>after</u> the Persians took over Babylon. Unger says his last prophecy (not including the latter half of his book) was around 518 BC, twenty years after Persia defeated Babylon and began its empire. In Zechariah's vision in chapter five, he sees a bushel basket called "wickedness." Two women with wings lift it up and carry it to the land of Shinar, the plain of Shinar, the land of Babylonia. It says a temple will be built for her and then she will be placed on her own pedestal (support for a statue, from the Hebrew word "to set up" or "place something on"—Strongs). Sounds like idolatry all over again—fitting in with the Book of Revelation (Zech.5:5-11; Dan.2, 3; Rev.13, 14, 17, 18).

John now receives the third vision in the Revelation he writes down and records for us ("in the Spirit" he was carried away; see similar in Ezk.11:1). One of the angels of the bowls of plagues guides him to see "the great harlot," reigning on the earth (vss.1, 5, 15, 18). She has affected ("infected") many kings and people on the earth with her immorality (vs.2). The woman (Babylon—vss.5, 18) sits on a scarlet beast (the Antichrist—6:1-4; 13:1-10; 18:24), full of blasphemous names (13:5, 6), having seven heads and ten horns (explained in vss.9-13; vs.3). The "harlot" is adorned in royalty—clothes and jewelry—and had a gold cup of her abominations of immorality in her hand (i.e., ready to pour it out, like God does the plagues; vs.4; 18:2, 3). In similar style as God did to His people (7:2-4), here a "mystery" (revealed by

God—remember her history; see Rev.1 for the word mystery), a name on her forehead—Babylon the great (it has been around awhile), "Mother of harlots" and the abominations of the earth, including blood of the saints, and witnesses of Jesus, vss. 5,6 (history past and presents bears this out—Dan.2, 3; Rev.6:1-4; 9-11; 13:1-18). The angel next reveals the "mystery" (that is, God reveals more about it—vs.7). He says the beast was, and is not and comes out of the abyss (for which see the commentary at the beginning of chapter nine; 11:7) and goes to destruction (vss.8, 11; Dan.9:27; 11:40-45; some say it is someone of the past or an impersonator of one in the past, or a takeoff of 13:3, 12, 14; see 2 Thess.2:8-12). The angel says the seven heads on the beast (vs.3) are seven mountains, which the woman sits (eight times in the Revelation the Greek word here translates it "mountains," referring to the kingdoms of the kings here in vs.10—"and they are seven kings;" see Dan.2 and Is.2). Babylon is responsible from the start of their first kingdom (Gen.10), all the way to their "pop up" ending, of the abominations of the earth (vss.4, 5; 18:2, 3) in the end times. They are also responsible for the starting and taking away of Israel's kingdom and capital city, Jerusalem, in 586 BC. Other kingdoms followed (called "the time of the Gentiles" (Lk.21:24)—Persia, Greece, Egypt and Assyrian kingdoms (see Dan.11—stated as the north and the south kingdoms then), followed by Rome that took over Palestine in 63 AD, (Unger), adding to their long dynasty of empire rule; kingdoms after this had nowhere near the reign and impact that Rome did in the world for over 14 centuries. The seventh is Babylon here in chapters 17 and 18. The beast only remains a little while (vss.9, 10; 13:5). He is also an "eighth" king, taking his rule with an alliance of 10 other kings, who give him their authority (eighth kingdom) for an even shorter period of time (vss.11-13). They all wage war against the Lamb, who will defeat them in His return to earth to rule and reign (vs.14; 1:5; 19:11-16). The ones with Him are His armies (the single article in the Greek include "called, chosen and faithful" together as one; not all fit this description, as much as we might like to think otherwise; see also His specific "armies" in 19:14; the Lord's main message of those who return with Him are His holy angels (Mt.16:27; 25:31; 1 Thess.3:13—to fit with the other Scriptures the Greek word "holy ones" here should be translated "holy ones" or angels; see also 2 Thess.1:7).

The angel goes on to explain the large vastness of Babylon's rule in the end times (vss.15, 18). Verse 16 says the ten kings who joined up with the beast to form the "eighth" kingdom (vss.11-13) will, along with the beast, turn against Babylon and burn it up to demonstrate their power as a new united alliance and kingdom (and fulfill God's word; see this prophecy in the Old Testament in the context of Babylon's destruction in Is.14:4, 18-22; also Jer.51:24-26, 56; Rev.18:4-6). Babylon thus receives its judgment and final removal from the earth (14:8; 18:2), as God executes His purposes and His prophetic word to put worldly kingdoms to an end and bring in the everlasting rule of His Son, King Jesus (vs.17; Lk.1:31-33; Rev.1:5, 6; 5:9, 10; 11:15; 19:11-16; 20:1-6; Is.46:8-11).

Rev.18—John is now given the vision of Babylon's destruction, its city and final end to its kingdom. One can see why after reading this chapter, especially vss.3, 24, and the previous chapter. He begins with the frequent words "after these things" (vs.1; 19:1). These words occur ten times in the Revelation, showing the continuation and sequence of events that John saw to record for Scripture. He sees another angel with strong authority and illuminating the earth with his glory (on his mission from God—vs.1). He declares that Babylon is fallen (see 14:8 for the preliminary announcement) and has become a dwelling place of demons and unclean and hated birds (vs.2; Jer.50:39; 51:37). The reason for it was given back in 17:4-6 in the description of Babylon, and now the kings and merchants of the earth are declared responsible with it, joining in its luxurious (living "wantingly") lifestyle (vs.3). God's people are instructed to stay away and out of their way of life and their sins, which have piled up to heaven, so as not to receive her plaques, for God has remembered their sins (vss.4, 5; 14:8; 16:19; Jer.51:9, 45). Babylon will be paid back double ("double unto her double according to her works"—KJ) for what she did to others, glorifying herself in her luxury (verb "luxury" of the noun in vs.3), living as a "worldly" queen (vss.6, 7; see the prophecy in Is.47:8-11 about Babylon; also Jer.50:15, 29; 51:56). For this, Babylon will be burned up in a single day (three times mentioned in "one hour," which in today's age may be literal), for God who judges her is strong (vss.8, 10, 17, 19; 17:16).

Three main groups of leaders responsible for committing these actions are—the kings of the earth, the merchants of the earth, shipmasters, all those traveling by sea, sailors and all those making their living by the sea (vss.9, 11, 17). Kings will lament and weep, watching Babylon burning, in fear of her torment, seeing the judgment take place (vss.9, 10). Merchants will lose their vast amount of various cargos, including animals, slaves and human lives involved (vss.11-13), along with all their own luxuries (vs.14). They react as the kings did in vs.10, seeing all the valuable things of their world they "depended" on, gone in smoke in "one hour" (vss.14-17). Those out at sea watch the "great city" (called by them all—vss.10, 16, 18, 19, 21) burning in smoke, where they live and deliver their products and became rich by the abundance of them—being destroyed in "one hour" (vss.17-19). Yet, the saints, apostles and prophets rejoice, because God has brought His judgment upon her ("for the way she treated you"—NIV; 6:9-11); vss.20, 24; 13:7; 16:5, 6; 17:3-6). Then a strong angel appears (see 5:2; 10:1) and fulfills the prophecy in declaration of Jer.51:62-64, showing how Babylon has disappeared and not to be found any longer (Jer.50:39)—throwing a millstone (used for grinding grains and usually turned by an animal—Vine) into the sea (with a rush, the Greek word here), taking all its various "lifestyles" (music, culture, crafts, business, manufacturing, marriages, etc.) with it (the Greek uses the emphatic negative, (two negative two letter words), to declare the final certainty of its disappearance, four times in vss.22, 23); for all the nations were deceived by Babylon's sorcery (Greek word is "pharmakeia," the use of drugs, that can also lead to sorcery; see this in 9:21, also), and in her was found the blood of prophets and saints who were killed on the earth (vs.24; 6:9-11; 13:7; 16:4-7; 17:3-6), and so, judged according to what they deserved (vss.5-8; 16:4-7; 19:1,2).

Rev.19—With the "great harlot" judged by God (17:5; 18:5, 6), the Lord Jesus is now about to return to earth, for the final judgment of the earth and begin His millennial reign. Four "hallelujahs"

("Praise the Lord") occur in heaven: first, for His righteous and true judgments on the great harlot, corrupting the earth with her immorality and taking the life of some of God's servants; for salvation, glory and power all come from the Lord (vss.1,2; 7:10; 12:10; 16:7; Dt.32; 4, 43; Ps.19:9); second, the judgment given the "great harlot" is eternal torment (vss.3, 20; 14:9-11; 16:5-7); third, the twenty-four elders and four living creatures around the throne join in worship and affirm the declarations with their "Amen" (so be it; remember their contributions in 5:8 and God's faithful answers—vss.1-4); a voice from the throne goes forth to God's servants in call to praise Him, those who revere Him, small and great, in unison with the moment at hand, and also knowing His supper is about to occur and the time to give them their rewards is soon to take place (vss.5, 7, 8; 11:18; 22:12); and the fourth "hallelujah" declares praise to the Lord our God Almighty because He reigns (vs.6; the Greek verb is past simple tense here and so, He "reigned," i.e., He won the victory, and is the Victor, all along—Col.2:13-15; Rev.1:17, 18; 19:11-21; Zeph.3:14-20; Is.52:7-10). This also is the introduction to the Marriage Supper of the Lamb (vss.7-9). People wonder and discuss in these four verses about where the Marriage Supper of the Lamb takes place. Looking over the context of these verses with the Book of the Revelation and any other related prophecy passages, I will share six reasons why I believe it occurs in heaven and also give a seventh proposition on how it may, in some capacity at least, carry over to the earth as well: 1) the "Hallelujahs" in this chapter are taken together beginning in heaven (vs.1) with no declared change of location going into the fourth one; 2) the declaration "Lord God

Almighty" occurs, seven times in the book, starting off by God Himself (1:8), one a reference to Him (21:22) and all the rest in strong affirmation to the Lord for who He is and what He has done in outward proclamation of worship in heaven (1:8; 4; 4:8-11; 11:17; 15:3; 16:7; 19:6); 3) the setting and description given in 19:6 is the same description given to us in 14:2 of the worship in heaven, minus the harps there for that context; 4) the praise and proclamation of "our Lord God Almighty reigns" recalls this great declaration from Is.52:7-10; this proclamation was given to God back at the seventh trumpet (11:15), as the angel disclosed this in 10:7. With the harvest now in (see the commentary on 14:14-16), this fulfills Jesus' statement at the Lord's Supper to the Apostles in Lk.22:15, 16. His promise is carried over in that chapter to vss.28-30, of them eating at His table and sitting on thrones judging the twelve tribes of Israel, which could only happen with them in heaven, where they are; 5) the "fine linen" given to the saints for their righteous deeds done unto the Lord in vs.8 are the same "linen" (and Greek word) that the Lord's armies wear in heaven (19:14); 6) with these "wedding clothes" in mind, this would put the "marriage feast" in Mt.22:1-14 in heaven, the point being there that one must come into the Kingdom God's way through the spiritual birth (Jn.1:12,13) and eventually with wearing His wedding clothes for the Bride (the believers) that the Lord gives them for the Marriage Supper of the Lamb (19:8); 7) it appears that this may carry over to some degree on earth, also, according to the promise given and exhortations stressed here to the believers and their faithful service to Him, when Jesus returns to earth (see Lk.12:35-40; Mt.25:1-13).

John in his reverence bows at the angel's feet but the angel will not allow it (vs.10) and reminds John to worship God (similar to 22:8, 9), for Jesus' testimony is the spirit of prophecy (here a descriptive genitive in the Greek; prophecy is the kind of spirit declared here, a telling forth of God's word, as Jesus is—the Word of God—vss.10, 13; Jn.1:1, 18), and so, to worship God.

John now sees heaven opened (4:1; Mt.3:16, 17) and Jesus on His white victory horse (see the delusion in 6:2), coming to conquer over sin and wickedness in the earth and rule and reign in His kingdom of righteousness (vss.11-21; Is.9:6, 7; 11:1-5; 49:7; 63:1-6; Ps.2). The description of the Lord returning here are fulfillments of many prophecies. "Faithful and True" recall the Lord's fulfilled ministry on earth (Jn.1:14, 17; 8:29, 30; 14:6; 17:4; Rev.1:5; 3:14), and righteously He judges and wages war (vs.11; Is.11:1-5; 42:1-4; 59:15-21; 63:1-6); Jer.23:5, 6; Jn.5:22-30). His eyes are a flame of fire (see 1:14; 2:18; Dan.10:6) and many diadems (kingly dignity and Lordship) are on His head; and He has a name which no one knows except Himself (vs.12; see 2:17, also). For His robe dipped in blood, see the prophecy in Is.63:1-6; and His name is the Word of God (vs.13; Jn.1:1, 14; Col.1:19; 2:9; Mt.24:35; Is.11:1-5). For the Lord's armies in vs.14, see the commentary on 17:14. For the "sharp sword" and "rod of iron"—vs. 15, see Ps.2:8,9 and Is.11:4; Rev.1:5; 12:5); for "treading the wine press," see chapter 14:14-20; for Jesus is the Salvation Harvester, and the Conquering King and Judge against wickedness, designated by God to carry out His judgment and wrath against all unrighteousness—vs.15; 6:9-11; 16:5-7, 19; 17:5; 18:3, 24; 15:3,4; Jn.5:22-30); for He is the King of kings and Lord of lords, which appears written on His robe and thigh (vs.16; 17:14; 1:5; see also Ps.2; Jer.10:6, 7, 10; Rev.15:3,4).

An angel announces the Lord's coming conquering victory over the armies of evil on the earth ("the war of the great day of God the Almighty"—vs.17, 18; 16:14, 16). The beast and the kings of the earth assemble in war against the Lord (17:3,14; 18:3, 8-10; Zech.14:3-5,9) and the beast and the false prophet (13:1-18) were captured and thrown alive in the Lake of Fire (vss.19, 20; see Mt.25:41); and the rest of their army were killed by the sword from the mouth of the Lord (vss.21, 15; Is.11:4,5; Mt.24:27,28; Zeph.3:14-20; Ezk.43:1-9; Ps.24).

Rev.20—This chapter of the Revelation declares to us the millennial reign of Jesus Christ on the earth (vss.1-7). The certainty and length of time of these years is made known to us in that the 1000 year reign is mentioned six times in the first seven verses (vss.2-7). Satan is bound in the abyss during all these years (see the details in vss.1-3; and then released for a short time (vs.3; see commentary on 9:1 for the "abyss" and 1:18). For the "thrones and judgment" taking place in vs.4, see Dan.7:9-14, 21, 22. Those who experienced martyrdom for the Lord (6:9-11) and those who did not worship the beast, his image or take his representative mark during the Great Tribulation, came to life and reigned with Christ for the 1,000 years (vs.4; 7:14-17). This is the first resurrection, and those to be judged will be in the second resurrection (vss.5, 6). His saints (the believers) will serve Him as priests in His kingdom and reign with Him the 1,000 years (mentioned twice, in vss. 4, 6; 1:5, 6; 5:10; 1 Pet.2:9, 10).

After the 1,000 years, Satan is released for a short time to deceive the nations, Gog and Magog (reference to the nations; some say "Gog" is the leader of Magog, while some others say Gog comes from Magog or is connected with it (vss.7, 8; see Gen.10:2; Ezk.38, 39). For the "broad plain" see Ezk.38:14-23. The last attempt to wage war on the saints will be met by fire from God on their enemies and they will be devoured (vss.7-9; see the same verb here in 11:5 under similar conditions) and the devil will be casted into the Lake of Fire, and tormented there day and night forever and ever (vs.10). For the "beloved city," see Ps.48 and Ps.87; (vs.9).

Now we see the final judgment for all time to take place. The dead from land and sea, death and Hades (for which see the commentary on 1:18) are given up and come before "the great white throne" (vss.11-13; 4:2; Dan.7:9, 10). Note they are judged by (according to) their deeds (vss.12, 13) and if their name is in the book of life (see 21:27, the "Lamb's book of life," i.e., belonging to Him, His people—3:4, 5; Lk.10:20; Jn.1:12, 13; 5:24; Phil.4:3). Anyone not found in the book of life was thrown into the Lake of Fire, with death and Hades, the second death (vss.14, 15; Mt.25:41-46; Jn.10:10, 27-30; 17:3; see the Prayer in back of the book).

Rev.21—John now receives the fourth and last of his visions for the Book of Revelation (vs.10). God's family for eternity is now complete (Lk.20:34-36) and He has prepared a city for them to dwell in and live with Him forever (vss.2, 3; see the Architect and Builder in Heb.11:10, 16 and that commentary). The judgments are finished and now God has created a new heaven and new earth and new Jerusalem for them to dwell in with Him forever (vss.1, 2).

Whether the new heaven and earth are brand new or the old restored has been discussed both ways. Peter's language appears to present a restored (purified) heaven and earth (2 Pet.3:10-13) and 2 Cor.5:17 uses the same root word in "passed away" with only a different prefix regarding the spiritual birth. Heb.12:27 seemed to point this way, also (see the prophecy in Is.65:17-23). From the beginning, God's heart has always been to dwell with His people (Family—Gen.1:27, 28; 3:8; 9:7; Ex.25:8; Lev.26:11, 12). Finally, after much patience (long-suffering) by God and purification of mankind and heaven and earth (1 Pet.1:17-21; Rev.12:7, 8; 19:20; 20:10), it all comes together and takes place (vss.2, 3, 7), and much to the comfort of His Family, who shared in the sufferings of the Lord they served, but not ever to see the likes of those sufferings and pains, including physical death, ever again (vs.4; 7:14-17; Is.25:6-9; 35:10; 51:11; 65:17-23; Jn.16:22; 17:20-24). For the Lord makes (present tense) all things new (vs.5; if restoration is seen in vs.1, then that would take on the meaning that the "things" of the earth and heaven passed away, much like the "elements" being burned by fire Peter refers to in 2 Pet.3:10, 12). God wants everyone to know that these words of His are faithful and true (vs.5). The saying "it is done" in vs.6 is actually plural, meaning "they are done" (what great planning by God! see Is.25:1; 46:8-11; Eph.1:7-12), and all given to the believers (His Family) as a free gift, like His salvation to mankind (Jn.1:12, 13; 3:16, 17), which includes being a son of God (vss.6-8; Is.55:1-5; Jn.7:37-39).

One of the angels who had one of the last plagues (Rev.16) next takes John in the Spirit to a great high mountain and shows him God's new and holy city Jerusalem, coming down out of heaven and having the glory of God (vss.9, 10; Ezk.40:2). Its brilliance was like a jewel of crystal-clear jasper (vs.11; see the commentary on 4:3). From now until vs.22, the concentration of John's vision is on the city itself, the wall and its foundation stones, and the cities gates (vss.12, 15-17, 19). The wall is great and high with twelve gates, three facing each direction (north, south, east and west), having twelve angels, and the name of the twelve tribes of Israel written on the gates (vss.12, 13). The wall has twelve foundation stones, with the twelve names of the twelve apostles of the Lamb on them (vs.14; the beautiful descriptions are given in vss.19-21). An angel was taking the measurements of the city, its gates and wall, using human measurements, which are also angelic measurements ("which the angel was using" (NIV), vss.15, 17). The city made of pure gold, like clear glass (vs.18), is laid out as a square (or others have said, by the description, a cube—length, width and height being equal, the Greek word here "four cornered"—vs.16; see 1 Kg.6:20). The city measured out to be about 1,500 miles (about half the distance, east to west, of the United States, vs.16) and the material of the wall was jasper (vs.18; 4:3), seventy-two yards long (New American Standard Bible, almost three-quarters of a football field—vs.17); and the city was pure gold, like clear glass (vs.18). Here are the twelve foundation stones that decorate the wall of the New Jerusalem (taken from Unger's Bible Dictionary): 1) jasper—colored translucent (light passes through but now transparent) varieties of quartz; sky-blue, green or rosy hues, as examples; see 4:3; 2) sapphire—an opaque stone that can come in a variety of colors, usually occurring as dark blue or different shades of blue; second in hardness to diamonds; 3) chalcedony—a greenish or bluish green silicate (glassy mineral found in various forms of quartz, opal or sand) of copper, found in mines at Chalcedon (northern Turkey); 4) emerald—usually a bright green color; 5) sardonyx—derived from two words—sard (like sardius, the next word in order) meaning a reddish-orange color; and onyx—a striped or clouded coloring, which can look off-white with striped colors; 6) sardius—a deep red or brown-red (including orange or orange-like color) varieties of chalcedony (silicate copper); 7) chrysolite—commonly topaz today, a variety of yellowish gems; 8) beryl—a hard mineral that can appear as deep varieties of green, as an emerald, or aquamarine (turquoise, sea-green) in color; 9) topaz—a variety of yellowish gems, peridot (yellowish-green), being one example; 10) chrysoprase—a light green chalcedony (word means "gold leek," like a green onion); 11) jacinth—reddish-orange or red-brown color; some have "hyacinth" here, like a blue in the sapphire; and 12) amethyst—purple or violet variety of quartz; there are few purple gemstones (Unger); see the "breastplate" jewels of Aaron in Ex.28:17-20.

The twelve gates were twelve pearls, each gate a single pearl, and the streets are as the city (vs.18)—pure gold like transparent glass (vs.21).

The city has no temple, for the Lord God Almighty and the Lamb are the temple (vs.22; see Jn.2:19; Is.66:1, 2). The light of the city will be the glory of the Lord, and its lamp is the Lamb (vs.23; see Ps.119:105; Prov.6:20-23; Jn.1:5, 9; 8:12). The nations now will walk by the light of the Lord (Is.60:3-5) and the kings of the earth will now bring their glory into it (Ps.72:10, 11, 18, 19), as the gates will never be closed with no more nighttime, celebrated by all God's Family (vss. 24-27; Ps.87).

Rev.22—As John comes to the completion of what he is shown about the New Jerusalem, the angel (21:9, 10) shows him a river of the water of life, clear as crystal, coming from the throne of God and the Lamb (vs.1). The "tree of life" was then seen on either side of the river, as the river traveled down the middle of the street (vs.2). The "tree of life" is bearing twelve kinds of fruit, yielding it's fruit every month, serving as healing for the nations (vs.21; "healing" here meaning life-giving health and nutrition for the people; see Gen.2:9, 16, 17; 3:22; note, couldn't eat off of both trees and live in Gen.2:16, 17). The setting here seems very similar to the setting in Ezk.47, yet, lets note some important distinguishing differences between them: In the millennial setting of the temple in Jerusalem (Ezk.40-48), in Ezk.47:7, 12, it states that "all kinds of trees" were located on the riverbank, while in Rev.22:2, the word "tree" of life, mentioned twice, is singular both times. One might wonder how such beautiful pure water could be existing in these two different places at two different times (the millennium and the new Jerusalem coming down out of heaven)? The answer is because God's throne is in <u>both</u> places, where the beautiful clear water comes from—the very throne of God (Ezk.43:1-9; Rev.22:1-3); and also in Gen.3:22, the "tree of life" was meant for those in the eternal state (i.e. would not die—Gen.2:16, 17; Rev.21:4), and so, after man sinned, he would be lost from God if taking this fruit in his fallen state (Gen.3:22-24);

and yet instead, God set out His plan to save him (Gen.3:15), so that he could live forever with God, as He intended from the very beginning (Gen.3:8; 2:9, 16, 17; Lev. 26:11, 12).

The curse will be gone forever in the new Jerusalem (21:4) and God's throne and the Lamb will then be in it, with His bondservants serving Him forever (vss.3, 5; 1:6; 5:9, 10; 7:14-17). And God's Family, being with Him forever (vs.3; 21:3, 7), will see God's face, with His name of ownership on their foreheads (vs.4; see 3:12; 14:1; Job 19:25, 26; Ps.16:7-11; 27:4; 84:4; Jn.3:16, 17; see the Prayer in back of the book); and with no more nighttime, God's Family will live by the light of the Lord—His glory!—and will reign with Him—their everlasting God and King—forever and ever (vs.5; 21:23-25; 19:16; Zeph.3:14-20; Is.9:6,7; Rev.1:8; 15:3,4).

The Book of Revelation closes with similar declarations, and encouragements as the book began. The faithfulness and truth of God's word are affirmed once again in vs.6 as stated in 21:5 (see also 19:11, 13). This follows supernaturally spoken through His prophets and sent angels to give to His servants what He wants them to know (Heb.12:9)—here, the things (literally) necessary to occur quickly (i.e., when they take place, they will occur quickly—vs.6, similar to Jesus' statement of His coming quickly—vs.7, 12, 20; and so to be ready, Mt.24:42, 44), and keep (heed) the words of the Book of Revelation (vs.7; 1:3; 16:15; 21:5-7). John's response to the angel is similar to his one previously in 19:10 (vss.8, 9; see that verse and commentary).

Unlike the Book of Daniel which many prophecies referred to the end times and were "sealed" up then (Dan.8:26; 12:4, 9),

John was told not to seal up the words of this prophecy, for the time is near (vs.10; see commentary on 1:3 for this; 10:7-11). For understanding of vs.11, see Ezk.3:27; Dan.12:10; Rev.6:15-17; 14:6-12. The Lord will reward every man according to the work he has done (vs.12; 1 Cor.3:11-15; Eph.6:8; Rev.2:23; 20:12; Mt.16:27), as the Lord sees all things, the One who is the first and the last, the beginning and the end (vs.13; 1:8, 17; 2:8; 21:6). For "washing their robes," see the commentary on 7:14; also see Is.1:18; Acts 2:38, 39; 22:16; Heb.9:11-14; so that they will be allowed to the "tree of life" (22:2) and may enter the gates of the New Jerusalem (vss.14, 15; 21:12).

John reminds and confirms that these things have been sent by Jesus through His angel to testify these things to the churches (vs.16; 1:1, 11). For "offspring of David," see 1 Chr.17:9-14; Is.9:6, 7; Mt.1:1; Lk.1:31-33; Rev.5:5; and for "the bright and morning star," see Mt.24:27, 30; 2 Pet.1:19; Rev.22:16. The invitation in the Book of Revelation to come to know the Lord Jesus, is given with a call by the Holy Spirit and the church—the bride of Christ—along with those who read and hear the words of this book (1:3), to those who are "thirsty" (for God's life and fulfillments) and whoever wishes to receive His gift of "the water of life" (note) without cost, to come to know and follow Him (vs.17; Jn.3:16, 17; 7:37-39; 6:50, 51; 11:25, 26; Is.55:1,2; Rev.21:6; 22:1, 2; see the Prayer in the back of the book). One is strictly warned not to add to or subtract from this prophecy, with the consequences written if such is done. God has given such warnings before not to add to or subtract from His word and commandments (Dt.4:2; 12:32; Prov.30:5, 6; see also Ps.12:6; 19:7-11).

John closes by giving his affirmation to Jesus' declaration that He comes quickly (see commentary on vs.6), and so John says, "Amen" to that; "Come Lord Jesus" (vs.20); and extends the encouragement that the grace of the Lord Jesus be with all (vs.21; 1:3-5).

Bibliography

Arndt, William F; Gingrich, F. Wilbur; Bauer, Walter; and Danker, Frederick W. A Greek-English Lexicon of the New Testament and Other Early Christian Literature. Chicago and London: The University of Chicago Press, 1979.

Strong, James. Strong's Exhaustive Concordance of the Bible. Public Domain.

Unger, Merrill F. The New Unger's Bible Dictionary. Harrison, R.K., Edit; Vos, Howard F, and Barber, Cyril J., Contrib. Edit. Chicago: Moody Press, 1988.

Vine, W.E. Vine's Expository Dictionary of New Testament Words. Nashville, TN: Thomas Nelson, Inc.; 1940.

All reprints used by permission of the publishers or are public domain.

Prayer

If you have never had this relationship before and desire to know Jesus and invite Him into your life, I encourage you to pray this prayer sincerely from your heart:

"Dear Lord Jesus…Thank You for coming to earth and being faithful to the Father, fulfilling the Old Testament Scriptures written about You. Thank You for dying for my sins and rising from the dead so I may receive Your gifts of eternal life and the Holy Spirit. I now turn from my sins and leave them at the cross that You died on for me. I ask You to come into my life as my Savior and Lord. Make my life what You want me to be and help me establish good relationships with other Christians. I will serve You as my Lord and King, now and forever in Your Kingdom that will never end. Amen."

If you prayed this prayer from your heart, seek out a good Bible believing and teaching church. Ask God to bring you together with good fellow Christian relationships and to help you grow and serve your Savior and Lord. Read the Bible every day for guidance and spiritual nourishment. Spend time praying and share your new found relationship with Jesus with others also, so that they may come to know the Creator, Savior and Lord of the universe, too.

The Family Bible Studies Series

Book 1—The Family of God—Foundation. Presents the character and functions of the Trinity and eight practical Bible studies throughout the Bible on a characteristic of God (Provider, Protector, our Guide in life, Giver of all good things, etc. 35 Pages.

Book 2—The Levels of Relationships. Provides Biblical understanding about the foundational words of relationships (stranger, acquaintance, friend, companion (three kinds in the Bible), etc. and how to determine if a relationship is growing or not. 48 pages.

Book 3—Growing In God's Wisdom. Gives definitions to the Hebrew words of the introduction to the Book of Proverbs, verses 1-7, and practical application of how to pray for these "ingredients" of God's wisdom. 102 pages.

Book 4—The Theology of the Bible—The Family of God. Presents the theme of the Bible, The Family of God, From Genesis 1 to Revelation 22; plus a Biblical outline and summary of the Creation Passage of Genesis 1 and 2. 41 pages.

Book 5—The New Testament Commentary for <u>The Family Bible Studies Series</u>.

Book 6—The Book of Revelation Commentary.

CPSIA information can be obtained
at www.ICGtesting.com
Printed in the USA
BVHW040916190419
546005BV00020B/266/P